N *atio*
an

Multinational Finance

Adrian Buckley
Cranfield School of Management

Philip Allan

First published 1986 by
PHILIP ALLAN PUBLISHERS LIMITED
MARKET PLACE
DEDDINGTON
OXFORD OX5 4SE

British Library Cataloguing in Publication Data

Buckley, Adrian
  Multinational finance.
  1. International business enterprises
  Finance
  I. Title
  658.1'599   HG4027.5

ISBN 0-86003-542-5
ISBN 0-86003-644-8 Pbk

Typeset by MHL Typesetting, Coventry
Printed in Great Britain by the Camelot Press, Southampton

To
three very special people –
Frances and Peter and David

Contents

Preface

This book describes the theory and practice of multinational finance. The increasing internationalisation of business, the breaking down of the fixed exchange rate system and the deregulation of capital markets around the world have made the study of multinational finance far more pertinent than heretofore.

Fifteen years ago the majority of financial executives in *The Times 1000* companies did not have to appreciate what impelled exchange rates to move, what were the opportunities to raise money outside the United Kingdom, what influenced the evaluation of overseas capital investment projects, and so on. The decisions to move away from the fixed exchange rate system and to abandon exchange controls in the UK were the most important factors which changed all that. The financial manager in Britain had to start to learn new tricks in the seventies. Those who were slow to learn made mistakes. They borrowed in Swiss francs because the interest cost was low; they failed to cover Deutsche Marks payable as sterling declined precipitously; they failed to realise the opportunities created by the demise of exchange controls; they did not appreciate the benefits that accrue from currency options; and so on.

The majority of financial executives are probably accountants and it·is to be regretted that the professional accounting bodies in the United Kingdom responded with too little, too late. In short, they have failed to provide an adequate test of knowledge in the field of multinational financial management as part of their professional training and examinations. This lacuna in their training, in conjunction with a paucity of coverage of the total treasury area – corporate finance, currency management, funding management and liquidity management – was one of the reasons for the growth and increasing importance in Britain of the Association of Corporate Treasurers. It is also a reason for the absence of a wide-ranging British text on multinational finance. This book is intended, in a modest way, to fill the gap and improve management practice in a most important area of business.

This text is primarily aimed at students on MBA electives in multinational finance or financial aspects of international business. But it is also intended to be used on final-year undergraduate options, and it is structured to meet the needs of aspiring accountants, bankers and treasurers. However, the emphasis on a student market is not to say that the book is not appropriate for the businessman who needs to know about finance in the international arena. The intention is that it should be relevant to the requirements of financial managers who want to study this special area of finance as well as for non-financial managers who need to know about international money and its implications. My intention is essentially practical. It is that this book should improve performance and awareness in the currency management area.

I am most grateful to the Association of Corporate Treasurers and to the Institute of Bankers for permission to reproduce some of their examination questions in the test banks. My thanks are also due to *The Financial Times* for permission to use certain of their tables on foreign exchange rates in Chapter 6 and to the International Monetary Fund for permission to use their table in Table 4.2. My thanks also go to the National Westminster Bank for permission to use the tombstone for their US $1 billion primary capital floating rate note issue of May 1985. And I am especially grateful to Sheila Hart who deciphered my handwriting and cheerfully typed this manuscript – her task was made more difficult by my consistent tendency to revise the text with excess frequency.

Adrian Buckley

1

Introduction

Financial management traditionally focuses upon three key decisions – the acquisition of funds, their investment and the payment of dividends. The former is termed the financing decision and it is concerned with obtaining funds, either internally or externally, at the lowest cost possible. The second key area of finance is the investment decision which is concerned with the allocation of funds to opportunities in order to earn the greatest value for the firm. The study of financial management is built upon the hypothesis that judicious financing, investment and dividend decisions positively affect the present value of shareholder wealth. Most writers on financial management arrive at these hypotheses by way of a process of deductive reasoning. They then present data from empirical tests of these hypotheses and from this base build an armoury of rules and recommendations which help us to analyse opportunities and choose the course of action which maximises shareholder value.

Domestic financial management is concerned with the costs of financing sources and the payoffs from investment. In the domestic arena, movements in exchange rates are substantially ignored. But when we move outside the purely domestic field, there is no way that we can analyse international financing and investment opportunities without an understanding of the impact of foreign exchange rates upon the basic model of financial management. We are still concerned with raising funds at minimum cost, but there are clearly complications of analysis if a UK-based company is raising funds by way of a Swiss franc borrowing. We are still concerned with investment opportunities chosen to create maximum shareholder value, but what if the income and cash flow of our UK-based company's investments arise from Germany in Deutsche Marks? Or from Brazil in cruzados? And what if exchange controls place barriers on remittances of some proportion of profit?

Obviously, multinational finance possesses a dimension that makes it far more complicated than domestic finance. Indeed, we make no bones about it – multinational finance is a complex area of study. It has been sired by the internationalisation of business. If money is the language of business, foreign exchange is the language of international business. We are therefore deeply concerned in this book with foreign exchange markets throughout the world and with the pressures that impel exchange rates to move upwards and downwards. In addition to evaluating theories of exchange rate movements, multinational finance is concerned with the risks that flow from holding assets and liabilities denominated in foreign currency. Clearly, the home currency value of such assets and liabilities changes as exchange rates move. Exposure to these changes creates foreign exchange risk. We are concerned not only with defining and classifying foreign exchange risk but also with reporting, managing and controlling that risk. But multinational finance is not only concerned with foreign exchange risk, it also embraces political risk, that is, the risk a firm takes on when it enters into business operations located overseas. Again, a practical orientation towards the study of multinational finance suggests that we should focus upon managing and controlling this risk. A systematic study of finance in the international arena requires that we consider the funding of international trade, the evaluation of the cross-frontier investment decisions and the financing of overseas associate and subsidiary companies, as well as understand international financial markets, the impact of tax regimes in different countries and the ways in which exchange controls affect multinational businesses. These topics are the subject matter of this book.

Multinational financial management is so riddled with complications – they far outweigh the complexities of domestic financial management – that there is a critical need to simplify the subject. One of the reasons for writing this book has been that most other texts which devote themselves to international money fail to present a clear picture to their readers. And when they do, they are invariably excessively wordy. Furthermore, most texts emanate from the United States of America. And there are also a good many texts on multinational finance which approach the subject at a high level of abstraction and with an emphasis upon mathematics that could easily be daunting to even the best of MBA students.

Given this background, the intention of the author is that this text should be orientated towards the requirements of the UK student of international finance who needs to understand the theory and practice of multinational finance. A certain amount of mathematics is necessary but the intention has been to keep it to a minimum.

The author's assumption is that the readership will be drawn not only from students but also from businessmen. Amongst student readers, it is anticipated that some will be aspiring accountants, bankers and treasurers, some will be undergraduates and some will be postgraduates, mainly on MBA programmes. This text should also appeal to businessmen drawn from the ranks of treasurers, accountants, bankers and corporate planners who require a coherent presentation of the theory and practice of multinational finance. However, inasmuch as there is an increasing need for non-financial managers – line managers and members of a company's top-level decision coalition – to understand finance in the international arena, it is intended that this text should meet their needs also.

It is assumed by the author that readers have a basic knowledge of financial management. This would probably embrace such topics as sources of corporate finance, the investment, financing and dividend decision and the efficient markets hypothesis – but such knowledge is not necessarily expected to be at a high level of competence. The line manager with a general manager's understanding of finance should not be disadvantaged as he explores most of the topics in this text.

Given the target audience of this book, the level of mathematics has deliberately been kept at a reasonably unsophisticated level. The author's desire is very much to present a complex subject in the style of a good communicator. And this means that mathematics is our servant, not our god.

Because the target audience substantially embraces students, there are four test banks of questions scattered through the book. The book is intended to be adopted by instructors for class use in teaching multinational finance. To help in this direction, a teacher's manual with suggested solutions to the test bank questions, plus further questions, is available to instructors from the publisher. The manual also contains a list of cases and suggests a structure for a case-based course in multinational finance which the author has found to be successful in the past.

Having studied the content of this book, the reader should be able to:

- appreciate the historic background and existing institutional framework of international money;

- understand the workings and methods of quotation in the foreign exchange markets;

- understand the theoretical relationship between spot and forward exchange rates, interest differentials, expected inflation differentials and expectations of future spot rates and know how well they stand up in the real world;

- understand the essence of theories for predicting future exchange rates;

- understand how to use purchasing power parity data plus balance of payments figures to forecast the future exchange rate (together with the frailties in this approach);

- estimate implied future exchange rates via the international Fisher effect;

- define and distinguish different types of foreign exchange risk and recommend appropriate management action given the existence of these different kinds of exposure;

- design an information system relevant to a multinational company's need to control, cost-effectively, foreign exchange exposure;

- appreciate the opportunities which the multinational has to control foreign exchange exposure internally – that is, without the need to enter into contracts with third parties;

- understand the essence of eliminating foreign exchange risk via forward markets, financial futures and currency options;

- understand the opportunities available to finance international trade and minimise credit risk;

- assess the international capital investment decision in a manner consistent with the parent company's desire to maximise the wealth of its shareholders;

- understand the sources and nature of political risk for the international company and, moreover, recommend appropriate management action to mitigate its impact in different circumstances;

- appreciate the problems in financing an overseas subsidiary and make recommendations on the most appropriate financial structure, given different sets of circumstances;

- understand the nature of and participants in the Eurocurrency markets and assess why there might be opportunities to borrow in the Euromarkets at rates below rates in comparable domestic markets;

- measure and compare the true cost of borrowing in the international financial arena;

- appreciate how currency swaps and Euronote markets work and how market imperfections create opportunities in these directions for the astute corporate treasurer;

- understand how corporate tax rules in many countries create opportunities and pitfalls arising from international financing and cross-frontier operations;

- obtain a general idea of the mode of working, opportunities and pitfalls created by exchange control regulations in countries in which the multi-national corporation operates;

- understand how and, more importantly, where market imperfections create profitable opportunities for the astute international financial manager.

The chapters in this book broadly follow the above list of objectives.

It is as well for the reader to remember that the analysis of international financial and investment opportunities with a view to maximising shareholder wealth for the multinational investor involves searching out market imperfections and temporary disequilibria. These are usually far more plentiful in the international arena compared with its domestic counterpart. Clearly, avoidance of those which are potentially adverse, and exploitation of those from which profitable outcome seems likely, is the recommended course of action.

Finally, the author wishes to warn readers that they may find the chapters on financial futures and currency options a little difficult. In anticipation of this, readers may wish to leave Chapters 16 and 17 to the end of their studies. They should not lose much by adopting this policy.

2

Some Key Facts about Multinational Finance

In this chapter we describe a few key facts which are pertinent to the study of finance in the multinational arena. They have been set out here because students of the subject repeatedly find themselves asking about these topics. It will therefore be as well for readers to bear them in mind as they peruse the text. The topics briefly considered here are the products which banks market, the creation of Eurocurrency and a range of facts about the size of and participants in the foreign exchange markets.

What do Bankers Sell?

Banks play a central role in financial management, whether in the domestic or international market place. Too often students of finance accept that banks occupy this vital position without asking themselves what kind of services bankers actually sell.

Most firms have a clearly visible product – Ford produces cars, Plessey produces communications equipment, ICL produces computers. But confusion surrounds what banks actually produce. The answer is that banks basically produce money in the form of demand and time deposits. Demand deposits are those where the investor places money with the bank but the money is repayable to the investor without notice – that is, on demand. This contrasts with time deposits where the investor places money with the bank but the money is only repayable (except with penalty) after the expiration of a fixed time. Most time deposits involve the bank in paying interest to the investor; some demand deposits also attract interest, but some do not. The receipts from these deposits provide the wherewithal to make loans and buy securities and other assets which yield an interest income for the bank. Banks have numerous other activities from which they receive fee income. They advise companies, manage trusts, and so on. But the bread-and-butter activity of banking involves trading in demand and time deposits and loans.

Banks deal with two groups of customers – depositors and borrowers. Most borrowers are also depositors; some depositors are also borrowers. Business firms tend to be predominantly borrowers. Households tend to be primarily depositors. Banks are intermediaries between the depositors who want a safe, secure and

5

convenient place to store some of their wealth, and borrowers, who want to expand their current production or consumption more rapidly than they can on the basis of their existing wealth and current income. The spread or markup between the interest rates bankers charge borrowers and the cost of borrowing covers their expenses and is the source of their profits.

Profits in banking depend on four factors. The first two are the bank's marketing skills in attracting deposits and its investment skills in making loans. Deposits coming in and loans going out appear on the bank's balance sheet respectively as liabilities and assets of the bank. The third source of profit is the banker's marketing, innovative and technical skills in rendering off-balance sheet services such as corporate finance advice and services relating to international trade. The fourth key to a bank's profit is, of course, management skills. Historically, the skills of bankers in terms of attracting deposits have been the key in determining how rapidly their banks grow. Recently, an emphasis upon off-balance sheet factors has become more evident − including the intermediation of money to borrowers from lenders without appearing on the banks' own balance sheets.

Investment skills involve matching the yields on loans and other assets with their risks. Riskier loans should attract higher yields. Banks seek those assets which offer the highest return for the risk. The banks that are best able to determine which assets are underpriced relative to their risks earn the highest returns. Banks which earn the highest returns are better able to increase the interest rates they pay on deposits and hence they can grow more rapidly than their competitors.

The Creation of Eurodollars

The traditional definition of a Eurodollar is a dollar deposited in a bank outside the USA.[1] A Eurodeutsche Mark is a Deutsche Mark deposited in a bank outside West Germany. A Eurosterling deposit is created by depositing British pounds in a bank account outside the UK. The term 'Eurocurrency' is used to embrace all forms of Euro-deposits. A certain amount of care needs to be exercised when interpreting information in this field because the term 'Eurodollars' is sometimes used as a generic term for all Eurocurrency deposits.

No mystery attaches to the production of Eurodollar deposits. In essence, the process is the same as when an individual with a deposit in one New York bank transfers funds to another bank in New York. The only difference is that the Euro-bank in London is across the Atlantic rather than across the Big Apple. If an individual with a dollar deposit in New York decides to move funds to the London branch of the same bank, the bank ends up producing an offshore dollar deposit. The London bank deposits the cheque in its account in a US bank. The investor now holds a dollar deposit in a bank in London as opposed to a dollar deposit in a

---

1. This definition is referred to as 'traditional' because, since December 1981, it has been possible for certain US financial institutions to establish, within the USA, international banking facilities, commonly termed IBFs. The IBFs accepting foreign deposits are exempted from reserve requirements and interest rate restrictions and can make loans to foreign borrowers. Under certain circumstances dollars deposited with an IBF effectively become Eurodollars. This topic is referred to again in more detail in Chapter 23.

bank in New York. Total deposits of the banks in the United States are unchanged. Individual investors hold smaller deposits in the United States and they hold larger deposits in London. The increase in the London bank's deposits in the New York bank is matched by the increase in dollar deposits for the world as a whole. But it is important to note that the volume of dollar deposits in New York remains unchanged, while the volume in London increases.

In the domestic economy, the capacity of banks to expand their deposits is limited by the monetary authorities. They determine both the reserve base of the banking system (the supply of high-powered money) and reserve requirements. But in the external currency markets, that is, the Euromarkets, there are no reserve requirements. Eurobanks sell additional deposits whenever the interest rates they are willing to pay are sufficiently high to attract new depositors.

The absence of reserve requirements on offshore deposits does not mean that there is the potential for an infinite expansion of deposits and credit. In the absence of reserve requirements domestically, there would not be an infinite expansion of domestic deposits and credit because bankers themselves would maintain prudential reserves. The growth of offshore deposits is limited by the willingness of investors to acquire such deposits in competition with domestic deposits. For investors, the relevant comparison involves the risk and return on offshore deposits and the risk and return on domestic deposits. The Eurobank system in dollars is an offshore extension of the domestic banking system, just as the Eurobank system in Deutsche Marks is an offshore extension of the domestic Deutsche Mark banking system. Eurobanks are offshore branches of the major international banks.

Dollar deposits in London differ from New York dollar deposits in terms of political risk. They are subject to the actions of a different set of government authorities. Maybe investors who continue to hold dollars in New York believe that London dollars are too risky, and that the additional interest income is not justified in terms of the possible loss if a move of funds back to New York were somehow restricted, perhaps as a package of exchange controls or an attack on the Eurobanking system. The continued growth in external deposits during the sixties reflected increasing investor confidence that the additional risks attached to external deposits were small. The risks of holding dollars offshore seemed small, particularly when viewed in the light of the differential in dollar interest rates on offshore deposits relative to domestic deposits.

One popular explanation for the genesis of the Eurocurrency markets in the fifties is that the Russian government agencies wanted to maintain currency deposits in dollars because the dollar was the most accepted currency for financing their international transactions. They were reluctant to hold their dollars in deposits in New York because of the threat that the US authorities might freeze these deposits. So the Russian dollars moved to London. The Russians effectively believed that the political risk of London dollar deposits was lower than in New York.

While the Russians may have been the cause of the rapid growth of offshore deposits during the fifties, the big growth in the sixties reflected other factors. The foremost of these was the increasing differential between Eurodollar and domestic interest rates, which made it increasingly profitable to escape national regulation. On top of this, growth was fuelled by the increasing size of the multinational firm and the great competitive expansion of banks.

Depositors contemplating a move of their funds to the Eurocurrency markets must decide whether to acquire external deposits in London, Zurich, Paris or some other centre. Depositors choose among centres on the basis of their estimates of political risk. This rules out a lot of potential centres where regulation or the threat of regulation is evident. Even though there may be an interest rate which would induce lenders to acquire dollar deposits in Sofia, banks issuing these deposits would not necessarily have the investment opportunities to justify paying such high interest rates.

Facts about the Foreign Exchange Markets

For the majority of foreign exchange markets, there are no individual, physical market places. The market is made up of banks and dealers carrying out transactions via the telephone and other telecommunication devices.

The total world foreign exchange market is the largest of all markets on earth. Trading around the world has been estimated (Group of Thirty 1985) to have doubled between 1979 and 1984, reaching $150 billion per day; this is well over fifty times the size of the New York Stock Exchange. The market is a twenty-four hour market which moves from one centre to another – from Tokyo to Hong Kong to Singapore to Bahrain to Beirut to London to New York to San Francisco to Sydney – as the sun moves round the world.

Between 90 and 95 per cent of all foreign exchange transactions involve banks. This high preponderance is reflected by banks taking and unravelling positions in currencies in order to offset imbalances created by their purchases and sales with customers. Some 99.5 per cent of all trades involve the US dollar. If a French importer wishes to pay a British exporter, the bank will calculate the French franc/sterling rate as the combination of the French franc/dollar rate and the dollar/sterling rate.

Nowadays, trade accounts for only a small proportion of foreign exchange deals – maybe 1 to 2 per cent of all transactions. The lion's share is made up of capital movements from one centre to another and the taking of positions by bankers in different currencies.

There is a spot market in which deals are arranged with effect immediately and there is a forward market in which purchase or sale is arranged today at an agreed rate but with delivery some time in the future. Forward markets do not exist for all currencies – for example, there is no forward Brazilian cruzado market. But, for a few currencies the forward market goes up to one year, and for many it is only in existence for up to six months. The term 'deep market' refers to those currencies which are widely dealt, for example sterling, Deutsche Marks, etc., and at the opposite end of the spectrum, the term 'shallow or thin market' is applied to currencies which are only occasionally traded. London is the largest foreign exchange centre, followed (a long way behind) by Zurich and Frankfurt in that order.

The foreign exchange market is the cheapest market in the world in which to deal. If one were to start with US $1 million and switch this into Deutsche Marks and then immediately reverse the transaction so that one returned to US dollars, the proceeds would be less than US $1 million by the amount of twice the bid/offer spread (the rate for selling and the rate for buying) for Deutsche Marks against US dollars − after all two deals have been done. But the total amount by which one would be out of pocket would only be $300 or so. For major currencies, the large banks act as market makers. This means that they hold stocks of foreign currencies and are prepared to deal in large amounts at stated prices. In other currencies, banks may operate as brokers, thereby avoiding the risk of price movements.

Foreign exchange dealers can make or lose a lot of money for the banks which employ them. Whilst they can make half a million dollars a day for the bank, they can also lose this sum. Their salaries and bonuses are high, too. Some make £150,000 per annum. But their business life is strenuous − watching currency movements for ten hours a day in the bank (and taking a Reuters foreign exchange rate mini-screen home) and dealing on the finest of margins takes its toll. Dealers on banks' foreign exchange desks seem to be aged between twenty and just over thirty. Perhaps beyond thirty, reflexes are slower; perhaps the adrenalin flows more slowly − or maybe dealers have made so much money already that motivation is not quite so great.

Reference

Group of Thirty (1985) *The Foreign Exchange Market in the 1980s*, Group of Thirty, New York.

3

The International Monetary System up to 1945

What do we mean by the international monetary system? Essentially, it encompasses the institutions, instruments, laws, rules and procedures for handling international payments, in particular those in final settlement of inter-country debts. Money has sometimes been defined as whatever is used in final settlement of debt. Internationally, central banks have come to be the institutions which make final settlements, and hence the assets they use may be termed international money. Central banks hold reserves of international money. These have also been termed reserve assets.

Prior to the Second World War there was no international central bank. Usually, central banks of individual countries made final settlements through transfers of gold or sterling or US dollars. A transfer of gold, sterling or US dollars from one country (other than the UK or the USA) to another (again leaving aside the UK and the USA) reduced the former's reserve assets and increased the latter's. A transfer of sterling from the UK to another country could be made by creating sterling deposit liabilities owed to the other country. The same was true for the USA. Thus reserve currency countries, as the UK and the USA came to be termed, had a different status from that of other countries. They could finance purchases, loans and investments by creating debt. They were effectively bankers to the world. They could create international money. If other countries had deficits in their balance of payments, they had to export gold or sterling or US dollars, thus reducing their holdings of international money. But as long as foreign countries accepted dollars or sterling, the USA and the UK could settle deficits by creating international money.

In this chapter we trace the international monetary system from before the First World War to the end of the 1939–1945 War. It was an era before the advent of the International Monetary Fund (see Chapter 4) and it was an era when gold, sterling and the US dollar occupied centre stage as media for international debt settlements.

The Gold Standard

The international monetary system that operated immediately prior to the 1914–1918 War was termed the gold standard. Then, countries accepted two major assets – gold and sterling – in settlement of international debt. So the term gold/sterling standard might be more appropriate.

Most major countries operated the gold standard system. A unit of a country's currency was defined as a certain weight – a part of an ounce – of gold. It also provided that gold could be obtained from the treasuries of these countries in exchange for money and coin of the country concerned.

The pound sterling could be converted into 113.0015 grains of fine gold, and the US dollar into 23.22 grains. The pound was effectively defined as 113.0015/23.22 times as much gold as the dollar – or 4.8665 times as much gold. Through gold equivalents, the pound was worth \$4.8665. This amount of dollars was termed the par value of the pound.

A country is said to be on the gold standard when its central bank is obliged to give gold in exchange for its currency when asked for it. When the UK was on the gold standard before 1914, anyone could go to the Bank of England and demand gold in exchange for bank notes. The UK came off the gold standard in 1914, but in 1925 it returned to a modified version termed the gold bullion standard. Individual bank notes were no longer convertible into gold, but gold bars of 400 ounces were sold and bought by the Bank of England. Other countries adopted either this system or the gold exchange standard, under which their central banks would exchange home currency for the currency of some other country on the gold standard rather than for gold itself. Britain was forced to abandon the gold standard in 1931.

The gold standard was a central pinnacle in the classical economic theory of equilibrium in international trade. The currency of countries on the gold standard was freely convertible into gold and this fixed exchange rates and enabled all international debt settlement to be in gold. A balance of payments surplus caused an inflow of gold into the central bank. This enabled it to expand its domestic money supply without fear of having insufficient gold to meet its liabilities. The increase in the quantity of money tended to raise prices resulting in a fall in the demand for

Table 3.1 Dates for the Adoption of the Gold Standard

Britain	1816
Germany	1871
Sweden, Norway and Denmark	1873
France, Belgium, Switzerland, Italy and Greece	1874
Holland	1875
Uruguay	1876
United States	1879
Austria	1892
Chile	1895
Japan	1897
Russia	1898
Dominican Republic	1901
Panama	1904
Mexico	1905

Source: Chandler (1948)

exports and therefore a reduction in the balance of payments surplus. In the event of a deficit in the balance of payments, the reverse was expected to happen. The outflow of gold would be accompanied by relative money supply contraction resulting in exports becoming more competitive and the deficit automatically becoming corrected.

The adoption of the gold standard began in Britain early in the nineteenth century. An attempt was made in the 1860s by a number of European countries to establish the Latin Monetary Union involving bimetallism for gold and silver. The intention was that both gold and silver should be used for international debt settlement. But the establishment of the gold standard in Germany in 1871, together with less demand for silver in other areas, led to a diminished use of silver as international money. The United States was forced to abandon redemption of paper money in metal during the Civil War, but the redemption of paper money for gold began in 1879. Key dates for the adoption of the gold standard in selected countries are summarised in Table 3.1.

The First World War had a serious effect on the international monetary system. Britain was forced to abandon the gold standard because of the wartime deficit on its balance of payments, and its reluctance at that time to provide gold to settle international differences. This was, perhaps, the beginning of a reduction in confidence in sterling as an international reserve asset.

Many other countries temporarily abandoned the gold standard, but none had the same significance as the action of Britain, because sterling had financed 90 per cent of world payments. The British government, recognising the importance of sterling and of British institutions in international finance, wished to return to the gold standard as soon as possible. Delay occurred because of the recession in the United States in 1920 and 1921, coupled with the post-World War I inflation which reversed itself as rapidly as it had occurred. Recovery in the United States came and a degree of recovery also occurred in Britain. After its disastrous hyper-inflation, ending with the value of the Mark at 4 trillion to the dollar, Germany also experienced stabilisation and it returned to the gold standard in 1924.

The gold standard to which major countries returned in the mid-twenties was different to that which had existed before the First World War. The major difference was that instead of two international reserve assets – gold and sterling – there were several. Both the USA and France had become much more important in international finance and dollar and franc deposits were used for much financing. However, generally speaking, countries other than Britain had only small amounts of gold. When some countries, including France, accumulated sterling balances, they sometimes attempted to convert these into gold, drawing upon Britain's gold reserves. When sterling, apart from gold, had been the only international currency, operating the international monetary system was not difficult, but when there were a number of countries whose bank deposits constituted international money, and when confidence in different currencies varied, the system became more difficult to operate.

A second important difference was that flexibility in costs and prices no longer existed as before the 1914–1918 War. This was especially important in Britain which had returned to the gold standard based on pre-War par values. But only with a decline in relative costs and prices could the former par value of the pound have been maintained in the long run. Given that flexibility in costs and prices was lacking, confidence in sterling deteriorated, culminating in the UK abandoning the gold standard in 1931. Most other countries followed the British example in quitting the gold standard.

But there were other forces impinging on Britain in the early thirties which also had a significant effect on her decision to discard the gold standard. Two of these were the Great Depression of the late twenties and early thirties and the international financial crisis of 1931; each of these topics will be summarised with a focus upon its impact on the international monetary system.

The Great Depression

Detailed discussion of the causes of the Great Depression are outside the terms of reference of a work of this sort. Nonetheless, various questions spring to the reader's mind. Some of these are pertinent to the international monetary system; some are not. To what extent was the stock market crash in 1929 a cause of the Depression? How did the big contraction in money supply contribute to a decline in business activity? Was the decline in rates of profit, which began in 1929, significant? Some of the explanations propounded do have significance in terms of their effects on Britain and the gold standard.

One such is the fact that the expansion of money and credit in the USA in the late twenties was greater than that needed for trade and commerce, and the excess found its way into stock market and real estate speculation. When the credit expansion ceased, stock market levels and real estate prices fell. A relevant question is why the expansion of money and credit did not result in a greater increase in either real output or prices of commodities and services. And one possible answer is that wage rates did not increase much, with the result that consumer spending did not rise sufficiently to cause any marked rise in either real or nominal GNP.

Interest rates and the availability of credit in the USA are inextricably linked to Britain's plight. Following the sharp rise in stock market prices in 1927 to 1929, the Federal Reserve Bank raised the discount rate as part of the classical precipitation for slowing the growth of money supply. This resulted in higher interest rates in the USA and this had the tendency to attract foreign funds – particularly from Britain. Remember that we are talking about an environment with fixed exchange rates. So funds moved out of the UK to take advantage of higher relative interest rates at the same time as gold was leaving the country because of Britain's overvalued exchange rate.

Discussing the Depression, Milton Friedman and Anna Schwartz (1963) have argued that what began life as a minor recession was transformed into a major depression because, as business declined, the money supply was reduced. With the US committed to deflation accompanied by a reduction in its money supply, the impact on the rest of the world was devastating. Friedman and Schwartz demonstrate impressive evidence of a correlation between declines in business activity and declines in the money stock, not only during the Great Depression, but in the five other instances between 1867 and 1960. They point out that in each case the decline in the money supply preceded the decline in business activity.

Furthermore, the USA had imposed import restrictions in 1922 and again in

1930. Countries heavily dependent upon exports found their incomes falling sharply, their unemployment levels rising and their consumption falling. They could neither finance their essential imports from their exports nor from their reserves.

Add to a world economic system under strain the precariousness of an international monetary system, balanced like an inverse pyramid upon a relatively small base of gold holdings, and our structure is weak indeed. Strains on those countries without substantial gold holdings could cause difficulties for the gold exchange standard countries. Moreover, strains on a gold standard country resulting in a flow of gold reserves to another country could easily precipitate a financial crisis. Many economists are convinced that the supply of gold at that time was inadequate to support the international financial structure of the day.

Exchange rates were out of line with cost structures in different countries. Britain's return to the old par value for sterling was undoubtedly an error; France's devaluation of the franc in the twenties was too great; fundamental disequilibria existed. And the system was inadequate to cope with them. Faced with an overvalued currency in deep depression, one of Britain's responses was to abandon the gold standard. The international financial crisis of 1931 was also a major contributor in the British decision.

The International Financial Crisis in 1931

The 1931 crisis began with the insolvency of a branch banking institution in Austria called the Kredit-Anstalt. Its failure created a lack of confidence wholly disproportionate with the bank's size. It first caused a withdrawal of funds from Austria and then there followed a flow of money out of Germany because German banks had large deposits in Austrian banks. British, American and French banks, acting together, could probably have made loans to Austria and prevented the spread of panic, but French banks were unwilling to co-operate in aid to Austria in view of its customs union with Germany, France's former enemy. Panic spread. Agreements were worked out to halt withdrawals of funds. Fearing that the pressures of the early thirties would now undermine the banking system, withdrawals from Britain commenced, and the pound was under heavy pressure. The Bank of France was a big seller of sterling and Britain decided that it could no longer support the value of the pound. This culminated in the abandonment of the gold standard on 20 September 1931. It was replaced by a system in which the pound did not have a fixed value in relation to gold or dollars. One of its major advantages as an international reserve asset disappeared.

Following the 1931 banking crisis, exchange controls were imposed in Austria and spread to Germany to prevent withdrawals of funds held in banks there. And as evasions of controls started, so the controls themselves became stricter. It is arguable that such controls had a material effect in the contraction of world trade in the thirties.

The economic and political uncertainties following the crisis of 1931 led to an outflow of gold from Europe to the USA. Flows of $1 billion per annum were usual and they were much more than this in some years. The term 'golden avalanche' was justly coined. It led to possession by the USA at one time in the thirties of 80 per cent of the world's monetary gold. Owners of gold, and indeed other assets, sought safety for their wealth by shipping them to the USA and purchasing dollar financial assets in return. At that time the dollar seemed safe and firmly fixed in value relative to gold. In fact, the dollar was devalued in 1933 by an increase in the price of gold from $20.67 to $35 an ounce. After the devaluation there seemed little reason to fear further decline in the dollar's value. The price of $35 per ounce made gold sales in the USA attractive. The dramatic shift of gold holdings from the rest of the world to the USA is shown in Figure 3.1. The change in the price of official gold is not taken into account in this figure. US gold holdings immediately after the Second World War were over $20 billion, or some 75 per cent of the world's monetary gold stock.

Note: Data in the figure do not allow for the change in the official price of gold effective from 1933.

Figure 3.1 US Gold Holdings from 1928 to 1940

The gold standard of the 1880 to 1914 period and the gold exchange standard of the 1925 to 1931 period gave way to a mixture of fluctuating exchange rates for some countries and strict exchange controls in others. The likelihood of a gold standard, in any form, being restored in the immediate future was gone.

Exchange Rates After 1914

With the First World War, the stability of exchange rates for major currencies ended. This had been a key feature in the international monetary system before 1914. When World War I began, the combination of payments via London for imports under bank credits and acceptances of London merchant banks combined with utter confidence in sterling – meaning that there were no significant with-drawals of sterling deposits – caused the exchange rate for the pound to rise sharply. Sterling rose as high as $7 to the £. But, as wartime expenditures occurred, the sterling exchange rate began to fall and dropped as low as $3.18 by early 1920.

As explained earlier in this chapter, the early thirties saw the international monetary system then in use begin to disintegrate. By the beginning of 1933 the major currencies of the world could be categorised as those of the gold bloc (France, Switzerland, the Netherlands and Belgium) which maintained their value in terms of gold, those which maintained their value by strict exchange controls (such as Germany's) enforced under a dictatorship, and those which were permitted to depreciate. Many currencies depreciated by as much as 35 to 50 per cent during the first half of the decade. Those countries which did not permit their currencies to depreciate, for example the USA, France, Belgium, Switzerland and the Netherlands, resorted to strong deflationary pressures. It was frequently complained that some countries deliberately encouraged currency depreciation, engaging in a beggar-my-neighbour policy. International trade was at a low level, and international capital flows virtually stopped.

The depreciation of currencies in the thirties, especially that of the pound – see Figure 3.2 – meant a decline in the foreign exchange component of international reserves relative to the gold component. With limited production of gold and with strong flows thereof to the USA, most countries found their gold holdings reduced.

With large fluctuations in exchange rates, accompanied by low levels of inter-national trade and world depression, there were influential calls in the late thirties and early forties in favour of a return to a stable exchange rate environment.

However, the Second World War led to more extensive and tighter controls on international trade and investment. Transactions with enemy countries became illegal and much of the trade between friendly nations consisted of munitions and warfare supplies. Private markets (as opposed to inter-governmental ones) for most currencies almost ceased to exist. Much of the trade that continued was under various inter-governmental agreements. But even the inter-governmental transactions that took place then were generally either barter transactions or grants made to carry on hostilities against the enemy. There was virtually no role for international finance. Foreign exchange markets, exchange rates, and other insti-tutional mechanisms were effectively suspended during the war and re-established when the war ended. Trade controls and exchange controls frequently meant that the usual methods of financing could not be used. So the financing of trade was not an urgent problem during the war.

By the end of the Second World War, many commentators, bankers and economists were agreed upon the need for a new monetary system. Sterling's dominance of international trade had gone; the era of the gold standard had passed.

Governments might have waited for a new international monetary order to

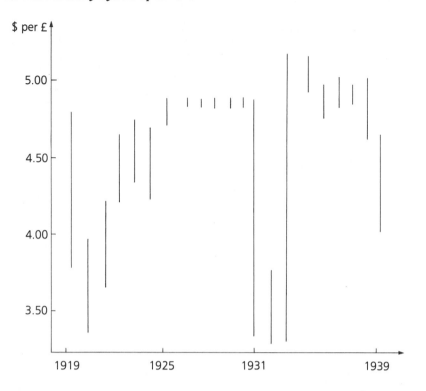

Figure 3.2 The Sterling/Dollar Exchange Rate 1919 to 1939 (Range Based on Monthly Averages)

evolve to replace the system which had worked well before 1914 but which had failed in the period from 1914 to 1944. But this would have meant uncertainty. Action was urgently needed. The action taken stemmed from the Bretton Woods agreement and saw the creation of a new international institution, the International Monetary Fund. The monetary system which emerged from Bretton Woods and occupied the international stage for the immediate post-war period through to 1971 is discussed in the next chapter.

Summary

The international monetary system based on the gold standard worked well from 1880 to 1914 – mainly because London was at the centre of the system and utter confidence in sterling and gold prevailed. In addition, there was no excessive inflation during that period and trade and investment were relatively free from controls.

International financial problems emerged after the First World War; they continued through the twenties and culminated in the financial crisis of 1931. The gold exchange standard revolving around competing international financial centres

– London, New York and Paris – did not work well and there was not enough gold at the fixed price for the system's needs. Second, inflation was sometimes a serious problem – especially the hyperinflation in Germany in the early twenties. Raising the price of gold then would have been likely to cause more inflation.

Furthermore, the USA ploughed a furrow which was hardly consistent with the smooth operation of an international monetary system. It made unwise foreign investments in the twenties and had almost ceased international lending and investing by 1930. It raised tariffs in 1922 and again in 1930 when world trade was declining. This fall in world trade and investment in the early thirties gave rise in many countries to competitive depreciation of currencies accompanied by exchange and trade controls.

A common belief emerged that international monetary problems might be attacked by the establishment of stable foreign exchange rates and the elimination of trade and exchange controls. It was against this background that governments sought, after the war, to design a new international monetary system which would achieve the kind of smooth operation that characterised the first part of the century. The need to search for this formula for international monetary order was universally accepted and it was accorded top priority.

References

Chandler, Lester V. (1948) *The Economies of Money and Banking*, Harper and Row.
Friedman, Milton and Schwartz, Anna J. (1963) *A Monetary History of the United States, 1867–1960*, Princeton University Press.

4

The International Monetary System Since 1945

The framework for a new international monetary system was created in July 1944 in the USA at Bretton Woods, New Hampshire. The prime movers were John Maynard Keynes and Harry Dexter White, the respective British and US representatives. The key innovations of the Bretton Woods agreement were:

1. A new permanent institution, the International Monetary Fund (IMF), was to be established to promote consultation and collaboration on international monetary problems and to lend to member countries in need due to recurring balance of payments deficits.
2. Each Fund member would establish, with the approval of the IMF, a par value for its currency and would undertake to maintain exchange rates for its currency within 1 per cent of the declared par value. Countries that freely bought and sold gold in settlement of international transactions were deemed to be adhering to the requirement that they maintain exchange rates within 1 per cent margins. Hence the USA, the only country that met this condition, was not expected to intervene in the foreign exchange markets. Other countries would intervene by buying or selling dollars against their own currencies, to keep their rates within 1 per cent of their parities with the dollar.
3. Members would only change their par values after having secured IMF approval. This approval would only be granted if there were evidence that the country was suffering from a fundamental disequilibrium in its balance of payments. It was generally agreed that a long and continuing large loss of reserve assets in support of an exchange rate would be evidence of this fundamental disequilibrium.
4. Each IMF member country would pay a quota into the IMF pool, one quarter being in gold, with the remainder in its own currency. The size of the quota was a function of each member's size in the world economy.
5. The IMF would be in a position, from the subscription of quotas, to lend to countries in ongoing deficit.

A new monetary framework was thus established which created fixed exchange rates subject to alteration should fundamental disequilibria emerge. Since there

19

was a mechanism for discontinuous adjustment to exchange rates, the system became known as the adjustable peg system.

During its early years, the Bretton Woods system played a positive part in a rapid expansion in world trade. However, its success obscured one of its basic shortcomings – there was no provision for expanding the supply of international reserves necessary to support growing trade flows. The unmet demand for international reserves eventually led to increased holdings of national currencies and in particular it strengthened the US dollar's position as an international reserve currency.

The dollar's expanding role in international trade and finance raised new problems in monetary relations. This difficulty has been referred to as the Triffin dilemma, named after Robert Triffin (1960) who focused attention upon it. Because the US dollar played the part of a reserve currency, US balance of payments deficits were necessary in order to increase international liquidity. But as US liabilities to foreign central banks grew, so confidence in the convertibility of dollars into gold wavered. US gold reserves were becoming a decreasing fraction of foreign liabilities. This method of providing international liquidity could only continue as long as no central bank attempted a run on the US gold reserves. Concern over this dilemma led to the introduction of a new international reserve asset administered by the IMF. This asset, the Special Drawing Right (SDR), was proposed and ratified in 1969.

SDRs were allocated to individual countries by the IMF through the deliberate decision of IMF members to accept them as a new form of international reserve. These credits were allocated to IMF members in proportion to their quotas – rather like a bonus issue of shares in a company. A country holding SDRs may use them to acquire foreign currency by transferring them, via the IMF Special Drawing Account, to another country in exchange for foreign currency. Only member states of the IMF and certain designated official institutions may legally hold SDRs.

The Role of Gold up to 1971

Gold had long existed as a medium of international exchange. But in its role as a reserve asset it has significant shortcomings. First, it is wasteful to use a commodity with a significant positive cost of production to perform a function which could equally well be performed by a financial instrument with a zero cost of production. Second, the use of gold gives benefits to the country where the gold is produced and which may not necessarily benefit the world economy. And there have been objections to the political nature of the world's largest gold producers, the USSR and South Africa. Third, the increase in the supply of gold may not reflect the world's increasing need for extra international liquidity. Indeed, increases in gold supplies may be unrelated to the world's needs. They may be substantially related to the need for foreign exchange on the part of the USSR and South Africa.

The price of gold was fixed in 1933 at $35 an ounce and this fixed value held up to the early seventies. Since the currencies were fixed in relation to the dollar, central banks could exchange their currencies for dollars and with their dollars they could obtain gold. The US Federal Reserve Bank was willing to buy and sell gold at this rate. This willingness of the USA to back the world monetary system is understandable given that the USA, at the end of the Second World War, had a gold stock valued at $20 billion, or 60 per cent of the total of official gold reserves. As long as the dollar and its gold backing were considered invulnerable, foreign central banks had an incentive to hold currencies, which earned interest, rather than gold, which earned nothing.

In 1954, a gold market was opened in London in which private buyers and sellers could operate. A central bank gold pool of $80 million was set up in 1962. The gold pool was an arrangement among eight countries, including the USA, to sell or buy gold in the free market to keep the price close to the official price of $35 an ounce. France left the gold pool in 1967.

By the late sixties there existed a situation whereby the dollar had become convertible into gold not only by foreign central banks but also by private speculators all over the world.

Until 1968, under gold pool arrangement, major central banks clubbed together to hold the gold price at $35 an ounce. As there was no prospect of the gold price going down, but a good prospect of it going up, this gave speculators a one-way option. In 1968, central banks were forced to set the gold price free for commercial transactions. But, for settlements between themselves, they agreed to stick to the old price and not to sell gold on the free market. The central banks expected that under this two-tier gold system, the free-market gold price would stay within easy reach of the official price. It did not do so for long.

Increasingly, fixed exchange rates were becoming more and more difficult to defend and various governments around the world were very reluctant to devalue and revalue despite what many would have described as fundamental disequilibria. In other words, international agreements were creating difficulties for the system.

In 1971 the system was clearly under pressure on two fronts – the fixed gold price and fixed exchange rates made little sense. Matters were brought to a head when President Nixon, as a preparation to the 1972 election, sought to expand demand in the USA. Speculation against the dollar mounted and many central banks in continental Europe and Japan were forced to buy dollars to keep their currencies within the narrow bands required by Bretton Woods – rather than allowing them to rise, which economic and speculative pressures were favouring. The free market gold price rose sharply. This led several countries to demand conversion of their surplus dollars into gold at the official price of $35 per ounce. The USA, with $10 billion in gold reserves versus liabilities of $50 billion in other countries' reserves, decided to suspend convertibility in August 1971 and the US dollar was set free to float.

Because of anxiety about the international monetary system, a conference of finance ministers was arranged in December 1971 at the Smithsonian Institute in the USA. The so-called Smithsonian Agreement resulted. This increased the fixed exchange rate band spread to 4.5 per cent, allowing central banks more room for manoeuvre before intervention became necessary. At the same time upward revaluations of various currencies against the US dollar were agreed, with the dollar formally devaluing against gold. The price of the metal was increased from $35 per ounce to $38 per ounce – an effective dollar devaluation of 9 per cent.

The dollar-based international monetary system continued to function for just over another year, when the failure of the US balance of payments to respond to the dollar's initial devaluation led to a second realignment. The dollar was devalued again in February 1973; this raised the official gold price to $42.22 per ounce. But this realignment was almost immediately brought under excessive strain when a new exchange crisis occurred in March 1973 and European central banks refused to buy dollars. In mid-March the Bretton Woods era finally crumbled when fourteen major industrial nations abandoned the adjustable peg and allowed their currencies to float against the dollar.

But we are not universally in a floating exchange rate world now – far from it, as will be seen under 'Exchange Rate Arrangements' later in this chapter.

The Second Amendment

Following abandonment of pegged exchange rates in March 1973, floating exchange rates were introduced for many countries. In Europe, the opinion was widespread that floating should be only temporary, a view most forcibly expressed by the French. In the USA, opinion favoured a continuing float.

Discussions at summit level moved from Rambouillet in France in November 1975 to Jamaica in January 1976 and culminated in a new IMF Article on exchange rate practices. This amendment, the second in the history of the IMF, was ratified by the required majority and became effective on 1 April 1978.

The Second Amendment provides for the reform of three key aspects of international monetary relations. Firstly, it allows substantially more flexibility in the management of exchange rates and expands the IMF's responsibility for supervising the international monetary system. Secondly, it alters the nature of the SDR to increase its attractiveness as an international reserve asset. And finally, it simplifies and expands the IMF's ability to assist members in financing short-term imbalances in their international payments accounts.

Under the first innovation, IMF members are expected to 'collaborate with the fund and other members to assure orderly exchange arrangements and to promote a stable system of exchange rates' (IMF 1978). Their method of collaboration is left to members' discretion. Members' obligations regarding their exchange practices are specified under Article IV of the fund's Articles of Agreement. Under this amended article (IMF 1978), each member shall:

1. endeavour to direct its economic and financial policies toward the objective of fostering orderly economic growth with reasonable price stability, with due regard to its circumstances;
2. seek to promote stability by fostering orderly underlying economic and financial conditions and a monetary system that does not tend to produce erratic disruptions;
3. avoid manipulating exchange rates or the international monetary system in order to prevent effective balance of payments adjustment or to gain an unfair competitive advantage over other members.

In April 1977, the IMF had adopted principles (IMF 1977) to provide additional guidance in the choice of an exchange policy. These principles of exchange rate management state that:

1. A member shall avoid manipulating exchange rates or the international monetary system in order to prevent effective balance of payments adjustment or to gain an unfair advantage over other members.
2. A member should intervene in the exchange market if necessary to counter disorderly conditions, which may be characterised *inter alia* by disruptive short-term movements in the exchange value of its currency.
3. Members should take into account in their intervention policies the interests of other members, including those of countries in whose currencies they intervene.

The above principles give members a great deal of latitude in the choice of an exchange rate policy. Members may peg, float, or manage their currencies to whatever degree they feel is consistent with their own domestic economic policies. The Second Amendment restricts the role of gold in the international monetary system. Par values may not be set in terms of gold and an official price for gold has been abolished. Members are expected to co-operate in reducing the role of gold with the intention that the SDR should become the primary reserve asset of the international monetary system. The IMF abolished requirements that members make some payments in terms of gold and has begun to dispose of its gold reserve.

The IMF may initiate consultations with members which it suspects of violating its obligations under Article IV. The key argument in favour of this kind of intervention is that nations have, in the past, waited too long before approaching the IMF with proposals for parity adjustment under the adjustable peg system. Other arguments are based on the necessity to restrict the freedom of members to manage their own exchange rate.

Consultation between the IMF and its members is carried out at various levels. Members' economic policies are reviewed. The IMF performs a broad review during the preparation of its annual world economic outlook. At that time, members' exchange rate practices are examined and their balance of payments objectives are checked for consistency. This review points out trouble spots for further attention. The second level of review occurs during regularly scheduled Article IV consultations with members. These consultations are conducted to review the economic policies of members in greater detail than is possible during the preparation of the world economic outlook. When possible, these consultations occur annually.

In addition to regular consultations, the IMF relies on a number of indicators to signal the need for special consultations concerning a member's economic policies. These consultations may be initiated should the indicators suggest that a member is not fulfilling its obligations under Article IV. The IMF's concern is aroused by (IMF 1977):

1. protracted large-scale intervention in one direction in the exchange market;
2. an unsustainable level of official or quasi-official borrowing, or excessive

and prolonged short-term official or quasi-official lending, for balance of payments purposes;

3. the introduction, substantial intensification, or prolonged maintenance, for balance of payments purposes, of restrictions on, or incentives for, current transactions or payments, or the introduction of substantial modification for balance of payments purposes of restrictions on, or incentives for, the inflow or outflow of capital;

4. the pursuit, for balance of payments purposes, of monetary and other domestic financial policies that provide abnormal encouragement or discouragement to capital flows;

5. behaviour of the exchange rate that appears to be unrelated to underlying economic and financial conditions, including factors affecting competitiveness and long-term capital movements.

In addition to these indicators, the managing director of the IMF can initiate supplementary consultations if it is believed that the current practices of a member have important effects on other members. These consultations can be initiated even when the surveillance indicators do not suggest the need (IMF 1979). This provides the IMF with an opportunity to investigate developments that might not otherwise come under review.

Through its surveillance, the IMF identifies members causing disruptive variations in exchange rates through their domestic economic policies. The IMF may then suggest alternative domestic policies which would have less of an effect on the exchange market. In 1980, the IMF initiated 94 consultations under Article IV.

Providing members with assistance in overcoming payments imbalances continues to be one of the IMF's prime objectives. A member in need of foreign exchange to finance short-term exchange rate intervention may apply to the IMF for borrowing assistance.

International Reserves

The IMF provides its members with international reserves through the SDR. Changes in the calculation of the value and interest rate earned on excess holdings of SDRs have increased its attractiveness as a reserve asset. The value of the SDR is no longer fixed in terms of the US dollar. Its value is now calculated using a currency basket that includes the five major member currencies. The quantities of each of the currencies included in this currency basket are reported in Table 4.1 along with the value of the SDR in terms of the US dollar on 11 July 1985.

The dollar value of the SDR is computed daily using the average of the buying and selling rates at midday on the London foreign exchange markets. The amounts of currency making up the SDR are fixed; changes in market exchange rates cause changes in the effective weights of the currency amounts over time. The interest rate paid to members holding more than their allocation of SDRs and owed to members holding less than their allocation is determined quarterly as a weighted average of market interest rates. The attractiveness of the SDR has also been

Table 4.1 Valuation of the SDR as at 11 July 1985

Currency	Currency amount	Exchange rate in dollars	US dollar equivalent
US dollar	0.5400	1.00000	0.540000
Deutsche Mark	0.4600	0.34264	0.157614
French franc	0.7400	0.11274	0.083428
Japanese yen	34.0000	0.00412	0.140080
UK pound	0.0710	1.38200	0.098122
			1.019244

increased by expanding the types of transactions in which it can be used. In addition to financing outright purchases of foreign currencies, members can now use SDRs in forward and swap transactions and they can donate SDRs and make SDR-denominated loans to other members and authorised non-member institutions.

Exchange Rate Arrangements

The current exchange rate practices of IMF members span the range of alternatives from pegging to floating. Pegged exchange rates generally are managed on a day-to-day basis through official intervention in the foreign exchange markets and by internal regulations limiting exchange market transactions. Exchange rate parities are set in terms of a foreign currency or group of currencies, and fluctuations in the exchange rate around this parity are achieved by official intervention.

Countries that peg their exchange rate may select from a wide range of alternatives. Many nations peg to a single currency. But it has become increasingly common to peg against a group of currencies. Pegging is attractive because it helps reduce the variability of prices in the domestic economy. But pegging has its costs. These flow from the need to regulate international transactions and intervene in foreign exchange markets. Exchange rate arrangements as of 31 March 1985 are summarised in Table 4.2.

Generally speaking, floating exchange rates are managed less closely, although practices vary. Some members refrain altogether from intervention, whilst others intervene strongly. In most cases, nations with developed financial markets prefer floating exchange rates.

Of the 147 nations that reported their exchange policies to the IMF on 31 March 1985, 94 pegged in terms of some currency or group of currencies and 53 floated their currencies. Thirty-four nations pegged their currencies to the US dollar, 14 to the French franc, one to the Indian rupee, one to the UK pound sterling, and two to the South African rand. Eleven nations pegged to the special drawing right and 31 pegged to some other currency basket.

The group of floating currencies included six that were really managed using

Table 4.2   Exchange Rate Arrangements as of March 1985

	Currency pegged to				Flexibility limited in terms of a single currency or group of currencies		More flexible		
US dollar	French franc	Other currency	SDR	Other composite	Single currency	Cooperative arrangements	Adjusted according to a set of indicators	Other managed floating	Independently floating
Antigua & Barbuda	Benin	Bhutan (Indian rupee)	Burma Burundi	Algeria	Afghanistan	Belgium	Brazil	Argentina	Australia
Bahamas	Burkina Faso		Guinea	Austria	Bahrain	Denmark	Chile	Costa Rica	Canada
Barbados	Cameroon	Gambia,	Iran, I.R. of	Bangladesh	Ghana	France	Colombia	Ecuador	Jamaica
Belize	C. African Rep.	The (pound	Jordan	Botswana	Maldives	Germany	Peru	Greece	Japan
Bolivia	Chad	sterling)	Kenya	Cape Verde	Qatar	Ireland	Portugal	Guinea-Bissau	Lebanon
Djibouti	Comoros	Lesotho	Rwanda	China P.R.	Saudi Arabia	Italy	Somalia	Iceland	Philippines
Dominica	Congo	(South	São Tomé &	Cyprus	United Arab	Luxembourg		India	South Africa
Dominican Rep.	Equatorial	African	Principe	Fiji	Emirates	Netherlands		Indonesia	Uganda
Egypt	Guinea	rand)	Seychelles	Finland				Israel	United
El Salvador	Gabon	Swaziland	Vanuatu	Guyana				Korea	Kingdom
Ethiopia	Ivory	(South	Viet Nam	Hungary				Mexico	United States
Grenada	Coast	African		Kuwait				Morocco	Uruguay
Guatemala	Mali	rand)		Madagascar				New Zealand	Zaire
Haiti	Niger			Malawi				Nigeria	
Honduras	Senegal			Malaysia				Pakistan	
Iraq	Togo			Malta				Spain	
Lao P.D. Rep.				Mauritania				Sri Lanka	
Liberia				Mauritius				Turkey	
Libya				Mozambique				Western	
Nicaragua				Nepal				Samoa	
Oman				Norway				Yugoslavia	
Panama				Papua New					
Paraguay				Guinea					
St. Christopher				Romania					
& Nevis				Singapore					
St. Lucia				Solomon					
St. Vincent				Islands					
Sierra Leone				Sweden					
Sudan				Tanzania					
Suriname				Thailand					
Syrian Arab				Tunisia					
Rep.				Zambia					
Trinidad and				Zimbabwe					
Tobago									
Venezuela									
Yemen Arab									
Rep.									
Yemen, P.D.									
Rep.									

Source: International Monetary Fund, March 1985.

indicator rules. It also included the nations that were participating in the group float of the European Monetary System (EMS), which is looked at more closely later in this chapter. The remaining 39 nations used other, less specific rules to govern their exchange market intervention.

In truth, countries which allow their currency to float do not commit themselves not to intervene. Indeed, they either manage exchange rates informally, or use some set of economic indicators or rely on a cooperative exchange rate agreement such as the European Monetary System. Informal managed floats are the most frequently used. Many of these floaters follow strategies of leaning against the wind. This approach involves official intervention to smooth short-term fluctuations in exchange rates without unduly restricting long-term trends. Other nations with informally managed floats set target exchange rates and intervene to move market rates toward these levels.

Some countries rely on objective indicators to provide signals rather than using either targets or leaning against the wind. These indicators are used to show the economic need for a devaluation or a revaluation. Parities are adjusted frequently, in small amounts, as dictated by the indicators. Exchange market intervention is used to limit exchange rate fluctuations around these central rates. The procedures followed by the central bank of Brazil are typical of this practice. During 1981, the cruzeiro's parity against the US dollar, the intervention currency, was revised 33 times. The central bank made these adjustments in response to signals from a set of economic indicators that included Brazil's overall balance of payments position; the level of official foreign exchange reserves; the performance of Brazilian exports; and differences in inflation rates between Brazil and its major trading partners.

When a country chooses to peg or float its currency, it is not obliged to cooperate with the IMF or any other nation in the day-to-day management of exchange rates. Although most members value this independence, some nations wish to maintain closer economic ties with their trading partners. Article IV does not prohibit these nations from cooperating with each other in the management of their bilateral exchange rates. This practice, classified by the IMF as a cooperative exchange arrangement, has become known as group floating, of which the EMS is the most well-known.

The European Monetary System

Between April 1972 and December 1978, the various EEC countries operated a joint float referred to as the Snake. Its workings were rather like the EMS described below. However, strains upon the system had led to numerous withdrawals from it as intervention became an excessive burden upon participants. Despite the comparative failure of the Snake to yield a smooth exchange rate environment for Europe, it was replaced in 1979 by the EMS.

All the members of the EEC were participants in the EMS but the UK did not become a party to the group float. Becoming operational in March 1979, the purpose of the EMS was to 'stabilise exchange rates between the currencies of the member states of the European Economic Communities and to contribute to the strengthening of international monetary relations. At the same time it is intended to give a new impetus to the process of European integration' (Deutsche Bundesbank 1979). The eight countries that initially joined the group float intervened to limit fluctuations in their bilateral exchange rates while managing the group's float against the dollar. Within the EMS, intervention was expected to be carried out using group currencies. Two mechanisms were used to trigger intervention within the EMS. These were a parity grid of bilateral exchange rates and a set of divergence indicators.

The parity grid defines the central rates and upper and lower intervention rates for each of the bilateral exchange rates among member currencies. The buying and selling rates of each central bank differ by 2.25 per cent in either direction from the central parities for every currency except the Italian lira. The lira's intervention limits are set 6 per cent above and below its central rates against the other currencies of the group. Each member of the group float is obligated to buy its currency when one of its bilateral rates approaches the lower intervention limit, and to sell when it approaches the upper limit. So, if the Belgian franc moves to its lower limit against the Deutsche Mark, the National Bank of Belgium would be required to buy Belgian francs in the foreign exchange market, financing this intervention by drawing on its Deutsche Mark reserves. At the same time, the Deutsche Mark would be moving towards its upper limit against the franc. This would signal the Bundesbank to sell Deutsche Marks in exchange for Belgian francs. This sharing of responsibility for intervention divides the burden of exchange rate management between strong-currency and weak-currency countries.

In many ways, the operation of the parity grid is similar to that of the adjustable peg. But it differs from the Bretton Woods system in at least one important regard. Under the Bretton Woods agreement, the US dollar developed a special role as reserve currency and numeraire of the international monetary system. Exchange market intervention was carried out primarily in dollars, and exchange parities were defined in terms of the dollar. In the EMS, no single currency serves as numeraire. Instead, the par values of each participating currency are defined in terms of the European Currency Unit (ECU). Like other currency baskets, the ECU is composed of predetermined quantities of each member currency, including sterling. These quantities are selected so that the value of each component roughly reflects the relative size and importance of that member economy in respect of trade within the EEC. Plans call for the re-examination of the ECU's composition at five-year intervals. The composition of the ECU is shown in Table 4.3.

Table 4.3 Valuation of the ECU as at 26 November 1985

Currency	Currency amount	Exchange rate in Deutsche Marks		DM equivalent
Deutsche Mark	0.71900	×	1.000000	0.7190
French franc	1.31000	÷	3.047	0.4299
Sterling	0.08780	×	3.775	0.3297
Lira	140.00000	÷	675.0	0.2074
Guilder	0.25600	÷	1.126	0.2274
Belgian franc	3.71000	÷	20.21	0.1836
Luxembourg franc	0.14000	÷	20.21	0.0069
Danish kroner	0.21900	÷	3.164	0.0606
Irish punt	0.00871	×	3.096	0.0270
Greek drachma	1.15000	÷	59.031	0.0195
				2.2110

The bilateral central rates of the parity grid are ratios of the central rates of each currency against the ECU. Although the use of the ECU as numeraire avoids the politically sensitive selection of a national currency for that role, it increases the intervention activities of the participating central banks.

The second mechanism triggering intervention between the EMS is referred to as the divergence indicator. The divergence of a member's economic performance is signalled by fluctuations in the market value of the ECU relative to its central rate. Divergence limits for the domestic currency value of the ECU are set using the bilateral intervention limits from the parity grid. The upper intervention limits of the bilateral rates are used to compute the upper divergence limit, and the lower intervention limits are used to compute the lower divergence limit. The divergence threshold is reached when the ECU moves 75 per cent of the way toward either of its divergence limits.

The divergence indicator operates independently of the parity grid system. A currency can cross its divergence threshold without reaching any of its bilateral exchange rate limits, and a bilateral limit can be reached without crossing the divergence threshold. This indicator's function is to signal when a member is pursuing economic policies which should lead to appreciation or depreciation of its currency within the group.

Although parity realignments have been frequent with the EMS, it continues to bind the original participants. This flexibility has been the key to its early success and the EMS has survived longer than many of its critics suggested it would. But its long-term success depends on the convergence of economic performance and the coordination of economic policy within the EEC.

Summary

The framework for the international monetary system in the period immediately following the Second World War was set out in the Bretton Woods agreement of 1944. The IMF was created to promote consultation and solve problems on the international monetary front and to lend to member countries with recurring balance of payments deficits. The Bretton Woods agreement advocated par values for currencies with requirements for central banks to maintain exchange rates in narrow bands of one per cent each side of the par value. Devaluations and revaluations were allowed for with IMF approval should countries find themselves in fundamental disequilibrium positions on their balance of payments.

The Bretton Woods system served the world well up to the late sixties. But the failure of many countries to undertake exchange rate changes despite apparent fundamental disequilibria and problems relating to the fixed price of gold led to a reappraisal of the system. From the early seventies the adjustable peg system favoured by the Bretton Woods agreement was replaced by widespread floating of currencies of major industrial countries and it is this environment in which we now operate. However, by no means all of the world's currencies are freely floating; in fact, the majority are pegged to major floating currencies or groups of currencies.

IMF regulations have reduced the role of gold in the international monetary system, the SDR having taken over much of the domain previously occupied by gold.

References

Deutsche Bundesbank (1979) 'The European Monetary System: structure and operations', *Monthly Report of the Deutsche Bundesbank*, vol. 31.

International Monetary Fund (1977) *Annual Report of the Executive Directors for the Fiscal Year ended 30 April 1977*, Washington DC.

International Monetary Fund (1978) *Articles of Agreement of the International Monetary Fund*, Washington DC.

International Monetary Fund (1979) *Annual Report of the Executive Directors for the Fiscal Year ended 30 April 1979*, Washington DC.

Robert Triffin (1960) *Gold and the Dollar Crisis*, Yale University Press.

Exchange Rates – The Basic Equations

Multinational finance and domestic finance have much in common – but there are also many ways in which they differ. International financial management usually involves manipulation with more than one currency. So its understanding necessarily involves questions about how foreign exchange markets work, why exchange rates change, how one can protect oneself against foreign exchange risk, and so on.

But before we can approach these topics, there are a number of basic relationships which must be examined. This chapter focuses upon one series of approaches to the determination of foreign exchange rates, but it is by no means the only one: we briefly examine some others in Chapter 8.

Foreign Exchange Markets

An American company importing goods from West Germany, with their price denominated in Deutsche Marks, buys Marks in order to pay for the goods. An American company exporting goods to Germany, again with the price denominated in Marks, receives Deutsche Marks which it then sells in exchange for dollars. The currency aspects of these transactions involve use of the foreign exchange markets. In most centres, the foreign exchange market has no physical central marketplace. Business is conducted by telephone or telex. The main dealers are commercial banks and central banks. Companies wishing to buy or sell currency usually do so through a commercial bank.

In the UK, exchange rates are quoted in terms of the number of units of foreign currency bought for one unit of home currency, that is £1. This method of quotation is termed the indirect quote. By contrast, exchange rates throughout continental Europe are quoted in terms of the number of units of home currency, that is the number of Deutsche Marks, French francs, or whatever, necessary to buy one unit of foreign currency. This is the direct quotation method. In the USA, the convention is to use the direct quote when dealing internally with residents of the USA and the indirect quote when dealing with foreigners. The exception to this rule is that the direct quote is used when dealing with British-based banks or UK businesses. This practice means that New York uses the same convention

when talking to foreign dealers as these foreign dealers use for their own transactions and quotations. A quote of $0.3636 DM in New York means that each DM
costs $0.3636. In other words, to put it in indirect terms, there are DM 2.7503 to
the $, given by 1/0.3636.

Buying or selling a currency at the spot rate of exchange implies immediate
delivery and payment, but the practice of the foreign exchange market is for
delivery to be at two working days after the deal – note that this only applies to
spot transactions.

There is also the forward market where deals are for future delivery – usually
in one, three or six months' time, although other durations can be dealt, assuming
the market in the currency concerned has sufficient depth. The forward market
enables companies and others to insure themselves against foreign exchange loss.
Thus, if one is going to pay out or receive foreign currency at some future date,
one may avoid any potential loss by buying or selling forward. If, for instance, one
needs DM 100,000 in 6 months' time, one can enter into a six-month forward
contract. The forward rate on this contract is the price agreed now to be paid in six
months when the DM 100,000 are delivered.

If the six-month forward rate for the DM against the $ is quoted at $0.3704 DM
as opposed to a spot price of $0.3636, the implication is that one pays more dollars
if one buys forward than if one buys Deutsche Marks spot. In this case the dollar is
said to trade at a forward discount on the Deutsche Mark. Put another way, the
Deutsche Mark trades at a forward premium on the dollar. Expressed as an annual
rate, the forward premium is:

$$\frac{(0.3704 - 0.3636)}{0.3636} \times \frac{12 \text{ months}}{6 \text{ months}} \times 100 = 3.74 \% \text{ p.a.}$$

Assuming that forward markets and interest rates are in equilibrium, the currency
of the country with the higher interest rate is said to be at a discount on the other
currency. At the same time, looking at things from the opposite side of the fence,
the currency of the country with lower interest rates will be at a premium on the
other currency.

The foreign exchange markets and their methods of quotation are considered
in far more detail in Chapter 6.

Some Basic Relationships

Why should one currency be quoted at a different rate in the forward market and
the spot market? The hypothesis – the whys and wherefores of which will be
examined later in this chapter – is that, in the absence of barriers to international
capital movements, there is a relationship between spot exchange rates, forward
exchange rates, interest rates and inflation rates. This relationship can be
summarised as shown in Figure 5.1.[1] The theoretical underpinning to the
hypothesised link between variables will now be examined.

---

1. For definitions of all notations used in the figures in this chapter see Table 5.1.

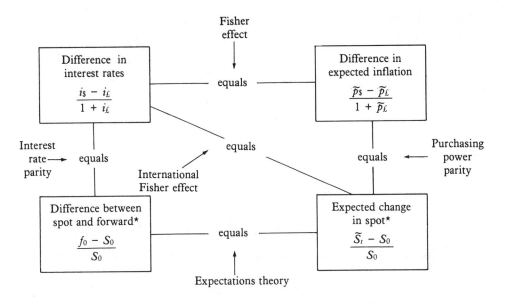

Important Note: Using the notation here, f_0, S_0 and $\widetilde{S}_t$ must be stated in terms of $/£$ (that is, the number of dollars to the pound). If the rate is quoted as $£/$ (that is, the number of pounds to the dollar), the expectations theory boxes should read:

$$\frac{S_0 - f_0}{f_0} \text{ and } \frac{S_0 - \widetilde{S}_t}{\widetilde{S}_t}$$

This should be self-evident. If it is not, consider the following situation. The $£/$ quotation is equal to:

$$\frac{1}{(/£)}$$

$$\frac{f - S}{S} \text{ can be shown to be equal to } \frac{1/S - 1/f}{1/f}$$

This is demonstrated below:

$$\frac{1/S - 1/f}{1/f} = (1/S - 1/f)\, f$$

$$= f/S - 1$$

$$= \frac{f - S}{S}$$

Great care must be taken on this point on all occasions when using the above formulations. We recommend that readers use the four-way model as set out above but always use the direct New York quote. When the dollar is not involved in a problem, be careful to get the substitution consistent with the formulations above. Generally, in using the formulae, values of i and $\widetilde{p}$ should be expressed in annualised terms as decimals and $(f_0 - S_0)/S_0$ and $\widetilde{S}_t - S_0/S_0$ should be annualised too. Thus a three-month forward premium or discount would have to be treated as $(f_0 - S_0)/S_0 \times 12/3$.

In practice, a slight modification is necessary because US dollar interest rates are quoted on a 360-day year basis, whereas sterling rates are quoted on a 365-day basis.

Figure 5.1   The Four-Way Equivalence in the Foreign Exchange Market

Interest Rates and Exchange Rates

Assume that an investor has £1 million to invest for a period of one year. The London quotation for the dollar is $1.3905 spot, and $1.3635 for twelve months forward. Twelve-month interest rates are $8\frac{25}{32}$ per cent in New York and $10\frac{15}{16}$ per cent in London. The investor may either:

1. invest £1m in London at $10\frac{15}{16}$ per cent for one year; or
2. convert £1m to $ at $1.3905; invest the proceeds in New York[1] for one year at $8\frac{25}{32}$ per cent and sell the calculated proceeds forward for one year at $1.3635.

What would the respective returns be?

1. Investing in London: proceeds at end of year = £1,109,375.
2. Investing in New York: the amount invested will be the proceeds from the spot transaction, namely $1,390,500. This will accumulate to $1,512,603 at the end of the year. And, having sold this calculated sum forward, the sterling proceeds will be:

$$£\frac{1,512,603}{1.3635} = £1,109,353$$

The two investment opportunities offer almost exactly the same return. Were this not the case, operators in the foreign exchange market would buy in one centre, ship money and invest in the other centre, taking profitable advantage of the imbalance in quotations.

The actions of arbitrageurs ensure that profitable opportunities based on the above kind of operation do not last for more than very short periods. Where profitable opportunities do exist, the market would say that there are opportunities for profitable covered interest arbitrage. But exploitation of these opportunities itself creates movements in exchange and interest rates, ensuring that the tendency in the foreign exchange market is towards equilibrium between differences in interest rates and differences between forward and spot rates.

Covered interest arbitrage involves borrowing in centre A for a specified period at a fixed interest rate and shipping the proceeds borrowed to centre B. The sum shipped is deposited there for the same specified period as the borrowing in centre A, again at a fixed interest rate. The total proceeds of investment in centre B that will accrue at the end of the investment period can be calculated, since the interest rate is fixed. Such proceeds are sold via the forward market for the period of the borrowing and lending, and the sum received in centre A from this forward transaction will more than repay the borrowing in centre A plus accrued interest. This profit is said to be a covered interest arbitrage profit.

By contrast, uncovered interest arbitrage involves a borrowing in centre A for a specified period at a fixed interest rate and shipping the proceeds borrowed to centre B via the spot market. The sum is again placed on deposit for the same

---

1. Or a location such as a Eurodollar banking centre. The point is, of course, that the deposit is a dollar deposit attracting an interest rate appropriate to dollar deposits.

period as that for which the borrowing was arranged in centre A and again it is at a fixed rate. This time the investor speculates that the proceeds from lending in centre B, when shipped to centre A at the spot rate prevailing at the end of the investment period, will exceed the borrowing plus accrued interest in centre A. Note that, under uncovered interest arbitrage, the operator speculates on the future spot rate. Any profit earned is a risky profit. Under covered interest arbitrage, the operator is not speculating but making a risk-free profit based on momentary disequilibria in interest differentials and forward and spot rates.

It should be noted in the numerical example above that we have used single (presumably middle) rates for quotations of interest and spot and forward rates. In reality, the investor needs to look at buy-and-sell rates in the spot and forward markets and at borrow-and-lend rates in interest markets.

The interest rate differential is termed the interest agio.[1] In the numerical example above it would be given by:

$$\frac{i_\$ - i_£}{1 + i_£} = \frac{8\frac{25}{32}\% - 10\frac{15}{16}\%}{1.10\frac{15}{16}}$$

$$= -0.0194$$
$$= -1.94\%$$

Note that calculating the interest differential in this manner – which is the precisely correct way – differs from taking a straight difference between interest rates, that is $(i_\$ - i_£)$. The rationale for using the precise calculation rather than the approximation is demonstrated algebraically at the end of this section.

The annual forward discount is termed the exchange agio. In the numerical example it would be equal to:

$$\frac{f_0 - S_0}{S_0} = \frac{1.3635 - 1.3905}{1.3905}$$

$$= -0.0194$$
$$\text{or } -1.94\%$$

If arbitrageurs' actions ensure that opportunities for profitable covered interest arbitrage are eliminated, the interest agio will equal the exchange agio: this is the essence of interest rate parity theory – see Figure 5.2.

The whole of the above theory is, of course, built upon the assumption that we are looking at markets in which money is internationally mobile. The majority of governments throughout the world restrict the mobility of money. But that does not invalidate the hypothesis. Furthermore, governments also frequently place restrictions on lending and borrowing rates charged in domestic interest rate markets. To avoid the effects of this market imperfection, we should look at free markets and these are available in the form of Eurocurrency markets. Clearly then, in applying the interest rate parity theorem, our attention should focus upon the comparative term structure of interest rates in the Eurocurrency markets.

We shall now consider the whys and wherefores of using the precise calculation

---

1. Agio means the sum payable for the convenience of exchanging one kind of money for another. The term originally derived from Italian moneylending in the Middle Ages.

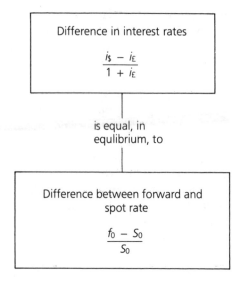

Figure 5.2   The Interest Rate Parity Theorem

rather than the approximation. Assume that a US exporter is due to receive £A in one year (or at time t where $t = 1$ year), and assume the notation in Table 5.1. The US exporter might avoid foreign exchange risk by using the forward market. His proceeds in US dollars at time t would be $\$f_0A$. Alternatively, he might avoid the risk by covering in the money markets. He could borrow

$$\frac{£A}{1 + i_£}$$

in London at time $t = 0$. At time $t = 1$, £A will be due to the lender and this will be

Table 5.1   Notation Used in this Chapter

S_0	=	spot $\$/£$ exchange rate now (direct New York quote)
f_0	=	forward $\$/£$ exchange rate now (direct New York quote)
$i_\$$	=	Eurodollar interest rate
$i_£$	=	Eurosterling interest rate
r	=	real return
$\tilde{p}_\$$	=	expected US inflation
$\tilde{p}_£$	=	expected UK inflation
$p_\$$	=	US price level now
$p_£$	=	UK price level now
$\tilde{S}_t$	=	expected spot $\$/£$ exchange rate at time t (direct New York quote)
$\tilde{f}_t$	=	expected forward $\$/£$ exchange rate at time t (direct New York quote)

obtained via payment of the receivable. Meanwhile, the US exporter would convert

$$\frac{£A}{1 + i_£}$$

to dollars at time 0 to give:

$$\frac{\$A}{1 + i_£} S_0$$

Investing this in the US money market would yield, at time t:

$$\frac{\$A}{(1 + i_£)} S_0 (1 + i_\$)$$

Assuming equilibrium between money markets and forward markets, each formula of cover will yield the same amount. So we can say that:

$$f_0 A = \frac{A}{(1 + i_£)} S_0 (1 + i_\$)$$

Rearranging this expression, we get:

$$f_0 = S_0 \frac{(1 + i_\$)}{(1 + i_£)}$$

and dividing through by S_0 and then taking 1 from each side gives:

$$\frac{f_0}{S_0} - 1 = \frac{(1 + i_\$)}{(1 + i_£)} - 1$$

from which it follows that:

$$\frac{f_0 - S_0}{S_0} = \frac{1 + i_\$}{1 + i_£} - 1$$

This yields the exact interest rate parity formula of:

$$\frac{f_0 - S_0}{S_0} = \frac{i_\$ - i_£}{1 + i_£}$$

This precise formulation, rather than the approximate one, is used by traders when dealing or making calculations for foreign exchange purposes. We shall now turn our attention to the second leg of the theoretical four-way equivalence in the foreign exchange markets.

Exchange Rates and Inflation Rates

Just like the above relationship between interest rates and exchange rates, there exists a similar one – again underpinned to some extent by the actions of arbitrageurs – relating inflation rates and exchange rates. This relationship is also best approached by a numerical example. If a commodity sells in the USA at $300 per kg, and in the UK for £250 per kg, and the exchange rate is $1.40 to the pound sterling, a profitable opportunity exists to buy the commodity in the USA, ship it to Britain and sell there – always assuming, that is, that the gross profit of $50 per kg [(250 × 1.40) – 300] exceeds shipping and insurance costs from the USA to the UK.

Were this profitable opportunity to exist, so the theory goes, arbitrageurs buying in New York and selling in London would increase the price in the USA and depress it in the UK, and this would go on until the profit potential was eliminated. Arbitrage ensures that, in the absence of market imperfections, the prices of a commodity in two centres should not differ. When talking about prices of a particular good in this way, economists are invoking the law of one price.[1] Applied to the case in point, one could say that:

£ price of a commodity × price of £ = $ price of the commodity, that is,

$$\text{Price of } £ = \frac{\$ \text{ price of the commodity}}{£ \text{ price of the commodity}}$$

This kind of relationship should tend to hold for all internationally traded goods. That is,

$$\text{Price of } £ = \frac{\$ \text{ price of the internationally traded commodity}}{£ \text{ price of the internationally traded commodity}}$$

Changes in the ratio of domestic prices of internationally traded goods in two centres should be reflected in changes in the price of currencies – the exchange rates.

In order to take the argument to the next stage, we should, strictly speaking, limit our attention to relative prices of internationally traded goods. But we approximate. Purchasing power parity (PPP) theory uses relative general price changes as a proxy for prices of internationally traded goods. And, applying it to the previous equation, we would obtain:

$$\text{Change in } \$ \text{ price of } £ = \frac{\text{change in } \$ \text{ price level}}{\text{change in } £ \text{ price level}}$$

Thus, if inflation is 8 per cent per annum in the USA and it is 12 per cent per annum in the UK, then, applying purchasing power parity theory, we would expect the pound sterling to fall against the dollar by

$$\frac{0.08 - 0.12}{1.12}$$

that is, 3.6 per cent. Again, this calculation is precise. A quick approximation based merely on straight inflation differentials would suggest a devaluation of 4 per cent per annum. The justification for using the precise formulation, rather than the approximate one, is considered in the algebraic formulation below.

Purchasing power parity theory, itself an approximation since it uses the general price level as a proxy for the price level for internationally traded goods,

---

1. Like all 'laws' in the social sciences, we should not give this one the status of immutability.

suggests that changes in the spot rate of exchange may be estimated by reference to expected inflation differentials. When looking at past exchange rate movements, the hypothesis might be tested by reference to actual price level changes. When making ex ante estimates of spot changes we should look at expected change in inflation rates. Figure 5.3 summarises the purchasing power parity hypothesis.

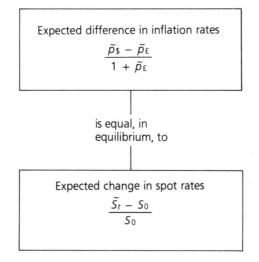

Figure 5.3   The Purchasing Power Parity Theorem

The precise formulation of the purchasing power parity theory, illustrated diagrammatically in Figure 5.3, can be easily substantiated by relatively simple algebra. Using the notation in Table 5.1, and given that the spot rate of exchange at any date is underpinned by relative price levels, it follows that the values of the respective spot rates of exchange at time 0 and those expected for time t are given by:

$$S_0 = \frac{p_\$}{p_£}$$

$$\tilde{S}_t = \frac{p_\$ (1 + \tilde{p}_\$)}{p_£ (1 + \tilde{p}_£)}$$

Substituting, we obtain:

$$\frac{\tilde{S}_t - S_0}{S_0} = \frac{p_\$}{p_£} \left[\frac{(1 + \tilde{p}_\$)}{(1 + \tilde{p}_£)} - 1 \right] \frac{p_£}{p_\$}$$

from which it follows that:

$$\frac{\tilde{S}_t - S_0}{S_0} = \frac{(\tilde{p}_\$ - \tilde{p}_£)}{(1 + \tilde{p}_£)}$$

At its simplest, then, purchasing power parity predicts that the exchange rate changes to compensate for differences in inflation between two countries. Thus, if country A has a higher inflation rate than its trading partners, the exchange rate of the former should weaken to compensate for this relativity. If country A's nominal exchange rate falls and if that fall is an exact compensation for inflation differentials, its real effective exchange rate is said to remain constant. Purchasing power parity predicts that real effective exchange rates will remain constant through time.

In terms of using purchasing power parity to forecast exchange rates, it should be clear that the predicted equilibrium rate will vary according to which year is chosen as a base date. Thus, referring to Figure 5.4, if 1980 is used as the base year with trade-weighted, inflation-adjusted exchange rates of currencies A, B and C fixed at 100 as of that date, then, as of 1985, currency A appears overvalued, currency B appears correctly valued and currency C appears undervalued. But if 1983 is taken as the base year, currency A appears undervalued by 1985; at this time currency B looks overvalued and currency C looks correctly valued. How does one get over this problem?

The answer is that one should start the analysis at a time when the exchange rate of the country being analysed is in equilibrium. And what is meant by the exchange rate being in equilibrium? We believe that the best approach is to commence at a time when the exchange rate is such that the overall balance of trade plus invisibles is equal (or approximately equal) to zero. In this sense, exchange rate equilibrium may be defined as that level at which its impact results in the balance on trade and invisibles coming out at zero overall. Now let us turn to the theoretical relationship between interest rates and expected inflation rates.

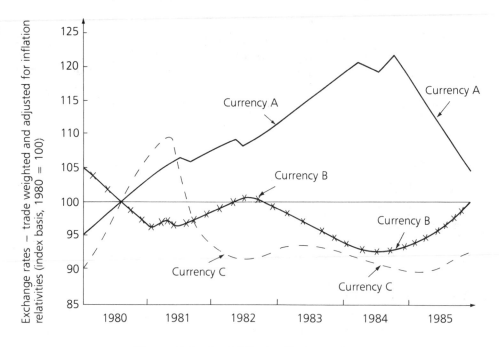

Figure 5.4   Real Effective Exchange Rates

Interest Rates and Inflation Rates

According to the Fisher effect, a term coined because it was observed by US economist Irving Fisher, nominal interest rates in a country reflect anticipated real returns adjusted for local inflation expectations. In a world where investors are internationally mobile, expected real rates of return should tend toward equality reflecting the fact that, in search of higher real returns, investors' arbitraging actions will force these returns towards each other. At least this should hold with respect to the free market Eurocurrency interest rates. Constraints on international capital mobility create imperfections which, amongst other things, prevent this relationship from holding in domestic interest rate markets. So nominal Euro-currency interest rates may differ for different currencies but, according to the Fisher effect, only by virtue of different inflation expectations. And these inflation differentials should underpin expected changes in the spot rates of exchange. In other words, we would expect US and UK free market interest investment to yield equal real returns. Differences in nominal returns would reflect expected inflation differentials. This would give us the theoretical relationship summarised in Figure 5.5.

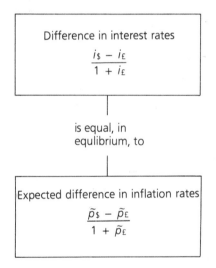

Figure 5.5 The Fisher Effect

Again, the implications of the Fisher effect (sometimes termed Fisher's closed hypothesis) can be followed through algebraically towards the formulation shown in Figure 5.5. Since the Fisher theorem suggests that local interest rates reflect a real expected return adjusted for inflationary expectations, when money is internationally mobile and market imperfections are eliminated, local interest rates will be equal to the international real return adjusted for domestic inflationary expectations. Put algebraically, the following two equivalences are implied:

$$(1 + i_\$) = (1 + r)(1 + \tilde{p_\$})$$

and

$$(1 + i_£) = (1 + r)(1 + \tilde{p_£})$$

A simple substitution gives:

$$i_\$ - i_£ = (1 + r)(\tilde{p_\$} - \tilde{p_£})$$

and this leads to:

$$\frac{i_\$ - i_£}{(1 + r)} = \tilde{p_\$} - \tilde{p_£}$$

Now, multiplying all through by $\dfrac{1}{1 + \tilde{p_£}}$ we get:

$$\frac{i_\$ - i_£}{(1 + i_£)} = \frac{\tilde{p_\$} - \tilde{p_£}}{(1 + \tilde{p_£})}$$

We now turn to the relationship between expected changes in the spot rate and the forward discount or premium on a currency.

Changes in the Spot Rate and the Forward Discount

This is the fourth side of the quadrilateral and must logically give rise to equality because of the hypothesised equality of the other three sides. This is the expectations theory of exchange rates and its implications are summarised diagrammatically in Figure 5.6.

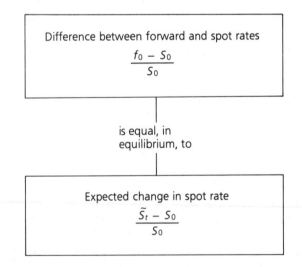

Difference between forward and spot rates

$$\frac{f_0 - S_0}{S_0}$$

is equal, in
equilibrium, to

Expected change in spot rate

$$\frac{\tilde{S_t} - S_0}{S_0}$$

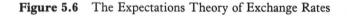

Figure 5.6   The Expectations Theory of Exchange Rates

This hypothesised relationship can be proved by a priori reasoning. If users of the foreign exchange market were not interested in risk, the forward rate of exchange would depend solely on what people expected the future spot rate to be. A twelve-month forward rate of $1.3635 to the pound would exist only because traders expected the spot rate in twelve months to be $1.3635 to the pound. If they anticipated that it would be higher than this, nobody would sell sterling at the forward rate. By the same token, if they expected it to be lower, nobody would buy at the forward rate.

Since traders do care about risk, the forward rate might be higher or lower than the expected spot rate. Suppose that a US exporter is certain to receive £1 million in six months' time: he might wait until six months have elapsed and then convert to dollars, or he might sell the pound forward. The first action involves exchange risk; the latter does not. To avoid foreign exchange risk, the trader may be willing to pay something slightly different from the expected spot price.

On the other side of the equation, there may be traders who wish to buy sterling six months away. To avoid the risk associated with movements in foreign exchange rates, they may be prepared to pay a forward price a little higher than the expected spot price.

Some traders find it safer to sell sterling forward; some traders find it safer to buy sterling forward. If the former group predominates, the forward price of sterling is likely to be less than the expected spot price. If the latter group predominates, the forward price is likely to be greater than the expected spot price. However, the actions of the predominant group are likely to adjust rates until they arrive at the hypothesised position in Figure 5.6.

Interest Rate Differentials and Changes in the Spot Exchange Rate

The hypothesis that differences in interest rate should underpin the expected movement in the spot rate of exchange is termed the international Fisher effect; it is sometimes also called Fisher's open hypothesis. Referring back to the original figure in this chapter (Fig. 5.1), international Fisher appears as one of the diagonals in the quadrilateral. What international Fisher predicts is summarised in Figure 5.7.

When discussing the interest rate parity theorem, we referred to covered and uncovered interest arbitrage. Effectively, the actions of arbitrageurs eliminate continuing opportunities to make riskless profits by covered interest arbitrage. Their operations bring into equilibrium interest differentials and spot and forward exchange rates.

A similar line of reasoning underpins the international Fisher effect – but this time it is uncovered interest arbitrage which is at the heart of the argument. Rational investors may make estimates of future spot rates of exchange. If their views were such as to justify expectations of profit (in excess of that commensurate with the risk involved) from uncovered interest arbitrage, their actions in purchasing one currency spot and selling another would move exchange rates so as to eliminate excess returns from the uncovered speculation. In a world of efficient markets, investors would use all available information to arrive at fair estimates of spot and future exchange rates so that the relationship between them would eliminate

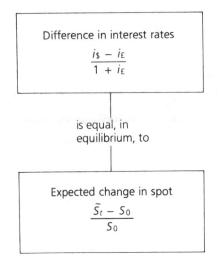

Figure 5.7   The International Fisher Effect

consistently profitable opportunities of uncovered interest arbitrage. The effect of this would, of course, be to bring interest rate differentials into line with spot exchange rates and expectations of future spot rates.

Summary

Whether we use deductive reasoning or elementary mathematics, we can justify the hypothesised relationship in Figure 5.1. This model, relating spot and forward exchange rates, interest differentials, inflation differentials and expected movements in spot, is most important. Indeed, in the study of multinational finance, it is perhaps the single most important set of theoretical ideas and it is stressed that readers should be very familiar with the four-way equivalence model.

The model itself is an equilibrium model. In the real world markets are rarely, if ever, in equilibrium. Therefore it should not be surprising if, for lengthy periods, parts of the model do not hold in the real world. Markets move towards equilibrium and the same is true of foreign exchange markets. But the test of a good theory is how well it stands up in the real world. In Chapter 11 we examine the empirical evidence relating to the hypothesised four-way equilibrium model.

6

The Foreign Exchange Market

The foreign exchange market is the framework of individuals, firms, banks and brokers who buy and sell foreign currencies. The foreign exchange market for any one currency, for example the French franc, consists of all the locations such as Paris, London, New York, Zurich, Frankfurt and so on, in which the French franc is bought and sold for other currencies. Foreign exchange markets tend to be located in national financial centres near the local financial markets. The most important foreign exchange markets are found in London, New York, Frankfurt, Amsterdam, Paris, Zurich, Toronto, Brussels, Milan, Bahrain and Tokyo.

There are five main types of transaction undertaken in these foreign exchange markets: spot transactions, forward deals, futures transactions, currency options and deposit market deals. The futures market and currency options are respectively considered in Chapters 16 and 17. This chapter focuses on the other three markets.

In the spot market, currencies are bought and sold for immediate delivery. In practice, this means that settlement is made two working days after the spot date. The intervention of these two days allows for necessary paperwork to be completed. In the forward market, currencies are bought and sold at prices agreed now but for future delivery at an agreed date. Not only is delivery made in the future, but payment is also made at the future date. In the deposit market, currencies are borrowed or lent with a view to undertaking associated foreign exchange deals. The mechanism of this market was considered in the previous chapter under the heading 'Interest Rates and Exchange Rates'. It should be noted that the initial borrowing may be of the domestic currency or of the foreign currency.

Participants

The main participants in the market are companies and individuals, commercial banks, central banks and brokers. Companies and individuals need foreign currency for business or travel reasons. Commercial banks are the source from which companies and individuals obtain their foreign currency. Through their extensive network of dealing rooms, their arbitrage operations ensure that quotations in different centres tend towards the same price. There are also foreign exchange brokers who bring buyers, sellers and banks together and receive

45

commissions on deals arranged. The other main group operating in the market is the central bank, the main part of whose foreign exchange activities involves the buying and selling of the home currency or foreign currencies with a view to ensuring that the exchange rate moves in line with established targets set for it by the government.

Not only are there numerous foreign exchange market centres around the world, but dealers in different locations can communicate with one another via the telephone, telex and computers. Furthermore, the overlapping of time zones means that, apart from weekends, there is always one centre which is open. This is shown in diagrammatic form in Figure 6.1. The capacity to take advantage of slightly varying quotations in different centres has been affected by computerised systems.

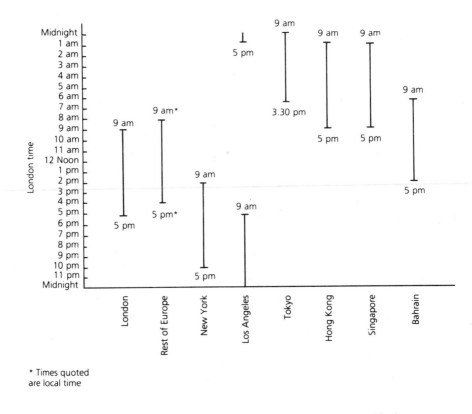

Figure 6.1   Time Overlap of World Foreign Exchange Markets

Methods of Quotation

A foreign exchange rate is the price of one currency in terms of another. Foreign exchange dealers quote two prices, one for selling, one for buying. The first aspect of the mystique in foreign exchange quotations arises from the fact that there are two ways of quoting rates. There is the direct quote and there is the indirect quote. The former gives the quotation in terms of the number of units of home currency necessary to buy one unit of foreign currency. The latter gives the quotation in terms of the number of units of foreign currency bought with one unit of home currency.

Continental European dealers normally quote via the direct method. In London dealers use the indirect method. In the USA both quotation methods are used. When a bank is dealing with a customer within the United States a direct quotation is given, but when dealing with other banks in Europe (except the UK), the indirect quotation is used.

Foreign exchange dealers quote two prices: the rate at which they are prepared to sell a currency and that at which they are prepared to buy. The difference between the bid rate and the offer rate is the dealer's spread which is one of the potential sources of profit for dealers. Whether using the direct quotation method or the indirect quote, the smaller rate is always termed the bid rate and the higher is called the offer, or ask, rate.

If we assume that the middle quote (that is, halfway between the sell and buy price) for Deutsche Marks to the US dollar is DM 2.55 = $1, then the New York internal quote for this rate would be $0.39216 and the Frankfurt quote would be DM 2.55. Where both centres use the same method of quotation (that is, they both use the direct quote or they both use the indirect method) and when they are both effectively quoting the same price – in other words there are no arbitrage opportunities – the quote in one centre is the reciprocal of the other. Thus two quotes multiplied together will equal 1.0. To the extent that this condition fails to hold, possibilities for profitable arbitrage – selling in one centre and buying in the other – exist. Of course, operators need to look at the buy rate in one centre and the sell rate in the other in terms of assessing arbitrage opportunities. In carrying out a profitable arbitrage, dealers force the prices in various centres towards equality.

If, in terms of the middle quote, the sterling/US dollar rate is $1.5015 equals £1, then the New York quote (using the local direct method) will be $1.5015 and the London quote (using the indirect method) will also be $1.5015. Where one centre uses the direct quotation method and the other uses the indirect method, the two quotations will, assuming no profitable arbitrage opportunities exist, be exactly the same.

The size of the bid/offer spread varies according to the depth of the market and its stability at a particular point in time. Depth of a market refers to the volume of transactions in a particular currency. Deep markets have many deals; shallow markets have few. Higher percentage spreads are associated with high uncertainty – perhaps due to impending devaluation – and low volumes of transactions in a currency. Lower spreads are associated with stable, high-volume markets. Deep markets usually have narrower spreads than shallow markets.

If US dollars are quoted in terms of sterling as $1.5050 to $1.5060, it means that the dealer is prepared to sell dollars at $1.5050 to the pound, or buy dollars at $1.5060. Conversely, the dealer is prepared to buy pounds at the rate of $1.5050 or sell pounds at $1.5060. In the above example the spread is equal to $0.0010, or 10 points. A point – or pip, as it is widely referred to – is a unit of a decimal, usually the fourth place to the right of the decimal point.

Next, it is necessary to consider the meaning of cross rates. A cross rate may be defined as an exchange rate which is calculated from two (or more) other rates. Thus the rate for the Deutsche Mark to the Swedish krona will be derived as the cross rate from the US dollar to the Deutsche Mark and the US dollar to the krona.

The practice in world foreign exchange markets is that currencies are quoted against the US dollar. If one bank asks another for its Deutsche Mark rate, that rate will be quoted against the US dollar unless otherwise specified. Most dealings are done against the US dollar; hence it follows that the market rate for a currency at any moment is most accurately reflected in its exchange rate against the US dollar. A bank which was asked to quote the £ against the Swiss franc would normally do so by calculating this rate from the £/US$ rate and the US$/SFr rate. It would therefore be using cross rates to arrive at its quotation.

Let us suppose that we require a quote for Swiss francs against the Deutsche Mark. The quotation which we would receive would be derived through the quote of both currencies against the US dollar. If these rates against the dollar were US$1 = SFr 2.2185/2.2195 and US$1 = DM 2.7955/2.7965, it would be possible to derive the cross rate for SFr against the DM. Our goal is to derive the selling and buying rates for SFr in terms of DM. If we are selling Swiss francs we will be buying Deutsche Marks. So we begin with the rate for selling Swiss francs and buying dollars; we then move to selling dollars and buying Deutsche Marks. The amalgamation of these two rates gives us the rate for selling Swiss francs and buying Deutsche Marks. The rate for selling Swiss francs to the dealer and buying dollars is SFr 2.2195; the rate for selling dollars and buying Deutsche Marks is DM 2.7955. So selling SFr 1 gives $0.450552. Selling $0.450552 gives DM 1.259518. Thus the rate for selling Swiss francs and buying Deutsche Marks is SFr1 = DM 1.259518, or DM1 = SFr 0.793955.

Similarly, if we are buying Swiss francs we will be selling Deutsche Marks. This time we begin with the rate for buying Swiss francs from the dealer and selling dollars to him, and then we move to buying dollars and selling Deutsche Marks. Amalgamating these two rates gives us the rate for buying Swiss francs and selling Deutsche Marks. The rate for buying Swiss francs and selling dollars is SFr 2.2185; the rate for buying dollars and selling Deutsche Marks is DM 2.7965. Selling DM 1 gives $0.357590. Selling $0.357590 gives SFr 0.793313. Thus the rate for buying Swiss francs and selling Deutsche Marks is DM 1 = SFr 0.793313, or SFr 1 = DM 1.260536. Thus the cross-rate quotation using direct Zurich figures would be SFr 0.793313/0.793955 = DM 1. And the direct Frankfurt quote would be DM 1.259518/1.260536 = SFr 1.

Forward Contracts and Quotations

It is necessary to consider next how forward rates are quoted by foreign exchange dealers. A forward foreign exchange contract is an agreement between two parties to exchange one currency for another at some future date. The rate at which the exchange is to be made, the delivery date, and the amounts involved are fixed at the time of the agreement. Such a contract must be distinguished from a foreign exchange futures contract. This is discussed in more detail in Chapter 16, but a brief definition is given here. A futures foreign exchange contract is a contract between two parties for the exchange of a standardised amount of foreign currency at a future date. In both the London International Financial Futures Exchange and the Chicago International Money Market the sterling/US dollar contract is for £25,000 with delivery dates in both markets fixed for the second Wednesday of the contract month which may be either March, June, September or December. A forward contract is usually completed by actual delivery of the currency involved or for part of the sum involved, whereas futures contracts are more usually closed out by completing a deal in the reverse direction before the maturity date, rather than actually taking delivery on the delivery date.

One of the major problems which newcomers to foreign exchange markets have is understanding how the forward premium and discount works and how foreign exchange dealers quote for forward delivery. Assume that a quoted currency is more expensive in the future than it is now in terms of the base currency. The quoted currency is then said to stand at a premium in the forward market relative to the base currency. Conversely, the base currency is said to stand at a discount relative to the quoted currency.

Consider an example in which the US dollar is the base currency and the Deutsche Mark is the quoted currency. Assume that the spot rate is US$1 = DM 2.7955. The rate quoted by a bank today for delivery in three months' time (today's three-month forward rate) is US$1 = DM 2.7698. In this example the dollar buys fewer Deutsche Marks in three months' time than it does today. So the Deutsche Mark is more expensive in the forward market. Thus the dollar stands at a discount relative to the Deutsche Mark; conversely, the Deutsche Mark stands at a premium relative to the dollar. The size of the dollar discount or Deutsche Mark premium is the difference between 2.7955 and 2.7698, that is, 2.57 pfennigs. The convention in the foreign exchange market is frequently to quote in terms of points, or hundredths of a unit. Hence 2.57 pfennigs is frequently quoted as 257 points.

In order to arrive at the forward prices, the Deutsche Mark premium or dollar discount must be subtracted from the spot rate. Were there a Deutsche Mark discount or dollar premium, this would be added to the spot rate. But care has to be taken: in our example we used a New York indirect quote; had we used a New York direct quote, the reverse would apply – in other words, the Deutsche Mark premium or dollar discount would have to be added to the spot quotation. A far easier way to deal with this little problem is always to remember – and this has never, in practice, been found to be otherwise – that the bid/offer spread on the forward quote is always wider than the spread on the spot figure. If this is remembered it is an easy process to compare the two spreads and, if the forward spread is narrower than the spot spread, the sums have been done incorrectly and recomputation is necessary.

Just as in the spot market, dealers quote selling and buying rates in the forward market, too. As in the spot market the convention, whether using direct or indirect quotation methods, is that the smaller rate is quoted first. In the above example the spot rate for DM to the US$ might be quoted as DM 2.7955/2.7965 and the three-month DM premium (or dollar discount) might be 257/252. Thus, if the foreign exchange dealer is buying dollars forward, there will be a Deutsche Mark premium of 257 points, or 2.57 pfennigs. But if he is buying the Deutsche Mark, the premium will only be 252 points or 2.52 pfennigs. Using the convention that the forward spread is wider than the spot spread, the full three-month forward quotation comes out at DM 2.7698/2.7713, given by:

	Bid rate	Offer rate	Spread in points
Spot quotation	2.7955	2.7965	10
Forward spread	257	252	−5
Subtract to make forward spread 15 points	2.7698	2.7713	15

Sometimes forward quotes are given as −10/+10 or 10P10. In this situation the forward market is said to be 'round par'. Thus, to get the forward rate, 10 points have to be added to either the bid or offer and 10 points have to be subtracted so that the forward spread widens on the spot spread. Thus, were we given quotations of:

2.7955/2.7965   −10/+10

the forward rate could be construed as 2.7945/2.7975. The forward rate may be quoted in full rather than as points distance from spot. This is called the outright forward price. It would be computed as shown below:

	Bid rate	Offer rate	Spread in points
Spot quotation	2.7955	2.7965	10
Forward spread	(10)	10	20
	2.7945	2.7975	30

Sometimes this kind of situation is quoted in terms of the spread from the spot rate as 10 pfennigs discount, 10 pfennigs premium.

It is important to bear in mind that the currency which is quoted at a discount in the forward market relative to another currency will have higher Eurocurrency interest rates than the currency which is at the premium. The rationale for this was discussed in Chapter 5 in some detail. As an adjunct to the above methods of quoting forward foreign exchange rates, we sometimes see the percentage per annum cost of forward cover. What does this mean? And how is it calculated?

It will be recalled that, in Chapter 5, the annualised exchange agio expressed as a percentage was calculated by reference to the formula:

$$\frac{\text{forward rate} - \text{spot rate}}{\text{spot rate}} \times \frac{12}{n} \times 100$$

where n is the number of months in the forward contract. This percentage is called the forward premium and it is frequently referred to in foreign exchange literature. It should be mentioned that small differences in the annual percentage cost of forward cover arise when using the direct quotation method as opposed to using the indirect quote. Slightly different results arise as well from using the buying rate as opposed to the selling rate or the middle price. The problem of differing costs of forward cover for buying and selling is a simply resolved problem. Whilst mathematically different figures are achieved, the relevant figure for a company executive using the forward market is the percentage cost of doing the transaction which he wishes to undertake.

Let us look at an example. Suppose again that we have a spot rate of US$1 = DM 2.7955/2.7965 and that the three-month forward quote is 257/252. The forward rate came out − see above − as DM 2.7698/2.7713. If we were a buyer of Deutsche Marks forward, the forward premium would be obtained by comparing the rates for buying Deutsche Marks − that is, DM 2.7955 spot and DM 2.7698 three months forward. The annualised forward premium for buying Deutsche Marks would therefore amount to:

$$\frac{2.7698 - 2.7955}{2.7955} \times \frac{12}{3} \times 100$$

$$= -3.68\%$$

The Deutsche Mark is said to be at an annualised premium of 3.68% in the three-month forward market based on rates for buying Marks. Of course, multiplying our quarterly rate of 0.92 per cent by four to give an annualised rate is slightly inaccurate because it fails to take account of compounding effects.

Main Purpose of the Forward Market

By entering into a forward foreign exchange contract, a UK importer or exporter is able to fix, at the time of the contract, a price for the purchase or sale of a fixed amount of foreign currency for delivery and payment at a specified future time. By so doing, he may eliminate foreign exchange risk due to future exchange rate fluctuations. This enables him to calculate the exact sterling value of an international commercial contract despite the fact that payment is to be made in the future in a foreign currency.

If a foreign currency stands at a premium in the forward market, it shows that the currency is 'stronger' than the home currency in that forward market. By contrast, if a foreign currency stands at a discount in the forward market, it shows that the currency is 'weaker' than the home currency in that forward market. The words stronger and weaker are put in inverted commas because, in the context of forward markets, strength and weakness merely take account of interest rate differentials, as suggested by the interest rate parity part of the four-way equivalence model encountered in Chapter 5.

How The Financial Times Quotes Currencies

Each day of its issue, a whole page of *The Financial Times* is devoted to rates and reports of trading in the foreign exchange markets and money markets. Since the foreign exchange markets run on through twenty-four hours a day with action moving from one centre to another, *The Financial Times* obtains a sample of rates from participants in the London foreign exchange markets at 5 p.m. (that is, 1700 hours) London time each trading day. By the time the reader of *The Financial Times* refers to rates on the following morning, the market will probably have moved. The rates quoted in the newspaper are therefore not up-to-the-minute. They merely provide a daily record of market activities. Two key tables specify the previous day's trading for the pound spot and forward and the US dollar spot and forward. Samples of these tabulations appear in Tables 6.1 and 6.2 respectively. They show prices for immediate delivery and for contracts involving settlement one month or three months ahead. For the sterling/dollar rate (see Table 6.1) six- and twelve-month forward rates are also given.

Table 6.1   *Financial Times* Table (12 September 1985) for the Pound Spot and Forward

Sept. 11	Day's spread	Close	One month	% p.a.	Three months	% p.a.
US	1.3000-1.3230	1.3075-1.3085	0.40-0.37c pm	3.53	1.03-0.98pm	3.07
Canada	1.7872-1.8097	1.7925-1.7975	0.01c pm-par	0.03	0.02pm-par	0.02
Nethlnd.	4.31$\frac{1}{2}$-4.36$\frac{1}{4}$	4.34$\frac{1}{4}$-4.35$\frac{1}{4}$	2$\frac{1}{4}$-2c pm	5.87	6$\frac{1}{8}$-5$\frac{3}{4}$pm	5.46
Belgium	77.56-78.36	78.00-78.10	22-15c pm	2.84	48-35pm	2.13
Denmark	13.97$\frac{1}{2}$-14.03$\frac{3}{4}$	14.02-14.03	4$\frac{1}{8}$-2$\frac{7}{8}$ore pm	2.99	11-9$\frac{1}{2}$pm	2.92
Ireland	1.2392-1.2469	1.2415-1.2425	0.27-0.11p pm	1.84	0.57-0.28pm	1.37
W. Ger.	3.85$\frac{1}{4}$-3.88$\frac{1}{4}$	3.86$\frac{3}{4}$-3.87$\frac{3}{4}$	2$\frac{1}{2}$-2$\frac{1}{4}$pf pm	7.36	6$\frac{3}{4}$-6$\frac{1}{2}$pm	6.84
Portugal	228$\frac{1}{4}$-232$\frac{1}{4}$	229-231	60-390c dis	-11.74	400-1385d	-15.52
Spain	226$\frac{3}{4}$-228$\frac{1}{2}$	227$\frac{1}{2}$-228	par-50c dis	-1.32	50-160dis	-1.84
Italy	2,551$\frac{1}{2}$-2,582$\frac{1}{4}$	2,573-2,574	1-6lire dis	-1.63	7-13dis	-1.55
Norway	1.23-11.28$\frac{1}{2}$	11.24$\frac{1}{2}$-11.25$\frac{1}{2}$	$\frac{1}{8}$-1ore dis	-0.60	2$\frac{1}{4}$-3$\frac{1}{4}$dis	-0.96
France	11.71$\frac{1}{2}$-11.83$\frac{3}{4}$	11.79$\frac{1}{2}$-11.80$\frac{1}{2}$	2$\frac{3}{8}$-1$\frac{3}{4}$c pm	2.10	5-3$\frac{5}{8}$pm	1.46
Sweden	11.28-11.35	11.30-11.31	3$\frac{1}{2}$-4$\frac{1}{8}$ore dis	-4.11	9$\frac{5}{8}$-10$\frac{3}{4}$dis	-3.60
Japan	316$\frac{1}{2}$-320$\frac{3}{4}$	318-319	1.47-1.37y pm	5.35	4.05-3.90pm	4.99
Austria	27.05-27.23	27.13-27.20	15$\frac{3}{4}$-14$\frac{3}{8}$gro pm	6.66	42-38pm	5.89
Switz.	3.17-3.20$\frac{1}{4}$	3.18$\frac{1}{2}$-3.19$\frac{1}{2}$	2$\frac{1}{8}$-1$\frac{7}{8}$c pm	7.52	5$\frac{1}{2}$-5$\frac{1}{4}$pm	6.74

Note: Belgian rate is for convertible francs. Financial franc 78.60-78.75. Six-month forward dollar 1.72-1.67c pm. 12-month 2.75-2.60c pm.

In *The Financial Times* table (Table 6.1), sterling is quoted in terms of the number of Deutsche Marks, US dollars, or whatever, to the pound – that is the indirect London quote. For the US dollar, the same convention holds, except that sterling and the Irish pound are quoted according to the direct New York quote. The tables detail the day's spread – the range from the highest to the lowest prices at which dealings have occurred in the spot market during the day – and the price at 5 p.m. in London based on a representative sample of quotations from market participants. The forward tabulations give the premium or discount to the spot rate. These premia or discounts are tabulated in two ways. They are both shown as an absolute difference from the spot rate and also as an annual percentage of the spot rate.

Table 6.2   *Financial Times* Table (12 September 1985) for the Dollar Spot and Forward

Sept. 11	Day's spread	Close	One month	% p.a.	Three months	% p.a.
UK†	1.3000-1.3230	1.3075-1.3085	0.40-0.37c pm	3.53	1.03-0.98pm	3.07
Ireland†	1.0490-1.0600	1.0500-1.0510	0.20-0.10c pm	1.70	0.55-0.35pm	1.70
Canada	1.3702-1.3724	1.3709-1.3714	0.08-0.11c dis	-0.83	0.27-0.32dis	-0.86
Nethlnd.	3.2975-3.3350	3.3235-3.3245	0.68-0.65c pm	2.40	2.05-2.01pm	2.44
Belgium	59.25-59.75	59.60-59.70	3-5c dis	-0.81	14-17dis	-1.04
Denmark	$10.62\frac{3}{4}$-$10.73\frac{3}{4}$	10.72-$10.72\frac{1}{2}$	par-$\frac{3}{4}$ore dis	-0.42	par-$\frac{3}{4}$dis	-0.14
W. Ger.	2.9330-2.9650	2.9605-2.9615	0.97-0.92pf pm	3.83	2.78-2.73pm	3.72
Portugal	$174\frac{1}{2}$-$176\frac{3}{4}$	$175\frac{1}{2}$-$176\frac{1}{4}$	100-350c dis	-15.32	450-1200d	-18.72
Spain	172.75-174.10	173.40-173.70	50-80c dis	-4.49	170-250dis	-4.83
Italy	1,952-1,969	1,967-1,968	9-10lire dis	-5.80	$23\frac{1}{2}$-25dis	-4.94
Norway	8.54-8.63	$8.59\frac{3}{4}$-$8.60\frac{1}{4}$	$2\frac{1}{4}$-$3\frac{1}{4}$ore dis	-4.18	$8\frac{1}{2}$-9dis	-4.06
France	$8.94\frac{1}{2}$-9.03	$9.01\frac{3}{4}$-$9.02\frac{1}{4}$	1.10-1.25c dis	-1.56	3.85-4.15dis	-1.77
Sweden	$8.58\frac{3}{4}$-8.66	8.64-$8.64\frac{1}{2}$	$5\frac{1}{4}$-$5\frac{3}{4}$ore dis	-7.63	$14\frac{1}{4}$-$14\frac{3}{4}$dis	-6.71
Japan	242.40-243.60	243.45-243.55	0.40-0.36y pm	1.87	1.21-1.16pm	1.95
Austria	$20.61\frac{3}{4}$-$20.79\frac{3}{4}$	20.70-20.75	$5\frac{3}{4}$-5gro pm	3.10	16-$13\frac{1}{2}$pm	2.84
Switz.	2.4190-2.4430	2.4385-2.4395	0.82-0.76c pm	3.89	2.26-2.20pm	3.66

Notes: † UK and Ireland are quoted in US currency. Forward premiums and discounts apply to the US dollar and not to the individual currency.

Belgian rate is for convertible francs. Financial franc 60.10-60.20.

Using the figures shown in Table 6.1 for sterling against the Deutsche Mark, it will be noted that the quotations under spot and one month forward are given as:

W. Ger. Close	:	$3.86\frac{3}{4}$ − $3.87\frac{3}{4}$
One month	:	$2\frac{1}{2}$ − $2\frac{1}{4}$ pf pm
% p.a.	:	7.36

To obtain the full forward quote, the one-month premium must be built upon the spot figure. In the table for the pound forward, the term discount or premium implies that the foreign currency is at a discount or premium as the case may be. So the Deutsche Mark is at a premium in the one-month forward market for the bid and the offer quotations. Therefore, less Deutsche Marks will be quoted in the forward market for pounds (put another way, the Deutsche Mark is hardening − or strengthening − in the forward market). Furthermore, it should always be borne in mind, when dealing with forward quotations, that the bid/offer difference (or spread) is wider in the forward market than it is in the spot market. This has been found to hold always and it turns upon the fact that forward rates are based on bid/offer quotations for spot plus or minus Euro-interest rate differentials. Forward quotations are based on the absence of covered interest arbitrage profit opportunities. These (see Chapter 5) are based on borrowing in one centre and lending in the other − interest rate quotations use the bid quote in one centre and the offer quote in the other. The fact that one is going through this route logically implies that the forward bid/offer spread should be wider than the spot bid/offer spread − and empirically this is found to be the case.

Returning to our numerical example, the Deutsche Mark is at a forward premium on sterling and the outright forward quote can be calculated as:

	Bid		Offer	Difference
Spot	3.8675	–	3.8775	1 pf = 100 pips
One-month premium	250	–	225	$\frac{1}{4}$ pf = 25 pips
Outright forward quote	3.8425	–	3.8550	$1\frac{1}{4}$ pf = 125 pips

The Financial Times also expresses the forward premium as an annualised percentage of the spot rate. This is a reminder that interest rate markets and currency markets are interlinked – see the discussion on the interest rate being part of the four-way equivalence model in Chapter 5. If it receives an order to supply Deutsche Marks for pounds in one month's time, the bank concerned may, out of prudence, decide to purchase Marks straight away and put them on deposit for one month. Should Deutsche Mark deposits yield less than sterling deposits, they will lose interest by moving from sterling into Deutsche Marks. The bank would pass this cost on to its customer by charging more for one-month Deutsche Marks than it would for Marks spot. In the forward market, Marks would be sold at a premium. Banks do not usually go through this kind of process – but the theory is nonetheless applicable.

The one-month premium of the Deutsche Mark on sterling in our example is (based on the middle-market quotation, halfway between bid and offer) 2.375 pfennigs. This compares with a middle-market close of DM 3.8725. The annual forward premium is calculated in *The Financial Times* as:

$$\frac{2.375 \text{ pfennigs}}{\text{DM } 3.8725} \times \frac{12 \text{ months}}{1 \text{ month}} \times 100$$

$$= 7.36\% \text{ p.a.}$$

This calculation is, of course, similar to the forward premium based on $(f - s)/s$ which was discussed in Chapter 5.

We now turn to a similar kind of example to the above, but based on Table 6.2. The method by which *The Financial Times* quotes spot and forward rates in its dollar tabulation is exactly the same as that for the sterling forward table, except that sterling and the Irish punt are quoted on the New York direct rate convention and the premium or discount quoted applies to the US dollar and not to the pound or the punt. Otherwise, the approach is exactly the same. Thus the outright one-month forward rate for the US dollar to the Deutsche Mark is given by:

	Bid	Offer	Difference
Spot	2.9605	2.9615	10 pips
Three-month forward	97	92	5 pips
Outright forward rate	2.9508	2.9523	15 pips

and the annualised premium is computed as:

$$\frac{0.00945}{2.96100} \times \frac{12 \text{ months}}{3 \text{ months}} \times 100$$

$$= 3.83\% \text{ p.a.}$$

Tables 6.1 and 6.2 detail the dollar and sterling against major currencies. A further table appears in *The Financial Times* headed 'Other Currencies'. An example of this is Table 6.3. This details sterling and dollar spot rates against second-line currencies for which some kind of free market exists – although in practice there may be a considerable degree of official exchange rate control. This table also gives details of rates at which banks deal between themselves in large quantities of bank notes. Since notes do not carry interest, their spreads for buying and selling are under those in the spot markets quoted in Tables 6.1 and 6.2.

Table 6.3 *Financial Times* Table (12 September 1985) for Other Currencies and Bank Notes

September 11	£	$		£ Note rates
Argentina Austl.	1.0416-1.0438	0.8000-0.8010	Austria	27.15-27.45
Australia Dollar	1.9325-1.9365	1.4820-1.4840	Belgium	78.55-79.35
Brazil Cruzeiro	9,537-9,590	7,325-7,360	Denmark	14.00-14.14
Finland Markka	8.1140-8.1365	6.2280-6.2300	France	11.79-11.90
Greek Drachma	182.25-186.18	138.70-141.60	Germany	$3.86\frac{1}{4}$-$3.89\frac{1}{4}$
Hong Kong Dollar	10.1970-10.2070	7.8145-7.8165	Italy	2565-2605
Iran Rial	118.00*	90.50*	Japan	320-324
Kuwait Dinar (KD)	0.4000-0.4010	0.30675-0.30685	Netherlands	4.34-4.38
Luxembourg Franc	78.00-78.10	59.60-59.70	Norway	11.24-11.35
Malaysia Ringgit	3.2755-3.2855	2.5100-2.5130	Portugal	223-238
New Zealand Dlr.	2.5340-2.5420	1.9435-1.9475	Spain	$220\frac{1}{2}$-229
Saudi Arab Riyal	4.7645-4.7740	3.6515-3.6520	Sweden	11.31-11.42
Singapore Dollar	2.9980-3.0080	2.2975-2.2995	Switzerland	$3.18\frac{1}{2}$-$3.21\frac{1}{2}$
Sth African Rand	3.1945-3.2180	2.4450-2.4630	United States	1.31-1.33
U.A.E. Dirham	4.7920-4.8015	3.6720-3.6730	Yugoslavia	400-450

Notes: *Selling rate.
Rand financial rate: 2.6845-2.7585 ($) and 3.5075-3.6040 (£).

In its Monday edition, *The Financial Times* gives a table of spot rates and one-, three-, six- and twelve-month outright forward rates for the US dollar, the Deutsche Mark, the French franc, the Swiss franc and the Japanese yen against sterling. This table merely shows middle rates rather than bid/offer figures. *The Financial Times* supplements this information by a weekly table showing the world value of the pound. This appears in Tuesday editions, and a similar table showing the world value of the dollar appears on Fridays. Many of the currencies shown are very strictly controlled by local monetary authorities and are not therefore openly dealt in foreign exchange markets but may be procured from the country concerned. An example of a world value of the pound table is given in Table 6.4.

Table 6.4   *Financial Times* Table (7 January 1956) for World Value of the Pound

£ WORLD VALUE OF THE POUND

The table below gives the latest available rate of exchange for the pound against various currencies on January 6, 1986. In some cases rate is nominal. Market rates are the average of buying and selling rates except where they are shown to be otherwise. In some cases market rates have been calculated from those of foreign currencies to which they are tied.

Abbreviations: (A) approximate rate, no direct quotation available; (F) free rate; (P) based on U.S. dollar parities and going sterling-dollar rates; (T) tourist rate; (Bas) basic rate; (bg) buying rate; (Bk) bankers' rates; (cm) commercial rates; (ch) convertible rate; (fn) financial rates; (exC) exchange certificate rate; (nc) non commercial rate; (nom) nominal; (o) official rate; (sg) selling rate; (c) controlled rate; (u) unified rate.

COUNTRY	CURRENCY	VALUE OF £ STERLING
Afghanistan	Afghani	99.00
Albania	Lek	10.06
Algeria	Dinar	(A)6.87
Andorra	{ French Franc / Spanish Peseta	10.77 / 220.17
Angola	Kwanza	43.1190
Antigua	E. Caribbean $	3.87
Argentina	Austral	1.1552
Australia	Australian $	2.1185
Austria	Schilling	24.79
Azores	Portugu'se Escudo	227.90
Bahamas	Ba. Dollar	1.4360
Bahrain	Dinar	0.5395
Balearic Isles	Spa Peseta	220.17
Bangladesh	Taka	43.60
Barbados	Barbados $	2.8620
Belgium	B. Franc	{ (cm) 71.95 / (fn) 72.80
Belize	B $	2.87
Benin	C.F.A. Franc	538.50
Bermuda	Bda $	1.4360
Bhutan	Ngultrum	17.25
Bolivia	Bolivian Peso	(o) 2238546.0
Botswana	Pula	2.92725
Brazil	Cruzeiro‡	15,378.0
Brit. Virgin Isles	U.S. $	1.4360
Brunei	Brunei $	3.0575
Bulgaria	Lev	1.4100
Burkino Faso	C.F.A. Franc	538.50
Burma	Kyat	11.3307
Burundi	Burundi Franc	161.00

COUNTRY	CURRENCY	VALUE OF £ STERLING
Greenland	Danish Kroner	12.8250
Grenada	E. Caribbean $	3.87
Guadaloupe	Local Franc	10.77
Guam	U.S. $	1.4360
Guatemala	Quetzal	1.4360
Guinea	Syli	32.28
Guinea-Bissau	Peso	244.30
Guyana	Guyanese $	6.03
Haiti	Gourde	7.17
Honduras	Lempira	2.90
Hong Kong	H.K. $	11.2725
Hungary	Forint	68.1945
Iceland	I. Krona	60.6650
India	Ind. Rupee	17.25
Indonesia	Rupiah	1,612.0
Iran	Rial	121.40(sg)
Iraq	Ireci Dinar	0.4600
Irish Republic	Irish £	1.1575
Israel	Shekel	2,148.0
Italy	Lira	2,394.50
Ivory Coast	C.F.A. Franc	538.50
Jamaica	Jamaica Dollar	8.00(sg)
Japan	Yen	290.0
Jordan	Jordanian Dinar	0.5300
Kampuchea	Riel	N/A
Kenya	Kenya Shilling	23.30
Kiribati	Australian $	2.1185
Korea (Nth)	Won	1.35
Korea (Sth)	Won	1,280.39

COUNTRY	CURRENCY	VALUE OF £ STERLING
Peru	Inti	exC(A)20,1250/(18
Philippines	Philippine Peso	26.50
Pitcairn Islands	{ £ Sterling / New Zealand $	— / 2.7580
Poland	Zloty	210.78
Portugal	Portuguese Escudo	227.90
Puerto Rico	U.S. $	1.4360
Qatar	Qatari Ryal	5.2100
Reunion Island	French Franc	10.77
Romania	Leu	{ (Cm) 5.74 / (N/C) 16.05
Rwanda	Rwanda Franc	139.07
St. Christopher	E. Caribbean $	3.87
St. Helena	St. Helena £	1.0
St. Lucia	East Caribbean $	3.87
St. Pierre	Local Franc	10.77
St. Vincent	E. Caribbean $	3.87
Samoa American	U.S. $	1.4360
San Marino	Italian Lira	2,394.50
Sao Tome & Prin.	Dobra	59.17
Saudi Arabia	Saudi Ryal	5.2705
Senegal	C.F.A. Franc	538.50
Seychelles	S. Rupee	9.42
Sierra Leone	Leone	(0) 7.50
Singapore	Singapore $	3.0575
Solomon Islands	Solomon Is. $	2.3239
Somali Republic	Somali Shilling	52.45

COUNTRY	CURRENCY	VALUE OF £ STERLING
Cameroon	C.F.A. Franc	538.50
Canada	Canadian $	2.0268
Canary Islands	Spanish Peseta	220.17
Cape Verde Is	Cape V. Escudo	127.92
Cayman Islands	Cay. Is $	1.1965
Cent. Afr. Republic	C.F.A. Franc	538.50
Chad	C.F.A. Franc	538.50
Chile	Chilean Peso	262.19
China	Renminbi Yuan	4.5298
Colombia	Col. Peso	(F)248.49
Comoro Islands	C.F.A. Franc	538.50
Congo (Brazzaville)	C.F.A. Franc	538.50
Costa Rica	Colon	(U) 76.52
Cuba	Cuban Peso	1.2755
Cyprus £	Cyprus £	0.7750
Czechoslovakia	Koruna	(oom) 9.35 / n/c 16.28 / 15.57
Denmark	Danish Kroner	12.8250
Djibouti	Djibouti Franc	245.0
Dominica	E. Caribbean $	3.87
Dominican Repub.	Dominican Peso	1.4360 / (o) 4.25(7)
Ecuador	Sucre	(o)137.81 / (F) 179.78
Egypt	Egyptian £	(o) 1.1895 / (T) 1.9000
El Salvador	Colon	(o) 3.5880 / (F) 7.0356
Equatorial Guinea	C.F.A. Franc	538.50
Ethiopia	Ethiopian Birr	2.9650
Falkland Islands £	Falkland Is £	1.0
Faroe Islands	Danish Kroner	12.8250
Fiji Islands	Fiji $	1.6045
Finland	Markka	7.7960
France	French Franc	10.77
French C'ty in Af.	C.F.A. Franc	538.50
French Guiana	Local Franc	10.77
French Pacific Is.	C.P.F. Franc	190.0
Gabon	C.F.A. Franc	538.50
Gambia	Dalasi	5.00
Germany (East)	Ostmark	3.5150
Germany (West)	Deutsche Mark	3.5150
Ghana	Cedi	86.2500
Gibraltar	Gibraltar £	1.0
Greece	Drachma	213.70

COUNTRY	CURRENCY	VALUE OF £ STERLING
Kuwait	Kuwaiti Dinar	0.4188
Laos	New Kip	50.16
Lebanon	Lebanese £	26.49
Lesotho	Maluti	3.5605
Liberia	Liberian $	1.4360
Libya	Libyan Dinar	0.4245
Liechtenstein	Swiss Franc	2.9725
Luxembourg	Lux Franc	71.95
Macao	Pataca	11.65
Madeira	PortugueseEscudo	227.90
Malagasy Republic	MG Franc	815.0
Malawi	Kwacha	2.3940
Malaysia	Ringgit	3.5100
Maldive Islands	Rufiyaa	10.03
Mali Republic	C.F.A. Franc	538.50
Malta	Maltese Lira	0.6050
Martinique	Local Franc	10.77
Mauritania	Ouguiya	110.34
Mauritius	M. Rupee	20.48
Mexico	Mexican Peso	(F)612.55 / (O)529.35
Miquelon	Local Franc	10.77
Monaco	French Franc	10.77
Mongolia	Tugrik	4.81
Montserrat	E. Caribbean $	3.87
Morocco	Dirham	13.52 (sg)
Mozambique	Metical	(A) 59.55
Namibia	S.A. Rand	3.5605
Nauru	Australian Dollar	2.1185
Nepal	Nepalese Rupee	29.38
Netherlands	Guilder	3.9550
Netherland Antilles	Antillian Guilder	2.58
New Zealand	N.Z. Dollar	2.7380
Nicaragua	Cordoba	(O)40.10
Niger Republic	C.F.A. Franc	538.50
Nigeria	Naira	1.432787(sg)
Norway	Norwegian Krone	10.38
Oman Sultate of	Rial Omani	0.4945
Pakistan	Pakistan Rpee	22.60
Panama	Balboa	1.4360
Papua N. Guinea	Kina	1.4527
Paraguay	Guarani	(343.80(10) / 937.29(7)

COUNTRY	CURRENCY	VALUE OF £ STERLING
South Africa	Rand	3.5605
Spain	Peseta	220.17
Spanish ports in North Africa	Peseta	220.17
Sri Lanka	S. L. Rupee	38.95
Sudan Republic	Sudan £	3.58
Surinam	S. Guilder	2.58
Swaziland	Lilangeni	3.5605
Sweden	S. Krona	10.9925
Switzerland	Swiss Franc	2.9725
Syria	Syrian £	(A)(T)9.0 / (CM) 5.62
Taiwan	New Taiwan $	57.13
Tanzania	Tan. Shilling	23.45
Thailand	Baht	37.75
Togo Republic	C.F.A. Franc	538.50
Tonga Islands	Pa'anga	2.1185
Trinidad	Trinidad & Tob $	5.16
Tunisia	Tunisian Dinar	1.0620(sg)
Turkey	Turkish Lira	832.91
Turks & Caicos	U.S. $	1.4360
Tuvalu	Australian $	2.1185
Uganda	Uganda Shilling	1,950.0
United States	U.S. Dollar	1.4360
Uruguay	Uruguay Peso	179.87
Utd.Arab Emirates	U.A.E. Dirham	5.3033
U.S.S.R.	Rouble	1.0979
Vanuatu	Vatu	145.0
Vatican	Italian Lira	2,394.50
Venezuela	Bolivar	(4) 6.16 / (5) 10.46 / (6) 21.1650
Vietnam	New Dong	(O) 18.64 (15)
Virgin Island U.S.	U.S. Dollar	1.4360
Western Samoa	Samoan Tala	(A) 3.2550
Yemen (Nth)	Ryal	(A) 10.0170
Yemen (Sth)	S. Yemen Dinar	0.4915
Yugoslavia	New Y Dinar	454.0354
Zaire Republic	Zaire	79.7497
Zambia	Kwacha	8.00
Zimbabwe	Zimbabwe $	2.3725

‡ Rate is the transfer market (controlled). ‡‡ Now one official rate. (1)Essential goods. (2) Preferential rate for priority imports such as foodstuffs.
(4) Preferential rate for public sector debt and essential imports. (5) Preferential rate. (6) Free rate for luxury imports, remittances of money abroad and foreign ravel. (7) Parallel rate. (9) Banknote rates. (10) Rate for exports. (14) Nearly all business transactions. (15) Vietnam:—1 new dong equals 10 old dongs. (16) Peru:—1 inti equals 1,000 soles.

The Financial Times also gives daily tables on currency movements and currency rates (see Table 6.5). The former gives details of trade-weighted percentage changes in the values of major trading currencies. The Bank of England indices are based to the average currency value as of 1975. The Bank of England index compares with a level of 100 at 1975. The figure for the Deutsche Mark of 123.8 indicates that the Deutsche Mark has strengthened by 23.8 per cent against the currencies of its trading partners, weighted by volume of trade, since 1975. The corresponding change based on an average over 1980 to 1982, the Morgan Guaranty calculation, is also shown. Over this period, the Deutsche Mark can be seen to have strengthened, in trade-weighted terms, by 7.6 per cent.

The table of currency rates (Table 6.5) first of all sets out the central bank discount rates for the various countries. Care needs to be taken in using these figures; this is because, in many countries nowadays, other market rates have greater influence on the level of market interest rates than the central bank discount rate. The table of currency rates also sets out the previous day's value of major currencies in terms of two international currency baskets – the Special Drawing Right of the International Monetary Fund and the European Currency Unit or ECU. Both comprise a predetermined amount of a number of different currencies – only five in the case of the SDR, and the currencies of the EEC countries in the case of the ECU. The former is the unit in which the IMF accounts are operated and the latter is used for transactions pertaining to the European Monetary System. Their composite character is such that these currency baskets are less volatile than their individual units, and they are being increasingly used for commercial purposes, from denominating exports and imports to denominating borrowings.

In Chapter 4 we briefly discussed the working of the European Monetary System. Daily details of the relationship with the ECU of currencies which are members of the European Monetary System are given in *The Financial Times* in a table headed 'EMS European Currency Unit Rates'. This table (Table 6.6) enables the rate of individual currencies against the ECU to be compared with the central rates, the fixed points against which EMS fluctuations are measured.

What does Table 6.6 mean? The Belgian franc's central rate is 44.8320 to the ECU. Its actual rate is 45.0005. The table shows a percentage change of plus 0.38 per cent from the central rate. The plus reflects a rise in the ECU. A positive change shows that the currency in question has weakened from its central rate. The last column in the table gives the divergence limit for each currency. This does not refer to the formal percentage by which the EMS currencies are permitted to fluctuate on either side of the ECU central rate. It amounts to $2\frac{1}{4}$ per cent for all currencies except the lira for which 6 per cent is specified.

It is usual for intervention, or other action to protect a weak EMS currency, such as a rise in interest rates, to commence before the currency reaches its floor level; and action to depress a currency against its EMS partners is taken before the ceiling is reached. For each currency the divergence limit, expressed as plus or minus a certain percentage movement from the ECU central rate, gives the level of deviation at which official action can be expected to commence. It is therefore a kind of early-warning system.

Because the EMS currencies have different weights in the basket from which

Table 6.5 Currency Movements and Currency Rates Tables from *The Financial Times* of 12 September 1985

Currency Movements

Sept. 11	Bank of England Index	Morgan Guaranty Change %
Sterling	79.9	−9.7
US dollar	142.4	+28.3
Canadian dollar	86.8	−7.5
Austrian schilling	114.3	+4.2
Belgian franc	90.1	−10.8
Danish kroner	78.3	−5.7
Deutsche Mark	123.8	+7.6
Swiss franc	144.9	+10.9
Guilder	114.6	+4.2
French franc	66.3	−14.4
Lira	44.0	−19.9
Yen	157.4	+13.3

Morgan Guaranty changes: average 1980–1982 = 100.
Bank of England Index (base average 1975 = 100).

Currency Rates

Sept. 11	Bank rate %	Special Drawing Rights	European Currency Unit
Sterling	—	0.767892	0.576671
US $	7½	1.01285	0.757457
Canadian $	9.20	★	1.03847
Austrian Sch.	4	20.8860	15.6566
Belgian Fr.	9½	60.1430	45.0005
Danish Kr.	7	10.7818	8.07335
D Mark	4	2.97656	2.22920
Guilder	5	3.34544	2.50377
French Fr.	9½	9.07868	6.79552
Lira	15½	1979.36	1481.21
Yen	5	246.021	183.911
Norway Kr.	8	8.67506	6.47891
Spanish Pta.	—	175.117	131.040
Swedish Kr.	10½	8.71203	6.52057
Swiss Fr.	4	2.45312	1.83721
Greek Dr'ch	20½	142.012	106.180
Irish Punt	13½	N/A	0.716271

*C$/SDR rate for Sept. 10: 1.38693.

Table 6.6 EMS European Currency Unit Rates as at 12 September 1985

	ECU central rates	Currency amounts against ECU Sept. 11	% change from central rate	% change adjusted for divergence	Divergence limit %
Belgian Franc	44.8320	45.0005	+0.38	+0.71	±1.5425
Danish Kroner	8.12857	8.07335	−0.68	−0.35	±1.6421
German D-mark	2.23840	2.22920	−0.41	−0.08	±1.1455
French Franc	6.86402	6.79552	−1.00	−0.67	±1.3654
Dutch Guilder	2.52208	2.50377	−0.73	−0.40	±1.5162
Irish Punt	0.724578	0.716271	−1.15	−0.82	±1.6673
Italian Lira	1520.60	1481.21	−2.59	−2.57	±4.0856

Note: Changes are for ECU, therefore positive change denotes a weak currency. Adjustment calculated by *Financial Times*.

the value of the ECU is calculated, divergence limits vary. The Deutsche Mark is given a smaller divergence up or down than other currencies. Compounding this difficulty, there is the sterling problem. Although not a member of the EMS, sterling has a large weighting in the ECU basket. Thus the stronger sterling is, the more the ECU is worth in terms of, for example, the Belgian franc. It then becomes more likely that the Belgian franc will move towards its lower divergence limit. The column '% change adjusted for divergence' takes into account these distortions. When all EMS currencies, including sterling, are within their divergence limits, the third and fourth columns of the table will be identical. Of course, should sterling become a full member of the European intervention mechanism, the means by which the exchange rates of the French franc and the Deutsche Mark are tied to other members would apply to sterling.

The last table in *The Financial Times* devoted solely to foreign exchange is headed 'Exchange Cross Rates' and it expresses the value of the world's main trading currencies in terms of each other. This table covers the US dollar, sterling, the Deutsche Mark, the yen, the French franc, the Swiss franc, the Belgian franc, the Dutch guilder, the Italian lira and the Canadian dollar. The table effectively shows direct and indirect quotes for each other. Thus the cross-rate table is based on reciprocals. The pound sterling rate to the dollar as shown in the first row of Table 6.7 is the usual indirect London quote of 1.308. In the second row the rate of 0.765 occurs. This is the less frequently used London direct quote which indicates that £0.765 buys US$1.

On the *FT* page devoted to foreign exchange rates there is also a foreign exchange market report typically describing the major events in the markets during the previous day's trading. Eurocurrency interest rates are linked with foreign exchange rates and *The Financial Times* publishes a table of such rates daily – see Table 6.8. The tabulation shows Eurocurrency interest rates for periods from overnight to one year for eleven currencies, the Asian dollar and the Belgian financial franc. At the foot of the table, which embraces rates obtained late in the European trading day, the newspaper quotes deposit rates for the Asian

Table 6.7 Exchange Cross Rates from *The Financial Times* of 12 September·1985

Sept. 11	Pound Sterling	US Dollar	Deutsche Mark	Japanese Yen	French Franc	Swiss Franc	Dutch Guilder	Italian Lira	Canadian Dollar	Belgian Franc
Pound Sterling	1.	1.308	3.873	318.5	11.80	3.190	4.348	2574.	1.795	78.05
US Dollar	0.765	1.	2.961	243.5	9.020	2.439	3.324	1968.	1.372	59.65
Deutsche Mark	0.258	0.338	1.	82.25	3.047	0.824	1.123	664.6	0.464	20.15
Japanese Yen 1,000	3.140	4.107	12.16	1000.	37.05	10.02	13.65	8080.	5.636	245.1
French Franc 10	0.847	1.108	3.282	269.9	10.	2.703	3.684	2181.	1.521	66.14
Swiss Franc	0.313	0.410	1.214	99.84	3.699	1.	1.363	806.7	0.563	24.47
Dutch Guilder	0.230	0.301	0.891	73.26	2.714	0.734	1.	591.9	0.413	17.95
Italian Lira 1,000	0.389	0.508	1.505	123.6	4.585	1.240	1.689	1000.	0.697	30.33
Canadian Dollar	0.557	0.729	2.157	177.4	6.574	1.777	2.422	1434.	1.	43.48
Belgian Franc 100	1.281	1.676	4.962	408.1	15.12	4.087	5.570	3297.	2.300	100.

Table 6.8 Eurocurrency Interest Rates from *The Financial Times* of 12 September 1985 (Market Closing Rates)

Sept. 11	Sterling	US Dollar	Canadian Dollar	Dutch Guilder	Swiss Franc	D-mark	French Franc	Italian Lira	Belgian Franc Conv.	Fin.	Yen	Danish Krone
Short-term	$11\frac{1}{4}$-$11\frac{3}{8}$	$8\frac{3}{8}$-$8\frac{1}{4}$	8-$8\frac{1}{2}$	$5\frac{3}{4}$-6	$2\frac{3}{4}$-3	$4\frac{3}{16}$-$4\frac{7}{16}$	$9\frac{1}{2}$-$9\frac{5}{8}$	11-13	$7\frac{1}{2}$-$7\frac{3}{4}$	$7\frac{1}{2}$-$7\frac{3}{4}$	$6\frac{1}{4}$-$6\frac{3}{8}$	8-$8\frac{1}{2}$
7 days' notice	$11\frac{1}{4}$-$11\frac{1}{2}$	$8\frac{1}{16}$-$8\frac{3}{16}$	$8\frac{3}{8}$-$8\frac{5}{8}$	$5\frac{3}{4}$-$5\frac{7}{8}$	$2\frac{1}{2}$-$2\frac{1}{4}$	$4\frac{3}{8}$-$4\frac{1}{2}$	$9\frac{1}{2}$-$9\frac{5}{8}$	$11\frac{1}{2}$-$14\frac{1}{2}$	$8\frac{1}{2}$-$8\frac{3}{4}$	$8\frac{1}{2}$-$8\frac{3}{4}$	$6\frac{1}{4}$-$6\frac{3}{8}$	9-$9\frac{1}{2}$
Month	$11\frac{9}{16}$-$11\frac{11}{16}$	$8\frac{1}{8}$-$8\frac{1}{4}$	$8\frac{5}{8}$-$8\frac{7}{8}$	$5\frac{3}{4}$-$5\frac{7}{8}$	$4\frac{3}{8}$-$4\frac{1}{2}$	$4\frac{7}{16}$-$4\frac{9}{16}$	$9\frac{5}{8}$-$9\frac{3}{4}$	$12\frac{1}{4}$-$13\frac{1}{4}$	$8\frac{3}{4}$-9	$8\frac{3}{4}$-9	$6\frac{7}{16}$-$6\frac{1}{2}$	$8\frac{3}{4}$-$9\frac{1}{4}$
Three months	$11\frac{1}{2}$-$11\frac{11}{16}$	$8\frac{1}{4}$-$8\frac{3}{8}$	$8\frac{7}{8}$-$9\frac{1}{8}$	$5\frac{3}{4}$-$5\frac{7}{8}$	$4\frac{1}{4}$-$4\frac{1}{2}$	$4\frac{1}{4}$-$4\frac{3}{8}$	10-$10\frac{1}{8}$	$12\frac{3}{4}$-$13\frac{1}{4}$	$9\frac{1}{4}$-$9\frac{1}{2}$	$9\frac{1}{4}$-$9\frac{1}{2}$	$6\frac{1}{8}$-$6\frac{7}{16}$	$8\frac{3}{4}$-$9\frac{1}{4}$
Six months	$11\frac{7}{16}$-$11\frac{9}{16}$	$8\frac{1}{4}$-$8\frac{1}{2}$	$8\frac{1}{2}$-$8\frac{5}{8}$	$5\frac{3}{4}$-$5\frac{7}{8}$	$4\frac{11}{16}$-$4\frac{13}{16}$	$4\frac{5}{8}$-$4\frac{3}{4}$	$10\frac{1}{2}$-$18\frac{3}{4}$	13-$13\frac{1}{2}$	$9\frac{5}{8}$-$9\frac{7}{8}$	$9\frac{5}{8}$-$9\frac{7}{8}$	$6\frac{3}{8}$-$6\frac{7}{16}$	$8\frac{7}{8}$-$9\frac{3}{8}$
One year	$11\frac{5}{16}$-$11\frac{7}{16}$	$8\frac{7}{8}$-9	$9\frac{5}{16}$-$9\frac{9}{16}$	$5\frac{3}{4}$-$5\frac{7}{8}$	$4\frac{11}{16}$-$4\frac{13}{16}$	$4\frac{3}{4}$-$4\frac{7}{8}$	$11\frac{3}{8}$-$11\frac{1}{2}$	$13\frac{3}{4}$-$14\frac{1}{4}$	$9\frac{3}{4}$-10	$9\frac{3}{4}$-10	$6\frac{3}{8}$-$6\frac{7}{16}$	$9\frac{1}{4}$-$9\frac{3}{4}$

Asian $ (closing rates in Singapore): Short-term $7\frac{7}{8}$-$8\frac{1}{16}$ per cent; seven days 8-$8\frac{1}{4}$ per cent; one month $8\frac{1}{8}$-$8\frac{1}{4}$per cent; three months$8\frac{1}{4}$-$8\frac{1}{2}$ per cent; six months $8\frac{1}{2}$-$8\frac{5}{8}$ per cent; one year $8\frac{7}{8}$-9 per cent. Long-term Eurodollars: two years $9\frac{3}{8}$-$9\frac{7}{8}$ per cent; three years $10\frac{1}{4}$-$10\frac{1}{8}$ per cent; four years$10\frac{3}{8}$-$10\frac{5}{8}$ per cent; five years $10\frac{5}{8}$-$10\frac{7}{8}$ per cent nominal. Short-term rates are call for US dollars and Japanese yen; others two days' notice.

dollar. These are offshore dollars traded in the Far East before the European markets open. The rate quoted is the closing rate in Singapore.

On the same page as that on which it details happenings in the foreign exchange markets, *The Financial Times* also has a section devoted to London money markets, and a section on financial futures in which it quotes rates in the London and Chicago financial futures markets. These quotations are in the standard financial futures format. Readers are advised to refer to Chapter 16 before venturing into *The Financial Times* quotes on futures.

Summary

Foreign exchange markets comprise the framework of individuals, firms, banks and brokers who buy and sell foreign currencies. In these markets there are five kinds of transaction: spot deals, forward deals, futures transactions, currency options and deposit market deals. The future and options markets are covered in Chapters 16 and 17 respectively. Market participants include companies, individuals, commercial banks, central banks and brokers. Between 90 and 95 per cent of all foreign exchange transactions involve banks. Trade accounts for only 1 or 2 per cent of all transactions nowadays.

Because of the overlapping of time zones around the world, the foreign exchange markets are effectively open all the time in one centre or another, except at weekends.

The essence of this chapter concerns the ways in which the financial community quotes foreign exchange rates – it is most important that students become fully conversant with this. An investment of time on this chapter will therefore be amply repaid as progress is made through the field of multinational finance.

TEST BANK
NUMBER ONE

FOREIGN EXCHANGE PROBLEMS

In these problems assume that all interest rates quoted are per annum rates. Calculate 90 day rates by taking one quarter of the annual rate. Also assume that, where only one rate is quoted, rather than a bid/offer rate, deals may be done at this rate whether they are purchase or sale deals, lend or borrow deals. This is, of course, a simplifying assumption. Also disregard any transaction costs; for substantial deals these are generally taken care of in the bid/offer spread.

1. The spot rate for the Deutsche Mark in New York is $0.40.
(a) What should the spot price for the US dollar be in Frankfurt?
(b) Should the dollar be quoted at DM 2.60 in Frankfurt, how would
    the market react?

2. When the Deutsche Mark spot rate was quoted at $0.40 in New York, the US market was quoting sterling at $1.80.
(a) What should the price of the pound be in Frankfurt?
(b) If sterling were quoted at DM 4.40/£ in Frankfurt, what profit
    opportunities would exist?

3. Your company has to make a US $1 million payment in three months' time. The dollars are available now. You decide to invest them for three months and you are given the following information:
– the US deposit rate is 8% per annum
– the sterling deposit rate is 10% per annum
– the spot exchange rate is $1.80/£
– the three-month forward rate is $1.78/£
(a) Where should your company invest for the better return?
(b) Assuming that interest rates and the spot exchange rate remain
    as above, what forward rate would yield an equilibrium situation?

(c) Assuming that the US $ interest rate and the spot and forward rates remain as in the original question, where would you invest if the sterling deposit rate were 14% per annum?

(d) With the originally stated spot and forward rates and the same dollar deposit rate, what is the equilibrium sterling deposit rate?

4. The spot rate for the French franc is $0.1250 and the three-month forward rate is $0.1260. Your company is prepared to speculate that the French franc will move to $0.1400 by the end of three months.

(a) Are the quotations given direct or indirect Paris quotations?

(b) How would the speculation be undertaken using the spot market only?

(c) How would the speculation be arranged using forward markets?

(d) If your company were prepared to put $1 million at risk on the deal, what would the profit outturns be if expectations were met? Ignore all interest rate implications.

(e) How would your answer to (d) above differ were you to take into account interest rate implications?

5. The six-month interest rate for the Canadian $ is 9% when the six-month interest rate for the US $ is 6.75%. At the same time the spot Canadian $ quotation in New York is US $0.9100 and the six-month forward rate is US $0.9025.

(a) Is interest rate parity holding? Why?

(b) If not, how could advantage be taken of the situation?

(c) If a large number of operators decide to do the arbitrage suggested under (b), what will the effect be upon spot and forward quotations and upon interest rates for the two currencies?

6. Set out below is a table of cross rates.

	Deutsche Mark	Dollar	French franc	Pound sterling
Frankfurt		2.2812	0.4712	4.0218
New York	0.4421		0.2110	1.8000
Paris	2.0949	4.7393		8.4301
London	4.0207	1.7775	8.4232	

Note that, for Frankfurt, New York and Paris, all quotes are direct; for London, all quotes are indirect.

    If all the above quotes were available at the same instant in time and assuming no transactions costs, how might a nimble trader take advantage of the situation?

7. A foreign exchange trader gives the following quotes for the Belgian franc spot, one-month, three-month and six-month to a US-based treasurer.

$0.02478/80   4/6   9/8   14/11

(a) Calculate the outright quotes for one, three and six months forward.
(b) If the treasurer wished to buy Belgian francs three months forward, how much would he pay in dollars?
(c) If he wished to purchase US dollars one month forward, how much would he have to pay in Belgian francs?
(d) Assuming that Belgian francs are being bought, what is the premium or discount, for the one-, three-, and six-month forward rates in annual percentage terms?
(e) What do the above quotations imply in respect of the term structure of interest rates in the USA and Belgium?

8. Imagine that you are a trader working for a New York bank. The spot exchange rate against the Canadian $ is US $0.9968 and the one-month and one-year forward rates are respectively US $0.9985 and US $1.0166. Twelve-month interest rates in the USA and Canada may be taken as 6.45% and 4.46% respectively.
(a) What is the forward premium as an annual percentage?
(b) Which currency is at a premium? Why?
    You become party to some inside information which suggests that US interest rates will rise by 1 per cent per annum during the next month. The bank has a rule that in the foreign exchange markets 'buy equals sell'. This means that for any currency the total of long positions must equal the total of short positions – but this aggregation disregards maturity.
(c) Indicate the mechanics of two operations by which you may trade in expectation of profit for the bank should the inside information turn out to be well-founded.

FOREIGN EXCHANGE RATES

Consider the tablulation below which is given by a bank to a customer. For questions 1 to 16, the required rate is against the home currency.

	$	Guilders	Escudos
Spot	1.3915–25	4.70–4.70¼	263.15–25
	Premium	Premium	
1 month forward	1–0.90 cents	4½–4¼ cents	15 cents pm
			10 cents dis
2 months forward	1.60–1.50 cents	8½–8¼ cents	17 cents pm
			8 cents dis
3 months forward	2.10–2.00 cents	10½–10¼ cents	19 cents pm
			6 cents dis

The word 'premium' or 'discount' implies that the foreign currency quoted at the head of each commn is at the premium or discount respectively.

1. At what rate will the bank buy spot dollars?
2. At what rate will the customer buy escudos three months forward?
3. At what rate will the customer sell dollars one month forward?
4. At what rate will the bank sell spot escudos?
5. At what rate will the customer buy guilders spot?
6. At what rate will the bank buy escudos two months forward?
7. At what rate will the customer buy dollars two months forward?
8. At what rate will the bank sell dollars two months forward?
9. At what rate will the bank buy guilders three months forward?
10. At what rate will the customer sell escudos one month forward?
11. At what rate will the bank buy dollars three months forward?
12. At what rate will the customer sell escudos three months forward?
13. At what rate will the customer sell dollars three months forward?
14. At what rate will the bank sell escudos one month forward?
15. At what rate will the bank buy guilders one month forward?
16. At what rate will the bank sell guilders three months forward?

For questions 17–22 calculate the annual forward premium/discount, state which currency is at the premium, and indicate where interest rates should be higher if interest rate parity holds.

17. Home currency versus dollars 1 month. Assume you are a buyer of dollars.
18. Home currency versus dollars 3 month. Assume you are a buyer of home currency.
19. Home currency versus dollars 3 months. Assume you are a seller of dollars.

20. Home currency versus escudos 3 months. Do the calculation on middle prices.
21. Home currency versus escudos 3 months. Assume you are a seller of home currency.
22. Home currency versus guilders 2 months. Assume you are a buyer of home currency.

EXAMINATION QUESTIONS

1. In Frankfurt the French franc is selling for DM 0.4343 spot and the 3-month forward rate DM 0.4300. The 3-month Eurodeutsche Mark interbank rate is 5.75% and the Eurofrench franc interbank rate is 9.00%.
(a) Are exchange rate and money markets in equilibrium? Why?
(b) Is there any way to take advantage of the situation? If so, how?
(c) What rate trends would appear in the market if a large number of operators took the actions indicated in (b)?

2. On 1 September 1985 the Peter Company Inc. bought from a foreign firm equipment that will require the payment of 9 million rurals on 30 November 1985. The spot rate on 1 September 1985 is 10 rurals per dollar; the expected future spot rate on 30 November is 8 rurals per dollar; and the three-month forward rate is 9 rurals per dollar. The US interest rate is 12 per cent per annum and the foreign interest rate is 8 per cent per annum. In this question please ignore taxation. The Peter Company is considering the following alternatives to deal with the foreign exchange risk problem:
(a) Use the forward market and buy 9 million rurals at the three-month forward rate.
(b) Borrow an amount in dollars to buy the rurals at the current spot rate. This money is to be invested at the interest rate prevailing in the foreign country. With the interest income, it will equal 9 million rurals on 30 November.
(c) Wait until 30 November and buy 9 million rurals at whatever spot rate prevails at that time.
According to the above data, which alternative should the Peter Company follow in order to minimise its cost of meeting the future payment in rurals? Explain.

3. You are given the following spot quotations in London:
   US$1 = SFr 1.6230/40
   US$1 = DM 1.8110/20
   £1   = US$2.2530/40

Calculate the following bid/offer quotations, also in London:
(a) SFr against DM
(b) £ against DM

4. Assume that you are a wealthy American investor. A New York foreign exchange trader gives you the following quotations over the phone for the Deutsche Mark spot, one, three, six and twelve months against the US dollar: $0.4164/66; 3/4; 10/11; 20/21; 36/38.
(a) Would you expect Euro $ or Euro DM interest rates to be higher? Why? Which currency is at a premium in the forward market?
(b) What would the trader charge in dollars to sell DM 5 million three months forward?
(c) If you want to sell DM to the trader six months forward, what would the FX trader pay in dollars per DM?
(d) Calculate the three-month forward premium/discount as an annual percentage. Assume that you, as a private individual, are selling dollars.

5. A UK company has a requirement for Swiss francs for 3 months. A proposition is put that the currency should be borrowed direct due to the low interest rate.
At 27 March 1985:

   £/SFr spot 3.2075–3.2175
   £/SFr three-month forward 2.75–2.25c pm
   £ three-month interest $13\frac{9}{16}$–$13\frac{11}{16}$
   SFr three-month interest $5\frac{3}{4}$–$5\frac{7}{8}$
Should the proposition be carried?

(Association of Corporate Treasurers: Part II, Specimen paper in Currency Management)

6. A UK company has excess cash for a period of 3 months. A proposition is put that it should be invested in Italian lire due to the high interest rate.
When the decision is to be made the rates are as follows:

£/lire spot	$2,507\frac{1}{2}$–$2,508\frac{1}{2}$
£/lire 3-month forward	9–13 dis
£3-month interest	$12\frac{3}{8}$–$12\frac{1}{2}$%
Euro-lire 3-month interest	$13\frac{3}{4}$–$14\frac{1}{4}$%

Required:
What would you do and why?

(Association of Corporate Treasurers: Part II, September 1985 Paper in Currency Management)

7. XYZ Ltd, an export company customer of your bank, has sold goods to a buyer in the USA for $100,000, to be paid for in exactly

three months' time against an accepted bill of exchange. The finance director of the company wishes to know which of the following methods of financing the transaction would be the more profitable for the company (which normally operates on overdraft):
(a) Borrow $100,000 now, convert the dollars immediately into sterling to provide working capital, and repay the borrowing from the dollar proceeds of the bill of exchange when it falls due.
(b) Borrow sterling through the company's ECGD Bill and Notes Scheme and repay from the proceeds of the bill of exchange (due in three months' time) which is covered forward (fixed).

Required:
Using the additional information given below, show by calculation which would be the more profitable method for your customer.

	Spot	Three months forward
(i) US dollar rates	$1.8950–1.9150	2.47–2.54c disc

(ii) US dollar three months' LIBOR rate is $17\frac{1}{8}\%$, and for this important customer you would apply a margin of $\frac{3}{4}\%$.
(iii) UK base rate is 12% for the whole period.
(iv) Three months can be regarded as exactly one quarter of a year.
(v) Interest in (a) is to be converted at the middle rate today of 1.905 (the correct rate would not be known at the time when the transaction was discussed with the customer, and this 'middle' rate is used to give the customer an indication of the amount of interest to be charged when effecting transactions of this nature).

Note: Under the ECGD Bills and Notes Scheme the interest rate is $\frac{5}{8}\%$ over UK base rate – thus the effective rate is $12\frac{5}{8}\%$.

(Institute of Bankers: Banking Diploma, April 1982 Paper in Finance of International Trade)

8. You have recently moved to a new branch and are endeavouring to meet the more important customers as quickly as possible. One of them, Harold Farmer, is a respectable local farmer and you have made an appointment to see him within the next few days. Prior to your meeting you discover that, nearly three years ago, he switched his £100,000 sterling overdraft borrowing into a three-year, fixed-interest-rate 450,000 Swiss franc loan. He has no foreign currency income, nor is he likely to have any in the foreseeable future. The currency loan will soon have to be either extended or repaid by the customer. You have ascertained that the loan was his own idea and that your predecessor did nothing either to encourage or discourage

the customer from taking out this form of borrowing. At the time of the switch from sterling into Swiss francs the relative rates were:

Swiss francs loan established at $4\frac{5}{8}$% per annum three years fixed
Sterling base rate 17% per annum
The margin over the basic rate for the Swiss franc loan was 1% and the sterling overdraft rate was 2% over base rate.

At the time that the Swiss franc loan was taken out the funds were switched from sterling into Swiss francs at the rate of Swiss francs 4.50 = £1. Interest has been charged and covered quarterly, but the principal sum is still outstanding.

You contact your foreign exchange dealers who advise you that at the maturity of the loan within the next few weeks they are likely to offer a loan with 3, 6 or 12 months' roll-over facilities. The current rates of interest are as follows:

Swiss francs   3 months $6\frac{1}{4}$% p.a.
                 6 months $6\frac{3}{8}$% p.a.
                 12 months $6\frac{3}{8}$% p.a.
UK base rate   11%

The bank's selling rate for Swiss francs today is 3.0625.
Required:
(a) Brief notes on the advantages/disadvantages to your customer of his continuing to borrow Swiss francs as opposed to sterling from both an interest and capital point of view.
(b) Using the rates mentioned above, calculate the total saving or cost for Harold Farmer if he switched his Swiss franc borrowing back to a sterling overdraft of approximately £100,000 on the repayment date.
Note: Assume that the conversion back from Swiss francs into sterling is by selling the customer Swiss francs at today's selling rate. In your calculations, assume that any sterling interest which might have been paid, had the original borrowing remained in sterling, would have been at the sterling rate quoted at the beginning of the loan, i.e. 17% plus the margin over base rate, and that the Swiss franc interest charged is calculated at the original exchange rate of 4.50 = £1.

(Institute of Bankers: Banking Diploma, Stage 2, September 1983 Paper in Finance of International Trade)

7

The Balance of Payments

The balance of payments position of a country is often claimed to be an important piece of information for anyone wishing to predict the future of a currency's strength in exchange rate terms. A recurring current account surplus is often associated with a strengthening of a country's exchange rate; a continual deficit on current account is frequently associated with a fall in a country's exchange rate. A surplus on current account is underpinned by an excess of exports over imports. Suppose that exports from a country are denominated in the home currency. Payment for them involves a foreigner in buying home currency and selling foreign currency. This tends to strengthen the home currency. Hence surpluses and the strengthening of the exchange rate tend to go hand in hand. Conversely, deficits on current account are associated with an excess of imports over exports. Therefore recurring current account deficits and weakening of the exchange rate are generally related.

There are, however, a good many frailties in a forecasting model based solely on current account outturns. The current account is only part of the balance of payments picture. The capital account has to be considered as well. Before we can truly discuss the problems of using balance of payments data to forecast foreign exchange rates, we need to consider a number of concepts associated with the balance of payments. This chapter attempts to describe these concepts and draws conclusions about foreign exchange rate forecasting using balance of payments information.

The Essence of International Trade

The basis of international trade has been explained in terms of the principle of comparative advantage. This presumes that, for a number of reasons, some individuals and some countries produce some goods and services more efficiently than others. It is conceivable that one particular country might produce every product more efficiently than any other country. Even if this were so, it might be to that country's advantage to apply all its skills and resources towards the production of only those goods or services which gave it the greatest pay-off and to buy in other products and services which gave a lower pay-off. It is, of course, extremely

73

unlikely that one particular country would produce all goods and services more efficiently than its international competitors. However, as long as one country has a greater advantage, a comparative advantage, in producing certain goods and services, it benefits by specialising in those lines, exporting those goods and services and importing other goods and services from other countries. A country gains, then, by specialising in products in which it has the greatest comparative advantage because any shift of resources to other products reduces output. Naturally, a country must produce enough of the goods and services in which it possesses a comparative advantage not only to meet its own needs but also to export, in exchange for imports of goods and services needed to meet demand.

International trade usually involves the cross-frontier payment of money to pay for goods and services. The word 'usually' is deliberately employed because a significant volume of international trade is by barter. Indeed, in dealing with certain countries which are short of foreign exchange, trade is largely via barter. But for most transactions, barter is as awkward internationally as it is domestically. Unless international trade is by barter alone, it must be financed.

One of the most valuable services rendered by the foreign exchange markets is the provision of a mechanism for transferring the money of one country into the money of another. As long as different countries exist, and as long as international trade embraces payment other than by barter, foreign exchange will be a necessary dimension of international trade.

The Balance of Payments and Foreign Exchange Rates

A foreign exchange rate is the price of one currency in terms of another. The balance of payments summarises the flow of economic transactions between the residents of a given country and the residents of other countries during a certain period of time.

The balance of payments measures flows rather than stocks. These flows represent payments and receipts. Balance of payments data only record changes in asset holdings and liabilities; they do not present the absolute levels of these items. So the balance of payments of a country is rather like the statement of sources and uses of funds of a firm. For a country, sources of funds are acquisitions of external purchasing power, rights a country has to claim goods and services or to invest in another country. For a country, uses of funds, in the context of the balance of payments, means a decrease in its external purchasing power.

For balance of payments purposes, a resident is any person, business firm, government agency, or other institution legally domiciled in the given country. Thus a subsidiary, but not a branch, of a company legally established in Britain would be treated like any other British enterprise for balance of payments purposes.

The balance of payments measures transactions among countries. Transactions that affect only local residents and only involve the national currency (in contrast to foreign exchange) are not recorded in the balance of payments. The balance of payments comprises three distinct types of account, namely:

- the current account
- the capital account
- the official reserves

Table 7.1 shows a simplified balance of payments format for Ruritania in 1984. It is simplified because it contains merely 23 lines of figures, whereas the full balance of payments as published by the IMF in *International Financial Statistics* contains over 50 lines. In terms of putting this rather complex presentation of data into a more readily handleable design for purposes of forecasting exchange rates, the model used in Table 7.1 is recommended.

Balance of payments information is compiled by government statisticians from questionnaires completed by companies, banks, export agencies and others. The overall balance of payments is, by definition, equal – the sum of the current and capital accounts equals the official financing. If the aggregate of data obtained by government statisticians does not balance, a heading called net errors and omissions is introduced. This item is a permanent feature of balance of payments figures. We shall now consider, in turn, the content of the current account, the capital account and the official financing parts of the balance of payments. In this description we shall constantly refer to data in Table 7.1 by way of illustration.

The current account records trade in goods and services and the exchange of gifts among countries. Trade in goods comprises exports and imports. A country increases its exports when it sells goods to foreigners; this is a source of funds. It increases imports when it buys goods from foreigners; this is a use of funds. The difference between exports and imports is called the trade balance. According to Table 7.1, Ruritania has a positive trade balance of $1,000 million in 1984. Sources of external purchasing power exceed uses thereof through trade by $1,000 million.

The difference on services is called the balance of invisibles. In balance of payments terminology, services include interest, dividends, travel expenses, shipping, property, banking, financial and other consultancy services. The rendering of these services to foreigners is a source of funds and their receipt from foreigners is a use of funds. Respectively they increase or reduce external purchasing power. Table 7.1 shows that Ruritania has a positive balance on invisibles of $500 million. In other words, sources of external purchasing power exceed uses by $500 million in respect of transactions in invisibles.

Gifts are recorded in the unilateral transfers account. This account is frequently called remittances or unrequited transfers. It embraces money that migrants send home, and gifts and aid that one country makes to another. A gift represents a use of external purchasing power. Ruritania has a negative balance on unilateral transfers amounting to $400 million. Uses of funds exceed sources by this amount.

The overall current account of Ruritania shows a positive balance of $1.1 billion, made up of positive balances in trade and invisibles and a negative balance on unilateral transfers.

Turning now to the capital account, this details international movements of financial assets and liabilities. These are classified in the balance of payments according to their maturity and according to the involvement of the owner of the asset or liability. There are a number of sub-divisions such as direct investment, portfolio investment, and private short-term capital flows. Direct investment and portfolio investment involve financial assets with an initial maturity of more than a year when issued. Short-term capital movements consist of claims with an original maturity of less than one year. The distinction between direct investment and portfolio investment is made on the basis of the degree of management involvement. In the case of direct investment, considerable management involvement is

Table 7.1   Simplified Balance of Payments Format for Ruritania in 1984
(Figures in $ million. Sources of funds given by +; use of funds given by −.)

CURRENT ACCOUNT			
Trade account			
Exports of goods	2,500		
Imports of goods	− 1,500		
Balance of trade		1,000	
Invisibles account			
Receipts from interest and dividends, travel and services such as shipping, property, banking and financial charges	1,000		
Payments for interest and dividends, and services such as shipping, travel, property, banking and financial charges	− 500		
Balance of invisibles (services)		500	
Unilateral transfers			
Gifts received from aborad	200		
Grants to foreign countries	− 600		
Balance in unilateral transfers		− 400	
Current account balance			1,100
CAPITAL ACCOUNT			
Long-term capital flows			
Direct investment			
Sale of financial assets	1,000		
Purchase of financial assets	− 2,000	− 1,000	
Portfolio investments			
Sale of financial assets	3,000		
Purchase of financial assets	− 1,500	1,500	
Balance on long-term capital		500	
Private short-term capital flows			
Sale of financial assets	5,000		
Purchase of financial assets	− 2,000		
Balance on short-term private capital		3,000	
Capital account balance			3,500
OVERALL BALANCE			4,600
OFFICIAL RESERVES ACCOUNT			
Gold decrease (+) or gold increase (−)			− 2,400
Decrease (+) or increase (−) in foreign exchange			− 2,200
TOTAL OFFICIAL FINANCING			− 4,600

presumed to exist; this is interpreted as a minimum of ten per cent ownership in a firm. No management involvement is presumed to exist for portfolio investment.

Ruritania has a deficit on direct investment to the extent of $1,000 million. Whilst foreigners invested $1,000 million in the country, Ruritania invested $2,000 million outside the country in respect of those situations where in excess of ten per cent ownership was acquired. Under the heading of portfolio investment, Ruritania has an inflow of $3,000 million compared with an outflow of $1,500 million. Together with the balance on direct investment, this gives a positive balance on long-term capital account of $500 million. In the private short-term capital account, Ruritania increased its liabilities to foreigners – a source of funds for the country – by $5,000 million, whilst Ruritania increased its claims on foreigners (a use of funds for Ruritania) by $2,000 million. These two items gave rise to a positive net balance on short-term capital account of $3,000 million. Summing long-term and short-term capital flows gives the balance on capital account. For Ruritania there is a positive capital account balance of $3,500 million. When the current account and capital account are added up, we get a total that is frequently called the overall balance. For Ruritania, this amounts to $4,600 million. In other words, Ruritania has acquired a net source of external purchasing power of this amount.

The official reserves account rounds off the balance of payments. It shows the means of international payment that the monetary authorities of a country have acquired or lost during a particular period. The term 'means of international payment' includes gold and convertible foreign currency. It must be borne in mind that only foreign currency holdings that are freely convertible are included in the official reserves. Really, this means that only a handful of currencies find their way into official reserves. Currencies such as the US dollar and sterling qualify as they are freely convertible at the present time. Most governments do not allow their country's currency to be freely converted to others, so holdings of Italian lire, Portuguese escudos, Spanish pesetas, and so on, would not be classified as official reserves.

If there is a surplus at the overall balance level on a country's balance of payments, there will be an inflow of official reserves. But we must bear in mind the notation used in balance of payments accounting. As we shall see later in this chapter, balance of payments accounting is just another variant of double-entry bookkeeping. For every debit there is a credit; for every plus entry on the balance of payments, there will be a compensating minus entry. So, in the official reserves part of the balance of payments, a negative entry implies an increase in reserves. In Table 7.1 Ruritania has expanded its gold reserves by $2,400 million and its foreign exchange reserves by $2,200 million. Care must be taken to interpret the sign in front of official reserves data correctly because of the counter-intuitive nature of the way in which information is recorded.

Movements in the official reserves may be interpreted as an indicator of the extent of direct intervention in the foreign exchange markets by the central bank. When the monetary authorities support the home currency (or associated currencies where there is a joint float), they do so by selling reserves and buying the home currency – this would reduce official reserves. Conversely, when they depress the home currency, they do so by buying in convertible currency and selling home currency – this would increase official reserves.

Balance of Payments Accounting

The balance of payments always balances. The sum of the debits and credits on the current account, the capital account and the official financing is always equal. This arises because balance of payments tabulations are built on double-entry book-keeping principles. Table 7.2 summarises the accounts used in balance of payments accounting. These accounts are numbered so that such numbers can be used as a form of shorthand in student exercises. The accounts are classified according to whether they are typically debit or credit − or both.

Table 7.2   Balance of Payments Accounting

Debit (−)	Credit (+)
1. Import of goods	
	2. Export of goods
3. Purchase of services from foreigners	
	4. Sale of services to foreigners
5. Interest, dividends, rents and royalties to foreigners	
	6. Interest, dividends, rents and royalties from foreigners
7. Gifts to foreigners	
	8. Gifts from foreigners

9. Direct investment
  · by residents in
    foreign countries
	· by foreigners in
	  home country

10. Portfolio investment
  · by residents in
    foreign country
	· by foreigners in
	  home country

11. Long-term claims on foreigners · increase	· decrease
12. Long-term liabilities to foreigners · decrease	· increase
13. Short-term claims on foreigners · increase	· decrease
14. Short-term liabilities to foreigners · decrease	· increase
15. Official reserves of gold · increase	· decrease
16. Official reserves of foreign exchange · increase	· decrease

Through a series of simple examples the essence of balance of payments accounting may be understood.

Example 1:   A resident of country X exports goods to a resident of country Y who signs a bill of exchange, denominated in country Y's currency which matures in ninety days. In country X's balance of payments, an export has occurred and a short-term claim on a foreigner has been acquired. The debit and credit position is therefore:

Dr   Short-term claims on foreigners (the bill of exchange)
Cr   Export of goods

Example 2:   The exporter in Example 1 holds the bill to maturity when he receives payment in country Y's currency. The exporter now has a claim (the payment in Y's currency) on a bank in country Y. Effectively, the debit and credit are therefore in the same account.

Dr   Short-term claims on foreigners (the amount in Y's currency)
Cr   Short-term claims on foreigners (the bill of exchange)

Example 3:   The exporter in the two previous examples now decides to convert the payment in country Y's currency to his own. He does this through his own clearing bank. Here the bank buys the foreign currency and sells the home currency in exchange. Now the bank in country X has acquired country Y's currency. The bank now has a short-term claim on foreigners. All that has happened is that the short-term claim on foreigners has been shuffled from one resident of country X, the exporter, to another, the clearing bank. From a balance of payments standpoint no entry needs to be made.

Example 4:   The clearing bank decides to sell the foreign currency acquired in the previous example to country X's central bank in exchange for home currency. Assume that country Y's currency is freely convertible in the foreign exchange markets. When the central bank acquires gold or freely convertible foreign currency, it increases the official reserves. So in this case the balance of payments entry is:

Dr   Official reserves of foreign currency
Cr   Short-term claims on foreigners (the amount in Y's currency)

Example 5:   If the previous example had differed in only one respect, namely that country Y's currency had not been freely convertible, there would have been no increment to the official reserves. In that case there would have been no balance of payments entry – the short-term claim on foreigners would merely have been shuffled from the clearing bank to the central bank and, since the short-term claim was not convertible foreign currency, it would not have counted as part of the official reserves. It would, in fact, have remained as a short-term claim on foreigners – but the claim would be held by the central bank rather than the clearing bank.

Example 6:   A US resident on holiday in country X changes dollar travellers cheques for country X's currency at an airport bank. All of it is spent on his vacation. In this case the balance of payments entry would be:

Dr   Short-term claims on foriegners (the holding of US dollars)
Cr   Travel services to foreigners (part of account number 4 in Table 7.2).

Example 7:   Had the airport bank in the previous example then sold the US dollars to the central bank, this would have increased the official reserves. The balance of payments entry would be:

Dr   Official reserves of foreign currency
Cr   Short-term claims on foreigners (the holding of US dollars)

The acquisition of convertible foreign currency within a country does not lead to an entry in the official reserves until that foreign currency finds its way to the central bank. This is a very important feature of balance of payments accounting which needs clearly to be understood.

Example 8:   A resident of country X sends a cheque to a relative in Australia. In country X's balance of payments the above transaction is shown as:

Dr   Gifts to foreigners
Cr   Short-term liabilities to foreigners (the cheque)

Example 9:   A foreign bank uses a deposit in country X's currency to buy country X's treasury bills. This transaction is classified as a reduction in short-term liabilities to foreigners (the deposit in country X's currency) matched by an increase in short-term liabilities to foreigners (the treasury bills). Note that, since treasury bills have a maturity of less than twelve months, they do not constitute portfolio investment. So the transaction is:

Dr   Short-term liabilities to foreigners − decrease (the currency deposit)
Cr   Short-term liabilities to foreigners − increase (the treasury bills)

It is worth pointing out that current account and capital account movements are termed autonomous in balance of payments parlance. These movements can be considered as a barometer of pressures on the exchange rate of the home currency. Official reserves movements are termed compensating or accommodating items. Sometimes this distinction is expressed in 'above the line' and 'below the line' terms respectively. Accounts 'above the line' embrace autonomous accounts whose balance determines whether the balance of payments is in surplus or deficit. Accounts 'below the line' represent compensating accounts that show how the balance of payments surplus or deficit was financed.

When the balance of payments is in surplus, the international purchasing power of a country has increased during the period in question; that is, autonomous receipts exceed autonomous payments. When balance of payments is in deficit, the international purchasing power of a country has decreased during the period in question: autonomous payments exceed autonomous receipts. A surplus in the autonomous account is accompanied by an increase in foreign reserves or a decrease in official liabilities in the compensating accounts. This puts an upward pressure on the external value of the home currency. A deficit in the autonomous accounts is associated with a decrease in foreign reserves or an increase in liabilities to foreigners. This tends to put a downward pressure on the external value of the home currency. Countries with continuous deficits in the balance of payments experience international currency depreciation.

In practice, balance of payments statistics are not compiled on an entry-by-entry basis. Only aggregates of transactions are measured for a period. The customs and excise authorities provide the main source for figures on exports and imports; financial institutions, government agencies and industry report the changes in foreign financial assets and liabilities to foreigners. Hence there is the almost perennial item in balance of payment accounting − net errors and omissions − which arises because sources and uses fail to balance.

Forecasting Exchange Rates and the Balance of Payments

The use of balance of payments data to forecast foreign exchange rates is predicated upon the assumption that, when a country's currency is in equilibrium, that country will display a break-even position in respect of trade and those invisibles which reflect the rendering of services (as opposed to the remuneration of capital, that is, interest and dividends). Although not exactly in accordance with the above formula, this is frequently interpreted as being equivalent to an even current account outturn. The other key assumptions in forecasting foreign exchange rates from the balance of payments are that currencies which are undervalued will have the effect of creating positive current account outturns and that currencies which are overvalued will have the effect of creating negative current account results.

These key underpinnings also assume that no market imperfections exist such as the absence of any significant valuable raw materials or trained labour force which typify so many third-world countries. So often one concludes that, on the basis of balance of payments data, there is no way to identify the exchange rate at which many third-world countries will break even on current account.

There are also frailties of the forecasting model which need to be borne in mind. These basically concern three key areas. The first of these relates to situations where exports are denominated in a third currency and where the exporter continues to hold the proceeds of an export sale in the said currency. Consider an example. Many raw materials are priced in US dollars. This is true of oil. A UK oil exporter will sell petroleum to Europe, for example, with price denominated in US dollars. When the European importer pays the UK oil company it will pay in dollars. The export will show as a positive increment to the British balance of payments current account. But if the exporter continues to hold the proceeds of the sale in a US-dollar bank account, it will not strengthen the pound sterling. As far as the balance of payments is concerned the dollar deposit will show as a short-term claim on foreigners. Now if the UK oil company were to sell its dollars for pounds via its clearing bank, this deal would tend to strengthen sterling. But even if the UK oil company sold its dollars to a clearing bank, the transaction would still show as a short-term claim on foreigners from a balance of payments viewpoint. But the claim is now held by the bank rather than the oil exporter. Clearly, from the standpoint of using balance of payments data to forecast exchange rates with great confidence, we have inadequate information based on the normal package of published figures.

The second frailty involves a country's capital account. Whilst it may experience substantial deficits on current account, a country may have substantial capital inflows from multinationals. These capital flows may exceed the current account deficit, resulting in an overall tendency for a country's currency to strengthen despite its negative current account balance. This situation underpinned the strength of the Mexican peso and the Indonesian rupiah in the early seventies, when inflows from oil companies undertaking exploration activities propped up deficits on current account and allowed the governments of both countries to postpone devaluations which were indicated by purchasing power parity.

The third frailty also arises in the area of the capital account. Amongst other things, the capital account includes borrowings from bankers or from the IMF. These would show as long-term liabilities to foreigners. The conversion of such borrowings from, say, US dollars to the home currency would tend to strengthen the home currency in the short term but would not, in the very short term, affect the current account of the country.

Evidently, using current account data as indicators of potential foreign exchange movements is fraught with pitfalls. The forecaster needs to tread very warily but, with care, he has a useful tool at his disposal.

Summary

Balance of payments data may be used to help forecast foreign exchange rates. The key premise is that, when a country's currency is in equilibrium, that country will display a break-even position in respect of trade accounts plus those invisible accounts which reflect the rendering of services (as opposed to the remuneration of capital). This is frequently, although not strictly correctly, interpreted as an even current account result.

Although there are a number of caveats concerning the ease of application of the above idea, it should be clear that, if balance of payments data are so useful in terms of forecasting exchange rates, it is as well that the student should understand how to read balance of payments information.

This chapter is concerned with communicating the essential features of balance of payments accounting and reporting to the reader. In terms of understanding multinational finance from the corporate treasurer's position, this topic is of a lower priority than the subject areas covered in many of the other chapters in this text.

8

Theories of Exchange Rate Movements

Explanations of economic phenomena often conflict. Hypotheses are advanced and tested. For a while it looks as if one particular series of explanatory variables is accounting for changes in the dependent variable – then the relationship breaks down. As social scientists we should not be surprised at the infuriatingly unpredictable way in which our world seems to work.

Multinational finance is no exception. The key question to which we seek a solution is: what makes foreign exchange rates move and can these movements be predicted? We are looking for the typical kind of regression equation in which the future spot rate is the dependent variable and there may be one or more independent variables whose coefficients can be estimated, hopefully with acceptably high levels of significance, and where the equation has a high R squared.

Unfortunately the models that have been developed do not necessarily hold for anything but shortish periods. So we do not have the kind of model which we can rely on with a high degree of certainty in terms of predicting movements in spot rates. So what are the competing hypotheses? And can we do anything about predicting movements in foreign exchange rates?

nflation and Interest Rate Differentials

s outlined in Chapter 5, one of the major deductive hypotheses about expected ovements in the spot exchange rate is underpinned by:

- expected inflation differentials
- interest rate differentials (and here we should be looking at free market interest rates such as Euro-rates)
- spot and forward rate differentials

he rationale for the hypothesised relationships is dealt with at length in Chapter The four-way equivalence model developed there is extremely important. It is of ence that readers understand the theoretical relationship between inflation ferences, interest rate differences, the forward premium/discount and expected t movements. It must be remembered, however, that the existence of non-traded ds logically gives rise to deviations from the purchasing power parity theory of

exchange rates. Also, systematic deviations from purchasing power parity theory are to be expected due to short-term capital flows and current account imbalances.

As we shall discuss in Chapter 11, the purchasing power parity theory of exchange rate movements holds up fairly well in the long term. The fact that short-term deviations abound has stimulated the search for a better model — one of these is the balance of payments approach.

The Balance of Payments Approach

There are various brands of a balance of payments explanation for exchange rate movements. The emphasis has tended to change through time as the international financial scene has itself undergone change.

In its original form, the explanation tended to ignore capital flows. Prior to the sixties, this was excusable since most major currencies were not convertible, with the consequence that there were minimal private capital flows. The current account theory can best be explained by approaching it under the two distinct systems of exchange rate regime — namely, fixed and floating.

Assume a fixed exchange rate regime first. The national income model suggests that the current account gets worse as national income rises. The basic tendency is then for the domestic currency to weaken (to pay for the increased imports) and the fixed exchange rate system requires that, should it fall beyond certain narrow limits, this should be countered by support from the domestic government. This might take the form of selling reserves of foreign currency in the foreign exchange markets. Usually, it would be accompanied by domestic severity to dampen home demand evidenced by a lower relative money supply growth, with consequent lower relative inflation leading to an improvement in exports and a lowering of imports. According to this formula — which looks fine on paper — the current account deficit is automatically corrected. And so is a surplus. Here, rather than selling foreign exchange reserves, the foreign currency is bought. To pay for this, borrowings are increased — probably by the issue of treasury bills. Being a reserve asset this results in an increase in money supply which in turn leads, *ceteris paribus*, to higher inflation. Remember that we are looking at a fixed parity regime; this means that exports become less competitive — hence the surplus reduces — again an automatic corrective mechanism.

On paper, then, the Bretton Woods system should avoid permanent disequilibria — after all, there are automatically correcting means of achieving current account stability at work. But empirically things did not turn out this way as anyone who has examined the evidence of Britain in the fifties and sixties knows. Of course, devaluation or revaluation were an available option designed to counter recurrent disequilibria. Predicting changes in exchange rates under these circumstances became a potentially fruitful area of investigation. An interesting study carried out in the seventies by Martin Murenbeeld (1975) is worth mentioning. Using discriminant analysis, Murenbeeld studied a series of devaluations and revaluations from the late fifties to early seventies and came up with a discriminating equation. His original hypotheses can be summarised in the format shown in Table 8.1.

Having obtained data on a number of currency realignments, the researcher

Table 8.1 Murenbeeld's Devaluation/Revaluation Hypotheses

Devaluation		Revaluation
		Revaluation
High	Inflation	
Up	Trend in unemployment	Low
Low	Ratio of reserves to imports	Down
Down	Change in level of reserves	High
		Up

arrived at a Z-score predictor of foreign exchange parity change using respective quarterly and monthly data as follows:

$$Z = -0.487 + 0.732RI + 0.058\Delta R - 0.123\Delta WP - 0.145 UNEM - 0.25OM + 0.167G$$

$$Z = 0.33 + 0.69RI + 0.17\Delta R - 2.29\Delta WP - 0.45 UNEM - 0.66M + 15.35G$$

where the quarterly and monthly independent variables are:

RI = ratio of reserves to imports
ΔR = % change in reserves
ΔWP = % change in wholesale price index
$UNEM$ = change in trend of number becoming unemployed as % of total number unemployed
M = change in trend of money supply as % of total money supply
G = change in trend of government budgetary surplus/deficit as % of GNP

According to Murenbeeld, quarterly Z scores in excess of 2.0 are indicators of a revaluation and scores below −1.5 indicators of devaluation. And for monthly data, discriminating scores are respectively 1.0 and −1.5. Interested readers are referred to the original.[1]

Having deviated slightly from the mainstream of this chapter, let us now return to it by examining the current account theory of the exchange rate under a floating currency regime. Again, in terms of illustrating the mechanism, let us begin with an increase in national income and a worsening of the current account balance. If we leave the capital account out of the equation for the time being, paying for the increased imports results in demand for foreign currency at the expense of the home currency. Buying foreign exchange for domestic currency weakens the local currency which then makes exports more competitive and (assuming that the Marshall−Lerner[2] conditions on elasticities are met) conse-

---

[1] If one is going to use the model, one should study the original Murenbeeld article to obtain the exact definitions of *UNEM*, *M* and *G*.
[2] The Marshall−Lerner condition states that, if the sum of the elasticities of demand for a country's exports and that for its imports exceeds unity, a devaluation will have a positive effect upon its trade balance. Alternatively, if the sum of these elasticities is less than one, revaluation should improve the trade balance. The Marshall−Lerner model is built upon a number of grossly simplifying assumptions.

quently improves the current account. By a reverse route in the argument, current account surpluses lessen with a strengthening exchange rate as the corrective mechanism.

So far, of course, our models have been simplistic to the extent that the capital account and the interest rate have been left out of the equation. Extending the argument now to make good this omission, we come up with the essence of the Mundell (1967) and Fleming (1962) models. The overall balance of payments is the current account plus the capital account. Using the simple example to illustrate the workings of the model, let us begin by assuming an increase in national income with an accompanying deterioration in the current account balance. If overall balance of payments equilibrium is to be maintained at zero as national income increases, the domestic real rate of interest must also rise – this improves capital flows to compensate for the initial deterioration on the current account. This increase in the interest rate dampens domestic demand which, in its turn, has the effect of reducing imports and consequently improves the current account. The mechanism of this version of the balance of payments model involves the interest rate increase as a means of avoiding a weakening in the domestic currency. This is in line with conventional wisdom – but does not accord with the monetary approach.

The Monetary Approach

In the world of classical economics, trade deficits were associated directly with money supply changes. In its more modern form, the monetary approach predicts that an excess supply of money domestically will be reflected in an outflow across the foreign exchanges.

Beginning with our example of growth in national income, under the monetary approach this will be associated with a growing demand for money for transaction purposes. An excess demand for money can be met in one of two ways – either through domestic credit creation or through a balance of payments surplus. This rationale explains the apparent paradox (remember the Keynesian model predicts that an increase in national income will be associated with a weakening current account balance) of fast-growing countries like West Germany which appear to have almost perpetual balance of payments current surpluses. Fast real growth causes a growth in transactions demand for money: the economy induces an inflow of money via the foreign balance to the extent that this money is not created by the central bank.

Assuming that two countries have equal real growth but one increases its money supply (or there is no money supply in either but there are different real growth rates) more than the other, rational expectations would suggest that relative interest rates and expected relative inflation would alter. Either through the purchasing power parity theorem or via the mechanism referred to in the last paragraph, the economy with the high relative money supply growth will have a weakening exchange rate. According to the monetary approach, high interest rates and weakening currencies both flow from high relative money supply growth.

So far in this chapter, we have looked briefly at a handful of economic means of predicting foreign exchange rates. But, as we shall see in Chapter 11, empirical tests indicate that we would not be well advised to risk large amounts of money on the forecasts produced by econometric models. So what about relying on charts?

There seem to be plenty of forecasters of exchange rates who produce charts. And how do charts work anyway?

Chartism

Applied to share price movements, commodity price movements and currencies, this technique involves the study of past price movements to seek out potential future trends. Implicit in this possibility is the assumption that past price patterns provide a guide to future movements.

Just in case readers are not familiar with what chartism — sometimes called technical analysis — does, this section attempts to give a very brief description. If readers want a more detailed review, especially of the point and figure approach which is most frequently used, they are referred to other specialist works on chart techniques (Beckman 1969). Chartists attempt to predict share price movements by assuming that past price patterns will be repeated. There is no real theoretical justification for this. Chartists do not attempt to predict every price change. They are deeply interested in trends and trend reversals (that is, when the price of a share or commodity has been rising for several months but suddenly starts to fall). Features of chartism that are considered important for predicting trend reversals include:

- the observance of resistance levels
- head and shoulders patterns
- double bottom or double top patterns

But there is a great deal more too: all that can be done in a general section of this sort is to give a flavour. The main features referred to can best be illustrated by examples.

Consider Figure 8.1. In this, the dotted line represents the lower resistance level on a rising trend. It will be noted that many of the troughs lie on this line, but only at the end is it breached. The chartist would tend to view this breach as an indication that the trend has been reversed.

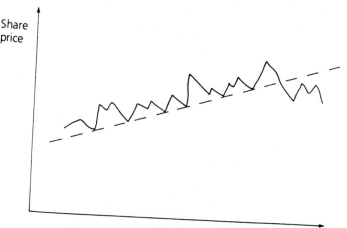

Figure 8.1   Breach of a Rising Trend

In Figure 8.2 the basic trend has been flat with oscillations within a channel. There are upper and lower resistance levels which bound this channel and, according to chartists, the breach of either of these will indicate a new trend. This sort of pattern arises from market indecision, as does the triangular pattern in Figure 8.3. In this exhibit the breach of the resistance lines is said to indicate a change of trend.

Let us now look at a resistance level on a double top. Suppose that the price of a share has been rising steadily for some time. Recently the price fell as some investors sold to realise profits and it then rose to its maximum level for a second time before starting to fall again. This is known as a double top and, based on experience, the chartist would predict that the trend has reversed. A typical double

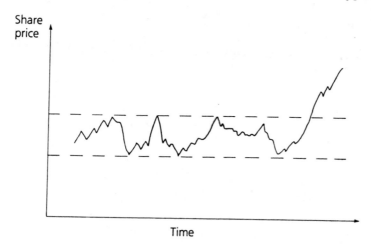

Figure 8.2   Movement out of a Channel

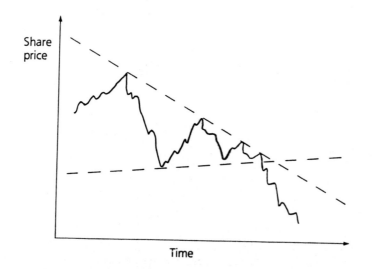

Figure 8.3   Breach of a Triangular Pattern

top might appear as shown in Figure 8.4. Double bottoms are interpreted in a similar – but reverse – way.

Another indication of a trend reversal is the head and shoulders formation of the type shown in Figure 8.5. In this kind of situation the chart might be interpreted as follows. The price has been rising for some time. At the peak of the left shoulder, profit taking has caused the price to drop. The price has then risen steeply again to the head before more profit taking causes the price to drop to around the same level as before – the neck. Although the price rises again, the gains are not as great as at the head. The level of the right shoulder, together with the frequent dips down to the neck, suggests to the chartist that the upward trend

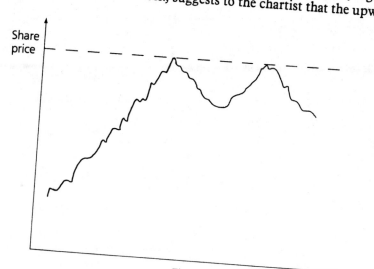

Figure 8.4   Double Top Formation

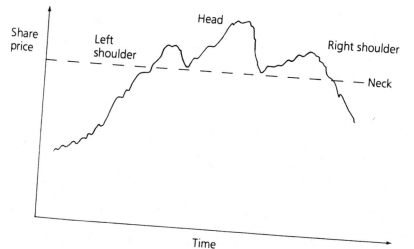

Figure 8.5   Head and Shoulders Formation

previously observed is over and that a fall is imminent. The breach of the neck line is the indication to sell. An inverse head and shoulders is interpreted using a reverse, but similar argument.

Modern financial theory based upon efficient markets has little time for chartist techniques in deep markets. But there is some evidence (see Chapters 11 and 12) that in foreign exchange markets chartism pays greater dividends than does reliance upon econometric models for forecasting exchange rates. Perhaps it is worth reminding readers of the essence of the efficient markets hypothesis.

The Efficient Markets Hypothesis

An initial, and very important, premise of an efficient market is that there are a large number of profit maximising participants concerned with the analysis and valuation of securities and that they are all operating independently of one another. A second assumption is that new information regarding securities comes to the market in a random fashion. The third assumption of an efficient market is especially crucial: investors adjust security prices rapidly to reflect the effect of new information. While the price adjustments made are not always perfect, they are unbiased − sometimes there is an overadjustment; sometimes there is an underadjustment. One does not know which it will be. Adjustment of security prices takes place rapidly because the market is dominated by profit-maximising investors. The combined effects of new information coming to market participants in a random, independent fashion plus the presence of numerous investors who adjust stock prices rapidly to reflect this new information means, according to efficient market theorists, that price changes are likely to be independent and random. According to chartism, of course, price changes are not independent − they are to some extent a function of past price movements. It is evident why efficient market proponents utterly reject the claims of chartists.

In our brief overview of efficient markets it should also be mentioned that, because security prices adjust to all new information and, therefore, supposedly reflect all public information at any point in time, the security prices that prevail at any point in time should be an unbiased reflection of all currently available information. Based on this brief description, an efficient market is evidently one in which security prices adjust rapidly to the infusion of new information, and current stock prices fully reflect all available information including the risk involved. Therefore, the returns implicit in a security's price reflect merely the risk involved, so that the expected return on a security is consistent with risk − nothing more. There are three gradations of efficient market − the weak form, the semi-strong and the strong form.

The weak form of the efficient market hypothesis assumes that current stock prices fully reflect all stock market information including the historical sequence of prices, price changes and any volume information. Because current prices already reflect all past price changes and any other stock market information, this implies that there should be no relationship between past price changes and future price changes. That is, price changes are independent of any trading rule − like chartism − that depends upon past price changes. In other words, past market data cannot be of any use in predicting future prices.

The semi-strong efficient market hypothesis asserts that security prices adjust rapidly to the release of all new public information. In short, stock prices fully reflect all publicly available data. Obviously, the semi-strong hypothesis encompasses the weak form hypothesis because all public information includes all market information such as past stock prices, trends and so on, plus all non-market information such as earnings, stock splits, economic news, political news. A direct implication of this hypothesis is that investors acting on important new information after it is public cannot derive above-average profits from the transaction, allowing for the cost of trading, because the security price already reflects the effects of this new public information.

The strong form efficient market hypothesis contends that stock prices fully reflect all information, whether public or otherwise. Hence it implies that no group of investors has a monopolistic access to information relevant to the formation of prices. Therefore, no group of investors should be able consistently to derive above-average profits. The strong form hypothesis encompasses both weak and semi-strong forms. Further, the strong form hypothesis requires not only efficient markets, where prices adjust rapidly to the release of new public information, but also perfect markets in which all information is available to everyone at the same time. This form of the efficient market hypothesis contends that, because all information is immediately available to everyone and is rapidly discounted by everyone, no group has monopolistic access to important new information and, therefore, no individual trader can consistently derive anything more than the average profits for all traders. The extent to which the stock market exhibits market efficiency is considered in other texts (Keane 1983); our concern here is with foreign exchange markets.

It will be recalled that, at the beginning of the discussion of the efficient market hypothesis, the basic premise of an efficient market was that there was a large number of profit-maximising participants. So there is in the foreign exchange markets. But there are also very large non-profit maximisers – central banks. Their intervention is not designed to make profits but to ease currency price movements designed to achieve a multiplicity of political objectives. The question is: does this intervention stop currency markets from exhibiting market efficiency? This is entirely an empirical question and it is looked at in Chapter 11. In addition to the studies referred to in that chapter, there are a great many others in Dornbusch (1979) and Kohlhagen (1978). To summarise the evidence – it is conflicting. The markets in some currencies exhibit efficiency some of the time, but not all of the time; probably this is because central banks intervene some of the time only. One opinion is that governments' direct intervention in foreign exchange markets and via the levels of interest rates is so great that currency markets cannot, from a deductive standpoint, be expected to exhibit all the characteristics of market efficiency with anything like consistency. The corollary to this is that chartism may well pay off in the foreign exchange markets, some of the time.

Capital Movements

According to purchasing power parity, exchange rates are determined by relative prices of goods exchanged between countries. Countries with above-average

inflation would, until their exchange rate fell, see their exports priced out of world markets and their home markets flooded with imports. The result would be a balance of payments deficit. But this scenario might be reversed by a currency realignment. Exchange rates would therefore move to equalise the prices of traded goods between rival economies and help to stabilise the system.

In the middle eighties, an observer would deduce correctly that international money flows from where it is cheap and plentiful to where it is scarce and expensive. It might be hypothesised that exchange rates move to equalise expected rates of return in rival financial centres. Money moves to where returns are anticipated to be highest. But, as well as interest received, returns include anticipated currency appreciation and depreciation. Hence there is a direct feedback. Currencies attracting funds rise and, in rising, become more attractive. The country perceived to offer the highest true return has the strongest currency. Its strong currency then prices its exports out of world markets and causes its home markets to be flooded with imports. Whereas, traditionally, a trade deficit caused a currency to weaken, it is possible to argue that in the middle eighties the relationship has been reversed. A strong currency causes a trade deficit.

This new order is decidedly unstable. Currencies overshoot due to the effects of positive feedback. Exchange rate movements operate to generate, rather than to correct, imbalances in trade and payments, and these imbalances may become both large and unbelievably long-lived by past standards. In this new world it is vital, but extremely difficult, to identify whether differing expected rates of return are due to real differences in the returns from capital investment in one economy rather than another. If they are, large imbalances can and do persist for longer than might be thought to be the case in more traditional models.

Summary

One of the key questions that students of multinational finance have long asked is whether there is any single model which can be relied upon for the purpose of predicting movements in exchange rates. Such students are seeking a deductive model which, when tested in the real world, stands up to rigorous statistical tests. Unfortunately the models that have been developed do not seem to hold in anything like a reliable way; so we do not have the sort of model which can be relied upon with a high degree of certainty in terms of predicting movements in exchange rates.

What we do have is a series of competing hypotheses. These range from the four-way equivalence model to which reference was made in detail in Chapter 5, to balance of payments based models (the subject of Chapter 7), monetary models, capital movements models and technical analysis, sometimes called chartism. All compete as tools to predict future exchange rate movements. This chapter has presented the sinews of the competing hypotheses. Our judgement as to which model is to be preferred must wait until we have considered how each stands up empirically in the real world. Suffice it to say, at this stage, that there are many competing explanations designed to be used to predict the dependent variable, the future spot exchange rate.

References

Beckman, R.C. (1969) 'Share price analysis', *Investors Bulletin*.

Dornbusch, Rudiger (1979) 'Monetary policy under exchange rate flexibility', in Donald E. Lessard (ed.), *International Financial Management: Theory and Application*, Warren Gorham and Lamont.

Fleming, J.M. (1962) *Domestic Financial Policies under Fixed and Flexible Rates*, IMF Staff Papers, November.

Keane, Simon M. (1983) *Stock Market Efficiency*, Philip Allan.

Kohlhagen, Steven W. (1978) *The Behavior of Foreign Exchange Markets – A Critical Survey of the Empirical Literature*, New York University Monograph.

Mundell, R.A. (1967) *International Economics*, Macmillan.

Murenbeeld, Martin (1975) 'Economic factors for forecasting foreign exchange rate changes', *Columbia Journal of World Business*, Summer.

9

Definitions of Foreign Exchange Risk

Foreign exchange risk management begins by identifying what items and amounts a firm has exposed to risk associated with changes in exchange rates. An asset, liability or expected future cash flow stream (whether certain or not) is said to be exposed to exchange risk when a currency movement changes, for better or worse, its parent or home currency value. The term exposure used in the context of foreign exchange means that a firm has assets, liabilities or expected future cash flow streams denominated in home currency or foreign currencies such that the home currency value of assets and liabilities or the present value in home currency terms of expected future cash flows changes as exchange rates change. Risk arises because currency movements may alter home currency values.

In this sense, assets, liabilities and expected future cash flow streams denominated in foreign currencies are clearly exposed to foreign exchange risk. But some expected future cash flows denominated in home currency terms may also be exposed. For example, a UK company selling in the home market may be competing with firms based in West Germany. In such circumstances changes in the Deutsche Mark/sterling exchange rate will almost certainly affect the present value of the UK company's expected cash flows by strengthening or weakening its competitive position against its German rivals. A similar line of argument applies to export sales and imported inputs (see later in this chapter).

Foreign exchange exposure is usually categorised according to whether it falls into one or more of the following categories:

- transaction exposure
- translation exposure
- economic exposure

Transaction exposure arises because a payable or receivable is denominated in a foreign currency. Translation exposure arises on the consolidation of foreign currency denominated assets and liabilities in the process of preparing consolidated accounts. This concept is essentially concerned with what might be called accounting exposure; indeed, translation exposure is often termed accounting exposure. Economic exposure arises because the present value of a stream of expected future operating cash flows denominated in the home currency or in a foreign currency may vary due to changed exchange rates. Transaction and economic exposures are

94

both cash flow exposures. Each of the three categories of exposure will now be examined and defined in more detail.

Transaction Exposure

Transaction exposure arises because the cost or proceeds (in home currency) of settlement of a future payment or receipt denominated in a currency other than the home currency may vary due to changes in exchange rates. Clearly, transaction exposure is a cash flow exposure. It may be associated with trading flows (such as foreign currency denominated trade debtors and trade creditors) or capital flows (such as foreign currency denominated dividends or loan repayments). Transaction exposure is a comparatively straightforward concept; translation and economic exposures are more complex.

Translation Exposure

Consolidation of financial statements which involve foreign currency denominated assets and liabilities automatically gives rise to translation exposure, sometimes also termed accounting exposure. Consolidation of foreign subsidiaries' accounts into group financial statements denominated in home currency requires the application of a rate or rates of exchange to foreign subsidiaries' accounts in order that they may be translated into the parent currency. Both balance sheets and income statements must be consolidated, and they both give rise to translation exposure. Translating foreign currency profit and loss accounts at either the average exchange rate during the accounting year or at the closing rate – the exchange rate at the end of the accounting year – will mean that expected consolidated profit will vary as the average or the expected closing rate changes. So the whole amount of profit earned in foreign currency is exposed to translation risk in the sense that the home currency consolidated profit may vary as exchange rates vary.

Balance sheet exposure is somewhat more complex. Some items in a foreign subsidiary's balance sheet may be translated at their historical exchange rates (the rate prevailing at the date of acquisition or any subsequent revaluation). Thus their home currency translated value cannot alter as exchange rates alter; such assets and liabilities are not exposed in the accounting sense. Other items may be translated at the closing exchange rate – the rate prevailing at the balance sheet date at the end of the accounting period. When the value of such items is fixed in the foreign subsidiary's currency, the amount translated into the parent currency will alter as the exchange rate alters. Hence all foreign currency items which are consolidated at current rates are exposed in the accounting sense.

Accounting exposure therefore reflects the possibility that foreign currency denominated items which are consolidated into group published financial statements at current or average rates will show a translation loss or gain as a result. This kind of exposure does not give an indication of the true effects of currency fluctuations on a company's foreign operations.

Economic exposure, to be discussed later, is a far better measure of true value exposure. Translation exposure, as will become clear later in this and the next chapter, is really a function of the system of accounting for foreign assets and liabilities on consolidation which a group of companies use. Clearly, it has little to do with true value in an economic sense.

There is an increasing consensus among major accounting standards setting bodies in different countries about consolidation and reporting of foreign assets and liabilities on consolidation which a group of companies uses. Clearly, it has little to we must first look at the contrasting effects of alternative reporting possibilities.

There are four basic translation methods. These are the current/non-current method (sometimes called the traditional or working capital method), the all-current (or closing rate) method, the monetary/non-monetary method, and the temporal method. These alternatives are considered in detail below but their essential rules of translation are summarised in Table 9.1.

The Current/Non-Current Method

This approach uses the traditional accounting distinction between current and long-term items and translates the former at the closing rate and the latter at the historical rate. Accounting exposure for a foreign subsidiary at a particular point in time is given by the net figure of assets less liabilities which are exposed to potential change should exchange rates alter (this figure is usually expressed in home currency terms). Evidently, according to the current/non-current method, the sum exposed is net current assets.

One of the implications of this method of translation is that inventory is exposed to foreign exchange risk but long-term debt is not. The logic of such an assumption is by no means apparent. Indeed, it should be clear that long-term debt is very much exposed to exchange risk. In home currency terms, the cash amount of a foreign currency denominated loan (whether a payable or receivable loan) will evidently change as exchange rates change. This lack of logic underpins the move away from the current/non-current method which has been witnessed over recent years.

The All-Current (Closing Rate) Method

This method merely translates all foreign currency denominated items at the closing rate of exchange. Accounting exposure is given simply by net assets or equity. This method has become increasingly popular over time and is now the major worldwide method of translating foreign subsidiaries' balance sheets.

The Monetary/Non-Monetary Method

Monetary items are assets, liabilities or capital, the amounts of which are fixed by contract in terms of the number of currency units, regardless of changes in the value of money. Translation via the monetary/non-monetary method involves monetary assets and liabilities being translated at the closing rate whilst non-monetary items are translated at their historic rate. Accounting exposure under

Table 9.1 Translation Rules Summarised

	Current/non-current method		All-current method		Monetary/non-monetary method		Temporal method
	Closing rate	*Historical rate*	*Closing rate*	*Historical rate*	*Closing rate*	*Historical rate*	
ASSETS							
Fixed assets		✓	✓			✓	Historic rate is applied to all items stated at historic cost. The closing rate is applied to all items stated at replacement cost, realisable value, market value or expected future value (see text for further detail)
Stock	✓		✓			✓	
Debtors payable in twelve months	✓		✓		✓		
Debtors payable beyond twelve months		✓	✓✓		✓✓		
Cash/Securities	✓		✓		✓		
LIABILITIES							
Creditors payable in twelve months	✓		✓		✓		
Long-term debt and creditors payable beyond twelve months		✓	✓		✓		
EQUITY	Residual		Residual		Residual		Residual

this method is given by net monetary assets. In terms of development of accounting reporting, this method of translating foreign subsidiaries' accounts seems to have been a halfway house between the current/non-current method and the all-current method.

The Temporal Method

The temporal method of translation uses the closing rate method for all items stated at replacement cost, realisable value, market value or expected future value (in other words, the closing rate is applied to all items stated at current cost) and uses the historic rate for all other items stated at historic cost. The rationale for the temporal approach is that the translation rate used should preserve the accounting principles used to value assets and liabilities in the original financial statements. According to the temporal method the translation rate for each asset or liability depends upon the measurement basis used in the foreign subsidiary's original accounts.

Applied to traditional historic cost accounts, the temporal and monetary/non-monetary methods give almost the same results. The main difference arises in the case of certain items of inventory. Where stock is stated in the original accounts at market value (where it is below historic cost) the temporal method would translate it at the current rate, whilst the monetary/non-monetary approach would use the historic rate of exchange. But it should be emphasised that the temporal method is by no means synonymous with the monetary/non-monetary approach.

Translation Exposure – A Numerical Example

It should be clear that identical firms with identical assets and trading results may show different translation gains and losses and different translated balance sheets depending upon the method used for converting foreign currency items to home currency values. This can easily be demonstrated with the help of a simple numerical example.

Assume that a UK company sets up a subsidiary in West Germany on 1 March and that the opening transactions are booked in the German company's accounts according to the prevailing exchange rate of £1 = DM4. The opening balance sheet is shown in Table 9.2. Assume further that no additional business or transactions go through the German company during March and consequently the Deutsche Mark balance sheet at the end of the month remains as at the beginning. But assume also that during March sterling falls against the Deutsche Mark and that the exchange rate at the end of the month is £1 = DM3.5. This means that the sterling translated balance sheet of the subsidiary will alter – and the extent of the change will differ according to whether the current/non-current, all current, or monetary/non-monetary method of translation is used. Table 9.2 shows the results.

From the table it will be noted that the translation gain or loss is equal to 12.5 per cent of the accounting exposure. This is, of course, consistent with the movement in sterling value versus the Deutsche Mark from 4 to 3.5. But it will further

Table 9.2 Example Illustrating Translation Exposure

	Subsidiary's balance sheet as at 1 March	Subsidiary's £ balance sheet as at 1 March	Subsidiary's £ balance sheet as at 31 March translated according to:		
			All-current rate	Current/non-current	Monetary/non-monetary
	DM 000	*£000*	*£000*	*£000*	*£000*
Fixed assets	8,400	2,100	2,400*	2,100	2,100
Inventory	4,200	1,050	1,200*	1,200*	1,050
Cash	3,164	791	904*	904*	904*
Total assets	15,764	3,941	4,504	4,204	4,054
Current payables	2,100	525	600*	600*	600*
Long-term debt	4,200	1,050	1,200*	1,050	1,200*
Equity	9,464	2,366	2,704	2,554	2,254
Translation gain/(loss)			338	188	(112)
Accounting exposure as at 31 March			2,704	1,504	(896)

Note: * = assets and liabilities exposed, as of 31 March, to translation exposure under different translation conventions.

be noted from the table that translation outturns range from a gain of over £300,000 to a loss of over £100,000. These differences arise merely due to varying accounting methods.

Whilst translation methods affect group balance sheet values, the key point is that they have nothing to do with economic value. The value of the German subsidiary in the example should not be affected by adopting a different method of accounting – its worth will be the same whether the all current, current/non-current or monetary/non-monetary method is used. In all probability its discounted net present value will have changed as a result of the strengthened Deutsche Mark. But this changed present value is hardly what we pick up by using different methods of translating balance sheets. Clearly, changes in value resulting from changed exchange rates show in terms of different present values. If we are concerned with how true value has changed due to exchange rate movements, we should be looking at economic value and how it changes in sympathy to moving exchange rates. This is what true exposure to exchange rate movements is all about.

Economic Exposure

Economic exposure is frequently referred to as cash flow exposure. It is concerned with the present value of future operating cash flows to be generated by a company's activities and with how this present value, expressed in parent currency, changes following exchange rate movements. The concept of economic exposure is most frequently applied to a company's expected operating cash flows from foreign operations, but – as mentioned earlier in this chapter – it can equally well be applied to a firm's home territory operations and the extent to which the present value of those operations alters resultant upon changed exchange rates. For the purpose of convenience the exposition which follows is based on a firm's foreign operations. Some experts classify transaction exposure as a sub-set of economic exposure. They take this view arguing that the present value of an uncovered foreign currency denominated receivable or payable will vary as exchange rates vary. Whilst we accept the logic of this view, in this book we prefer to treat economic and transaction exposures separately. This perspective on the topic is adopted because of the relative ease with which the multinational can monitor and control transaction and economic exposures (see Chapters 12 and 13).

The value of an overseas operation can be expressed as the present value of expected future operating cash flows which are incremental to that overseas activity discounted at the appropriate discount rate. Expressing this present value in terms of the parent currency can be achieved via the formula set out below – but remember that incremental cash flows to the whole group of companies include management fees, royalties and similar kinds of flows as well as direct cash flows from trading operations. The present value of the foreign subsidiary may be expressed as:

$$PV = \sum_{t=0}^{n} \frac{(CI_t - CO_t)e_t}{(1 + r)^t}$$

where PV is the parent currency present value of the foreign business; CI represents estimated future incremental net cash inflows associated with the foreign business expressed in foreign currency; *CO* represents estimated future incremental net cash outflows associated with the foreign business expressed in foreign currency; *e* is the expected future exchange rate (expressed in terms of the direct quote in the home territory); *r* is the appropriate discount rate, namely the rate of return which the parent requires from an investment in the risk class of the overseas business; *t* is the period for which cash flows are expected; and *n* is the final period for which all flows are expected. The above formulation assumes that all net incremental cash flows accruing to the overseas operation are distributable to the parent company in the home country.

At first sight the reader might conclude that quantifying economic exposure and the impact of changing exchange rates is fairly straightforward. For example, assume that a British company has a wholly-owned French subsidiary with a net present value of FF120 million. If the exchange rate is £1 = FF10 and it subsequently moves to £1 = FF12, presumably the value of the subsidiary has moved from £12 million to £10 million. Such a conclusion would, in all probability, be incorrect. It is necessary to be far more analytical to reach a worthwhile conclusion on valuation.

Devaluation will affect cash inflows and cash outflows as well as the exchange rate. Consider a company competing in export markets. Whilst devaluation will not affect the total market size, it should have a favourable market share effect. The company in the devaluing country should increase sales or profit margins – in short, it should benefit. Similarly, companies competing with imports in the domestic market should also gain since a devaluation will tend to make imported products more expensive in local currency terms. However, this benefit may be offset to some extent by domestic deflation which frequently accompanies devaluation. Thus, in the import competing sector of the domestic market, there will be beneficial and negative impacts. Also, in the purely domestic market, devaluation may lead to reduced company performance in the short term as a result of deflationary measures at home which so often accompany currency depreciation.

All of the above factors affect cash inflows. Devaluation also affects cash outflows. Imported inputs become more expensive. If devaluation is accompanied by domestic deflation it will probably be the case that suppliers' prices will rise as their financing costs move up. Furthermore, the level and value of working capital carried may be affected by devaluation. An inverse line of reasoning applies with respect to revaluation of a currency.

In summary, getting to grips with economic exposure involves us in analysing the effects of changing exchange rates on:

- export sales, where margins and cash flows should change because devaluation should make exports more competitive;
- domestic sales, where margins and cash flows should alter substantially in the import competing sector;
- pure domestic sales, where margins and cash flows should change in response to deflationary measures which accompany devaluation;
- costs of imported input, which should rise in response to a devaluation;
- cost of domestic inputs, which may vary with exchange rate changes;
- levels of working and fixed capital.

The analysis is clearly complex but it is necessary in order to assess fully how the home currency present value of overseas operations is likely to alter in response to movements in foreign exchange rates.

So far it has been assumed that the parent's present value of its foreign subsidiary is a function of that subsidiary's estimated future net cash flows. In other words, there is an assumption that all cash flows are distributable to the parent. In fact, host governments frequently restrict distribution to foreign parents by exchange controls. This topic is considered in more detail in Chapters 19 and 25 on 'International Capital Budgeting' and 'Exchange Controls' respectively. Suffice it to say in this section that, where distribution of cash flows to the parent is limited, the present value formula needs to be adjusted a little – see below:

$$PV = \sum_{t=0}^{n} \frac{(Div_t + OPF_t)e_t}{(1 + r)^t} + \frac{TV\, e_n}{(1 + r)^n}$$

The notation is as before except that *Div* represents the expected net dividend inflow in a particular year, *OPF* represents other parent flows such as royalties and management fees in a particular period, and *TV* represents the terminal value remittable over the foreign exchanges at the end of the project's life.

The reader should always bear in mind that economic exposure is equally applicable to the home operations of a firm inasmuch as a change in exchange rates is likely to affect the present value of its home operations; this may arise for all the reasons which impinge upon foreign businesses.

It can be seen that assessing economic exposure necessarily involves us in a substantial amount of work on elasticities of demand and behaviour of costs in response to changes in exchange rates. Numerical examples of economic exposure calculations are available in some of the longer texts (Shapiro 1986; Eiteman and Stonehill 1986) on international financial management. But the critical question that we would ask is whether economic exposure – or transaction exposure or translation exposure for that matter – is of any relevance to the financial manager of an international company. This topic is addressed in Chapter 12 called 'Does Foreign Exchange Exposure Matter?'.

Summary

Foreign exchange risk arises because the home firm has assets or liabilities or expected future cash flow streams the value of which (in home currency terms) may alter as a result of exchange rate movements. Changes in exchange rates can change the parent currency value of those assets, liabilities or expected future cash flow streams. Foreign exchange risk falls into one or more of three basic categories: transaction exposure, translation exposure and economic exposure. The first and last of these exposure types are underpinned by expected future cash flows denominated in foreign currencies.

Transaction exposure relates to situations where a business has payables or receivables denominated in foreign currency terms. Translation exposure arises simply where the application of different exchange rates to foreign currency denominated assets and liabilities and/or profits and losses would result in different home currency balance sheet amounts and/or different home currency profit and loss account amounts respectively. Economic exposure arises because the present value of a stream of expected future operating cash flows may alter, in home currency terms, due to changed exchange rates.

A particular item may be classified under more than one heading. For example, a long-term foreign denominated borrowing is certainly both a transaction exposure, because the home currency equivalent to repay the loan varies as exchange rates change, and a translation exposure (under all translation methods other than the current/non-current method). We prefer not to call it an economic exposure as well because our definition is restricted to operating cash flows – but some commentators would also categorise it as an economic exposure.

As a result of classifying foreign exchange risk according to the three headings discussed in this chapter we would advocate that (1) some categories of exposure should be actively managed by the headquarters treasury; (2) other categories should be ignored since, as they do not matter greatly, there is little point in applying treasury time to avoid the risk. These topics are taken up in more detail in Chapters 12, 14 and 15.

References

Eiteman, David K. and Stonehill, Arthur I. (1986) *Multinational Business Finance*, 4th edn, Addison Wesley.
Shapiro, Alan C. (1986) *Multinational Financial Management*, 2nd edn, Allyn and Bacon.

10

Financial Accounting and Foreign Exchange

In the previous chapter we discussed the nature of translation exposure and showed how it could change with different accounting conventions used to record foreign operations. The accounting profession in much of the capitalist world has addressed itself to this problem and in many countries has come up with a series of rules for reporting to shareholders.

This chapter focuses upon the methods recommended in the USA and in the UK. These are respectively embodied in FASB 52 and SSAP 20 which are very similar in terms of their prescriptions. Prior to the introduction of FASB 52 in the USA, there was an extended debate about the implications of the previous accounting standard, FASB 8.

In summary, the recommendations of FASB 52 and SSAP 20 are as follows. The closing rate method is to be used to convert foreign subsidiaries' balance sheets. Gains and losses on exchange arising from mere translation exposure are to be taken direct to the balance sheet and dealt with as movements on reserves. The only foreign exchange gains or losses to be credited or debited to profit and loss account are transaction (i.e. cash flow) gains or losses.

According to FASB 52, profits earned by foreign subsidiaries and reported in their income statements are to be consolidated in the group accounts in home currency terms at an average exchange rate for the accounting period. The UK standard, SSAP 20, permits the use of either the average method or the closing rate method.

The procedures put forward in the new standards differ substantially from that promulgated by FASB 8. Under the old standard, both translation and transaction gains and losses were to be recorded to the group income statement – a procedure which resulted in heated debate in the financial community. All three standards are now looked at in more detail.

FASB 8

Issued in 1975, the objectives of FASB 8 were 'to measure and express in dollars and in generally accepted principles the assets, liabilities, revenues, or expenses that are measured or denominated in foreign currency' (FASB 1975). Under FASB 8,

US firms were required to translate financial statements into US dollars according to the temporal method. The stated objective was to produce the same results as if the foreign entity's books had been maintained in the parent currency. Cash, receivables and payables would be translated at the current rate. Assets and liabilities carried at historic prices would be translated at the historical exchange rate. Assets and liabilities carried at current prices or at future exchange prices would be translated at the current exchange rate. Revenues and expenses in the profit and loss account would be translated at average rates for the accounting period, except for those items relating to assets carried at past exchange prices, such as depreciation (relating to fixed assets) and cost of goods sold (relating to inventory). These items would be translated at historical rates. All gains and losses, whether arising on translation of profit and loss accounts or balance sheets, would be taken direct to the income statement.

A substantial section of the US financial community was of the opinion that reporting results according to such a formula produced distortions which would mislead rather than inform. Clearly the income statement of a US multinational might receive a big increment or decrement as the dollar respectively weakened or strengthened. And this would flow through to earnings per share. The pressure group that built up felt that gains and losses on foreign currency transactions should be taken directly to the consolidated income statement, but that gains and losses arising from mere translation should be taken out of income.

Another concern was that certain items were not being translated logically. Inventory, for example, was translated primarily at historical exchange rates. So a rate change in one period might not affect profits until the period in which the inventory was sold. Many accountants were also concerned about the practical problems involved in keeping track of the historic costs and historical exchange rates for inventory, an asset which turns over very quickly. They preferred to translate inventory at current rates.

Another problem area was long-term debt. Although seemingly logically translated at current rates and hence exposed to exchange rate changes, many financial executives considered that it was incorrect to translate a fixed asset at historic rates and thus have the asset sheltered from any foreign exchange gain or loss, whilst the debt used to finance the asset was exposed to exchange rate changes. Commentators were by no means unanimous in terms of suggesting alternatives. Some proposed that the asset should be translated at the current rate in order to match the exposure of the debt. Others suggested that the translation methods for long-term debt and fixed assets were logical but that the gain or loss on the debt translation should be taken out of the income statement.

Mounting influential criticism, coupled with opinions within the Financial Accounting Standards Board and the American accounting profession to the effect that FASB 8 created misleading distortions to reported profits of multinationals, led to its withdrawal and its replacement by FASB 52.

FASB 52

In 1982, FASB 52 replaced FASB 8 as the guiding standard for translation of foreign currency accounts by US corporations. The new standard's stated objective was to 'provide information that is generally compatible with the expected economic effects of a rate change on an enterprise's cash flows and equity and, secondly, to reflect in consolidation statements the financial results and relationships of the individual consolidated entities as measured in their functional currencies in conformity with US generally accepted accounting principles' (FASB 1981). Unlike FASB 8, which permitted only the temporal method of translating financial statements, FASB 52 permits the use of two different methods, depending upon circumstances.

Before going into the mechanics of FASB 52, it is important to appreciate one of the standard's key concepts – namely that of the functional currency. An entity's functional currency is the currency of the primary economic environment in which the entity operates. In the case of a US exporter, the functional currency is normally the US dollar. In this case, the functional currency is also the reporting currency, as the US exporting company generates its financial statements in US dollars. If a US corporation had an independent subsidiary in France that exported goods to the UK, the functional currency of the French subsidiary would, most probably, be the French franc. However, the reporting currency of the US parent of the French subsidiary would be the US dollar, the currency in which its consolidated financial statements are prepared.

In the case of a US company becoming involved in a foreign currency transaction, each asset, liability, revenue, expense, gain or loss arising from the transaction is to be recorded in the firm's functional currency at the exchange rate in effect at the transaction date. At each subsequent balance sheet date, any balances that are denominated in a currency other than the functional currency of the entity should be recorded at the new balance sheet rate, namely the current rate. So, if a US importer expects to pay a UK exporter in pounds sterling for goods bought, the liability is denominated in pounds sterling and its dollar value must be adjusted on each balance sheet to reflect the current exchange rate. The change in dollar value is treated as a foreign exchange gain or loss and, since it is a transaction gain or loss, it should be included in the determination of net income in the period in which the rate changes.

An example may usefully explain the point here. Assume that a US importer buys goods from a UK exporter on 1 December for £1 million with payment to be made on 20 January following. Assume further that the US importer closes his books on 31 December and that the exchange rate moves from $1.6805 = £1 on 1 December to $1.6407 = £1 on 31 December, and to $1.6100 = £1 on 20 January. As can be seen from Table 10.1, the purchase of goods is booked on 1 December at the exchange rate prevailing then. But at the company's year-end, 31 December, the payable is revalued at the exchange rate prevailing then and the difference is taken to an exchange gain account which will, in turn, be taken to the credit of the company's profit and loss account. On 20 January settlement of the debt takes place at the exchange rate prevailing on that date so that a further exchange gain is then booked.

Note that under FASB 52 the gain on foreign exchange goes directly to the income statement in the period when the exchange rate changes, even though the liability has not been settled and the exchange rate could subsequently go the other way before ultimate settlement. In the example, the $39,800 is taken to the credit of the income statement before the debt is settled. This kind of treatment is in

Table 10.1 US Company's Books – Transaction in £ Sterling

		Dr	Cr
Dec. 1:	Purchases	$1,680,500	
	Accounts payable		$1,680,500
	Purchase of goods at £1mn converted at $1.6805		
Dec. 31:	Accounts payable	$39,800	
	Foreign exchange gain		$39,800
	Revaluation of payable of £1mn at $1.6407		
Jan. 20:	Accounts payable	$1,640,700	
	Foreign exchange gain		$30,700
	Cash		$1,610,000
	Payment of £1mn to creditor at $1.6100 and foreign exchange gain versus previous balance		

breach of the realisation principle, one of the canons of accounting. Clearly it contravenes the prudence concept in accounting under which revenues and profits are not anticipated, but are recognised by inclusion in the profit and loss account only when realised in the form either of cash or of other assets, the ultimate cash realisation of which can be assumed with reasonable certainty.

In the above example it was assumed that the US importer did not cover the sterling payable. He could have done so by entering into a forward contract. In terms of FASB 52, forward contracts create a number of problems which result in different accounting treatments according to the nature of, and the rationale for, the forward contract.

There are several reasons for entering into a forward contract. These may be:

- to cover a transaction such as the import mentioned above
- to speculate on currency movements
- to hedge a net investment in a foreign currency
- to hedge a foreign currency commitment

All of these give rise to different accounting treatments under FASB 52.

In the example described above, the US importer must deliver foreign currency to the UK exporter on 20 January and is unsure as to the future spot rate. To avoid this uncertainty, the importer may enter into a forward contract on 1 December with a banker to deliver dollars in return for pounds on 20 January. In these circumstances the cost of goods is effectively $1,680,500 plus or minus the forward discount or premium. Looked at another way, the importer then has a foreign currency receivable from the bank to offset the foreign currency payable to the exporter. Assuming that the size of the forward contract equals the size of the account payable, then every time the exchange rate changes, the value of the receivable changes, giving rise to a gain or loss that is exactly equal and opposite to the gain or loss on the foreign currency account payable. This gain or loss on the forward contract receivable is recognised in the income statement immediately, so it offsets the gain or loss on the account payable. The only accounting cost to the importer would then be the premium or discount on the forward contract, and that is written off over the life of the contract. The accounting treatment of forward contracts to cover a foreign currency transaction is to create a neutral income statement effect.

If a firm enters into a forward contract to speculate on expected currency movements rather than to cover an exposure, any gains or losses on that contract are recognised immediately in income. The gain or loss is determined by multiplying the amount of the contract by the difference between the forward rate available on the balance sheet date and the original contracted rate, or the forward rate last used to measure a gain or loss.

If a US parent decides to enter into a forward contract or other foreign currency transaction – like a borrowing in the same currency – to hedge an investment in a foreign entity, the parent may include any gain or loss on the contract as a separate component of stockholders' equity rather than incorporating it in the income statement.

A firm may enter into a foreign currency commitment and hedge it with a forward contract. Here the premium or discount on the contract, as well as any gain or loss resulting from exchange rate changes, is deferred until the transaction date and included in the foreign currency transaction. Thus the US importer may have entered into a commitment with the British exporter in October to receive goods on 1 December. At the same time, the US importer might have entered into a forward contract to hedge its commitment. On 1 December, any gains or losses and amortisation of premium or discount would be added to the cost of the goods purchased from the exporter.

The idea of a borrowing to hedge an investment in a foreign entity is important. Take the example of a US parent company with a net investment in a Swiss subsidiary, for which the Swiss franc is the functional currency. Assume that the US parent borrows Swiss francs and designates the Swiss franc loan as a hedge of the net investment in the Swiss firm. The loan is in Swiss francs which are not the functional currency of the US parent. The loan is therefore a foreign currency transaction. The loan is a liability and the net investment in Switzerland is an asset. Should the dollar/Swiss franc exchange rate move subsequently, the adjustment resulting from translation of the Swiss subsidiary's balance sheet would go in the direction opposite to the adjustment resulting from translation of the US parent company's Swiss franc debt. Should the adjustment from translation of the Swiss franc loan (after tax effects, if any) be less or equal to the adjustment from translation of the Swiss subsidiary's balance sheet, both adjustments would be included in the analysis of changes in the cumulative translation adjustment and reflected in equity movements. However, should the adjustment from translation of the US parent's Swiss franc debt (after tax effects, if any) exceed the adjustment from translation of the Swiss subsidiary's balance sheet, the excess is, in FASB 52 terms, a transaction gain or loss which would be included in the consolidated income statement.

Ordinarily, for a borrowing to hedge a net investment, it should be in the same currency as the functional currency of the net investment hedged. But the standard allows for exceptions such as those relating to currencies which move in tandem.

But where a foreign currency borrowing is not in the same currency as a net investment in a foreign country, FASB 52 does not recognise a hedged position and in this case the gain or loss resulting from changes in the exchange rate against the currency of the borrowing would be viewed as an income statement item.

Reverting to forward contracts, it is important to realise that in order for the separate accounting for forward contracts against foreign currency commitments to hold, two conditions must be met. First, the forward contract must be designated as a hedge on a foreign currency commitment; and second, the foreign currency commitment must be firm. The forward contract may be for an amount equal to the commitment on an after-tax basis, but any foreign exchange gains or losses on an amount in excess of that must be taken into the income statement rather than being dealt with via reserve accounting in the balance sheet. The idea of accounting for forward contracts is to match the recognition of contract gains and losses with those of the foreign currency transaction.

Earlier in this chapter we discussed the relevance of the functional currency for FASB 52 accounting. As defined earlier, the functional currency is that of the primary economic environment where the entity operates. A US-owned French corporation that produces and sells for the French market might consider the French franc as its functional currency and the currency in which it also keeps its books and records. The functional curency would be translated into the parent company's reporting currency using the current rate method. This means that all assets and liabilities – bar equity – would be translated at the current rate. In addition, all revenues and expenses would be translated at a weighted average exchange rate for the accounting period concerned.

If it were decided that the functional currency was something other than the currency of the country where the entity was operating and that in which its books and records were being kept, then those books and records would have to be translated into the functional currency. Generally, in these circumstances management would decide that the reporting currency of the parent would be the functional currency. Translation would take place under the temporal method, as with FASB 8. Again the translation process is designed to produce the same results as if the books and records had been maintained in the functional, rather than the local, currency.

Generally, the functional currency would be the local currency if the local operations are relatively self-contained and integrated with the environment. The parent's reporting currency is normally considered the functional currency if the foreign entity is an extension of and fairly dependent on its dealings with the parent. Management is responsible for deciding which is the functional currency and FASB 52 gives a series of guidelines for its selection. The standard uses a series of indicators which it classifies as:

- cash flow indicators
- sales price indicators
- sales market indicators
- expense indicators
- financing indicators
- inter-company transactions indicators

For further detail on these indicators, interested readers are referred to the actual standard; but the gist of the matter is that the choice of functional currency should flow from the question: in what currency are the above indicators designated?

Once the decision has been made as to which currency is the functional currency, translation can take place. The mechanics of translation are not difficult, but a few problems need to be resolved. For example, a foreign entity might be conducting multiple business activities through branches or divisions, each with a different functional currency requiring a different translation method. A French subsidiary of a US corporation may have African subsidiaries that are considered an extension of the French firm. The African operations would be translated into French francs using the temporal method. If the French firm were considered fairly independent of the US parent, the French statements would be translated on consolidation into US dollars at the current rate.

Another problem concerns entities operating in highly inflationary countries, defined in FASB 52 as those in which cumulative inflation over a three-year period totals 100 per cent or more. Balance sheets of entities in these countries would be highly distorted if they were translated at the current exchange rate, so the standard requires that the functional currency should be the parent currency, with the use of the temporal method.

Finally, there is the question of how gains and losses are treated. When the functional currency is considered to be the local currency, any gains or losses that arise merely from translating the financial statements into the parent currency using the current rate method are taken to a separate component of stockholders' equity rather than through the income statement. This is a major departure from FASB 8. If the temporal method is used for cases where the local currency is not considered to be the functional currency, the foreign exchange gain or loss is taken directly to the income statement, as under FASB 8.

Compared with FASB 8, its successor allows a good deal of flexibility in terms of choice of method of translating financial statements. This recognises the fact that there are inherent differences in foreign operations that require different methods of translation. However, lest the standard appear too flexible, it is important to note that, once management decides which is the functional currency of a foreign operation, it is not permitted to change without a significant change in the economic facts and circumstances prevailing relative to those at the time of the original choice.

Much more important, though, is the fact that translation gains and losses where the functional currency is the local currency are treated as a separate component of shareholders' equity, thereby taking these gains and losses out of the income statement. Finance directors, accountants and analysts have generally regarded this as a more realistic approach than that proposed by FASB 8.

One of the objectives of FASB 52 is to provide information compatible with the economic effects of a rate change on an enterprise's cash flows and equity. The new standard, for firms whose functional currency is the local rather than parent currency, will always place such companies in a net exposed asset position, since net worth is the only section of the balance sheet that is not translated at the current rate. This means that a parent with a subsidiary operating in a country whose currency is strong relative to the parent currency will recognise foreign exchange gains upon translation since the dollar value of the net asset position rises as the foreign currency hardens. This is claimed to be consistent with the cash flow picture since the dollar value of dividends also rises as the foreign currency hardens.

The current rate method does not totally eliminate the impact of exchange rate changes on the income statement. This is because the subsidiary's income statement must still be translated into dollars. If the foreign currency is weakening relative to the dollar, the dollar equivalent of net income will fall. This was experienced by US corporations with operations in Europe during the recession of the early eighties. Income in local currency was not advancing much because of the recession but the strong dollar magnified this weak income picture. The result was very poor dollar increments in some cases and declines in others.

Of course, where inflation is exceedingly high, the use of the temporal method is still recommended under FASB 52 so, to an extent, the objections to the temporal method remain.

Certainly FASB 52 avoids the distortions in reported profit brought about by taking translation gains and losses to the income statement – as recommended by FASB 8. So it is claimed that published accounts become more relevant to managers and to the financial community. However, most of the serious evidence (see the next chapter) is that financial analysts were not deceived by the inclusion of translation gains and losses in the income statement and that the reporting requirements of FASB 8 had no significant effect on security values of multinational corporations reporting under the old standard.

SSAP 20

The UK accounting profession has made recommendations very similar to its counterpart in the USA. Although much less detailed and rigorous than FASB 52, the application of the UK standard produces such similar results that it would be an exercise in duplication to summarise them here. Suffice it to say that one minor material difference is that SSAP 20 permits translation of the foreign subsidiary's income statement at either the closing rate or at an average exchange rate for the period, provided that the method selected is consistently applied from one period to another. Otherwise the summary of FASB 52 given above is a fair reflection of the content of SSAP 20.

Summary

The accounting professions in the USA and UK now have almost identical rules for accounting for foreign currencies in published accounts. Generally speaking, translation of foreign balance sheets uses the current rate method. Transaction gains, whether realised or not, are accounted for through the profit and loss account. But there is a major exception. Where a transaction profit or loss arises from taking on a foreign currency borrowing in a situation in which the borrowing can be designated as a hedge for a net investment denominated in the same foreign currency as the borrowing, then the gain or loss on the borrowing, if it is less than the net investment hedged, would be accounted for by movements in reserves rather than through the income statement. If this kind of transaction gain or loss exceeds the amount of the loss or gain respectively on the net investment hedged, the excess gain or loss is to be reported in the profit and loss account. Non-transaction gains and losses are to be dealt with by reserve accounting direct to the balance sheet rather than through the profit and loss account.

According to the US standard, FASB 52, translation of foreign currency revenues and costs — the essence of the income statement — is to be made at the average exchange rate during the accounting period. The British standard, SSAP 20, allows the use of either the current rate or the average rate for this purpose. However, it is fair to say that opinion in the UK is moving towards the average exchange rate.

References

Financial Accounting Standards Board (1975) *Statement of Financial Accounting Standards No. 8*, Stamford, Ct., October.
Financial Accounting Standards Board (1981) *Statement of Financial Accounting Standards No. 52*, Stamford, Ct., December.

Kohlhagen, Steven W. (1975) 'The performance of the foreign exchange markets 1971–1974', *Journal of International Business Studies*, Fall, pp. 33–38.

Kohlhagen, Steven W. (1978) *The Behavior of Foreign Exchange Markets – A Critical Survey of the Empirical Literature*, New York University Press.

Levich, Richard M. (1978) 'Further results of the efficiency of markets for foreign exchange', in Jacob A. Frenkel and Harry G. Johnson (eds), *Managed Exchange Rate Flexibility: The Recent Experience*, Federal Reserve Bank of Boston, Conference Series No. 20, Boston.

Levich, Richard M. (1981) 'How to compare chance with forecasting expertise', *Euromoney*, August, pp. 61–78.

Levich, Richard M. (1982) 'How the rise of the dollar took forecasters by surprise', *Euromoney*, August, pp. 98–111.

Levich, Richard M. (1983) 'Currency forecasters show the way', *Euromoney*, August, pp. 140–147.

McKinnon, R.I. (1979) *Money in International Exchange*, Oxford University Press.

Marston, Richard C. (1976) 'Interest arbitrage in the euro-currency markets', *European Economic Review*.

Oxelheim, Lars (1985) *International Financial Market Fluctuations*, John Wiley.

Pedersson, George and Tower, Edward (1976) *On the Long and Short Run Relationship Between the Forward Rate and the Interest Parity*, Duke University, Mimeograph.

Pippinger, John E. (1973) 'The case for freely fluctuating exchange rates: some evidence', *Western Economic Journal*, September, pp. 314–326.

Poole, William (1967) 'Speculative prices as random walks: an analysis of ten time series of flexible exchange rates', *Southern Economic Journal*, April, pp. 468–478.

Robinson, Bill and Warburton, Peter (1980) 'Managing currency holdings: lessons from the floating period', *London Business School Economic Outlook*, February, pp. 18–27.

Rogalski, Richard J. and Vinso, Joseph D. (1977) 'Price variations as predictors of exchange rates', *Journal of International Business Studies*, Spring–Summer, pp. 71–83.

Roll, Richard W. (1979) 'Violations of the Law of One Price and their implications for differentially denominated assets', in Marshall Sarnat and George Szego (eds), *International Finance and Trade*, vol. 1, Ballinger.

Roll, Richard W. and Solnik, Bruno H. (1975) *A Pure Foreign Exchange Asset Pricing Model*, European Institute for Advanced Studies in Management, Working Paper No. 75, August.

Stein, Jerome L. (1965) 'The forward rate and interest parity', *Review of Economic Studies*, April.

Taylor, Dean (1982) 'Official intervention in the foreign exchange market, or, bet against the central bank', *Journal of Political Economy*, April, pp. 356–368.

Treuherz, Rolf M. (1969) 'Forecasting foreign exchange rates in inflationary economies', *Financial Executive*, February, pp. 57–60.

Upson, Roger B. (1972) 'Random walk and forward exchange rates: a spectral analysis', *Journal of Finance and Quantitative Analysis*, September, pp. 1897–1905.

Wong, S.K.O. (1978) *The Forward Rate as Predictor of the Future Spot Rate*, MBA dissertation, University of Bradford.

Yeager, Leland B. (1958) 'A rehabilitation of purchasing power parity', *Journal of Political Economy*, December, pp. 516–530.

12

Does Foreign Exchange Exposure Matter?

Most of the arguments about whether or not foreign exchange exposure matters draw on material summarised in the earlier chapters on the four-way equivalence model, definitions of foreign exchange exposure and the empirical work on the four-way model. Foreign exchange exposure can be looked at under three separate headings, namely transaction exposure, economic exposure and translation exposure: an earlier chapter provided a discussion on these different perspectives of foreign exchange exposure. In this chapter we shall consider the extent to which each should be a relevant factor for the corporate treasurer in his objective of playing a role in the maximisation of the present value of the firm.

Transaction Exposure

Transaction exposure is concerned with how changes in exchange rates affect the value of anticipated foreign currency denominated cash flows relating to transactions already entered into.

According to the bulk (although by no means all) of empirical work on the expectations theory part of the four-way equivalence model, the current forward rate is an unbiased predictor of the future spot rate. If using the forward rate to approximate the future spot rate results in the long term in being on the high side as often as on the low side — which is what the term 'unbiased predictor' means — then it follows that covering forward will be of little worth to the firm that has a large number of foreign currency denominated transactions. That firm might as well not cover forward but take the spot rate at the time the payable or receivable matures, since the results from adopting the strategy of covering forward will, in the long run, equal the results achieved from running the debt to maturity and taking the spot rate. Indeed, given that foreign exchange dealers charge their customers a wider bid/offer spread on forward contracts compared with spot transactions, it follows that avoiding cover should be more profitable in the long run.

This can, however, also be an extremely dangerous policy. By failing to cover transaction exposure, a firm may incur a vast loss on a single very large receivable or payable denominated in a foreign currency. This may result in an overall loss for the firm in a particular financial period which could, in its turn, lead to all sorts of financial distress. It is not much comfort to the finance director of a company which has just failed as a direct result of not covering transaction exposure that it would have been all right in the long run because at some time in the future it could have hoped to win on another contract the amount that it had just lost on the present one. There is little consolation in the company being all right in the long run, if it is dead in the short run. Bearing this in mind, the prudent finance director will argue that covering forward reduces potential variability in home currency cash flows as well as in profits. Thus covering forward reduces some of the threat of short-term financial problems. In the longer term, the cost of such insurance against foreign exchange risk is small since it effectively amounts to the dealer's spread on forward transactions, less the spread on spot deals. It may not be the case that this policy maximises profits in the long run but, from the standpoint of a risk-averse satisficer, it has clear appeal.

It is understandable that the firm which enters into very few foreign currency denominated transactions may cover all of them. It is also understandable that risk-averse managers in companies with a vast number of foreign currency denominated transactions will make a habit of covering them. However, treasurers in such firms usually adopt policies of selective covering. The rationale of this tactic and its frequent mode of operation are considered further in Chapters 13 and 15.

The same kind of argument – but with some essential differences – applies with respect to lending and borrowing denominated in foreign currencies. Most lending or borrowing involves respective receipt or payment of interest at regular intervals with capital repayment at a specified date. According to the international Fisher effect, the penalty for borrowing in a hard currency will be exactly offset by the benefit of a low interest rate. Perhaps this can best be illustrated by an example. Assume that the expected inflation in the UK is higher than that in Switzerland. If we begin from a base year in which exchange rates between sterling and the Swiss franc are in equilibrium, we shall anticipate, via purchasing power parity, that the Swiss franc will strengthen against sterling. And, via the Fisher effect, we shall expect interest rates in Switzerland to be lower than sterling interest rates. Thus the international Fisher effect will suggest a weakening of sterling against the Swiss franc compensated for by lower Swiss franc interest rates. So a company considering raising £5 million might do so in sterling and it would then expect to pay a higher interest rate than would be the case were that same company to raise the money in Swiss francs. But raising the money in Swiss francs would have the drawback that, when repayment was due, the company would probably have to find in excess of £5 million sterling because of the strengthening of the Swiss franc during the period that the loan was outstanding. Leaving aside imperfections in the market created by the taxation treatment of foreign exchange losses on loans (see Chapter 24, but note that in the real world these market imperfections created by non-symmetrical tax treatment are far too important to be left aside), the international Fisher effect predicts that the gain resulting from the lower interest rate on the Swiss franc borrowing would be exactly offset by the loss on capital repayment at maturity.

The above situation is illustrative of how the international Fisher effect underpins the argument that foreign exchange exposure on borrowings does not matter. But, of course, we have seen in our overview of empirical investigations of the four-way equivalence relationship that our deductive, theoretical model does not always hold in the real world. Some studies suggest that international Fisher holds in the medium to long term but there is other work that suggests that we can wait an awfully long time for international Fisher to assert itself. For the international company these findings are crucial. In the long run our company borrowing in hard currencies might expect to come out even and thus be indifferent to the currency denomination of its borrowings, but in the short run its Swiss borrowing might wipe it out.

This kind of problem has dramatically affected more than a few British companies. Laker Airways arranged lease finance denominated in US dollars for the bulk of its aircraft at a time when the dollar was extremely strong. And J. Lyons, another UK company, had a wealth of Swiss franc borrowings on its balance sheet at a time when sterling was weak against the Swiss franc. Laker went out of business partly, but by no means solely, due to its dollar borrowings; Lyons was rescued when it was taken over by Allied Breweries, but its plight was largely a result of its uncovered hard-currency debt.

The problem that treasurers of international companies have is not just that international Fisher is found empirically to be a long-run phenomenon, but that when they undertake a foreign currency denominated borrowing the exchange rates between the home currency and the foreign one may not be in equilibrium. Subsequent correction of the disequilibrium can incur a vast loss (or profit) for the international borrower.

Perhaps it is fair to conclude that, were the four-way equivalence model to hold in the real world immutably and with no time lags, and were the tax treatment on repayment of foreign denominated loans (see Chapter 24 for details on this topic) on the same footing as interest paid and received, then transaction exposure would not matter. That the real world is not so convenient as the theoretical one, that the four-way equivalence model does involve time lags (and very big ones), and that tax treatment of interest and currency gains and losses is not symmetrical means that transaction exposure is very important to international financial executives. In short, it needs to be managed.

Economic Exposure

Economic exposure refers to the possibility that the present value of future operating cash flows of a business, expressed in parent currency, may change due to a change in foreign exchange rates. According to purchasing power parity theory, exchange rate changes are associated with different relative rates of inflation. The argument that economic exposure does not matter draws on the purchasing power parity theorem.

Devaluation of the home currency tends to favour companies competing in export markets. It also has a favourable impact in import-competing areas. And it creates advantages for firms which are domestically sourced (imports become relatively more expensive) and domestically financed. Revaluations have inversely opposite effects.

A relatively high home country inflation rate, if not accompanied by devaluation, has an adverse effect on companies competing in export markets and those competing domestically with imported goods. It affects adversely firms which are domestically sourced and (because the tendency will be for the home interest rate to rise) domestically financed.

Devaluation creates advantages which correct disadvantages flowing from high relative inflation rates. The benefits created for some firms by devaluation should offset earlier adverse effects created by inflation. If relative inflation rates are accompanied by appropriate exchange rate adjustments, as predicted by purchasing power parity, it may be argued that we have a situation where the overall effect is neutral. The benefits of devaluation exactly offset the earlier penalties of inflation. But should this be universally true? Maybe the above argument would be applicable to the firm whose costs were all inflating at the same rate as the general level of inflation in the country in which it was based. The devaluation or revaluation would then exactly offset movements in the firm's specific costs. In these circumstances economic exposure would not matter to the firm.

Of course, it is unusual for the firm's individual costs to move in line with general inflation. And where they do not, economic exposure will matter to the firm. Indeed, multinationals consider relocating or switching manufacture from one country to another in order to correct for local costs which have inflated in excess of general inflation levels or, more specifically, in excess of competitor nations' costs.

If, then, economic exposure does matter to the international company, should it endeavour to hedge this exposure through forward market purchases or sales of currency? We believe that the answer to this question veers towards the negative. We have reached this conclusion not because economic exposure is based on uncertain cash flows, nor because it is difficult to quantify since it involves detailed analysis of elasticities of demand. But we believe that there are easier ways to deal with the fact that the present value of expected cash flows accruing from operations may alter in response to changes in exchange rates. The simple way involves financing operations, either partially or wholly, in the foreign currency (or currencies) which is judged as having a significant impact upon the present value of operations. It should be mentioned that this approach does not provide an exact cover for economic exposure. This arises because the hedge via financing is a function of relative inflation rates with differences corrected via purchasing power parity. The changing value of operating cash flows is affected by relative specific price and cost increases and these are only partially corrected by changing exchange rates based on general inflation levels.

It should be mentioned that the author has come across anecdotal evidence of international companies actively managing economic exposure via forward markets and via currency options. This involves the calculation of exposed net present values based on anticipated operating cash flows, deducting from them the hedge effect achieved by financing and then using forward and/or option markets to hedge net exposure should this be deemed to be the advantageous course of action.

We would mention that there is a strong case for monitoring and managing economic exposure by entering into forward or option markets to protect the present value of expected future cash flows where the tenor of the firm's involvement in a particular overseas environment has a finite time horizon, such as a joint venture which will terminate after, say, three years of operation. Since the firm's involvement does not span sufficient time to ensure a cycle running through to equilibrium, economic exposure can be material. However, this kind of situation has more of a transaction exposure dimension since the residual value of the project will, presumably, be remitted to headquarters at the end of the period of overseas involvement.

Translation Exposure

Translation exposure arises as a result of the process of consolidation of foreign currency items into group financial statements denominated in the currency of the parent company. It was discussed in Chapters 9 and 10. Some items frequently viewed as being solely translation exposure are essentially transaction exposure items. This is the case with respect to foreign currency denominated borrowings or lendings under the current rate method. Repayment of the loan requires cash to pass from borrower to lender and this creates a cash flow exposure. With respect to the question of whether foreign exchange exposure matters for this kind of item (which may be classified as both transaction exposure and translation exposure), the answer should flow from viewing it as a transaction, rather than translation, item.

It will be recalled from earlier chapters that different translation methods may have different impacts upon a firm's reported earnings per share. But do these different accounting methods affect the valuation of the firm? Clearly, from a theoretical standpoint, the accounting methods of reporting for overseas subsidiaries' results should not impact on their own upon valuation of a subsidiary. Its valuation to the parent company should be a function of expected future cash flows which are distributable to the parent. Admittedly this may alter as exchange rates alter. We would argue theoretically that subsidiaries' values change in response to movements in exchange rates because their present value, in home currency terms, is perceived by investors to have altered. Note that this theoretical argument has nothing to do with accounting reporting for foreign operations.

But the key question is: how does the investment community interpret changing subsidiary results based on changed translation methods? In other words, whether translation exposure matters is essentially an empirical question. Our answer therefore draws on empirical investigations. Since the relevant studies have not yet been referred to elsewhere in this book, it is necessary to spend some time discussing them.

Under FASB 8, translation gains and losses were included in the group consolidated profit and loss account and caused wide fluctuations in reported corporate profits and earnings per share. Referring to the impact of the US standard, Shapiro (1982, p. 141) comments that 'nothing is surer to upset a chief executive than an accounting provision that disturbs the smooth year-to-year earnings gains so cherished by securities analysts'. This kind of reasoning on the part of some large multinationals has undoubtedly led to some questionable decisions designed to hedge translation exposure by incurring transaction exposure. Srinivasula (1983) describes a situation where ITT, the US-based multinational, sold forward $600 million worth of foreign currencies with a view partially to hedging its balance sheet exposure. The dollar fell relative to most foreign currencies and this resulted in a translation gain and an offsetting loss on forward cover. This gain was unrealised but the forward loss involved a cash loss in the order of $48 million. Although ITT achieved its objective of partially hedging balance sheet exposure, we would argue that such transactions make little or no economic sense. Of course, FASB 52 obviates the need for any company to take this illogical action. It is worth mentioning that ITT was by no means alone in its response to accounting exposure under FASB 8. A number of studies reported similar actions by US-based multinationals designed to counter translation exposure by incurring transaction exposure. A paper by Paul Griffin (1979) summarises a number of studies by other researchers into the effects FASB 8 had on corporate financial policy. It should be noted, though, that it was a minority of US multinationals which responded to exposure under FASB 8 by taking on transaction exposure in the opposite direction.

But did the reporting requirements of FASB 8 affect the stock market performance of companies reporting translation gains and losses? Clearly this is entirely an empirical question. There have been two major investigations in this area. These have been undertaken by John Makin (1977) and Roland Dukes (1978); their results are by no means identical. Makin assessed share price performance for three sample groups comprising typical multinational companies, comparable domestic companies and, thirdly, a group of multinationals which were considered to be particularly sensitive to FASB 8 reporting requirements. He found that the accounting standard requirements did not affect share price performance for the typical multinational group but he did find a downgrading in share price for the sensitive group. Whilst he interprets this as implying that FASB 8 reporting requirements may affect share prices, Ian Giddy (1978) has challenged this interpretation because, as he points out, the sensitive group of multinationals would not only be affected in terms of income statement reporting but it would also be affected in terms of dollar remittances from dividends declared by overseas subsidiaries – an area to which Makin's study failed to address itself. Roland Dukes (1978) sought to investigate the stock market effect of FASB 8 reporting requirements in a study in which he compared security returns from a sample of 479 multinational companies with a control sample of domestic firms. The empirical results were that the security return behaviour of portfolios of multinational firms, despite the impact of FASB 8 on reported earnings, is not significantly different from the return behaviour of comparable portfolios of domestic firms. Although Dukes' methodology can be challenged, his conclusions are that the US stock market is not kidded by pure translation gains and losses. Moreover, the actions of some multinationals in hedging translation exposure with transaction exposure are seen not only to be illogical from a deductive standpoint but also to be unjustified empirically since stock market analysts seem not to be interested in pure translation gains and losses.

If portfolios of multinational corporations were found to be more affected than matched samples of domestic companies, the question of identifying whether this flowed from foreign currency translation of income statements as opposed to alterations in aggregate investor views on the present value of future dividends from overseas subsidiaries remains. Indeed, this would seem to be a complex, if not intractable, problem. Certainly there appears to be a reasonable case for

investors to reappraise multinationals in response to changes in currency rates –
but this logical reassessment derives from economic and transaction exposure
rather than translation exposure. This deductive interpretation is consistent with
empirical conclusions that pure translation exposure does not matter.

Forecasting Exchange Rates

Perhaps the general conclusion of the foregoing discussion in this chapter is that
pure translation exposure can be ignored for all practical purposes. In the long
run, taking on transaction exposure should result in gains equalling losses, but in
the short run gains or losses may accrue. From a practical point of view we would
recommend selective cover of transaction exposure for the large international
company and (maybe) blanket cover for the very occasional exporter/importer or
company who is only casually involved in cross-frontier financial exposure. We
believe that economic exposure is best countered by financing in those currencies
which materially create the exposure.

Our conclusion in favour of selective covering of transaction exposure begs
the question of whether or not buying professional forecasts of exchange rates
might be helpful. The conclusions on selective cover and buying forecasts of
foreign exchange rates are really interrelated. We now examine the evidence. If
forecasts consistently achieve better results than the use of forward rates we may
wish to buy them to help us take selective action on transaction exposure. And we
may wish to use them to make speculative profits or to undertake leading and
lagging operations (which will be discussed in Chapter 14) in advance of devaluations and revaluations of currencies. Robert Aliber's (1983, p. 58) cynical comments
epitomise the negative point of view on buying foreign exchange forecasts. He
observes that 'since 1973, about twenty firms have been established to sell
forecasts of exchange rate movements. One inference is that they can make more
money selling forecasts than using them.' This view may have a lot of substance
during those periods when foreign exchange markets are displaying the characteristics associated with market efficiency. The contrary view, namely that
forecasting foreign exchange rates can lead to consistently profitable results, is
based on evidence to the effect that the foreign exchange market does not always
display the typical features associated with efficient markets. Chapter 11 was
devoted to a review of the available evidence.

The fact that Murenbeeld (1975) and various others, for example Armington
(1977), have developed models for predicting devaluations and revaluations and
these models have reasonably good track records presumably argues in favour of
forecasting. That Robinson and Warburton (1980) – see Chapter 11 – have
developed filter rules for locating funds for maximum profit; that Goodman (1978,
1980, 1981, 1982) and Goodman and Jaycobs (1983) have shown that some
technically-based forecasts consistently perform well; that Levich (1981, 1982,
1983) has identified some (but by no means total) persistence in forecasters'
superior performance – all combines to underwrite the potential value that may
accrue from selectively using foreign exchange forecasts. Giddy and Dufey's
(1975) finding that under clean floats the foreign exchange markets are efficient
and do not afford forecasters the opportunities consistently to make profits is

reconcilable with the opinion about the virtues of forecasting since we rarely find ourselves in clean float situations for long.

Summary

Transaction exposure is concerned with how changes in exchange rates affect the value of anticipated foreign currency denominated cash flows relating to transactions already entered into. Empirically it is generally found that the forward rate is an unbiased predictor of the future spot rate. This means that failing to take cover but running with the spot rate should yield similar results in the long run. Indeed, failing to cover should yield higher long-term results because the spread on the forward rate is wider than the spread on the spot rate. However, failing to cover may have disastrous short-term results. Avoiding these potential financial pitfalls by selective covering is therefore a logical strategy. It is little compensation to the uncovered firm that has just gone bust to argue that it would have been all right in the long run.

Economic exposure relates to the possibility that the present value of future cash flows of a firm may change due to foreign currency movements. But exchange rate changes are related, via purchasing power parity, to differences in relative inflation rates. The firm whose foreign operation experiences cost inflation exactly in line with general inflation should be returned to its original value by changes in the exchange rate exactly in line with purchasing power parity. In these circumstances it may be argued that economic exposure does not matter. But most firms experience specific cost inflations which differ from general inflation. In this situation, which is the usual one, economic exposure does matter. Our recommended approach to minimising this kind of exposure is to finance operations in the currency to which the firm's value is sensitive.

Translation exposure arises as a result of the process of consolidation of foreign currency denominated items into group financial statements denominated in the currency of the parent company. Whether it matters is purely an empirical question. Research work has tended to indicate that pure translation exposure does not matter and it is consequently recommended that pure translation exposure should not be covered.

References

Aliber, Robert Z. (1983) *The International Money Game*, 4th edn, Macmillan.

Armington, P.J. (1977) *Floating Exchange Rates. The Balance of Payment and the Global Equilibrium of Asset Markets*, Forex Research Paper No. 3, July, pp. 3–12.

Dukes, Roland E. (1978) *An Empirical Investigation of the Effect of Statement of Financial Accounting Standard No. 8 on Security Return Behavior*, FASB, December.

Giddy, Ian H. (1978) 'What is FAS No. 8's effect on the market valuation of corporate stock prices?', *Business International Money Report*, 26 May, p. 1665.

Giddy, Ian H. and Dufey, Gunter (1975) 'The random behaviour of flexible exchange rates', *Journal of International Business Studies*, vol. 6, no. 1, Spring, pp. 1–32.

Goodman, Stephen H. (1978) 'No better than the toss of a coin', *Euromoney*, December, pp. 75–85.

Goodman, Stephen H. (1980) 'Who's better than the toss of a coin?', *Euromoney*, August, pp. 80–89.

Goodman, Stephen H. (1981) 'Technical analysis still beats econometrics', *Euromoney*, August, pp. 48–59.

Goodman, Stephen H. (1982) 'Two technical analysts are even better than one', *Euromoney*, August, pp. 85–96.

Goodman, Stephen H. and Jaycobs, Richard (1983) 'Double up and prosper', *Euromoney*, August, pp. 132–139.

Griffin, Paul (1979) *FASB Statement No. 8: A Review of Empirical Research on its Economic Consequences*, Graduate School of Business, Stanford University Research Report No. 482, January.

Levich, Richard M. (1981) 'How to compare chance with forecasting expertise', *Euromoney*, August, pp. 61–78.

Levich, Richard M. (1982) 'How the rise of the dollar took forecasters by surprise', *Euromoney*, August, pp. 98–111.

Levich, Richard M. (1983) 'Currency forecasters lose their way', *Euromoney*, August, pp. 140–147.

Makin, John H. (1977) 'Flexible exchange rates, multinational corporations and accounting standards', *Federal Reserve Bank of San Francisco Economic Review*, Fall, pp. 44–45.

Murenbeeld, Martin (1975) 'Economic factors for forecasting foreign exchange rate changes', *Columbia Journal of World Business*, Summer.

Robinson, Bill and Warburton, Peter (1980) 'Managing currency holdings: lessons from the floating period', *London Business School Economic Outlook*, February, pp. 18–27.

Shapiro, Alan C. (1982) *Multinational Financial Management*, 1st edn, Allyn and Bacon.

Srinivasula, S.L. (1983) 'Classifying foreign exchange exposure', *Financial Executive*, February, pp. 36–44.

TEST BANK
NUMBER TWO

EXAMINATION QUESTIONS

1. Manana SA is the Coluvian subsidiary of a US manufacturer. Its local currency balance sheet is shown below. The current exchange rate is 20 pesos to the US dollar.

Figures in million pesos

Shareholders' funds	42	Fixed assets	36
Long-term debt	9	Debtors	12
Current liabilities	3	Cash	6
	54		54

(a) Translate the peso balance sheet of Manana SA, into dollars at the existing exchange rate of 20 pesos to the dollar. All monetary items in Manana's balance sheet are denominated in pesos.

(b) If Manana's balance sheet remained as above but the peso moved to 25 pesos per dollar, what would be the translation gain or loss if translated by the monetary/non-monetary method? by the current/non-current method? or the all-current rate method?

(c) If the peso moved to $0.06, what would be the translation gain or loss according to the three accounting translation methods referred to under (b)?

(d) What is Manana's translation exposure under the three accounting methods?

2. Indicate briefly what empirical evidence is available about how the four-way equivalence model holds up in practice.

3. It was 16 November 1979. Bob Dixon sat at his Sao Paulo office reviewing some figures which had been passed to him by his chief accountant. Bob had been sent to Brazil by the US multinational,

David Industries Inc., on 1 April 1979. As vice-president of the Brazilian subsidiary he had been concerned about the state of the economy ever since and his own boss was due to arrive at the beginning of December with the Group Treasurer of David Industries.

Bob was worried because of the widespread talk in Sao Paulo of an impending devaluation. He had asked his accountant for an evaluation. But as he closed the accountant's report he felt that the writer was sitting on the fence. The report had reviewed the development of the Brazilian economy commenting that the inflation of the early sixties, which had run at 150 per cent per annum, had been brought under control by the early seventies but that it had got out of control again through the decade. The report commented that exchange rate policy had moved from one of steep, infrequent devaluations to one of mini-devaluations with the cruzeiro devalued by 1 or 2 per cent every four to six weeks. The policy was to devalue the cruzeiro by the difference between Brazilian inflation and US inflation. Allegedly this made it easier for businessmen to plan their currency flows.

The accountant had presented some figures in his report comparing price indices in Brazil and in the USA, showing the exchange rate and the trade position of Brazil since 1972. A discontinuity in the trade figures occurred following the oil price hike of 1973/74. Because Brazil imports all its oil, the economy was thrown into disarray. Inflation began to creep back up, the balance of trade deteriorated, and Brazil was forced to borrow heavily to finance its oil imports and pay off debt obligations.

	Increase in price index Brazil (%)	Increase in price index US (%)	Exchange rate (Cr./$)	Trade Exports (millions of US$)	Imports (millions of US$)
1972	16.7	3.3		3,940	4,190
1973	12.6	6.2	6.220	6,090	6,150
1974	27.6	10.9	7.435	7,810	12,560
1975	28.9	9.2	9.070	8,490	12,040
1976	41.9	5.8	12.345	9,960	12,350
1977	43.7	6.5	16.050	11,920	12,020
1978	38.7	7.5	20.050	12,470	13,630
1979 (est.)	70–75	10–11	?	15,200	18,000
1st quarter			23.130		
2nd quarter			25.655		
July			26.115		
August			27.775		
September			29.825		
October			30.415		

The accountant's report pointed out that Brazil's external debt was expected to be about $50 billion by the end of 1979 and that its ratio of net debt to total exports had climbed from less than 1 in 1973 to $2\frac{1}{2}$ by 1978.

Bob had heard from other expatriate Americans that their companies were getting out of dollar debt and borrowing cruzeiros in anticipation of a major devaluation. Since the accountant's report failed to tell Bob what he wanted to know he began to do some calculations himself.

You are required to answer the four questions below:

(a) According to the indicators provided by Bob's accountant, what do you think will happen to the cruzeiro?

(b) In trying to figure out what would happen to the cruzeiro, what other information would you look at?

(c) Given Brazil's balance of trade position and the history of the value of its currency, what are some other exchange rate policies you would expect the Brazilian government might implement?

(d) Why are other US multinationals moving out of dollar debt and replacing it by cruzeiro financing? What other policies might they follow in anticipation of a devaluation of the cruzeiro?

Justify all your answers.

4. (a) What is the difference between accounting risk and economic or true risk?

   (b) Which risk should the treasurer be most concerned with?

(Association of Corporate Treasurers: Part II, Specimen paper in Currency Management)

5. Outline the major factors affecting exchange rates and discuss the relative importance of each.

(Association of Corporate Treasurers: Part II, Specimen paper in Currency Management)

6. (a) You have decided recently to hold a position long in Belgian francs. A bank with whom you have a very good relationship telephones you to say that a 'double top' is forming. What does this mean? Would you act on this information?

   (b) You have an agreement to add one person to your treasury staff to improve forecasting ability. Would you choose a chartist or an economist or another specialist? Would the nature of your business influence your decision?

(Association of Corporate Treasurers: Part II, September 1985 Paper in Currency Management)

13

Information for Exposure Management

Management of foreign exchange exposure is an integral part of the treasury function in the multinational company. Rational decision taking presupposes that relevant information pertinent to the decision is available. This generalisation is no less true of treasury management than it is of any other aspect of business. To make logical decisions on foreign exchange exposure, relevant information is required. This chapter is devoted to the topic of an information system for exposure management.

But what is the problem? Maybe an example would help. Suppose that one wholly-owned subsidiary of a UK-based group has a receivable of FF5 million due in three months' time whilst another wholly-owned subsidiary has a FF payable of FF5 million three months away. It would make no sense for the two subsidiaries each to cover their exposure by respectively selling and buying FF5 million three months forward. Obviously, these two exposures cancel out when viewed on a group basis. Maybe the boards of directors of the two wholly-owned subsidiaries would each reach a decision to the effect that they would want to cover their exposure. It is no problem to ensure that for internal management accounting purposes or for performance appraisal a notional hedge is done. Most multinationals achieve this by requiring that divisions wishing to cover foreign exchange exposures do so by buying or selling forward with the group treasury. But reverting to our numerical example, the point is that, from a group standpoint, there is no need to cover the receivable and payable referred to because setting the long position in one wholly-owned subsidiary against the short position in the other wholly-owned subsidiary provides an exact cancelling out. The difficulty for the multinational in this area is that it needs continuous flows of information from all subsidiaries on their foreign exchange exposure. But before getting to grips with information for exposure management, we need to ask ourselves with which definition of exposure the firm is concerned.

Which Kind of Foreign Exchange Exposure is Significant?

We have classified foreign exchange exposure under three headings, namely, transaction exposure, translation exposure and economic exposure. In the chapter immediately preceding this one we argued that the firm should be crucially con-

140

cerned with transaction exposure and economic exposure since these two classifications of exposure are essentially underpinned by cash flows. This contrasts with pure translation exposure where differences arise due to accounting conventions in the process of consolidation of the financial accounts of companies within a group. Generally, pure translation gains and losses are now dealt with by way of reserve accounting under the consolidation procedures of US and UK companies according to the accounting standards in these two countries. This means that distortions to earnings per share and profit trends which were brought about by the requirements of the US accounting standard FASB 8 have been eliminated. Furthermore, the indications of most serious empirical studies are that security analysts are sufficiently sophisticated not to be deceived by the inclusion of these translation gains and losses in income statements and, since they do not seem to affect security prices, the conclusion follows that translation exposure should not matter to the multinational company. And if companies need not worry about translation exposure, it follows that collecting information on it is not a worthwhile process. Furthermore, companies should not enter into transactions to hedge pure translation exposures. In this connection it should be reiterated that gains and losses arising from converting foreign currency denominated borrowings and lendings are clasified in this book as transaction gains and losses and are therefore left out of our definition of pure translation exposure. Should information be required on pure translation exposure, it is our belief that the normal rolling budgets which most large companies prepare ought to be sufficient to meet any needs of users.

Having argued against the inclusion of pure translation exposure within the exposure information system, we shall now turn to economic exposure and transaction exposure. The computation of economic exposure is a complex process, requiring as it does detailed analysis of elasticities of demand, competitor appraisals and other aspects discussed in Chapter 9. Identifying economic exposure presupposes that corporate executives are able to specify how the value of the firm will respond to exchange rate changes. Since, as we have argued elsewhere in this book, economic exposure matters, presumably treasurers in multinational companies will wish to manage it. The sort of information necessary to manage economic exposure concerns the impact of exchange rate changes upon the value of the firm. With rapidly changing exchange rates and a competitive world, economic exposure may also change regularly. But keeping track of this class of foreign exchange exposure is difficult. It clearly requires the input of very skilled executive time and as such is not easily amenable to being systematised. Given this background we would argue that if economic exposure is being actively managed, it is necessary to update information about it regularly. But, given that identification of economic exposure should be based upon the sensitivity of the present value of the firm to changes in exchange rates, we believe that this is so complex an issue that we would not recommend it to become the subject of a routine, simple information system. However, if a firm is actually managing economic and transaction exposure, it needs to equip itself with current figures on both kinds of exposure. For economic exposure, this would mean that regular net present value details of operating cash flows would be necessary for all of a multinational company's operations, plus details of the extent to which they are hedged by local and other financing.

The other class of exposure which is also based on cash flows is, of course, transaction exposure. We have argued in Chapter 12 that transaction exposure matters to the firm. Identification of transaction exposure is not difficult, unlike economic exposure. Unmanaged transaction exposure may result in foreign currency denominated loans being left exposed whilst the foreign currency strengthens dramatically. This may have very far-reaching effects on the firm, as we pointed out in the previous chapter. And passively managed transaction exposure may result in subsidiary companies in a group pursuing policies which are optimal for them but sub-optimal for the group. The example of the FF5 million exposure is a case in point which would cost the group two bid/offer spreads to cover exposures when an internal cover was already available. Managing transaction exposure presupposes that the group treasury has information on its magnitude and maturity. We shall now attempt to outline an information system for transaction exposure that is relatively easy and inexpensive to operate.

The Transaction Exposure Information System

Although no single transaction exposure information system will be universally applicable to every business, there are certain features which should be present in all. First, the information system should be forward looking. Given that we are concerned with taking decisions about future events, it follows that we need information about anticipated outturns. Second, the frequency of reporting needs to be adequate. What constitutes sufficient frequency is entirely a practical question but we have found that, for most companies with significant international operations, monthly reporting bolstered by telex communications to the centre on additional exposures taken on is adequate. But, clearly, very large groups, or those with vast foreign currency denominated items, may wish to shorten this reporting time scale. Third, the flow of information should be direct to the treasury rather than via other departments, such as accounting departments, which can create delays. Finally, the need for information must be sold to management in subsidiary companies. It is essential that such managers comprehend the rationale for data on foreign currency commitments, and it is essential that subsidiary company performance should not be distorted. We shall return to this topic under the heading of 'Reporting Performance' towards the end of this chapter. Failure in these areas usually results in reduced motivation on the part of subsidiary management and a weak and tardy system of control.

Information systems should be timely, succinct and orientated to decision and control. There is no place for irrelevant information. Thus the routine exposure information system should home in solely upon transaction exposure. Some other texts (McRae and Walker 1980) extend the currency exposure information system to translation exposure. For reasons set out above, we believe this to be unnecessary and unjustified.

Our concern is with transaction exposure, using a minimum monthly reporting frequency. Reports are essentially forecasts specifying foreign currency denominated receipts and payments to be made. They should focus upon currency of denomination, maturity and cover already taken. It is recommended that reports should distinguish four key data. These embrace intercompany versus third-party flows, capital versus trading items, firm contractual flows versus probable flows and finally, details of covered and uncovered flows. Table 13.1 is an example of such an exposure forecast. Although it does not split out capital and trading items or firm and probable flows as such, this can easily be achieved by entering the respective initials *C* or *T* and *F* or *P*. Thus the treasury at the UK holding company level would require from the US subsidiary a schedule like Table 13.1 showing all non-US $ exposures which had been taken on by that subsidiary. Similar schedules would also be required from all other subsidiaries showing transaction exposures in currencies other than the local currency. In addition to these schedules, material changes would be immediately communicated by telex to the group treasury. This would enable the group treasury to coordinate covering activities in response to the overall transaction exposure position. Where subsidiaries are permitted to hedge externally with local banks as well as with the group treasury, the exposure schedule should show details of external cover already taken.

Where global computer information systems are employed in a multinational group, communication of transaction exposure data is greatly facilitated. Some international banks and treasury consultancies provide appropriate services.

Receipt of transaction exposure schedules from all around the world enables the central treasury to prepare a group exposure statement. Like the previous schedule this is usually prepared monthly; an example of such a summary report appears in Table 13.2. It will be noted that currencies are categorised according to whether a forward market exists or not. This is a useful distinction since ease of action to obtain cover is more readily available when a forward foreign exchange market exists. However, where forward markets do not exist, cover may be synthesised by borrowing or lending in the local currency, assuming that financial markets have sufficient depth for this strategy to be pursued. It is also useful to categorise currencies according to their membership of joint floats, such as the EMS currencies. It will be noted that this has been done in Table 13.2. The value of this kind of device lies in the fact that sometimes large companies cover against the net cash flow exposure, having netted out positions with respect to all currencies in a joint float.

Histogramming

Having obtained transaction exposure data on a group basis and after duly allowing for foreign currency denominated overdrafts and bank accounts, net exposure positions can be estimated. The question for the treasurer is then what to do about exposure. Decision on action is clearly a function of the management's view on the directions in which exchange rates are likely to move. Here the histogramming technique is frequently used. This involves obtaining and giving weight to estimates of exchange rate movements from well-informed parties inside and outside the company. Sources inside the company might include the group treasury, the economics department, local management and various others. Sources outside the company would include bankers and forecasting groups. The technique involves each forecaster in assigning probabilities to a range of estimated future exchange rates over various periods. It should be noted that ranges, rather than single point estimates, are usually used. Table 13.3 shows a format which might be used for this process. As can be seen, it contains a weighting factor in addition to the actual forecast. Weightings are built into the process by reference to individual

Table 13.1   Transaction Cash Flow Exposure Schedule

Company: US Sub Inc.   Currency: $/£   Prepared by: AB   Rate: $ v. £ as at 24.12.84
Country: USA   Forecast period: 6 mths to 30.6.85   Date prepared: 24.12.84   Spot: 1.4200   1 mth 1.4300   3 mths 1.4500

Figures in £000	Jan.	Feb.	Mar.	Apr.	May	June	Beyond June	
RECEIPTS								
Third party	2,000	3,000	1,000	1,000			1,000	Due Sept. 85
Intercompany Swedish Sub		2,000						
TOTAL RECEIPTS	2,000	5,000	1,000	1,000			1,000	
PAYMENTS								
Third party	3,000	3,000						
Intercompany German Sub			2,000				2,000	Due Oct. 85
TOTAL PAYMENTS	3,000	3,000	2,000				2,000	
NET RECEIPTS/(PAYMENTS)	(1,000)	2,000	(1,000)	1,000			1,000 (2,000)	Sept. 85 Oct. 85
COVER AGAINST RECEIPTS								
COVER AGAINST PAYMENTS	1,000	1,000	1,000				2,000	
NET EXPOSURE	—	1,000	—	1,000			1,000	
DETAILS OF FORWARD COVER* (specify contact date; settlement date; rate amount)	1.8.84 Jan. 1.4350 1,000	1.9.84 Feb. 1.4450 1,000	30.9.84 Mar. 1.4550 1,000				16.10.84 Oct. 1.4580 2,000	

Note: *Details of forward cover frequently appear on a separate schedule.

Table 13.2 Group Cash Flow Exposure Schedule

Prepared by: . . . . Date prepared: . . . . Forecast period: . . . .

Figures in £000	Jan.	Feb.	Mar.	Apr.	May	June	Beyond June
CURRENCIES WITH FORWARD MARKET							
EMS Currencies							
− Belgian franc							
− Dutch guilder							
− French franc							
− German Mark							
− Italian lira							
− Other EMS							
Total EMS							
Canadian $							
Danish Kr.							
Swedish Kr.							
Swiss Fr.							
US $							
Others (specify)							
TOTAL							
NO FORWARD MARKET							
Argentine austral							
Brazilian cruzado							
Others (specify)							
TOTAL							

Table 13.3   Currency Forecast: £/$

	Forecaster:	Group treasurer	Current spot rate:	$1.2750 = £1	
	Currency:	£/$	Forward rate:	$1.2800 = £1	
	Forecast period:	3 months	Date prepared:	. . . .	

Expected range	Mid-point	Probability	Forecaster weighting	Weighted probability
1.2400 to 1.2699	1.2550	0.05	0.20	0.0100
1.2700 to 1.2999	1.2850	0.30	0.20	0.0600
1.300 to 1.3299	1.3150	0.35	0.20	0.0700
1.3300 to 1.3599	1.3450	0.25	0.20	0.0500
1.3600 to 1.3899	1.3750	0.05	0.20	0.0100
		1.00	0.20	0.2000

forecasters' previous track records. The sum of the weightings for all forecasters must equal 1.00. With reference to Table 13.3, the probability assigned by the forecaster is multiplied by the forecaster's weighting to give a final weighted probability. These weighted probabilities are brought together in a summary histogram – see Table 13.4 – and they may then be compared with the forward rate for the purpose of decision taking.

Let us revert to Table 13.3: this shows a format for individual forecasts – in this case for the treasury. Forecasts of this kind will be prepared by each of the forecasting participants for one month, two months, three months forward and so on. These forecasts are weighted according to each forecaster's past record – this has been done in Table 13.4 over three months – and histograms as shown at the foot of the table can readily be prepared for one month, two months, three months forward, and so on. In the example, the forecasting participants are group treasury, group economics, local treasurer, group financial planning, the company's bankers and a consultant foreign exchange forecasting company. The respective weights given to each party are 20%, 15%, 15%, 20%, 15% and 15%.

From Table 13.4 it can be seen that the weighted forecast suggests a very high probability that the exchange rate in three months time will be within the range 1.27 to 1.33. If the forward rate for three-month dollars is $1.28 to £1 – see Tables 13.3 and 13.4 – then, if the company expected to be short of dollars against the pound three months away (that is, it had to buy in dollars for pounds in three months' time), it would most probably benefit by waiting and buying dollars through the spot market in three months' time. In other words, according to the histogram, there is a good chance that the dollar will have weakened in three months' time; and the histogram promises a better payoff by using the spot rate in three months' time rather than the forward rate.

By contrast, were our company long of dollars three months away it might decide, logically according to the implications of the histogram, to sell dollars for-

Table 13.4 Summary Histogram: £/$

| | Currency: £/$ | Forecast period: 3 months | | | |
| | Date prepared ...... | Forward rate: $1.2800 = £1 | | | |

	Forecast range				
	1.2400 to 1.2699	1.2700 to 1.2999	1.3000 to 1.3299	1.3300 to 1.3599	1.3600 to 1.3899
Group treasurer	0.01	0.06	0.07	0.05	0.01
Group economics	0.01	0.08	0.05	0.01	0
Local treasurer	0	0.08	0.07	0	0
Financial planning	0.01	0.09	0.07	0.02	0.01
Banker	0.01	0.07	0.07	0	0
Forecaster	0.01	0.06	0.07	0.01	0
TOTAL:	0.05	0.44	0.40	0.09	0.02

Summary:

Confidence level

	1.2400 to 1.2699	1.2700 to 1.2999	1.3000 to 1.3299	1.3300 to 1.3599	1.3600 to 1.3899
	5%	44%	40%	9%	2%

ward. Thus the histogramming technique facilitates rational selective hedging. If selective hedging of this kind is undertaken, it is most important to monitor its effectiveness. The recommended post-audit procedure should compare the out-turns achieved from selective hedging with those that would have resulted from a policy of hedging everything in the forward market; it should also compare selective hedging achievements with results based on hedging nothing at all in the forward market. Clearly one needs to do this kind of post audit over a fairly lengthy time span, including periods when the home currency is rising and falling. If selective hedging is to be pursued, the results of post audits must justify the choice of this strategy. Such post audits need to be undertaken regularly. Individual forecaster weightings may also be changed as a result of this process. It cannot be stressed too much that the post audit is an essential part of a selective hedging policy.

Reinvoicing Vehicles

Many multinational companies have turned their treasury department into a separate company. All intergroup trade is then invoiced through this central company. Such companies are known as reinvoicing vehicles, or netting vehicles, or multicurrency management centres. Practice varies from company to company, but the general outline set out below is reasonably typical.

Group companies invoice exports to other group companies through the reinvoicing company in the currency of the exporter. The reinvoicing company in its turn invoices the importing company in its home currency. This means that neither exporter nor importer has any exchange risk; this is borne by the reinvoicing company which ultimately takes all covering decisions on a basis which it views as reflecting a balance of future outturns and the extent of its risk aversion.

Exports outside the group are either invoiced in the exporter's currency or, if the importer requires a different currency of sale, the exporter bills the invoicing centre in his own currency and the reinvoicing company bills the customer in the currency agreed between seller and purchaser. Again, all currency risk is concentrated into the reinvoicing centre. Imports are handled in the same manner enabling all currency risk to be borne by the invoicing company. Of course, the reinvoicing centre does become the legal owner of the goods in these transactions and should therefore have little difficulty in obtaining exchange control permissions to cover its exposure in countries where exchange controls are in place.

This technique concentrates all currency exposure in the reinvoicing centre. It therefore becomes an ideal vehicle for controlling and monitoring the group's foreign exchange exposure. In addition, the reinvoicing centre frequently acts as the banker to the group. In such circumstances cash management is centred in the reinvoicing company, as are group borrowings. Such fully-fledged, sophisticated and (frequently) costly vehicles are appropriate to large international groups with substantial cross-frontier trade, international borrowings and cash flows.

Strategies for Exposure Management

We have argued that firms should take management action in the foreign exchange markets to counter cash flow exposure. But there is another basic question which top management needs to answer. Is its posture one of making as much profit as it can through changes in foreign currency rates? Or is it basically in the business of making and selling goods or services with a foreign exchange stance designed to minimise losses through changing rates? There is no universal, clear-cut response to these questions. Different firms will adopt different postures because of their varying degrees of risk aversion. Maybe their postures on foreign exchange risk will vary from time to time. The firm which seeks to maximise profits in the foreign exchange markets is termed the aggressive firm; its counterpart, which aims merely to minimise potential losses resulting from changed exchange rates, is termed the defensive firm. In reality, judged by their overall strategies and tactics, firms rarely fall neatly into one category or the other but rather lie on a continuum of foreign currency risk between aggressive and defensive. Sometimes a particular firm will adopt an aggressive policy; at other times the same firm will pursue a defensive policy.

The aggressive posture will involve the firm in deliberately seeking and leaving open foreign exchange positions in currencies in which it expects to make profits. The defensive posture involves the avoidance of foreign exchange exposure by the techniques referred to in the next two chapters. In countries without foreign exchange controls it is easy for the aggressive firm to back its judgement on future currency movements by opening up exposure unrelated to trade via the forward markets or the futures or options markets. In countries with exchange controls, the only substantial opportunity open to the firm legally to take currency positions is

874770.

from which potential employees could deduce the requisite qualities of the successful SIA worker. A booklet explaining the Company's team philosophy was made available when applicants first filled out applications. Area newspapers ran several articles focusing on the company's 'new style' of management based on a team concept which stressed cooperation and quality.

In addition to giving the company ample time for selecting what it perceived as the most qualified workers, the selection process has the potential to effect behaviour on the shop floor. Since it was not necessary that an inherent liking for team participation be part of one's personality, the goal of the process is to select workers who outwardly adapt to management's efforts at structuring behaviour. To get the job in the first place, one had to be willing to play by the rules.

Orientation and training

Management's second mechanism, aimed at social control on the shop floor, emerged through the company's orientation and training programme. Every worker underwent one week of orientation and a minimum of two weeks of classroom training. The instruction fell based on trade transactions. An example of the aggressive stance in an environment with exchange controls is that of an exporter who might endeavour to invoice a sale in the currency which he expected to be hard relative to his own currency. An aggressive posture would also involve covering a foreign currency receivable only when the forward rate of exchange was more favourable than the expected spot rate on the settlement date. By contrast the defensive firm would seek to invoice in its own currency and, where it had a foreign currency receivable or payable, it would cover automatically in the forward market. It should be reiterated that when there are no exchange controls it is far more logical for the firm to take open positions via the forward, future or options markets than via trade transactions.

With respect to decisions of a long-term nature, the aggressive firm would similarly seek to obtain debt denominated in a soft currency relative to its own – having due regard to interest costs taken together with expected currency depreciation/appreciation. The defensive firm might endeavour to match the currency denomination of cash inflows and outflows, thereby minimising cash flow exposure, or to match the currency denomination of assets and liabilities.

A firm's posture on foreign exchange risk is usually a function of two key factors. The first is the aggregate risk aversion of the key members of the organisation's decision coalition. The second relates to the firm's ability to forecast exchange rates and its ability to beat the forward market. This latter factor takes us back to the whole range of questions concerned with efficiency of foreign exchange markets and the ability of forecasts consistently to yield excess returns.

Were foreign exchange markets efficient and subject to no imperfections there would be no systematic biases in rates and management's currency expectations would be synonymous with those of the market as embodied in forward rates. According to this scenario, consistent profit opportunities would not exist. But in a world in which governments create market imperfections by intervening in foreign exchange markets – this is termed dirty floating under the current floating exchange rate regime – and interest rate markets, these actions are likely to create systematic deviations between realised rates and expectations of future rates as embodied in forward rates. Certainly, as we saw in Chapter 11, there have been consistent and persistent biases which have continued for substantial periods suggesting that recurring profit opportunities do accrue to investors in foreign exchange markets. So the aggressive stance may be justified by two factors. First, market imperfections, such as government intervention in foreign exchange markets, may result in sustained periods when markets fail to demonstrate the features of efficiency. Second, it may be the case that forecasters have special opportunities based on access to information not available to most other participants in the market, or the firm or forecaster may have special expertise in interpreting available information. As we have pointed out earlier, firms adopting aggressive exposure policies need to monitor the results of pursuing such tactics carefully.

The essence of the defensive strategy varies according to the nature of the company concerned. For the basically domestic company which occasionally exports or imports, the low-risk policy involves consistent use of the forward markets. For the significant exporter, the defensive policy most frequently used involves forward markets or currency of financing policy. This latter approach is best illustrated with an example. If a firm's operations generate exposed assets or cash inflows, these exposures may be countered by taking on financial liabilities or cash outflows in the same currencies. According to this formula, a company with significant exports denominated in foreign currencies would try to match this by holding part of its liabilities in these currencies.

For the truly multinational company which has interrelated operations in many countries, the defensive financial strategy involves use of forward and options markets but it also has a significant further policy at its disposal. This involves protection of expected profit and cash flow levels against changes in foreign exchange markets and financial markets by adjusting operating and financial variables. Operating responses consist of alteration to sourcing, product, plant location, market selection, credit, pricing and currency of invoicing policies; these will be considered in Chapter 14. Adjustments of financial variables to protect profit and cash flows generally occur on the liabilities side. A company may finance itself in those currencies with which its operating cash flows are positively correlated. For example, consider a US holding company with a UK subsidiary exporting in Deutsche Marks to West Germany. Operating returns of the UK subsidiary are positively correlated with movements in the Deutsche Mark and the subsidiary might threfore decide to raise finance in Deutsche Marks. A movement in the Deutsche Mark against sterling would affect not only operating returns but also financing costs. The change in the one would be countered by changes in the other, thereby reducing foreign exchange risk.

Reporting Performance

Care must be taken when devising information systems designed to facilitate optimal action at the group level lest they affect motivation at the subsidiary level adversely. In this chapter we have suggested an information system designed to aid optimum foreign exchange action from the group viewpoint. We shall now stand back and look at financial performance measurement in the light of foreign exchange considerations. In this section we shall address the question of which financial figures to use for evaluating foreign affiliates and how to design control and reporting systems to ensure that the group optimising techniques advocated in this chapter do not distort subsidiary reporting performance evaluation and managerial motivation.

The major disadvantage of comparing actual performance with budgeted performance in terms of the parent or home currency is that changes in exchange rates which do not coincide with those budgeted for will affect translated results, irrespective of whether the current rate or the average rate method is used to translate the profit and loss account of the subsidiary. The overseas operating company will have budgeted its profit outturn in local currency and should hence be evaluated in profit terms using local currency. Just as UK operating subsidiaries budget in sterling and have their performance measured in sterling, so the congruent course for overseas subsidiaries is to use local currency for evaluating performance. Just as depreciation or appreciation of sterling can affect the profit and loss account results relative to budgeted performance, so devaluations and revaluations of overseas currencies can affect overseas operations. But, logically, local currency terms should be used.

Performance of subsidiaries may also be distorted by the introduction of non-operational factors into management accounts. Thus the impact of non-arm's-length transfer pricing should be eliminated for performance evaluation, as should variation of inter-affiliate credit terms which may be triggered by impending devaluations or revaluations; see Leading and Lagging in Chapter 14.

There is also the question of covering. Foreign operational management may wish to take cover from transaction exposure. If this is the case, performance evaluation should allow for covering even though all covering is only carried out at group level. International companies often introduce reporting systems of the type recommended in this chapter. It is usual to require that divisions do not use outside bankers to cover foreign exchange exposure but that all hedging be dealt with according to one of three approaches. These are:

- that subsidiaries hedge all foreign exchange transaction exposures with the group treasury;
- that subsidiaries hedge only those foreign exchange transaction exposures with the group treasury which they consider wise;
- that subsidiaries hedge no foreign exchange transaction exposure at all.

Whichever system is used, all transaction exposure should be reported to the group treasury. And where the central treasury is used for covering, it is required to quote to divisions the finest market rates for forward cover.

For reporting purposes, we believe that the middle course is the preferred one. It ensures that subsidiaries are responsible for their selective hedging actions. Using this system, divisional management accounts will reflect operational outturns and the results of covering on the part of subsidiaries. It should be recalled that, even though this system is used, all hedging is done with the centre and the group treasury obtains information on all transaction exposures whether hedged or not. So it can take action in response to this total group exposure.

Neither the first system nor the last gives operating management any discretion on hedging and we feel that the withdrawal of this discretion may be a demotivating factor. Given that we wish our control system to be functional as well as being a motivator, we prefer the system where divisions report all transaction exposures but may hedge whatever they wish of this exposure with the head office treasury. This system is also preferable where there are minority interests in a subsidiary. Clearly, selective hedging at the level of the partly-owned subsidiary may be beneficial to minority shareholders. If a system is to be designed that does not act against the interest of minority shareholders, which the 'hedge everything' or 'hedge nothing' system may do, then care must be taken to ensure that subsidiary results are not distorted by requirements which may be optimal at the group level but not at the subsidiary level.

Summary

One foreign subsidiary of a UK-based international company may have a FF5 million receivable due in three months' time whilst another subsidiary has a FF5 milion payable in three months' time. Without an information system which reveals the existence of this kind of internal hedge, divisions may both cover this exposure.

To avoid the above kind of illogical action, this chapter has suggested the framework for an information system to communicate transaction exposures to head office. Our recommended system involves all foreign and home subsidiaries reporting all foreign currency denominated transaction exposures to the group treasury. On the basis of such reports, we would suggest that the group treasury has the information necessary to take decisions which may optimise at the level of the overall group.

Care must be taken in terms of setting up systems and evaluating subsidiary performance to ensure that, whilst divisions report all transaction exposures to the group treasury, they also have discretion to adopt a policy of selective hedging – preferably with all hedging from subsidiaries being with the group treasury rather than with an outside banker.

Reference

McRae, Tom and Walker, David (1980) *Foreign Exchange Management*, Prentice-Hall.

14

Internal Techniques of Exposure Management

There is a wide range of methods available to minimise foreign exchange risk. This chapter and the following one focus respectively upon internal and external techniques. Internal techniques use methods of exposure management which are part of a firm's regulatory financial management and do not resort to special contractual relationships outside the group of companies concerned. External techniques use contractual means to insure against potential foreign exchange losses.

Internal techniques of exposure management aim at reducing or preventing exposed positions from arising. External techniques insure against the possibility that exchange losses will result from an exposed position which internal measures have not been able to eliminate.

Internal techniques embrace netting, matching, leading and lagging, pricing policies and asset/liability management. External techniques include forward contracts, borrowing short-term, discounting, factoring, currency overdrafts, currency swaps, government exchange risk and guarantees, financial futures and currency options. Frequently some of the above methods are unavailable to the multinational company – netting, matching and leading and lagging are illegal in some countries and restricted in others. It should also be borne in mind that many less developed countries have no forward market in their currencies. We shall now examine, in turn, netting, matching, leading and lagging, pricing policies and asset/liability management.

Netting

Netting involves associated companies which trade with one another. The technique is simple. Group companies merely settle inter-affiliate indebtedness for the net amount owing. Gross intra-group trade receivables and payables are netted out. The simplest scheme is known as bilateral netting. Each pair of associates nets out its own position with the other and cash flows are reduced by the lower of each company's purchases from or sales to its netting partner. Bilateral netting involves no attempt to bring in the net positions of other group companies.

Bilateral netting is easily illustrated by an example. Assume that the UK subsidiary in a group owes the French subsidiary of the same group the FF equivalent of $6 million and that at the same time the French company owes the UK company the sterling equivalent of $4 million. The actual remittance to clear the intercompany accounts would be netted down to the equivalent of $2 million (in an agreed currency which may – or may not – be dollars, sterling, French francs or any other currency) to be paid by the UK subsidiary to the French counterpart. Between them, the two companies have saved the transfer and exchange costs on the equivalent of $8 million. Netting basically reduces the amount of inter-company payments and receipts which pass over the foreign exchanges. Fairly straightforward to operate, the main practical problem in bilateral netting is usually the decision about what currency to use for settlement.

Multilateral netting is more complicated but in principle it is no different from bilateral netting. Multilateral netting involves more than two associated com-panies' intergroup debt and virtually always involves the services of the group treasury. Bilateral netting involves only two sides and it is usually undertaken without the involvement of the corporate centre. Of course, it is true that many subsidiaries may involve themselves in bilateral netting. Figure 14.1 shows how three subsidiaries in a group might be involved in bilateral netting with each other by netting off balances due between pairs of subsidiaries. But the scheme involves three lots of bilateral nettings.

Multilateral netting is easily exemplified. Consider a group of companies in which the UK subsidiary buys (during the monthly netting period) $6 million worth of goods and services from the Swiss subsidiary and the UK company sells $2 million worth of goods to the French subsidiary. During the same month, assume that the Swiss company buys $2 million worth of goods and services from the French subsidiary. The potential for multilateral netting is shown in the matrix in Figure 14.2. It can be seen that settlement of the intercompany debt within the three subsidiaries ends up involving a payment of the equivalent of $4 million from the UK company to the Swiss subsidiary.

Unlike the instance referred to in Figure 14.1, where bilateral netting could be achieved by a number of subsidiaries netting off balances between each other in pairs, multilateral netting always involves the group treasury as the centre of net-ting operations – see Figure 14.3. Participating subsidiaries report all inter-company balances to the group treasury on an agreed date and the treasury subsequently advises all subsidiaries of amounts to be paid to and received from other subsidiaries on a specified date. Multilateral netting yields considerable sav-ings in exchange and transfer costs but it requires a centralised communications

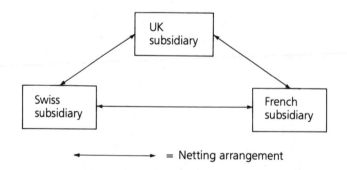

Figure 14.1   Scheme for Bilateral Netting

Figures in $mn		PAYING SUBSIDIARY			Total receipts	Net receipts	Eliminated
		Swiss	UK	French			
RECEIVING SUBSIDIARY	Swiss		6	0	6	4	2
	UK	0		2	2		2
	French	2	0		2		2
Total payments		2	6	2	10		
Net payments			4			4	
Eliminated		2	2	2			6

Netting potential: Gross flows $10mn
Net flows $ 4mn
Eliminated flows $ 6mn

Figure 14.2 Multilateral Netting Matrix

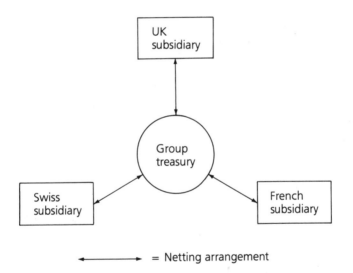

= Netting arrangement

Figure 14.3 Scheme for Multilateral Netting

system and discipline on the part of subsidiary companies. It should be noted that many countries' exchange controls put restrictions on bilateral and multilateral netting. Exchange control regulations need to be investigated carefully before embarking on a policy of netting.

Systems of netting used by international groups of companies involve fairly tight timetables in the period immediately prior to settlement. They usually vary around the following kind of basic schedule:

- Fix settlement day (e.g. the 6th of every month).
- 5 days before settlement day all participating subsidiaries telex inter-

company balances to the centre stating the currencies of the debt and translating them into a common currency at specified exchange rates.
- 4 days before settlement day intercompany balances are reconciled.
- 3 days before settlement day group treasury calculates the extent of netting to be used. The centre then issues instructions on payment to subsidiaries.
- 2 days before settlement day subsidiaries instruct their banks to make payments two days hence.
- settlement day is when payments and receipts occur.

Netting reduces banking costs and increases central control of intercompany settlements. The reduced number and amount of payments yields savings in terms of buy/sell spreads in the spot and forward markets and reduced bank charges. It is difficult to estimate total benefits but, as a guide to the extent of gains flowing from netting techniques, McRae and Walker (1980) estimate that savings approximate one-sixth of one per cent of the flows eliminated.

Matching

Although netting and matching are terms which are frequently used inter-changeably, there are distinctions. Strictly speaking, netting is a term applied to potential flows within a group of companies, whereas matching can be applied to both intra-group and third-party balancing.

Matching is a mechanism whereby a company matches its foreign currency in-flows with its foreign currency outflows in respect of amount and approximate timing. Receipts in a particular currency are used to make payments in that currency, thereby reducing the need for a group of companies to go through the foreign exchange markets to the unmatched portion of foreign currency cash flows.

The prerequisite for a matching operation is a two-way cash flow in the same foreign currency within a group of companies; this gives rise to a potential for natural matching. This should be distinguished from parallel matching, in which the matching is achieved with receipt and payment in different currencies, but these currencies are expected to move closely together, near enough in parallel. An example is the EMS currencies. Of course there is always the chance with parallel matching that the currencies concerned may move away from their previously parallel paths, for example in a realignment within the EMS. In this case the expected match fails to be realised.

The practical mechanics of matching is rather like multilateral netting since it involves the group treasury and gives rise to the need for information centralisa-tion with the group finance function just before settlement. Practical problems may arise because of the uncertain timing of third-party receipts and payments. Unexpected delays can create problems for the multinational treasury in its endeavours to match receipts and payments. The possibility that receipt of a sum due on a certain settlement day is postponed, but payment is nonetheless made on that same date as originally anticipated, creates obvious difficulties.

For this reason, success in matching is very much a function of the quality of information coming to the corporate financial centre, including realistic and accurate predictions of settlement dates. Like netting, the extent of matching is constrained by the exchange controls of some countries.

Leading and Lagging

Leading and lagging refers to the adjustment of credit terms between companies. It is most usually applied with respect to payments between associate companies within a group. Leading means paying an obligation in advance of the due date. Lagging means delaying payment of an obligation beyond its due date. Leading and lagging are aggressive foreign exchange management tactics designed to take advantage of expected devaluations and revaluations of currencies.

An example may help to indicate the processes involved. Suppose that subsidiary *b* in country *B* owes money to subsidiary *a* in country *A* with payment due in three months' time and with the debt denominated in US$. Suppose further that counry *B*'s currency is expected to devalue within three months relative to the US$ and also *vis-à-vis* country *A*'s currency. Obviously, if company *b* leads – that is, if it pays early – it will have to part with less of country *B*'s currency to buy US$ to make payment to company *A*. So the temptation to lead is attractive. However, decision takers need to look a little further than this. Should the international Fisher effect be holding in the short term, then the interest rate on deposits in country *B*'s currency should exceed the interest rate on US$ deposits by the amount of the expected devaluation. Decisions on leading and lagging need to take account of relative interest rates as well as expected currency movements. And there is a third relevant dimension – namely the effective tax rates on interest in differing countries. So, reverting to our example, we need to compare the net of tax cash flow effects after allowing for interest from a group standpoint. Should company *b* lead, it will save in terms of country *B*'s currency by beating the impending devaluation. But the group will then receive a US$ interest rate rather than an interest rate based on the currency of country *B* – and this US$ interest rate should be lower than that of country *B*'s currency. All this has to be taken into account on a net-of-tax basis over the period of the lead.

A similar example could be devised for lagging. Should country *B*'s currency be expected to revalue or harden against the US$, then lagging would, on the face of things, be suggested. But once again, as is always the case with leading and lagging decisions, we need to consider from a group standpoint the combined impact of:

- the expected currency change and its timing
- relative interest rates
- after-tax effects

As with matching, the group treasury is usually involved to ensure that the timing of intercompany settlement is functional from a group standpoint rather than merely from a local one. It is also worth mentioning that performance measurement may be affected if some subsidiaries are asked to lead and some to lag. Clearly, the subsidiary which does the leading loses interest receivable and incurs interest charges on the funds led. To overcome this problem, evaluation of performance is frequently done on a pre-interest, pre-tax basis.

The existence of local minority interest gives rise to complications on leading and lagging decisions. Significant local shareholders in the 'losing' subsidiary always raise strong objections because of the added interest costs and lower profitability resulting from the consequent local borrowing. In such cases, the interests of the minority shareholders appear to be subordinated to those of the majority shareholder, the parent company. The existence of strong local minorities frequently results in companies refraining from lead and lag techniques.

Leading and lagging may also be constrained by exchange control regulations. Leading and lagging affect balance of payments figures as well as exchange rates. Because of this, host governments frequently impose allowable bands on credit terms which must be followed in all international trading.

The application of leading and lagging techniques extends beyond the realm of pure risk minimisation in exposure management. Opportunities are created for taking aggressive stances on financing. It should be understood that this aggressive strategy is based upon the view, borne out by empirical evidence, that the international Fisher effect does not hold in the short term. Thus an expected devaluation in a host country would probably cause an international company to consider raising local finance to repay foreign currency denominated borrowings.

Pricing Policy

In exposure management terms, pricing policy embraces two strategies, namely price variation and currency of invoicing. Under these headings there are two subsets which are functions of whether trading is with third parties or inside a group of companies. Each of these is now considered.

Price Variation

Price variation involves increasing selling prices to counter the adverse effects of exchange rate changes. This tactic raises the question as to why the company has not already raised prices if it is able to do so. In some countries, price increases are the only legally available tactic of exposure management. In most South American countries this is true since many other methods are illegal, there is no forward market, and local financial markets are so shallow as to make borrowing with the objectives of achieving exposure management impossible.

We now turn to price variation on intercompany trade. Transfer pricing is the term used to refer to the pricing of goods and services which change hands within a group of companies. As an exposure management technique, transfer price variation refers to the arbitrary pricing of intercompany sales of goods and services at a higher or lower price than the fair, arm's-length price. This fair price would be the market price if there were an existing market or, if not, the price which would be charged to a third-party customer. Taxation authorities, customs and excise departments and exchange control regulations in most countries require that arm's length pricing be used; and in virtually all countries in the world tax authorities have the power to impute a price where transfer price manipulation is suspected; and customs and excise departments base excise duty on an imputed price when the transfer price is not considered to be a fair one. Having said all this, many multinationals nonetheless attempt to maximise after-tax group cash flows by transfer pricing to minimise tax payable.

Invoicing in Foreign Currency

Companies engaged in importing and exporting, whether of goods or services, are concerned with decisions relating to the currency in which goods and services are to be invoiced. Trading in a foreign currency gives rise to transaction exposure with its attendant risks and opportunities. Although trading purely in a company's home currency has the advantage of simplicity, it fails to take account of the fact that the currency in which goods are invoiced has become an essential aspect of the overall marketing package given to the customer.

A seller will usually wish to sell in his own currency or the currency in which he incurs cost; this avoids foreign exchange exposure. But buyers' preferences might be for other currencies. Many markets, such as oil or aluminium, effectively require that sales be made in the same currency as that quoted by major competitors, which may not be the seller's own currency. In a buyer's market, sellers increasingly tend to invoice in the buyer's ideal currency. The closer the seller can approximate the buyer's aims, the greater chance he has to make the sale.

Should the seller elect to invoice in foreign currency, perhaps because his prospective customer prefers it that way, or because sellers tend to follow the market leader, the seller should then only choose a major currency in which there is an active forward market for maturities at least as long as the payment period. Currencies which are of limited convertibility, chronically weak, or with only a limited forward market in London, should not be considered.

Where there is the prospect of a major export to a country with a small economy, so that the value of the contract is likely to be a significant factor in that country's balance of payments, further considerations apply. The seller is advised to avoid the buyer's currency. Where the government itself or one of its agencies is the customer, it behoves the seller to bear in mind that the customer himself is able to devalue the currency prior to payment, effectively reducing proceeds in the currency of the exporter.

The seller's ideal currency is either his own or one which is stable relative to his own. Often the seller is forced to choose the market leader's currency. Anyway, the chosen currency should certainly be one with a deep forward market. For the buyer, the ideal currency is usually his own or one that is stable relative to his own, or it may be a currency of which he has reserves, or a currency in which he earns reserves. Strong buyers may be in a position to insist on their own currency being used for pricing; it is often a condition of any deal and quotes in other currencies are simply ignored. An advantage to the seller when selling in the purchaser's currency is that payment is rendered simpler for the buyer; all he must do is make a payment in his own currency. In these circumstances payment is usually much more rapid, and this may constitute a good reason for invoicing in the buyer's currency.

Of course, many international traders seek to buy in the same currencies as those in which they receive income, in order to net out exposure at source. This will not necessarily be their home currency. Furthermore, many markets are economically structured in such a way that competitors follow the market leader. In such circumstances it is often the practice of participants to quote in the same currency as that in which the market leader quotes – and this may be neither the home currency of the buyer nor of the seller.

Occasionally it happens that the invoice currency becomes a bone of contention between seller and buyer. Often a proxy currency, namely one that moves similarly to the buyer's currency, is resorted to as a way of resolving the impasse. Another technique, which was popular in the past although it is less frequently used now, is the use of a currency clause whereby payment is made in one currency but the amount due is fixed by reference to another.

Usually, in export contracts, at least one party enters into a foreign exchange transaction. It may be the exporter if he is selling in a foreign currency; it may be the importer if he is buying in a currency other than his own. If the currency of the contract is not the home currency of either the importer or the exporter, both will have to undertake a foreign exchange transaction. Given this background, it is eminently sensible to arrange matters in such a way that the cost of doing the foreign exchange contract is minimised. Foreign currency markets within Europe vary widely in their competitiveness and spread or commission structure. For example, in France exchange controls require that a French company does its foreign exchange transactions with a bank in France where costs are high by London standards. The same is true in Scandinavian countries. For those who are able to access it, the London market is the cheapest foreign exchange market to deal in throughout the world. Where one of the parties to a trade is based in a country where exchange controls make it relatively expensive to use local foreign exchange markets it may be wise to structure the deal in such a way that the cheaper London market may be accessed. This is pertinent for intergroup trading. For an Anglo-French trade it may be worthwhile to invoice in French francs so that no foreign exchange transaction will arise in France and it will be in London that the foreign exchange deal takes place.

The arguments which we have set out above all relate to marketing aspects of the question of invoicing in foreign currency. None relates to aspects such as seeking to invoice in strong currencies, which seems to concern a great number of companies. Our view is that, in countries without exchange controls, devoting time to seeking to invoice in strong currencies is a waste of effort since, if the company wishes to be long in particular currencies, it is free to buy these whether or not there is any underlying trade. Forward markets, futures and currency options all provide scope for the aggressive company to take positions in currencies if its top management so desires. This would seem to be a more direct method of backing one's judgement on currencies without involving directly the basic business operations of the company.

Having said this, there are commercial reasons why a company in a country with or without controls might prefer to use a strong currency as the medium in which it invoices in international trade. The most frequently quoted reason is to enable the firm to maintain stable price lists in circumstances where new price lists are expensive to alter. In countries with exchange controls, it is usually the case that trade represents the only mechanism by which a company is able, legally, to take positions in foreign currencies.

Many companies with strong positions in markets where they are under short-term pressure from competitors may decide to invoice in a currency expected to be weak. Thus as the currency of invoicing depreciates, so the customer receives an increasing discount on the goods without the company formally announcing a price cut. This tactic enables the company to protect market share whilst market conditions are poor. Conversely, a company in a strong market position in a seller's market might, in the short term, specify a strong currency for invoicing thus obtaining the benefit of a continuously rising price in home currency without formally changing its price.

In countries where exchange controls limit the taking of positions in foreign currencies, international companies use cross-frontier trade as one of the very few mechanisms available to back their commercial judgement on future exchange rate payments. In these circumstances, and with respect to third-party trade, the defensive strategy is to attempt to invoice all exports and have all imports invoiced in the home currency irrespective of the strength and weakness of other currencies. By contrast, the aggressive tactic is to seek to invoice export sales in hard currencies and seek to obtain purchases invoiced in relatively soft currencies. When exchange controls are in place and forward markets are expensive to use, the currency of invoicing technique becomes pertinent. Customers frequently seek to buy goods in weak currencies whilst the selling company may prefer to invoice in strong currencies. So there is a clear conflict of interests. Marketing executives may prefer to close a sale by whatever means possible and may be functionally influenced to choose the weak currency although this policy is dysfunctional from a total company standpoint. Evidently there should be some marketing systems control mechanism which prevents this dysfunctional tactic.

We now turn to currency of invoicing in the context of intercompany trade. Analysed from a pre-tax point of view, the distinction between aggressive and defensive currency of invoicing disappears when looking at intercompany trade between subsidiaries of equal ownership status – but this is not so where there are minority interests. Currency of invoicing is a zero-sum game and therefore the potential benefit from currency of invoicing to one subsidiary equals the potential loss to the other. However, after-tax effects must never be left out of our decision-making criteria and in this context there may be gains to be achieved from currency of invoicing techniques. Consider two subsidiaries, *A* and *B* (both in different countries), which trade with one another. Suppose that *A* pays a higher marginal tax rate than *B*. In these circumstances, and with all other things being equal, *A* might logically invoice *B* in a weak currency whilst *B* invoices *A* in a strong currency. This policy concentrates exchange profits in *B* and puts losses into *A*, hence increasing overall after-tax income and cash flow.

Asset and Liability Management

We shall now consider the final internal technique of exposure management: this is known as asset and liability management. It can be used to manage balance sheet, income statement or cash flow exposures. As we have stated earlier, we believe that concentration on cash flow exposure makes economic sense, but emphasis on pure translation exposure is misplaced. Hence our focus here is on asset/liability management as a cash flow exposure management technique.

In essence, asset/liability management can involve aggressive or defensive

162 *Multinational Finance*

postures. In the aggressive attitude the firm simply increases exposed cash inflows denominated in currencies expected to be strong or increases exposed cash outflows denominated in weak currencies. By contrast, the defensive approach involves matching cash inflows and outflows according to their currency of denomination, irrespective of whether they are in strong or weak currencies.

Commentators frequently distinguish between operating variables and financing variables. This distinction is useful from an asset/liability standpoint. Manipulation of operating variables to manage cash flow exposure can best be illustrated by an example. Suppose that a UK exporter with an ongoing inflow from sales in Deutsche Marks wishes to avoid the Mark exposure: he will most probably use the forward market to do this. However, he might decide to source a significant volume of purchases from West Germany, such purchases being denominated in Deutsche Marks. By adopting this policy there is a partial match of currency denomination of inflow with currency denomination of outflow.

With respect to financing variables, the international company has considerable discretion in terms of asset/liability management. The aggressive stance will be to increase exposed cash, debtors and loans receivable in strong currencies (duly taking consideration of interest impact, currency movements and tax effects) and increase borrowings and trade creditors in weak currencies (again allowing for interest effects, currency depreciation and tax impacts). At the same time, policy will involve reducing exposed borrowings and trade creditors in strong currencies and reducing cash, debtors and loans receivable in weak currencies. In the multinational company operating in a weak currency country, the aim will be to acquire local debt and remit cash balances as quickly as possible to the hard currency parent either as dividend remittances or as parent loan repayments. The capital structure of subsidiaries based in weak currency countries may be organised to facilitate transfer of funds. For example, retained earnings may not be capitalised so that dividend flexibility is maintained by keeping up revenue reserves. Also, a high ratio of intercompany debt to parent equity in the subsidiary company's capital structure might help the repatriation of money in circumstances where a high dividend payment might be restricted or discriminated against from the tax point of view.

However, some of these financial strategies are constrained in many countries by a paucity of local financial sources. Furthermore, host governments often impose limits for debt-to-equity ratios and restrict dividend repatriation to certain percentages of capital raised outside the host country. Host governments frequently also penalise, with heavy taxes, dividends in excess of certain stipulated levels.

Summary

Internal techniques of exposure management are techniques which do not resort to special contractual relationships outside the group of companies concerned. Internal techniques include netting, matching, leading and lagging, pricing policies and asset/liability management.

Netting involves associated companies which trade with each other. Associates simply cancel out amounts owed with amounts due and settle for the difference. Bilateral netting is the simplest version of the technique; the more complicated version is termed multilateral netting and use of this technique requires that the group treasury play an active part in co-ordinating affiliates' settlement payments.

Matching is a term applied to a technique which is available for simplifying payments between affiliates and between third parties too. The company matches foreign currency inflows with foreign currency outflows – receipts in a particular currency are used to meet payments in that currency reducing the need to use foreign exchange markets to make purchases and sales of foreign currency.

Leading and lagging are techniques which are resorted to in the light of expected devaluations or revaluations. The mechanism involved is simply to advance or delay payment of intergroup amounts due and denominated in foreign currency. The objective of the exercise is to reduce the amount of local currency needed to settle a debt.

Pricing policy involves increasing prices to allow for expected changes in exchange rates or invoicing in a foreign currency to reduce the risk associated with invoicing in the host currency when a devaluation is expected.

Asset and liability management may involve manipulation of operating or financing variables. The former method involves, for instance, a UK subsidiary in obtaining Deutsche Mark input partially to match the fact that its sales are denominated in Deutsche Marks. Manipulation of financial variables involves seeking opportunities to raise finance in weak currencies. It also embraces considerations about the capital structure of subsidiaries designed to remit funds more readily to the parent company.

Reference

McRae, Tom and Walker, David (1980) *Foreign Exchange Management*, Prentice-Hall.

15

External Techniques of Exposure Management

External techniques of exposure management resort to contractual relationships outside a group of companies in order to reduce the risk of foreign exchange losses. External techniques include forward exchange contracts, short-term borrowing, financial futures contracts, currency options, discounting bills receivable, factoring receivables, currency overdrafts, currency swaps and government exchange risk guarantees. Each of these is considered in this chapter. But because of their specialist nature, financial futures and currency options are the subject of chapters devoted solely to their mechanics; Chapters 16 and 17 are the respective sections involved. It should be mentioned at this point that there is a big difference between a currency option and a forward option (or option dated contract, or option forward, as it is sometimes called). The currency option is rather like a stock market traded option but the forward option is simply a kind of forward contract in which the final settlement date is left flexible. Most of the attention in the current chapter is devoted to the first two methods of neutralising foreign exchange exposure, namely forward covering and short-term borrowing. However, currency swaps also receive significant coverage.

Forward Contracts

Forward markets are available in most major currencies of the world. But by no means all currencies have forward markets. A summary of forward market availability appears in the appendix to this chapter. Even though a market may be indicated by the list in the appendix as being available, the period of cover and the amount involved can be relevant. In some markets very large sums may be difficult to deal. Forward markets for periods beyond twelve months are frequently so thin as to be non-existent even for relatively popular currencies. Forward markets in major currencies are readily available for periods of up to twelve months. This is true for the US dollar, sterling, Deutsche Mark, Swiss franc, yen, guilder, French franc, Canadian dollar, Belgian franc, lira, Danish krone, Swedish krona, and so on. Generally speaking, the larger the deal, and the longer the settlement date is away, and the more exotic the currency involved, the less is the likelihood that a forward contract may be obtainable.

The way in which forward contracts work is best explained by reference to a numerical example. In reality it would be more likely for the company in the example to cover via a forward option, but for the purposes of explanation it is easier to keep the forward option until later. Assume that on 28 September 1984 a British firm enters into an export contract with a French customer. Goods are shipped immediately, the credit period is two months and the goods are invoiced at FF 5 million. On 28 November 1984 the UK company expects to receive FF 5 million. The receivable is booked at the spot exchange rate on 28 September 1984 – namely FF 11.531 = £1, giving a sterling equivalent of £433,614.

But what sterling amount will the British company actually receive for its FF 5 million on 28 November 1984? If the franc/sterling spot rate remains constant over the exposure term (the period during which the receivable or payable is exposed which in this case is the credit period of 2 months) there will be no discrepancy between the sterling equivalent receivable booked and the actual sterling receipt. Such stability is unlikely in a floating exchange rate environment. Should the French franc strengthen against sterling at the end of the exposure period compared to the rate at the start, the British exporter will receive more, in sterling terms, than the amount at which the receivable was originally booked. Should the pound be stronger against the franc in the spot market on 28 November compared with the rate on 28 September, the UK exporter will realise less, in sterling terms, than the amount originally booked. The treasurer in the UK exporting company can eliminate this uncertainty by using the forward market. How would he do this? Simultaneously with the signing of the export contract, the UK company treasurer might sell FF 5 million in the forward exchange market at a fixed price for delivery on the receivable payment date. He does this by a word-of-mouth contract over the telephone with his banker, the contract being confirmed in writing subsequently during the day. The fixed price will be the two-month forward rate for selling French francs and buying sterling. As Table 15.1 shows, this rate is FF 11.546. By this mechanism the UK exporter has contracted to deliver FF 5 million in two months' time at the forward rate of FF 11.546 = £1. Whatever happens to the franc/sterling spot and forward rates over the next two months, the contracted forward rate is irrevocably fixed. On 28 November 1984 the UK exporter should receive the French importer's payment of FF 5 million. This is then delivered to the bank handling the forward deal and, as agreed in the forward contract, the British exporter will receive a sterling credit of £433,050.

As a direct result of covering forward, the exporter or importer need no longer worry about the exchange risk element in the foreign currency denominated transaction. He continues to bear bad debt risk, of course. In our example, should the French importer fail to pay or go bankrupt, the British exporter stands to lose. To overcome this problem, bad debt insurance can be bought through various agencies such as ECGD in Britain – this topic is discussed further in Chapter 18. It should also be mentioned that there is a possibility that the bank with whom the exporter has arranged the forward contract fails or has to cease operations before the contract matures. In such a case the foreign currency would not be delivered to the failed bank. The company would not then be covered and it would have to close out the export deal by buying or selling, as the case may be, in the forward or spot market.

The annualised forward premium or discount as a percentage per annum is the cost of covering forward. This is sometimes stated in sterling terms by compar-

Table 15.1   Forward Cover Example

Contract data

Seller:	UK exporter
Buyer:	French importer
Contract date:	28 September 1984
Credit term:	2 months
Expected payment date:	28 November 1984
Invoice value:	FF 5 million

Exchange rate quotes at 28 September 1984

Spot:	11.521–11.531
1 month forward:	1/8 c pm − 5/8 disc
2 months forward:	1/2 c pm − 1 1/2 disc
3 months forward:	1 c pm − 2 1/4 disc

Exchange rates

Spot: 11.521–11.531

Forward bid/offer spread widens versus spot. Since quotes are pm/disc, one must be added to and the other must be subtracted from the spot rate to obtain the forward rate.

1 month forward: (11.521 less 1/8c) − (11.531 add 5/8c)
                              11.51975–11.53725

2 months forward:	11.516 −11.546
3 months forward:	11.511 −11.5535

Mechanism of forward contract

28 September 1984:	UK exporter sells FF 5 million forward 2 months at 11.546
28 November 1984:	UK exporter receives FF 5 million from French importer
	UK exporter delivers FF 5 million and receives sterling at the rate of FF 11.546 = £1. For FF 5 million he receives £433,050

---

ing the amount of the booked receivable − that is, the foreign currency amount converted into home currency at the spot rate at the invoice date − with the amount received under the forward contract. This is the *ex ante* cost and in our example it amounts to £564, given by £433,614 less £433,050. A slightly different measure of the cost of forward cover is the *ex post* cost which compares the amount that would have been received had the firm run the receivable to maturity (without forward cover) with the amount received via covering forward.

Of course, the reality of the business world is such that one cannot be certain when a customer will pay a bill. He may pay before the due date or he may pay after the due date. In other words, settlement date may not be known for certain.

In the example above it was assumed that the French customer would pay on 28 November 1984 – that is, two months after invoice date. Let us revert to the example, but suppose that the French purchaser is expected to pay on some uncertain date between 28 October and 28 December.

The British exporter may decide to cover despite an uncertain payment date via a forward option. How does the forward option work? Like all forward contracts, the exchange rate is irrevocably fixed when the contract is made. But with a forward option contract the precise maturity date is left open – it is for the company to decide subsequently. However, there is a caveat: the maturity date must fall within a specified option period. Reverting to our numerical example, the UK exporter expects payment between 28 October and 28 December – that is, between one month and three months from the invoice date. Since the bank giving the option does not know when the option will be taken up, it will charge the premium or discount for the most costly of the settlement dates within the customer's option period. In other words, the bank charges its customer the worst rate during the option period. In our example, the forward option is over the second and third months. Referring back to Table 15.1, it will be seen that the rate is therefore FF 11.5535; in this case (but not always) the rate to the seller of francs is the full three months discount. This is the worst rate between month one and month three for selling French francs. It should be noted that the British exporter might as well make his option over the whole three months, since the worst rate between invoice date and month three remains 11.5535.

Had the situation been different, with the UK company importing goods from France at an invoiced price of FF 5 million, and had the UK importer decided to buy francs forward with an option over the period from 28 November to 28 December (that is, over the whole third month), the price of French francs would have been 11.511. Again, this is the three-month rate. But it is not always the case that the rate for the furthest month is the relevant one. Let us look at an example.

Assume that a dealer has given us quotations for the Ruritanian grock as follows:

2.674/76   1 cent pm/1 disc   4/2   8/5

for spot, one month, two months and three months forward. The relevant rates are therefore:

Spot	2.674–2.676
1 month	2.673–2.677
2 months	2.670–2.674
3 months	2.666–2.671

For an option between month one and month three, the option determining rate, should one be buying grocks, is 2.666; were one selling grocks the option forward rate over the period from month one to month three would be 2.677.

It should be clearly understood that the forward option contract, or optional date forward contract as it is sometimes called, is not a currency option. The forward option is optional in terms of the date of delivery – currency must be delivered under the contract. However, under a currency option, currency need not be delivered; the distinction will become very clear after progressing to Chapter 17.

Another method of dealing with unspecified settlement dates is by a swap deal. This method is much less frequently used than forward options. A swap involves the simultaneous buying and selling of a currency for different maturities. Swap deals used for forward cover are of two basic types. There are forward/forward swaps and spot/forward swaps. In either case the exporter begins by covering the foreign currency transaction forward to an arbitrarily selected but fixed date, just as in an ordinary fixed-date forward contract. Then, if the precise settlement date is subsequently agreed before the initial forward contract matures, the original settlement date may be extended to the exact date by a forward/forward swap. Alternatively, if an exact settlement date is not agreed by the date when the initial forward contract matures, the forward cover may be extended by a spot/forward swap. In case this sounds rather complicated, we shall take a closer look at the mechanism.

A forward/forward swap or forward swap, as it is sometimes called, is merely a pair of forward exchange contracts involving a forward purchase and a forward sale of a currency, simultaneously entered into but for different maturities. A numerical example may help describe how forward/forward swaps work.

Assume that the details of an export contract from Britain to France are as set out in Table 15.1 except that the expected settlement date is uncertain (maybe because delivery date is equally uncertain). The British exporter takes out a forward contract on 28 September 1984 (the date of the sale contract with the French importer). This forward contract is for an arbitrary period – say, two months. So he sells FF 5 million forward for delivery on 28 November 1984. Now let us suppose that, on 13 October 1984, the UK exporter and the French purchaser agree that settlement will take place on 13 December. What the British exporter needs to do now is to counter the original forward sale of francs for settlement on 28 November and replace it with a contract for delivery on 13 December. This he does by buying FF 5 million for delivery on 28 November 1984 (thereby creating a contra to his original forward sale of francs) and simultaneously selling FF 5 million forward two months – thereby extending delivery to 13 December. Let us further assume that on 13 October the bank gives the UK exporter the following quotes:

Spot	11.55–11.56
1 month forward	1/2 c–1 1/4 c disc
45 days forward	1 c–2 c disc
2 months forward	2 c–3 c disc

Turning these quotes into full forward data, remembering that the bid offer spread is wider in the forward market than in the spot market, we obtain:

Spot	11.55–11.56
1 month forward	11.5550–11.5725
45 days forward	11.56–11.58
2 months forward	11.57–11.59

Thus, the overall covering mechanism can be seen to involve the transactions as set out below:

		£
28 September	Sell FF 5mn for £ forward 2 months at 11.546 (delivery 28 November)	433,050
13 October	Buy FF 5mn with £ forward 45 days at 11.56 (delivery 28 November)	(432,526)
13 October	Sell FF 5mn for £ forward 2 months at 11.59 (delivery 13 December)	431,406
	Net sterling proceeds	431,930

As can be seen from the figuring above, leg two of the total mechanism reverses leg one. Legs two and three are the opposite sides of the forward swap.

The effect of the above forward swap deal is that the British exporter has locked in as of 28 September at the forward rate for two months' cover adjusted for the premium/discount for a further 15 days given by the bid/offer spread incurred on the forward/forward swap. Of course, as at 28 September, the exporter does not know what the premium/discount will be on extending the contract, neither will he know what the bid/offer spread will be on the swap. The unknown premium/discount is a function of interest rate differentials prevailing on Euro-sterling and Euro-French francs at the date when the forward swap is done.

The above forward swap deal will mean that on the first two legs the UK exporter makes a profit which will be received from the bank on 28 November. The UK exporter's cash flow on the foreign exchange cover becomes:

		£
28 November	Profit received from bank	524
13 December	Sale of receivable at 11.59	431,406
		431,930

Rather than doing a forward/forward deal, the bank would be prepared to roll forward the contract for their customer. Rolling this old contract forward would work as follows. The market rate for rolling the contract forward by 15 days is 3 centimes (11.59 less 11.56). So the bank will adjust the original forward deal by 3 centimes. For settlement on 13 October, the bank would charge 11.576 and the sterling proceeds, payable on 13 October, would be:

$$\frac{5,000,000}{11.576} = £431,928$$

This amount is approximately the same as from the forward/forward swap. Differences are frequently much greater than the small variation in our example. However, this rolling approach is inherently incorrect and can cost the bank's customer dear at times.

A spot/forward swap is similar to a forward swap. It again involves a simultaneous pair of foreign exchange contracts, one of which is a spot contract whilst the other is a forward contract. Reverting to our numerical example, the original forward deal would be for the arbitrarily-set two-month period. But the exporter would wait until 28 November to reverse this deal and to extend maturity to the expected settlement date, namely 13 December. The mechanism might then be summarised as:

		£
28 September	Sell FF 5mn for £ forward 2 months at 11.546 (delivery 28 November)	433,050
28 November	Buy FF 5mn with £ spot at (say) 11.62	(430,293)
28 November	Sell FF 5mn for £ forward 15 days at (say) 11.6525 (delivery 13 Dec.)	429,092
		431,849

The fact that the net proceeds are less under the spot/forward swap than under the forward swap is merely coincidental. No rules about which alternative is cheaper can be given. Under the spot/forward swap the UK exporter's cash flow would be:

		£
28 November	Profit received from bank	2,757
13 December	Sale of receivable at 11.6525	429,092
		431,849

Had the customer rolled the old contract forward on 28 November, the proceeds as of December 13 would have been:

$$\frac{5,000,000}{11.5785} = £431,835$$

Again, this is not far out compared with the spot/forward method.

In practice the option forward is the preferred method of dealing with uncertain settlement dates. It is also a useful mechanism for dealing with a continuing stream of foreign currency payments or receipts. Where a firm's sales include a large number of small transactions denominated in foreign currency terms it is both expensive in transaction and administrative costs to cover each individual deal. This problem may be overcome by taking out a single large forward option contract to cover the approximate expected total cash value of the large number of different receivables or payables. Although the large number of small exports would normally have different settlement dates, forward options are ideally suited to this kind of situation. The amount of the forward contract is usually rounded off, thereby reducing the higher transaction costs asociated with odd values. Because of this it is usually necessary to close out bulk forward contracts of this sort by a spot purchase or sale.

As an example assume that a British exporter is expecting a series of Austrian Schilling receipts during the course of the six months from 10 January to 10 July. The rough total is estimated at AS 10 million. To cover this, the exporter sells AS 10 million on a six-month forward option with the option over the whole period. Assume that the rate is AS 26.56 to the pound and that the Austrian Schilling receipts delivered from proceeds of sales are as follows:

			£
16 February	AS 2.4mn @ 26.56	=	90,361
21 March	AS 2.6mn @ 26.56	=	97,892
16 June	AS 3.1mn @ 26.56	=	116,717
21 June	AS 1.5mn @ 26.56	=	56,476
Sterling proceeds from AS 9.6mn @ 26.56		=	361,446

Thus the exporter has delivered AS 9.6mn. If no more Schilling receipts come in from sales up to 10 July, the exporter must close out the deal by buying in AS 400,000 in the spot market on that date and delivering this against the balance of the forward option contract. If the spot rate on 10 July is AS 27.10, the receipts for the forward option come out at:

	£
Sterling proceeds from sale of AS 9.6mn (as above)	361,446
Cost of buying in AS 0.4mn on 10 July at spot rate of AS 27.10	(14,760)
Sterling proceeds from sale of AS 0.4mn at AS 26.56	15,060
Net sterling proceeds	361,746

Had our exporter actually received in excess of the AS 10 million during the forward option period, the excess would be sold spot for sterling.

Financial Futures and Currency Options

These are specialised topics; their markets are more complicated than basic forward exchange markets. Because of this they are respectively covered in Chapters 16 and 17.

Short-Term Borrowing

Short-term borrowing provides an alternative way of covering a receivable or payable denominated in a foreign currency. The availability of this technique as a practical tool of exposure management is subject to local credit availability and transactions must conform to exchange controls, which may restrict its use.

The mechanism is best illustrated by a numerical example and for this purpose we return to the data in Table 15.1. In it our UK exporter had a two-month exposure of FF 5 million from the contract date of 28 September 1984 through to settlement date on 28 November 1984. Assume this time that our exporter decides to use short-term borrowing to cover his transaction exposure. Simultaneously with the signing of the contract, he should borrow a sum in French francs so that with interest the expected receipt of FF 5 million in two months' time will repay the principal and accrued interest. The French franc sum should immediately be switched to sterling via the spot market. With French two-month interest rates equal to $11\frac{1}{8}$ per cent per annum, the sum to borrow would be FF 4,908,979 since this would mean that FF 5 million would be payable to clear the loan and interest in two months' time. Converting the borrowing to sterling at the spot rate of FF 11.531 = £1 would yield £425,720 and, if this were immediately put on deposit at the UK investment rate of $10\frac{5}{16}$ per cent per annum it would grow to £433,037 (given by £425,720 × 1.0171875) at the end of two months. This is approximately the same as the yield on the forward transaction – see Table 15.1.

In practice it would be more probable for our exporter to borrow FF 5 million on the signing of the contract and at the same date to buy FF 92,708 forward (made up as FF 5 million × $11\frac{1}{8}$ per cent per annum × 2/12). He would simultaneously sell the FF 5 million for sterling via the spot market. Thus the UK exporter is completely covered against exchange risk. On 28 November 1984 the UK company receives FF 5 million from its French customer and this is used to repay principal of the French franc borrowing. The exporter simultaneously receives FF 92,708 from the forward contract and this amount is used to cover accrued interest. All these transactions can be tied in at rates determined on 28 September and then rates are unaffected by subsequent currency and/or interest rate movements over the exposure period. If the proceeds of the FF 5 milion borrowing are switched to sterling at the spot rate on 28 September 1984, the overall proceeds of the deal are as follows:

28.9.84 Borrow FF 5 million at $11\frac{1}{8}$% p.a.
Buy FF 92,708 forward 2 months at 11.516
Sell FF 5 million spot to give £433,614 at 11.531
Invest £433,614 for 2 months at $10\frac{5}{16}$% p.a.

28.11.84 Receive FF 5 million from customer. Use this to repay principal of loan
Deliver FF 92,708 to cover loan interest
This comes from forward contract   (£8,050)
Receive proceeds of sterling loan given by £433,614
× $10\frac{5}{16}$p.a. × 2/12   £441,067

                                                                      £433,017

The slightly different proceeds from this transaction arise because the amount borrowed is FF 5 million as opposed to FF 4.909 million.

By this kind of mechanism any receivable or payable which can be covered by a forward contract may be covered by short-term borrowing assuming credit is available and assuming exchange controls do not prohibit any leg of the transaction.

Just as we looked at imprecise settlement dates and how to cover these via a forward option, so we can cover this eventuality by taking an overdraft type of loan. Rather than doing a forward option for, say, between three and six months, we could arrange an overdraft borrowing for the amount of a receivable for a period of up to six months and remit the proceeds of the borrowing via the spot market to the home country. A complication arises because interest rates on overdraft loans float up and down. Therefore interest is usually catered for by a spot transaction at the date when the borrowing is repaid. Consequently, interest payable cannot be tied in for certain. But by the same token the proceeds of the borrowing remitted to the home country via the spot market at the date the borrowing is drawn down will earn interest and this will vary according to market conditions in the home country. Thus the interest payable and receivable may both be left to market conditions. Hence the receivable is substantially, although not completely, covered against exposure risk.

Earlier in this chapter, we briefly considered how a continuing stream of foreign currency exposures could be covered using the forward market. This kind of situation can also be covered via short-term borrowing. The company in the home country arranges a borrowing facility, either in the currency of invoicing (in the case of the exporter) or the home currency (for the importer). This technique can be used simultaneously to handle the problems of continuing foreign currency exposures and uncertain settlement dates. Assume that we have a UK exporter with a continuing stream of Austrian Schilling export receipts. These can be covered by arranging a fixed rate Schilling borrowing. When each export contract is finalised, the exporter immediately draws down the Schilling loan by the amount of the sale and converts the proceeds into sterling. As the receivables are settled, the Schillings are paid into the exporter's Schilling account so that the borrowing is reduced. As long as the Schilling borrowing rate is fixed over the exposure term, the receivable is fully covered against exchange risk.

Discounting Foreign Currency Denominated Bills Receivable

Discounting can be used to cover export receivables. Where an export receivable is to be settled by a bill of exchange, the exporter may discount the bill and thereby receive payment before the settlement date. The bill may be discounted either with a bank in the customer's country, in which case the foreign currency proceeds can be repatriated immediately at the current spot rate; or it can be discounted with a bank in the exporter's country so that the exporter may receive settlement direct in home currency. Either way, the exporter is covered against exchange risk, the cost being the discount rate charged by the bank.

Factoring Foreign Currency Denominated Receivables

Like discounting, factoring can be used for covering export receivables. When the export receivable is to be settled on open account, rather than by a bill of exchange, the receivables can be assigned as collateral for bank financing. Normally such a service gives protection against exchange rate changes, though during unsettled periods in the foreign exchange markets appropriate variations in the factoring agreement are usual. Commercial banks and specialised factoring institutions offer factoring services. For the exporter, the technique is very straightforward. He simply sells his export receivables to the factor and receives home currency in return. The costs involved include credit risks, the cost of financing, and the cost of covering exchange risk. For these reasons, factoring tends to be an expensive means of covering exposure, although there may be offsetting benefits such as obtaining export finance and reducing sales accounting and credit collection costs.

Currency Overdrafts

Overdrafts in Eurocurrencies are available in the London money markets in all major currencies although banks tend to specialise by currency. The US dollar and the Deutsche Mark are the currencies in which the greatest amounts are advanced.

In terms of avoidance of exposure, all that a company needs to do is maintain the amount of its foreign currency receivables in a particular currency equal to the balance on the overdraft in that currency. However, if the company uses the proceeds of the receivables to run down the overdraft, it also needs to draw down as sales denominated in foreign currency are made. Some companies find it more convenient to sell the proceeds of foreign denominated receivables spot rather than perpetually to adjust the level of the overdraft. However, if the level of the currency overdraft remains constant, there is an assumption that new sales denominated in foreign currency are exactly offsetting incoming foreign receipts. This may not be realistic. If this is the case then, even with this method, it becomes necessary to refer to the level of foreign currency receivables and increase or run down the overdraft to ensure that exposure is being covered.

The currency overdraft is a particularly useful and economical technique of exposure management where a company carries a large number of small items denominated in foreign currency, all with uncertain payment dates.

In some countries use of the currency overdraft exposure management technique may be limited by exchange controls which prevent residents from using foreign currency denominated bank accounts.

Another linked technique is the currency bank account. This is particularly useful where a company engaged in international trade has receivables in excess of payables in the same currency. The company opens a foreign currency denominated deposit account into which receivables in a particular currency are paid and out of which foreign denominated payments in that currency are made. For example, should a UK company have a US dollar receivable of $2 million due on 31 October and a payment to be made on 30 November of $1.5 million, the company might open a dollar denominated deposit account into which it pays the $2 million. Of this, $0.5 million would be remitted via a previously arranged forward deal for delivery on 31 October and $1.5 million would remain in the account to meet the payment due on 30 November. In addition, at the end of November some interest would have accrued on the US dollar bank account.

This kind of exercise is designed to save making a large number of forward deals which are priced to the bank's customer on the basis of interest differentials. In the above example, the trader received US dollar interest on the deposit he left in the currency account. Had he remitted all proceeds from the initial receivable to the UK, he could have obtained a UK interest rate on the proceeds. It can be seen that the essential net saving for the company arises from eliminating the bid/offer spread on amounts left in the currency account to meet future payables. However, careful evaluation comparing the expected proceeds from the currency account technique with the outturns from doing a large number of forward deals should be made since the currency account may not always be the better alternative. Remember that the pricing of forward deals is based on interbank Eurocurrency interest differentials and using markets based on these differentials may give a superior result to the reliance on bank deposit accounts, where interest rates differ from interbank rates.

Currency Swaps

Swaps basically involve the exchange of interest or foreign currency exposures or a combination of both by two or more borrowers. They do not involve the legal swapping of actual debts but an agreement to meet certain cash flows under loan or lease agreements.

In essence, currency swaps enable a borrower who is, for example, in a relatively favourable position to raise long-term fixed-rate US dollar funding but who in fact wants floating rate yen, to marry his requirements with those of another borrower of relatively high standing in the yen market who does not have similar access to long-term fixed-rate dollars. The gain accrues to each corporation swapping liabilities through its respective abilities to trade market imperfections; the effect is to broaden the access of borrowers to international lending markets. They help the corporate treasurer to manage his liability portfolio using techniques very familiar to asset managers – for example, pension fund managers. Currency swaps enable the treasurer to alter the mix of his liabilities and assets.

Swap transactions may be set up with great speed and their documentation and formalities are generally much less detailed than in comparable deals: swap agreements are normally shorter and simpler than those relating to term loan agreements. Transaction costs are relatively low too; they are unlikely to exceed $\frac{1}{2}$ per cent of the total sum. Furthermore, swaps can be unwound easily.

The need to tailor-make swaps to meet individual needs of customers and to match them with a range of counterparties has fostered the prominence of a small number of major intermediaries, such as Citibank, Morgan Guaranty and Bankers Trust among commercial banks and Salomon Brothers and First Boston amongst investment banks. Leading London merchant bankers in the market are Kleinwort Benson and Schroder Wagg.

In analysing the swap markets it is possible to distinguish four distinct classes of swap. These are:

- the interest rate swap
- the fixed-rate currency swap
- the currency coupon swap
- the basis rate swap

The combined total of all swaps certainly exceeded $75 billion in 1984 and it is probable that the 1985 volume was even greater. The interest rate swap is the largest segment of the market, worth a total of between $40 billion and $50 billion in 1984, although the fixed-rate currency swap market is the oldest. We shall now set out the essential features of each of the above kinds of swap.

The interest rate swap involves the exchange between two counterparties of fixed-rate interest for floating-rate interest in the same currency calculated by reference to an agreed notional amount of principal. This amount, which normally equates to the underlying assets or liabilities being swapped, applies only for the purpose of calculating the interest to be exchanged under the swap. At no time is any principal amount physically passed between the parties. The counterparties are thus able to convert a fixed-rate asset/liability into a floating-rate asset/liability and vice versa. Cost savings are obtained by each party. These arise from differentials in the credit standing of the counterparties and other market imperfections. Usually investors in fixed-rate instruments are more sensitive to credit quality than floating-rate lenders. Thus a larger premium is demanded of issuers of lower credit quality in the fixed-rate debt market than in the floating-rate market. The counterparties to an interest rate swap effectively obtain an arbitrage advantage by drawing down funds in the market where they have the greatest relative cost advantage, subsequently entering into an interest rate swap to convert the cost of the funds so raised from a fixed rate to a floating rate and vice versa.

The methodology of the arbitrage and its cost saving potential can be seen by reference to an example involving two companies, X and Y. The former has a higher credit rating as can be seen from the data in Table 15.2. It superior credit standing gives it a 110 basis point advantage in the fixed-rate funding market and a 50 basis point advantage in the floating-rate market. Despite the fact that company X can raise funds more cheaply than company Y in both markets, a potential for interest rate arbitrage exists. Company X draws down funds in the fixed-rate market whilst company Y borrows on a floating basis. Each then enters into an interest rate swap requiring the payments from one to the other as shown under the heading of swap payments in Table 15.2. It can be seen by comparing the all-in cost of funding line in the table with the cost of direct funding line that each party has saved 30 basis points on the swap. The interest rate flows are summarised in Figure 15.1 in which the direction of the arrows represents the direction of interest rate flows.

The ability to transfer relative cost advantages in the manner shown in Table 15.2 and Figure 15.1 has led to many highly credit-worthy companies issuing fixed-rate Eurobonds solely with the purpose of swapping and frequently obtaining funding at an effective sub-LIBOR cost. In the early phase of the interest rate swap market, a triple-A issuer could expect to achieve between 75 and 100 basis points below LIBOR on a swap. Nowadays gains for a comparable borrower might bring the cost of funding down to 25 to 30 basis points below LIBOR.

Table 15.2   Example of an Interest Rate Swap

	Company X	*Company Y*
Credit rating	AAA	BBB
Cost of direct fixed-rate funding	10.40%	11.50%
Cost of direct floating rate funding	six-month LIBOR* + 0.25%	six-month LIBOR + 0.75%
Funds raised directly:		
Fixed rate by company X	(10.40%)	
Floating rate by company Y		(six month LIBOR + 0.75%)
Swap payments:		
Company X pays company Y	(six-month LIBOR)	six-month LIBOR
Company Y pays company X	10.45%	(10.45%)
All-in cost of funding	six-month LIBOR − 0.05%	11.20%
Comparable cost of direct funding	six-month LIBOR + 0.25%	11.50%
Saving	30 basis points	30 basis points

Note: *London Interbank Offer Rate

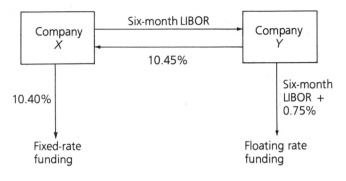

Figure 15.1 Direction of Interest Flows

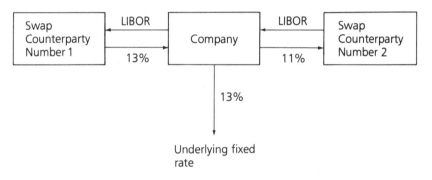

Figure 15.2 Position of Company Following Two Swaps

Besides providing cost advantages, interest rate swaps enable borrowers effectively to access markets which might otherwise be closed to them, for example by virtue of credit quality, lack of a familiar name, or because of excessive use. Even private companies are enabled to tap particular markets without the need to comply with disclosure requirements, credit ratings and other formal requirements. Swaps based upon commercial paper as the underlying floating-rate instrument are a growing segment of the interest rate swap market.

Interest rate swaps may be used as a means of reducing interest rate exposure or as a pure financing tool. They may also be used to enable a corporate treasurer to back his judgement on future trends in interest rates. For example, consider a company with fixed-rate debt costing 13 per cent per annum at a time when the treasurer expects a decline in interest rates to occur. The company might enter into a swap to obtain LIBOR-based funding and leave this swap in place during the period when interest rates were falling. At the end of the decline, the company might enter into a second swap to lock into the new lower fixed rate of, say, 11 per cent per annum. The company's position would then be like that summarised in Figure 15.2.

The interest rate swap process has the advantage of utter simplicity. It is often conducted by telephone and confirmed by telex subject to agreement on documentation which usually incorporates the minimum of restrictive covenants. There are both primary and secondary interest rate markets. The whole market centres on New York with London and Tokyo following – but not too closely.

We now turn to the fixed-rate currency swap, which is the oldest of the four sub-classifications of swap market. A fixed-rate currency swap involves one counterparty exchanging fixed-rate interest in one currency with another counterparty in return for fixed-rate interest in another currency. Currency swaps usually involve three basic steps; these are:

- initial exchange of principal
- ongoing exchange of interest
- re-exchange of principal amounts on maturity

The initial exchange of principal works as follows. At the outset, the counterparties exchange the principal amounts of the swap at an agreed rate of exchange. This rate is usually based on the spot exchange rate, but a forward rate set in advance of the swap commencement date may also be used. This initial exchange can be on a notional basis, that is, with no physical exchange of principal amounts or, alternatively, on a physical exchange basis. Whether the initial exchange is on a physical or notional basis, its importance is solely to establish the reference point of the principal amounts for the purpose of calculating first the ongoing payments of interest and secondly the re-exchange of principal amounts under the swap.

The ongoing exchange of interest is the second key step in the currency swap. Having established the principal amounts, the counterparties exchange interest payments on agreed dates based on the outstanding principal amounts at the fixed interest rates agreed at the outset of the transaction.

The third step in the currency swap involves the re-exchange of principal amounts. Agreement on this enables the counterparties to re-exchange the principal sums at the maturity date. This three-step process is standard practice in the currency swap market and it effectively transforms a fixed-rate debt raised in one currency into a fully-hedged fixed-rate liability in another currency.

Essentially, the currency swap is similar to a conventional long-date forward foreign exchange contract. Like interest rate swaps, the currency swap market is advantageous because it enables borrowers to reduce the cost of borrowing by accessing markets that might otherwise be closed to them. For example, a strong borrower in the Swiss franc market may obtain a finer fixed US dollar rate by raising funds directly in fixed Swiss francs and then swappping them into US dollars. Besides cost advantages, the currency swap market enables borrowers effectively to access foreign capital markets and obtain funds in currencies which might otherwise be unobtainable except at the highest premium.

Currency swaps are again briefly considered under the heading of 'Managing Overseas Funds' in the chapter on Exchange Controls.

The most important currencies in the currency swap market are the US dollar, the Swiss franc, Deutsche Mark, ECU, sterling and the Canadian dollar. The market is dominated by the US dollar on one side but direct swaps have been frequent in yen/Swiss franc, yen/ECU and Deutsche Mark/Swiss franc.

The currency swap is one further tool which enables corporate treasurers to manage currency exposure and reap cost benefits at the same time. We now turn very briefly to the third class of swap – the currency coupon swap. Essentially, this is a combination of the interest rate swap and the fixed-rate currency swap.

The transaction follows the three basic steps described for the fixed-rate currency swap, with the exception that fixed-rate interest in one currency is exchanged for floating-rate interest in another currency.

The final classification of swap is the basis rate swap. This is a fast growing segment of the swap market. The structure of the basis rate swap is the same as the straight interest rate swap, except that floating interest calculated on one basis is exchanged for floating interest calculated on a different basis. The origin of this kind of swap was the US dollar prime rate/LIBOR swap. However, a larger market has developed for the exchange of one-month US dollar LIBOR for six-month US dollar LIBOR, and also the exchange of US dollar LIBOR for US dollar commercial paper.

Government Exchange Risk Guarantees

As part of a series of encouragements to exporters, government agencies in many countries offer their businesses insurance against export credit risks and certain export financing schemes. Many of these agencies offer exchange risk insurance to their exporters as well as the usual export credit guarantees. The exporter pays a small premium and in return the government agency absorbs all exchange risk – thereby taking profits and absorbing losses.

The precise details vary from one export finance agency to another and the exact offerings should be checked with such bodies as ECGD in the UK, HERMES in West Germany, COFACE in France, Netherlands Credit Insurance Company in Holland, Eximbank in the USA and so on. Nowadays most countries have export credit and other similar government agencies offering to absorb foreign exchange exposure risk on export and import transactions in return for a fee.

Counterparty Risk

In providing forward cover for customers, banks take on risk. And just as they do for loans, they evaluate this risk and set credit limits. In this section we consider how a bank might go about this process of risk evaluation. The risk that the bank runs arises from two areas – there is the risk on unmatured forward contracts and there is settlement risk. We shall consider the risk on unmatured contracts first.

When a bank contracts a forward foreign exchange deal with its customer, it will wish at the same time to enter into an opposite transaction so that the net effect is for the bank to have a square position or balanced book. If the bank's customer should go bankrupt prior to the maturity of the contract, the bank knows that it will not receive the funds from the customer to satisfy the matching deal done in the market. The bank will enter the market again to buy in the necessary funds to meet the deal at current exchange rates. This will probably be at a different rate from that at which the original deal was done. This difference will cause the bank to incur either a loss or maybe a profit resulting from the financial failure of its customer.

Because of this, banks set limits on the extent of the risk they are prepared to run on each customer on their books. This credit assessment is done in the normal manner by reference to the company's balance sheet and other indicators of financial health. The setting of a limit for foreign exchange deals is exactly similar to setting a limit for the amount and period of an unsecured loan. But it is less easy to establish the extent of the risk represented by an unmatured forward contract. One might set a limit on the total deals outstanding to each counterparty as a gross total. But clearly this implies that all unmatured deals carry an equal degree of risk. An improvement would be an acceptance that deals with a short maturity involve less risk than longer ones and to allow for that in calculating exposure. In fact, banks have computer programmes designed to estimate their exposure to each customer allowing for such factors as past exchange rate volatility between currencies, period to run to maturity, and whether the existing contracts would show a profit or loss if the customer failed and it became necessary to replace them at ruling market rates.

We now turn to settlement risk. This may arise should the customer fail to deliver the currency concerned to the bank on settlement day and then go bankrupt. The bank's problem is that settlement of a foreign exchange contract is simultaneous – the bank pays away the currency due to the customer or his supplier in expectation of simultaneous receipt from the customer of countervalue. Banks are not usually in a position to ensure that countervalue has been received prior to paying away the currency amount. So if the customer fails just after the bank has paid away currency without receipt of countervalue from the customer, the bank has lost this amount. This kind of risk is only present on and immediately after settlement day up to when settlement is made. Most banks operate a system of settlement limits fixing a maximum amount for the settlement to be made on one date for each customer prior to receipt of countervalue.

Having calculated a limit for a customer, the essence of what banks do in terms of estimating whether a limit is breached is to weight contracts which are near to maturity by a small amount and those far from maturity by a larger figure. Thus a bank might adopt a policy of weighting contracts with one month or less to run to maturity by 0.10, contracts with up to three months to run by 0.15, contracts with up to six months to run by 0.20, and contracts with over six months by 0.25.

Summary

External techniques of foreign exchange exposure management use contractual relationships outside a group of companies in order to reduce the risk of losses following exchange rate changes.

The best known of these involves the forward currency market which may not only be used to cover receivables and payables but also to speculate on foreign currency movements. Although this market may be used to cover a receipt or payment denominated in a foreign currency when the date of receipt or payment is known, it can readily be adapted to allow for situations when the exact payment date is unknown. Techniques here include the forward option, the forward/forward swap and the spot/forward swap. It should be noted that a forward option (or option forward as it is sometimes called) is not a currency option. A forward option involves a right and an obligation to deal in foreign currency – the option is merely as to timing. Purchasers of currency options are considered in Chapter 17 of this book.

Short-term borrowing is another technique for covering receivables and payables and cover may also be bought by discounting foreign currency denominated bills of exchange, by factoring foreign currency denominated receivables, and by purchasing government exchange risk guarantees.

APPENDIX 15

Availability of Spot and Forward Foreign Exchange Markets

	Currency unit	London spot market	London forward market	Local forward market
Algeria	dinar	X	X	X
Argentina	austral	sellers only	X	X
Austria	Schilling	√	√	√
Australia	Australian dollar	√	√	√
Bahrain	dinar	√	√	√
Bangladesh	taka	sellers only	X	X
Belgium	Belgian franc	√	√	√
Bermuda	Bermudan dollar	√	X	X
Brazil	cruzado	sellers only	X	X
Burma	kyat	√	X	X
Burundi	Burundi franc	X	X	X
Canada	Canadian dollar	√	√	√
Chile	Chilean peso	X	X	X
China	Ranminbi yuan	√	√	√
Colombia	Colombian peso	sellers only	X	X
Denmark	Danish krone	√	√	√
Egypt	Egyptian pound	X	X	X
Finland	markka	√	√	√
France	French franc	√	√	√
French Africa	CFA franc	√	√	√
Ghana	cedi	√	X	X
Greece	drachma	√	X	√
Hong Kong	Hong Kong dollar	√	√	√
India	Indian rupee	√	X	X
Indonesia	rupiah	sellers only	X	X
Italy	lira	√	√	√
Japan	yen	√	√	√
Kenya	Kenyan shilling	√	√	√
Kuwait	Kuwaiti dinar	√	√	√
Malawi	kwacha	√	√	√
Malaysia	ringgit	√	√	√
Mexico	Mexican peso	√	X	X
Morocco	dirham	√	X	X
Netherlands	guilder	√	√	√
Netherlands Antilles	Antillian guilder	√	X	X
New Zealand	NZ dollar	√	√	√
Nigeria	naira	√	X	X
Norway	Norwegian krone	√	√	√
Oman	rial Omani	√	X	X
Pakistan	Pakistan rupee	√	X	X
Peru	sol	X	X	X
Philippines	Philippine peso	sellers only	X	X
Portugal	escudo	√	√	√

	Currency unit	London spot market	London forward market	Local forward market
Qatar	Qatari riyal	√	√	√
Rwanda	Rwanda franc	X	X	X
Saudi Arabia	Saudi riyal	√	√	√
Sierra Leone	leone	√	X	X
Singapore	Singapore dollar	√	√	√
South Africa	rand	√	√	√
Spain	peseta	√	√	√
Surinam	Surinam guilder	sellers only	X	X
Sri Lanka	Sri Lankan rupee	√	X	X
Sweden	Swedish krona	√	√	√
Switzerland	Swiss franc	√	√	√
Taiwan	Taiwan dollar	X	X	X
Tanzania	Tanzanian shilling	√	X	X
Thailand	baht	sellers only	X	X
Trinidad & Tobago	Trinidad & Tobago dollar	√	X	X
Tunisia	Tunisian dinar	sellers only	X	X
Turkey	Turkish lira	X	X	X
Uganda	Ugandan shilling	√	X	X
United Arab Emirates	UAE dirham	√	√	√
United Kingdom	pound sterling	√	√	√
Uruguay	Uruguay peso	sellers only	X	X
USA	US dollar	√	√	√
West Germany	Deutsche Mark	√	√	√
Zaire	zaire	X	X	X
Zambia	kwacha	√	X	X
Zimbabwe	Zimbabwe dollar	X	X	X

Key: √ = available
      X = not available

Note: The availability of forward markets varies from time to time.

16

Financial Futures and Foreign Exchange

This chapter on financial futures may appear a little difficult upon first reading. The topic itself is complicated. It is suggested that readers make their way carefully through it, though; light dawns later on. However, re-reading may be necessary.[1]

A financial futures contract is an agreement to buy or sell a standard quantity of a specific financial instrument at a future date and at a price agreed between the parties through open outcry on the floor of an organised financial futures exchange. With respect to standard quantity, each contract for a given type of financial instrument is for the same standard quantity, for example $100,000. The term 'specific financial instrument' implies that the contract specification lays down not only the type of financial instrument, for example a 20-year gilt-edged stock or a foreign currency, but also its quality in terms of such factors as coupon rate and maturity. With respect to future date, the delivery of the amounts specified in the contract must take place on one of four specified dates in the forthcoming year. The vast majority of financial futures deals are reversed before delivery date – thus most purchase deals are reversed by matching sale deals, thereby avoiding the need for delivery physically to be effected. Standardisation as to quantity and type of instrument enables easy transferability of futures contracts to be achieved. Financial futures contracts are negotiable via the financial futures network.

Someone who buys an interest rate future has the right and obligation to deposit money to the nominal amount contracted for at a specified rate for a specified period with the seller. Someone who sells an interest rate future makes himself available to take a deposit amounting to the nominal amount contracted at a specific rate of interest for a specific period of time.

Trading in financial futures markets is by open outcry as opposed to by

---

1. A good basic understanding of financial futures can be reinforced by reference to the LIFFE publication, *An Introduction to the London International Financial Futures Exchange*. Also recommended for a good overview on financial futures and currency options is John Heywood (1984) *Using the Futures, Forwards and Options Markets*, Adam & Charles Black.

telephone or telex which is the usual means in the forward markets. A principal may give instructions to his broker by telephone but the broker will effect the deal for his client on the financial futures floor (or pit, as it is called). Users transact business only through authorised brokers who receive a commission.

A Clearing House exists to ease the funds flow from the execution of contracts. In financial futures trading, the Clearing House evolved to assume the credit risk in futures transactions by guaranteeing the performance of buyer and seller to each other.

Whilst all financial futures transactions must have a buyer and seller, their obligation is not to each other but to a Clearing House. After a transaction is recorded, the Clearing House substitutes itself for the other party and becomes the seller to every buyer and the buyer to every seller. In this way the Clearing House achieves its primary objective which is to guarantee the performance of every transaction done on the floor of the financial futures exchange. Trading on margin is a feature of financial futures. Only a small fraction, called the initial margin, of the underlying instrument's value has to be placed by the parties as a surety for their performance. This amount varies according to the contract which is being dealt in, but it is typically between 1 per cent and 5 per cent of the instrument's value. Clearly this produces gearing which may be attractive to market operators. Gearing acts to the advantage of the operator in terms of magnifying his gains when markets are moving in his favour. But the reverse holds when markets move against the operator. Margin positions are revised daily, accounts are debited or credited according to movements and margin calls are made to cover accrued losses to top up subsequent margin to the required level.

The essential differences between the mechanics of financial futures and forward foreign exchange transactions are summarised in Table 16.1.

Financial futures markets are currently recording deals at the rate of some $38 billion a day in the USA. The main rationale for their existence and growth lies in the need for protection against adverse movements in interest rates which have experienced increasing volatility since the middle sixties. This volatility has greatly magnified the financial risks to which businesses are exposed. Interest rate futures were the first kind of financial future contract.

Financial futures perform three broad economic functions. They transfer risk from a hedger to a speculator who seeks to profit from his expectations of future price movements. Second, financial futures provide a convenient hedging mechanism for banks and other financial institutions relative to alternative hedging media. A bank may wish to hedge a maturity mismatch between customer deposits received and loans made. This mismatch arises because the maturity of deposits differs from the maturity of loans. The bank could enter the interbank deposit market and contract for matching placements. This simply involves borrowing and lending with other banks in order to iron out the mismatch. Alternatively, the bank might seek a forward/forward loan or deposit (this is a fixed loan or deposit beginning at a future date) to hedge the mismatch. But there is no ongoing deep market in forward/forwards suitable for hedging a continually changing asset/liability structure, and in any case bid/offer spreads are wider than for normal interbank dealings. Financial futures contracts solve these problems and they are accounted for off balance sheet, they are traded competitively and their credit risk is assumed by the Clearing House. By purchasing or selling a particular

Table 16.1 Comparison of Forward and Futures Markets in Foreign Exchange

	Financial futures	*Forward markets*
Location	Future exchanges	Banks and other traders – no single location
Trading medium	Open outcry	Telephone/telex
Contract size	Standardised	As required by customer
Maturity/delivery date	Standardised	As required by customer
Counterparty	Clearing House	Known bank or other trader
Credit risk	Clearing House	Individual counterparty
Commissions	Always payable. Flat rate for small deals; otherwise negotiable.	Negotiable or implied in dealer's spread when no specific commission is payable.
Security	Margin required	Counterparty credit risk. Banks set this against credit limits according to their own house rules.
Liquidity	Provided by margin payments	Provided by credit limits
Leverage	Very high	No formal gearing. But since payment is not required until delivery, although credit limits are used, effectively gearing may be achieved.
Settlement	Via Clearing House	Via arrangements with banks

type of contract, the bank may effectively agree to deposit or take deposit of money for a specified period in the future. By this means, ironing out of maturity mismatch can be achieved. Third, the futures market in interest rates creates an expression of expectations of the shape of the term structure of interest rates derived from a much wider spectrum of financial operators than those with access to traditional cash money markets. For readers unfamiliar with the concept, there is a section in Chapter 23 devoted to the Term Structure of Interest Rates.

There are two main uses of financial futures. One is hedging; the other is trading. Hedging is used to reduce the risk of loss through adverse price movements in interest rates or currency rates by taking a position in futures contracts that is equal and opposite to an existing or anticipated position in the cash market. Hedging may benefit banks, financial institutions, corporate treasurers and pension funds. As an illustration of the use of financial futures in banking, two examples are given. The first involves locking into a future lending rate and the second involves locking into a future borrowing rate. In the first example, assume that a financial manager knows that he will be receiving cash from the sale of an investment in three months' time. Rather than waiting for the prevailing interest rate at that time, he may lock into today's quoted rate by buying financial futures contracts for delivery in gilt-edged stock in three months' time. If yields decline, the price which the investor would have to pay for gilt-edged stock will be higher. And the rate at which the financial manager will place his money on deposit in three months' time will fall. However, as interest rates fall, so the price quotation (see next section on Financial Futures Quotations) of the future contract will rise and the manager can sell his contracts at a higher price than he paid. This profit will effectively offset the opportunity loss resulting from falling interest rates on the money to be deposited. The use of financial futures contracts locks the manager into rates currently prevailing and, if they were to move in the opposite direction to his expectation, there would be a loss on futures contracts offsetting the corresponding gain in the cash market. Either way he would have locked in the rate which prevailed when he bought the futures contract.

Our second example involves locking into a future borrowing rate. Managers of a company with a borrowing requirement in six months' time might consider that interest rates will rise. Thus they would sell interest rate futures contracts for delivery in six months. If rates did rise, the profit resulting from being short of the futures contract would approximately equal the additional borrowing cost.

In a similar way, financial futures provide a means of hedging for those who wish to lock in current exchange rates on future currency transactions. So foreign currency receivables and payables may be hedged via financial futures if a market exists in the foreign and home currency. In fact financial futures markets in foreign currencies exist for only a small spectrum of currencies; these are listed later in this chapter.

Financial futures may be traded by those who are willing to assume risk and wish to profit from the rises or falls they expect to occur in interest rates or exchange rates. This enables users to take a view about trends of rates without actually having to purchase or sell the underlying currency or financial instrument. They may sell short when they feel that it is likely that interest rates will rise or a currency's value will decline.

Hedgers and traders each have an important role to play in creating efficient operations in financial futures markets. Traders provide liquidity to the market enabling hedgers to buy or sell in volume without difficulty. Only a small percentage of futures contracts is held until delivery. The reason for this is that most hedgers have no further need for the hedge once they have traded out of their position in the cash market. Traders usually close their position once they have achieved their profit objectives or decided to cut their losses. A buyer closes his position by making an offsetting sale of the same contract; a seller makes an offsetting purchase.

There are two key elements of cost involved in dealing in financial futures. These are direct costs and margin costs. Members charge a negotiated commission for executing orders for a customer. Commission is charged for a round trip. This covers both the opening and the closing of a position and is normally payable either when the position is closed or when delivery takes place. This is the direct cost element.

Margin works differently. When a deal has been done, both buyer and seller have to put up margin to the Clearing House (either cash or collateral) to provide against adverse price movements of the futures contract. The minimum level of this margin, the initial margin, is set by the Clearing House and reflects the volatility of the underlying instrument. Typically, margin may range from 1 per cent to 5 per cent of the face value of the contract. As prices fluctuate daily, the value of outstanding contracts (open positions) will change. The amount of each day's gain or loss (called variation margin) is added to or subtracted from the margin account. Daily profits may be drawn by the investor. However, in order to maintain the initial margin intact, any losses have to be paid to the broker. Because the initial margin is greater than the likely daily movement of the underlying cash instruments, losses on a given day will not generally exceed the amount in a customer's margin account. If a contract is held until delivery, the buyer has to pay the seller the full value of the contract.

Financial Futures Quotations

Financial futures exchanges trade a number of contracts such as those on interest rates, currency exchange rates and stock market levels. Interest rates futures contracts cover long-term and short-term contracts, including instruments such as 90-day US treasury bills, US domestic certificates of deposit and three-month Eurodollar deposits. As an example of how such contracts are quoted, consider the London International Financial Futures Exchange (LIFFE) three-month Eurodollar deposit contract. This contract is based on three-month LIBOR. It is for a $1 million three-month deposit commencing on the second Wednesday in March, June, September or December. Dealings take place concurrently in all the different delivery months giving users a wide choice in the periods for which they can cover. The price of the contract for any futures month is determined by supply and demand for time deposits to be placed at that specified date. Prices are quoted as 100 minus the annual rate of interest on the deposit. So an interest rate of 10 per cent gives a price of 90. Should rates rise to 11.5 per cent, the price falls to 88.5. If rates fall to 8.24 per cent, the price rises to 91.76. The contract may be employed when operators expect a significant change in Eurodollar interest rates. The contract is sold in anticipation of a rise in interest rates. When rates rise the price of the contract falls, enabling the operator to close out the deal by purchasing at a lower price than that at which he originally sold. Inversely, an expected fall in rates would involve purchasing the contract because its price would subsequently rise when interest rates fell.

The minimum price movement in a contract (the last decimal place quoted by dealers) is known as a tick; for the three-month Eurodollar contract on LIFFE it is 0.01 per cent, often referred to as 1 basis point. Since this represents a 0.01 per cent per annum change in the rate of interest on a three-month Eurodollar deposit of $1 million, each tick has a value of $25 made up as follows:

$$\frac{0.01}{100.00} \times \$1,000,000 \times \frac{3 \text{ months}}{12 \text{ months}}$$

$$= \$25$$

Prices of contracts, like Eurodollar interest rates, are volatile. Since trading in the contract started on LIFFE in September 1982, the average daily change in its value has been $250, or 10 ticks. The maximum movement on any one day was $1,850; that is, 74 ticks.

Margin payments regulate dealings in LIFFE contracts. Buyers and sellers each have to place initial margins of $1,000 per Eurodollar contract with their LIFFE broker. This margin is set at a level sufficient to cover the likely maximum daily change in the value of a contract. The initial margin is held until the client closes his position by an equal and opposite transaction in the financial futures market or by arranging a deposit on the specified delivery date. Virtually all positions are closed prior to maturity. Futhermore, buyers' and sellers' accounts are debited and credited each day with changes in the value of the contracts in which they hold open positions. These debits and credits are known as variation margins. The volatility of the Eurodollar contract plus its low initial margin requirement make it a highly geared means of trading in Eurodollar rates.

The LIFFE Eurodollar contract means that traders may take positions in anticipation of changes in interest rates on deposits for different time periods. They are then trading in yield curve movements. How this is done requires a knowledge of forward/forward rates, that is, a rate of interest covering the period from one forward date to a later forward date. Although not excessively complicated, these kinds of financial futures trades are beyond the scope of this book. Interested readers are referred to the trading guidelines published by LIFFE or by the Chicago International Monetary Market.

Traders also have opportunities to arbitrage between financial futures exchanges and the underlying markets in the financial instruments themselves.

Since we are concerned in this book with foreign exchange, we now examine currency contracts traded on financial futures exchanges. For purposes of our analysis we look at the LIFFE contracts in currencies. These cover the dollar against sterling, the Deutsche Mark, the Swiss franc and the Japanese yen. Sizes and key data for LIFFE futures contracts appear in Table 16.2.

Currency Contracts

Financial futures contracts in currencies are priced in terms of the underlying exchange rate. The sterling future contract (that is, sterling against the US dollar) might be quoted one day at 1.2800 and at 1.2950 on the next day. The pricing system is similar to that in the interbank foreign exchange market. Other LIFFE currency contracts in yen, Deutsche Marks and Swiss francs are quoted in terms of the number of dollars per unit of foreign currency, that is, equivalent to the direct quote as in New York. As shown in Table 16.2, the tick value is 0.01 cents per unit of foreign currency. With this background, let us consider a simple example. A trader buys three sterling currency contracts at a price of $1.2800; he may find that within a week the position is closable at a price of $1.3300. This would yield a profit of $3,750, as calculated below:

3 contracts × 500 ticks

or

$$\$\frac{(1.3300 - 1.2800)}{0.0001} \times 2.50 \ (\$ \ \text{per tick}) \times 3 \ \text{contracts}$$

= $3,750 (total profit)

Table 16.2 Summary of LIFFE Futures Contracts – Late 1985

Contract	Unit of trading	Delivery months	Delivery date	Quotation	Minimum price movement (tick size and value)	Initial margin	Straddle margin
Twenty-year gilt interest rate	£50,000		Any business day in delivery month	Per £100 nominal	£1/32 (£15.625)	£1,000	£250
Three-month sterling interest rate	£500,000		Second Wednesday in delivery month	100 minus rate of interest	0.01 (£12.50)	£1,000	£500
US treasury bond	US $100,000		Any business day in delivery month	Per $100 par value	$1/32 ($31.25)	$1,250	Zero
Three-month Euro-dollar interest rate	US $1,000,000	March/June/Sept./Dec. for all contracts	Second Wednesday in delivery month	100 minus rate of interest	0.01 ($25)	$1,000	Zero
Sterling	£25,000		Second Wednesday in delivery month	US $ per £	0.01 cents per £ ($2.50)	$1,000	$100
Deutsche Mark	DM125,000		Second Wednesday in delivery month	US $ per DM	0.01 cents per DM ($12.50)	$1,000	$100
Swiss franc	SF125,000		Second Wednesday in delivery month	US $ per SF	0.01 cents per SF ($12.50)	$1,000	$100
Japanese yen	Y12,500,000		Second Wednesday in delivery month	US $ per Y	0.01 cents per Y ($12.50)	$1,000	$100
FT-SE 100	£25 per full index point		First business day after last trading day	FT SE 100 Index ÷ 10	0.05 (£12.50)	£750	£250

The trader always works out his overall profit or loss on an open position by multiplying the number of contracts by the number of ticks that the price has changed by the tick value. These three contracts would require initial margin of $3,000 outstanding for one week.

It should be noted that rates of initial margin quoted apply only between clearing members of LIFFE and the Clearing House. Margin arrangements for others may vary. A member may insist on being paid higher initial margins than those stated; the effect of this is to provide a cushion to cover variation margin calls and obviate the need for frequent charges or payments for small price changes on futures contracts.

It is important to note that much lower initial margins are required for what are termed straddle positions. A straddle position is defined as a simultaneous long and short position in different months of a single futures contract. A typical straddle might be to buy one September contract and sell one December contract. The initial margin on LIFFE for a pair of contracts in a straddle position is as follows:

- 3-month sterling interest rate £500
- 3-month Eurodollar zero
- 20-year gilt contract £250
- all currencies $100

The rationale for the lower level of straddle margin relative to initial margin is that the exposure on a buy/sell deal for different maturities is effectively the exposure on the period not overlapping and this should be less volatile than the absolute price changes in either month. It should be noted that the straddle rate does not apply if either contract is in its spot period; that is the period commencing seven business days prior to the first possible delivery date for the gilt contract and on the first business day of the delivery month for all other contracts.

The key factor regarding margin is to know exactly how much cash will be needed to take up the desired futures position, and to relate interest foregone on financing the deal to potential trading profits.

The financial futures markets do not claim to be superior to forward markets in terms of covering foreign exchange risk. However, they may be used to enable a company respectively to cover a receivable or payable by selling or buying the appropriate foreign currency. Clearly there are disadvantages compared with forward markets. Financial futures markets have only four delivery dates per year; deals are done for standard quantities of currency; only a small number of currencies are dealt. These difficulties mean that the financial futures markets are not the best markets for corporate treasurers who wish to avoid foreign exchange risk. But, if it is desired to overcome these difficulties, there are ways of doing so.

The problem of specific delivery dates can be overcome by trading such a number of contracts of one delivery date and such a number of contracts for another delivery date as to give a weighted average equal to the receivable or payable date. Since arbitraging between financial futures currency quotations and forward markets tends to lead to equality of quotations, it should be the case that the profit or loss on the financial futures currency contract used to cover an exposure should approximate the profit or loss accruing where cover is achieved through the forward markets. However, it is normally the case that the costs of dealing forward are significantly less than those incurred through using the financial futures markets.

Standardisation of size of financial futures contracts is a problem for the corporate treasurer seeking cover for foreign exchange exposure via financial futures. This is easily overcome by taking that number of contracts which approximates the value of the desired exposed amount – but of course this method cannot yield an exact hedge.

Although LIFFE only quotes a small number of currencies, the Chicago International Monetary Market deals the following currencies against the US dollar:

- Mexican peso
- Swiss franc
- Sterling
- Deutsche Mark
- Canadian dollar
- Japanese yen
- Dutch gilder
- French franc

It is interesting to note that, whilst no forward market in the Mexican peso exists, the Chicago International Monetary Market enables cover to be achieved. Clearly treasurers wishing to effect Mexican peso cover cannot do so in forward markets and must therefore rely on financial futures markets to hedge Mexican pesos.

The range of contracts offered is expanding all the time as new financial futures centres open. For example, the Sydney Futures Exchange deals in the Australian dollar and the New Zealand Futures Exchange quotes a New Zealand dollar contract.

The financial futures markets are much more frequently used for currency trading and speculation than for corporate covering. Trading may involve taking a plain open position in a financial futures contract. This occurs when the trader backs his opinion that exchange rates are going to move in a particular direction and when he believes that the general expectations of rates which are reflected in the current level of futures prices do not fully or even correctly discount likely events enabling a position to be taken that will show a profit should rates move in the way the trader predicts.

Furthermore, financial futures markets are appropriate to spread trading. In spread trading, the trader essentially takes a view on the relationship between two futures prices. Spread positions usually display less volatility than a pure open position. A spread is defined as the purchase of one futures instrument and the simultaneous sale of a different but related futures instrument. This differs from a straddle. It will be recalled that a straddle is a specific type of spread involving the simultaneous purchase and sale for different delivery months but in the same contract. Straddle trading involves much lower margin requirements than other types of spread. As an example of a currency straddle, consider a quotation of sterling on 26 March:

sterling June contract at $1.2825
sterling December contract at $1.3105
spread = $0.0280

If the trader expects the spread to narrow – reflecting a narrowing of interest rate differentials in Eurodollar and Eurosterling markets – the following action may be implied. He should buy the spread involving the purchase of one June contract (£25,000 at 1.2825) and the simultaneous sale of one December contract (£25,000 at 1.3105). Should the spread subsequently narrow as expected, say, by 16 April, he should close out the transaction by selling the spread; this means selling one June contract (£25,000 at, say, 1.2935) and simultaneously purchasing one December contract (£25,000 at, say, 1.3130). The profit on the one contract spread trade would be $212.50. The spread has narrowed as expected from $0.0280 to $0.0195 giving a net gain of:

$$85 \text{ ticks or } \$\frac{(0.0280 - 0.0195)}{0.0001} \times \$2.50$$

$$= \$212.50$$

Underpinning the profit on the above contract is a narrowing of interest rate differentials. Rather than doing the above deal through the currency financial future, the dealer might have been able to achieve the same result by intercontract spreading. This is a somewhat more complicated – and in the example given a less practical – type of spread trade. It involves the simultaneous purchase and sale of futures contracts written on different financial instruments, either on the same or on different financial futures exchanges. An intercontract spread on LIFFE might involve purchasing a June three-month Eurodollar interest rate contract and selling a June three-month sterling interest rate contract. Doing an intercontract spread of different exchanges might involve the simultaneous purchase of a June three-month Eurodollar interest rate contract on LIFFE and sale of a June treasury bill contract on the International Monetary Market in Chicago. Setting up spread deals of this type is complex. In this book, we have given a flavour of their means of operation. For a more detailed explanation of their mechanism, interested readers are referred to more specialised financial futures literature.

Hedging a Borrowing

One of the most useful features of hedging via financial futures concerns the rolling over of floating rate borrowings. The financial futures markets enable an investor or borrower to tie in to a fixed rate; the way in which futures may be used to achieve this with respect to a borrowing is best explained with the help of a numerical example. Suppose that it is 1 February. A borrower has a three-month Eurodollar loan of $1 million at a rate of 8 per cent per annum which is due to be rolled over on 31 May. The borrower suspects that by that date rates will have risen. By using the LIFFE three-month Eurodollar interest rate contract the borrower may cover the risk of higher interest rates. The contract is for a three-month deposit of 1 million Eurodollars beginning in March, June, September or December. Since the March contract will have matured before the 31 May rollover date, the borrower selects the June delivery month for covering. The contract is priced in the normal way by deducting the deposit interest rate from 100.00. On 1 February the interest rate is 8 per cent, giving a contract price of $92.00. The contract tick size is 0.01 cents and the value of one tick is $25. Because he is concerned that interest rates will rise, the borrower sells one June contract at $92.00. By 31 May, when the borowing is due to be rolled over, assume that Eurodollar interest rates for the month deposits have risen to 10 per cent per annum. The result of the hedge is as follows:

1 Feb. Sell one June contract at $92.00
31 May Buy one June contract at $90.00
Profit on deal = 200 ticks at $25
                        = $5,000

The profit on the financial futures deal exactly offsets the extra cost of interest amounting to $5,000 given by:

$$\text{Additional interest paid } 2\% \times \frac{3 \text{ months}}{12 \text{ months}} \times \$1,000,000$$

$$= \$5,000$$

The hedge has worked perfectly because the cash market interest rates have moved exactly in line with financial futures prices. In practice such perfect matching is rare – futures prices and cash market rates do not move exactly in line.

Summary

Financial futures markets are used for trading and hedging. Trading refers to speculation on future price movements. Financial futures hedging is used to reduce the risk of loss through adverse price movements in interest rates, currency rates or share prices by taking a position that is equal and opposite to an existing or anticipated position in the cash market. Basically, hedging allows lenders and borrowers to lock into existing interest rates, currency rates or share prices even though a lending or borrowing is not made until some time in the future.

Financial futures also provide markets for arbitrage and spreading. Additionally, although we have not considered them in this chapter, the financial futures markets trade options including currency options, and it is to this topic that we shall turn in the next chapter.

17

Currency Options

Like the previous chapter on financial futures, this one on currency options is a little complex.[1] Again, re-reading may be necessary.

Since December 1982, the Philadelphia Stock Exchange has been trading standardised foreign currency option contracts. As of late 1985, Philadelphia offers a competitive marketplace in which to buy and sell options against the US dollar on sterling, Deutsche Marks, Canadian dollars, Swiss francs, Japanese yen and French francs. Philadelphia options are traded on three-, six- and nine-month cycles.

Philadelphia was the first trading centre to deal in currency options and it remains the world market leader although it has been joined by other centres, such as the Chicago International Monetary Market, the Montreal Stock Exchange, the Amsterdam Stock Exchange and the London Stock Exchange. The International Monetary Market in Chicago trades currency options in the dollar against sterling, Deutsche Marks and Swiss francs; Montreal offers US dollar currency options against sterling, the Deutsche Mark, Swiss francs, Japanese yen and Canadian dollars; and Amsterdam deals in currency options for the dollar against sterling, Deutsche Marks, Dutch guilders and the ECU. Relative to Philadelphia's, all these centres deal in different standardised contract sizes. The range of traded currency options available seems likely to expand as more financial futures centres around the world come on stream.

Since May 1985 the London Stock Exchange has been trading a dollar/sterling option. More recently it has introduced dollar/Deutsche Mark options and it plans to expand the range of currencies traded. The London Stock Exchange options follow exactly the same rules, contract sizes, dealing-date requirements and quotation methods as those of Philadelphia. LIFFE also introduced a dollar/sterling option in London in mid-1985 but its contract size and other characteristics differ from the London and Philadelphia Stock Exchanges. However, the method of

---

1. Interested readers are referred to the May 1985 issue of *The Treasurer* on the theme of currency options. LIFFE has also published a useful guide called *Currency Futures and Options* and the London Stock Exchange has issued a booklet called *The Currency Options: Traded Options on Foreign Currencies*.

quotation and its means of operation are as described in this chapter. Here, we shall focus upon Philadelphia options. The chapter begins with a description of how currency option markets work; this is linked with a discussion of currency option terminology; this in turn is followed by a discussion relating to currency option pricing and then comes a section devoted to the use of currency options as risk-reducing instruments available to the corporate treasurer.

How Currency Option Markets Work

In this section we focus upon the way in which the Philadelphia Stock Exchange trades currency options. Philadelphia currency options are similar to options on ordinary shares. The buyer of an option cannot lose more than the cost of the option and is not subject to any margin calls. The Philadelphia Stock Exchange offers investors an organised marketplace in which to buy and sell options on sterling, Deutsche Marks, Canadian dollars, Swiss francs, Japanese yen and French francs, all against the US dollar. Options are traded on three-, six- and nine-month cycles. Currency options provide the right, but not the obligation, to buy or sell a specific currency at a specific price at any time prior to a specified date. That options give a right but not an obligation means that commercial users of the market are able to obtain insurance against an adverse movement in the exchange rate while still retaining the opportunity to benefit from a favourable exchange movement. At the same time the maximum risk to the buyer of an option is the actual cost of the option. Currency options have not been designed as a substitute for forward markets but as a new, distinct financial vehicle that offers significant opportunities and advantages to those seeking either protection or profit from changes in exchange rates.

Currency option markets, like traded options in shares, have a jargon of their own, although this language has much in common with that of traded options. Because we shall frequently use the jargon in this chapter, a short list of currency option terms and definitions follows:

American option	An option which can be exercised on any business day within the option period.
European option	An option which can only be exercised on the expiry date.
A call option	An option to purchase a stated number of units of the underlying foreign currency[1] at a specific price per unit during a specific period of time.
A put option	An option to sell a stated number of units of the underlying foreign currency[1] at a specific price per unit during a specific period of time.
Option buyer	The party who obtains the benefit under an option by paying a premium. These benefits are the right –

---

1. By 'underlying foreign currency' we refer to the currency which is not the US dollar. Thus the term 'underlying foreign currency' could refer to sterling in the context of a US dollar/sterling currency option.

but not the obligation – to buy the currency if the option is a call, or to sell the currency if the option is a put. The option buyer is known as the option holder.

Option seller	The party who has the obligation to perform if the option is exercised. He will have to sell the foreign currency at a stated price if a call is exercised, or buy the foreign currency at a stated price if a put is exercised. The option seller is also known as the option writer.
Exercise price, or exercise rate, or strike price	The price at which the option holder has the right to purchase or sell the underlying currency. Except for the French franc and Japanese yen, exercise prices are stated in US cents. Thus a DM 35 call would be an option to buy Deutsche Marks at $0.35 per Mark. Strike prices for options on the French franc are stated in tenths of a US cent. The holder of a French franc 107 call option has a right to purchase the underlying French francs at $0.107 per franc. The Japanese yen option exercise prices are stated in hundredths of a cent, so a yen 54 call entitles the holder to purchase the underlying yen at $0.0054 per yen.
Expiration months	The expiration months for options are March, June, September and December. At any given time trading is available in the nearest three of these months.
Expiration date	The last date on which an option may be exercised. For foreign currency options this is the Saturday before the third Wednesday of the expiration month.
Option premium	The option premium is the price of an option, that is, the sum of money that the buyer of an option pays when an option is purchased, or the sum that the writer of an option receives when an option is written.
Intrinsic value	The extent to which an option would currently be profitable to exercise. In the case of a call, if the spot price of the underlying currency is above the option exercise price, this is its intrinsic value. In the case of a put, if the spot price is below the option exercise price, this is its intrinsic value. Options with intrinsic value are said to be in-the-money. If the spot DM price is $0.35, a DM 32 call would have an intrinsic value of $0.03 per DM, but a DM 32 put would have no intrinsic value.
Time value	That part of the premium representing the length of the option, that is, the premium less the intrinsic value.

Notice of exercise	Notice given by an option holder to an option writer that an option is being exercised. Only an option holder may exercise an option. The option holder may exercise his option and the option writer may be assigned a notice of exercise at any time prior to expiration of the option.
Opening transaction	A purchase or sale transaction which establishes an option's position.
Closing transaction	A transaction which liquidates or offsets an existing option's position. Option holders may liquidate their positions by an offsetting sale. An option writer may liquidate his position by an offsetting purchase.
At-the-money	An option whose exercise price is the same as the spot price.
Out-of-the-money	A call whose exercise price is above the current spot price of the underlying currency, or a put option whose exercise price is below the current spot price of the underlying currency. Out-of-the-money options have no intrinsic value.
In-the-money	A call whose exercise price is below the current spot price of the underlying currency, or a put whose exercise price is above the current spot price of the underlying currency. In-the-money options have intrinsic value.

Currency option contracts are standardised. Contract sizes on Philadelphia are set out below for each currency against the US dollar:

Deutsche Marks	DM62,500
Swiss francs	SF62,500
Canadian dollars	C$50,000
Sterling	£12,500
Japanese yen	Y6,250,000
French francs	FF125,000

It is the intention that these standard sizes should apply to currency options traded on the London Stock Exchange. It was mentioned that the Amsterdam Stock Exchange adds some breadth to the range of currency options by trading a guilder/dollar contract. Delivery dates conform to Philadelphia expiration months and the contract size is $10,000.

When trading is introduced in an option with a new expiration month, the practice is for one option to be introduced with an exercise price above the current spot price and one to be introduced with an exercise price below the current spot price. As the spot price of a currency changes over time, additional options are introduced with the same expiration month but higher or lower exercise prices. The exercise price intervals are $0.01 for Deutsche Marks, Swiss francs and Canadian dollars, $0.05 for sterling, $0.0001 for Japanese yen and $0.005 for French francs. Thus, if Deutsche Mark options with a September expiration are introduced when the spot price is $0.35, exercise prices will normally be established at 34, 35 and 36. If the spot price were to change to $0.36, a new series of options having the same expiration date would be introduced with an exercise price of 37.

Prices, or premiums, for foreign exchange options are arrived at through open competition between buyers and sellers on the floor of the Philadelphia Stock Exchange. The premium quoted represents a consensus opinion of the option's current value and will comprise either or both intrinsic value and time value. Intrinsic value is the amount, if any, by which an option is currently in the money. Time value is that sum of money which buyers are willing to pay over and above any intrinsic value. Such buyers hope that, before expiration, the option will increase in value and may be sold or exchanged at a profit. If an option has no intrinsic value, its premium will be entirely a reflection of its time value.

The price or premium of an option reflects changes in the spot price of the underlying currency and the length of time remaining until expiration. Thus, with the spot DM price at $0.35, a DM 33 call with three months until expiration may command a premium of $1,600. Of this, $1,250 (given by $0.02 × DM62,500) is intrinsic value and the remaining $350 is time value. It should be borne in mind that an option is a wasting asset. Its sole value at expiration will be its intrinsic value, if any. Without intrinsic value, it will expire worthless. Thus, if the DM spot price in the previous example is still $0.35 when the DM call expires, the value of the option will be its intrinsic value of $1,250; it can no longer have time value. Of course, if the spot price had fallen by expiration to $0.33 or below, the DM 33 call option would expire as worthless. Factors influencing option premiums and their behaviour are briefly considered in the section headed Option Pricing Models.

It should be noted that option premiums are quoted in US cents per unit of the underlying currency with the exception of the Japanese yen and French franc. Thus an option premium quotation of 1.00 for a DM option is 1 cent per DM. Each option is for a standardised value of DM62,500 so the total option premium would be $625 (given by 62,500 × $0.01). An option premium quotation for the DM contract of 0.76 would represent $0.0076 per Deutsche Mark. The option premium would be $475 (given by 62,500 × $0.0076).

Similarly, if the premium quoted for an option on sterling is 8.4, the total premium amount would be $1,050 (given by 12,500 × $0.084). For a Japanese yen contract a premium quotation of 2.0 would be 2.0 one hundredths of a cent ($0.0002). The premium would thus be $1,250 (given by 6,250,000 × $0.0002). The simple arithmetic for translating these quotations into the cost per option contract should become second nature to an investor contemplating trading in options.

Currency option markets aim to provide a continuously active and liquid market in put and call options on foreign currencies. Orders to buy and sell options on foreign currencies are transmitted through brokers to the trading floor of the Exchange in the same way as transactions involving shares, but currency options, like other types of options, are investments not backed with a certificate of any sort.

We shall now outline some strategies for buying and writing options on foreign currencies. First, we shall consider a situation in which there is a profit potential in buying call options to exploit a foreign currency's strength or the dollar's weakness. A call option entitles the holder to purchase units of the foreign currency at the option price stated in US dollars. The option holder will therefore make a profit if the value of the option at expiration is greater than the premium paid to acquire the option – put another way, profit will accrue if the spot market price of the currency is above the option exercise price plus the initial option premium. As an example, assume that in March an investor pays $750 to buy a DM September 35 call and that by the expiration date in June the DM spot price has risen to 38, that is, $0.38. Since the call option with an exercise price of 35 (that is, $0.35) gives the investor the right to purchase Deutsche Marks at 3 cents below their current market value, the option is in the money by 3 cents. Thus, through selling or exercising the option, the investor will realise $1,875 ($0.03 × 62,500). This amount, less the $750 originally paid for the option, produces a profit of $1,125 over a six-month period. If the DM spot price at expiration had been $0.35 or below, the option would have expired worthless. The investor would have lost the $750 premium. But under no circumstance could his loss have exceeded the $750 paid for the option.

If the initial premium cost of a DM 35 call is $750, the following tabulation indicates the investor's profit or loss depending upon the DM spot price at the time the option expires.

DM spot at expiration	Profit or (loss)
$0.35 or below	($750)
0.36	(125)
0.37	500
0.38	1,125
0.39	1,750
0.40	2,375
0.41	3,000
0.42	3,625
0.43	4,250

The presence of high gearing for relatively low risk is evident from the above figures. The call option buyer has an unlimited profit potential, whereas his potential loss is limited to the cost of the option itself.

Of course, even when purchase of a call option is indicated, the investor seeking to profit from the currency change must still decide which call option to purchase. Options differ in the length of time remaining until expiration and in their exercise price. On a given date in April, there will be trading in Deutsche Mark options expiring in June, September and December. Assuming a DM spot price of $0.35, options may be available with exercise prices ranging from $0.33, say, to $0.37.

Options with more distant expiration months command a higher premium because they provide more time for the investor's expectations to be realised. Thus an at-the-money DM 35 call with three months to expiration may command a premium of $750. A DM 35 option with six months to expiration may be priced at $1,150, and a similar option with nine months to expiration may cost $1,500. The tendency amongst option traders is to err on the side of conservatism by allowing too much time for an expected event to occur.

In-the-money options always cost more than at-the-money options which in turn cost more than out-of-the-money options. Although the in-the-money option costs most in terms of investment it also yields the greatest profit potential for any given increase of a foreign currency against the dollar.

There is no simple answer to the question of which option to select. There is no formula for arriving at such an answer. The key thing to bear in mind is that, for a call option buyer to make a net profit at expiration, the spot currency price must be above the option exercise price by an amount greater than the premium paid for the option.

Just as call options provide profit opportunities, so put options can do the same. Thus investors expecting a particular currency to decline in value relative to the US dollar may seek to profit by the purchase of put options. These options convey the right, but not the obligation, to sell the foreign currency at an agreed price. Assume that, at a time when the DM spot price is $0.35, an investor expecting the DM to weaken relative to the US dollar pays $450 to purchase an at-the-money DM 35 put option with six months to run to expiration. Should the DM have dropped by expiration to, say, $0.32, the option may be sold or exercised at its intrinsic value of $1,875 and the investor's profit will be $1,425.

Assuming that the investor pays a premium of $450 to purchase a DM put option with an exercise price of 35, the tabulation below indicates his profit potential at various expiration spot prices:

DM spot at expiration	Profit or (loss)
$0.35 or above	($450)
0.34	175
0.33	800
0.32	1,425
0.31	2,050
0.30	2,675
0.29	3,300
0.28	3,925
0.27	4,550

Considerations involved in buying put options are the inverse of those applicable to call options. Again, an option with a long period of time until expiry normally commands a higher premium than an otherwise identical option with a short period till expiration. It is worth bearing in mind that the premium for an out-of-the-money option is low because such an option is less likely to become profitable to exercise.

Since the middle of 1985, LIFFE has been dealing in a US dollar/sterling currency option. Its standard size is £25,000 with expiry months of March, June, September and December. Like stock exchange currency options, quotation is in terms of US cents per £ with a minimum price movement of 0.01 cents per £ giving a tick size of $2.50. Exercise prices are at 5 cent intervals, for example $1.15, $1.20 and so on. Like most financial futures contracts, initial margin is required. But because of varying risk factors (see below) initial margins vary from day to day. The contract price on LIFFE currency options is payable by the buyer to the seller on exercise or expiry of the option, not on purchase. Like other financial futures contracts, positions are marked daily with the usual variation margin implications.

Like traded options on shares, it is possible to write currency options for investment income. The writer of an option is obligated, if the option is exercised, to perform according to the terms of the option contract. Thus he must sell and deliver the required number of units of the underlying currency at the option exercise price if the option is a call, or purchase the required number of units at the option exercise price if the option is a put. Investors considering writing options must remember that the holder of an option may exercise his rights under the option at any time. Of course, option writing (unless covered) involves substantial and potentially unlimited risk. The limited risk of option trading applies only to the option buyer – not to the option writer. However, the terms of an option can make option writing a potentially attractive source of profit.

There are ways in which writers of currency options can cover themselves. The detail of covering strategies is outside the scope of this book, but it is worthwhile to spend a little time on the generalities of covering option writing.

Assume that, at the time a call option is written, the pound spot rate is $1.20, the exercise price of the call option is $1.20 and the price of the call is 4 cents per dollar. A UK exporter expects to receive $100,000 in six months' time. He can guarantee a minimum rate of exchange by buying a six-month call on sterling. At the maturity of the option, if the spot rate is above $1.20, the option will logically be exercised and the $100,000 converted to sterling at $1.20 rather than at the spot rate. This guarantees that the net proceeds of the trade will be at least £83,333 minus the £3,333 paid for the call.

In this example, at the time the call is written, sterling is trading at $1.20 and the value of the call is 4 cents. If sterling were to rise to $1.22, the call premium might rise to 5 cents; if sterling were to fall to $1.18, the call premium might fall to 3 cents. So, for every 2 cents move in the spot price, there is a 1 cent move in the option value. The call is behaving like a spot position equal to half the currency on which the call is written. The ratio of the move in the call value to the move in the spot price is known as the hedge ratio or delta of the position. In our example, the delta is 0.5.

The importance of the delta is that it tells the writer of the option how much spot currency to hold in order to eliminate the risk of the option. In this example, if the writer of the option had held sterling of an amount equal to £41,667, half the face value of the call, he would not have been exposed to the change in the value of the currency option. Over a particular period, if the spot rate rose to $1.22, the call value would have risen in value by $1,000 and the spot sterling position would also have changed by the same amount offsetting the loss on the written call.

It must be stated that, as the spot price moves, so the delta may change and the spot position that is equivalent to the option changes accordingly. To construct a spot position that is equivalent to the option over its entire life, the amount of spot currency held to hedge the option must therefore change in response to the spot price. As a result, if a call is written and a spot position in delta is taken, and delta is revised frequently enough, the net position will be riskless over the entire life of the option. This forms the basis of one approach to covering for banks that write options. By following a delta strategy in the spot market, they can eliminate the risk of the option position. For more detail on this topic, interested readers may pursue some of the more specialist articles.[1] We now turn to the complexities of theoretical option pricing.

Option Pricing Models

A mathematical model for pricing stock market traded options has been developed by Black and Scholes (1973). Their model has been adapted by Garman and Kohlhagen (1983) for pricing currency options. It is perhaps worth spending a little time explaining the option or warrant pricing model developed by Black and Scholes. The assumptions in deriving their model are important. They are as follows:

1. The option can be exercised at maturity only.
2. There are no transaction costs and no taxes.
3. The risk-free rate of interest is constant for the life of the option.
4. The shares carry no cash dividends.
5. Share prices follow a random walk and the variance of the return on the share is constant over the life of the option. The variance can, for purpose of the model, be estimated using past data.

Black and Scholes developed deductively and tested empirically the following model:

$$C = SN(\text{dist } 1) - \frac{EN(\text{dist } 2)}{e^{rt}}$$

In the above formulation

C = price of the option
S = current price of the shares
E = exercise price
t = time remaining before expiration of the option, usually expressed as a proportion of a year
r = the continuously compounded riskless rate of interest
e = the base of the natural logarithm, or 2.71828
$N(\text{dist } 1)$ and $N(\text{dist } 2)$ = the value of the cumulative normal density function. This is a statistical term and is easily found from tables showing the area of the normal distribution that is a specified number of standard deviations to the left or right of the mean.
σ^2 = the variance of the continuously compounded rate of return on the share:[2]

---

1. Good general introductions appear in the supplement to the February 1985 issue of *Euromoney* which is titled 'Controlling Risk with Foreign Currency Options'.
2. Thus σ equals the standard deviation of the continuous compounded rate of return on the shares.

$$\text{dist } 1 = \frac{ln(S/E) + (r + \frac{1}{2}\sigma^2)t}{\sigma\sqrt{t}}$$

$$\text{dist } 2 = \text{dist } 1 - \sigma\sqrt{t}$$

The above formulation is complex and its derivation obviously involves mathematics beyond elementary levels. But since readers may be more interested in its application, rather than its proof, a numerical example is appended. Assume that the current share price is £2.36 and the strike price is £1.90 and that there are 22 days of the option to run to expiration. With a risk-free rate of return of 9 per cent and a variance rate of return of 16 per cent, found by contrasting the performance of the company's shares against the market, we can now find the likely value of the option according to the Black and Scholes model.

From statistical tables $N(\text{dist } 1)$ and $N(\text{dist } 2)$ can be found to be 0.990 and 0.987 respectively. The theoretical value of the option in pence can be found from the formula to be:

$$236 \times 0.990 - \frac{190 \times 0.987}{2.71828^{0.0925 \times 0.06027}}$$

This simplifies to 47 pence. The answer can easily be checked in general terms. The value of the option must be at least the difference between the stock price and the exercise price, namely 46 pence. Since the option period is short, the option premium should be near to this figure.

The Garman–Kohlhagen model for pricing currency options is an adaptation of the Black and Scholes model applied to a slightly different environment. Their model for the valuation of a currency call option at an exercise price of E is given by:

$$O = \frac{FN(\text{dist } 1) - EN(\text{dist } 2)}{e^{pt}}$$

In this case the notation (where different from Black and Scholes) is:

O = price of the currency option
F = the forward exchange rate
E = the exercise price
p = the risk-free interest rate differential (that is, domestic rate less foreign rate for comparable deposits) expressed on a continually compounded basis
σ^2 = the variance of the continuously compounded annual rate of change of the exchange rate:

$$\text{dist } 1 = \frac{ln(F/E) + (r + \frac{1}{2}\sigma^2)t}{\sigma\sqrt{t}}$$

$$\text{dist } 2 = \text{dist } 1 - \sigma\sqrt{t}$$

Although the model is still being evaluated, nowadays most banks use computer models based on formulations similar to the above for pricing currency options. Some institutions are using their own in-house formulae for valuing currency options but these are similar to the Black and Scholes or Garman and Kohlhagen models.

In our brief overview of currency option pricing models, it is now necessary to introduce another new concept. This is volatility. Consider an option held as cover – that is, for insurance purposes. The value of the option depends upon the chance that the spot price will be above or below the exercise price of the option at the maturity date. In turn, this probability depends upon the uncertainty about the spot rate at the time the option matures. The standard deviation of the distribution of possible levels of the spot rate at the maturity date describes this uncertainty – and this is what volatility is all about. There is a simple relationship between volatility over a short period and over a long period. The standard deviation over t days is equal to the square root of t times the daily standard deviation. The standard deviation over three months is equal to approximately eight times the standard deviation over 1 day, since there are about 63 trading days in a quarter and the square root of 63 is approximately 8. Table 17.1 sets out standard deviations over different time periods. All of these are equivalent to a standard deviation of 10 per cent per annum. The market has adopted the convention of always quoting volatilities on an annualised basis, just as interest rates and forward premiums are always quoted on an annual basis.

Table 17.1 Volatility over Different Time Periods

	Standard deviation
1 year	10.0%
9 months	8.7%
6 months	7.1%
3 months	5.0%
1 day	0.6%

Volatility does not increase linearly with time. Over three months there is half as much volatility as over one year. Table 17.2 illustrates why this is so. Assume that a currency rate can move up or down by 1 per cent or stay the same over a single day. The standard deviation is 0.82 per cent. Over two days the standard deviation is 1.15 per cent, equal to the square root of 2 times 0.82 per cent. The two-day moves are not twice as scattered as the one-day moves, since sometimes when the currency moves up on the first day it moves back down on the second day, and vice versa. This offsets part of the volatility contributed by the first day, resulting in the two-day standard deviation being less than twice the one-day standard deviation. Having said this, if both are annualised, they will give the same number.

Most currency options are hedged by some party. It may be that the bank writing the option takes cover; it may be that the market maker in the option market carries out the delta hedging strategy. In theory, the company could, instead of buying an option, perform these trades itself and thereby replicate the option. Potential competition from company synthesisers of their own options

Table 17.2 Volatility Over 1 and 2 Days

Over one day		Over two days	
Move	*Probability*	*Move*	*Probability*
+1%	1/3	+2%	1/9
0	1/3	+1%	2/9
−1%	1/3	0	3/9
		−1%	2/9
		−2%	1/9
Standard deviation		Standard deviation	
0.82%		1.15%	

forces prices towards the option model prices. This means that the spread of the market price over the model price is limited by the possibility of corporations and others synthesising their own options. The actual price paid by a corporation in the currency option market is likely, therefore, to be equal to the model price plus transaction costs of hedging by the option writer, plus a premium for risk of volatility changing, plus a pure profit spread.

Companies synthesising their own currency options would save on the pure profit spread. Their cost would be based upon the model price plus transactions costs of replication by the corporation, plus a premium for the risk of volatility changing.

Corporate Use of Currency Options

If a company wishes to leave open the possibility of making a currency gain on a receivable or payable whilst protecting itself against adverse movements in the exchange rate, it can do so via the currency option market. Currency options are of particular interest to the treasurer when a future currency cash flow is uncertain, as in the case of putting in a contract tender, or issuing a foreign currency price list. In the case of a tender, if the contract is not awarded, the company merely lets the currency option lapse − or, if it pays to do otherwise, it sells it on at a profit. If the company obtains the contract tendered for, it would exchange the currency option for a forward option running out to the payment dates under the contract.

But treasurers may also use currency options to hedge a contractually agreed deal in order to protect the downside exchange risk on a receivable or payable whilst leaving open the upside potential. Currency options have become particularly attractive to corporate treasurers in times when there is substantial volatility in the foreign exchange markets. In 1984 the dollar was strengthening rapidly against most currencies although many corporate treasurers felt that it was clearly overvalued in terms of purchasing power parity criteria. Given that trends in the market and purchasing power parity considerations pointed in opposite directions, it might have been an apposite time to use currency options. After the event, of course, it would have been better not to hedge dollar receivables at all, but this view only emerges with the benefit of hindsight.

A price has to be paid to secure the benefit of an option. This is the front-end non-returnable premium which the option writer receives whether or not the company exercises its option. The decision to use currency options needs to be carefully assessed by taking into account the likelihood of the currency flow taking place, the volatility of the exchange rate until the funds are received and the cost of the premium. The answer to the criticism that some treasurers make to the effect that currency options are expensive comes back loud and clear: why not write options yourself, then?

Of course, one of the major problems with currency options traded on the Philadelphia, London or Amsterdam stock exchanges is that they have specific expiration dates which will usually differ from the date up to which cover is required. Because of this there has developed an over-the-counter (OTC) market in which tailor-made options are bought and sold privately between banks and their customers. The growth of exchange-traded and OTC currency options is really complementary. The exchange-traded markets are used most frequently by banks hedging OTC positions. The OTC currency option business is largely made up of corporate activity. Increased volume in one market supports increased activity in the other. There are obvious reasons why a large volume of corporate currency option business has been channelled through the OTC rather than directly through exchange markets. First and foremost is the fact that OTC options are tailor-made to meet a company's specific needs. A company may therefore ask a bank to quote a price on a currency option which matches exactly its hedge requirements with respect to the currency to be bought and sold, the amount, the price and the time period to be covered. The option specifications of exchange-traded products are standardised so that a company's precise needs will not easily be met through this marketplace.

Corporate treasurers are also attracted by the fact that OTC transactions are operationally straightforward and are rather similar to forward foreign exchange dealing procedures. It should be noted that there is no formal secondary market in OTC currency options, which makes them less flexible than exchange-traded options. The company can only sell its OTC option back to the bank writing it, but OTC options have far greater flexibility for companies in terms of expiry dates, amounts involved and the possibility of dealing in currencies not quoted on the traded exchanges. Banks may be prepared to tailor options in a wider range of currencies than those quoted on the currency options markets. In Table 17.3 a comparison between exchange-traded and OTC options is tabulated.

The currency option market is an innovative one and a variant of the basic option contract which has been introduced is the cylinder option (McFarlane 1985). Its interest to corporate treasurers arises because in times of high volatility it enables the treasurer to lock into a narrow band in the exchange rate range. The workings of the cylinder option will become apparent with the help of a numerical example.

Assume that a UK company has a dollar receivable. The treasurer has a range of possible options in respect of the asset. He may, amongst other alternative actions:

- leave the dollars uncovered
- sell the dollars forward

Table 17.3 Exchange-Traded and OTC Options Compared

	Exchange-traded	*OTC*
Contract terms, including amounts	Standardised	Fixed to suit circumstances – terms are not standard
Expiration	Standardised	Determined by requirements of customer
Transaction method	Stock exchange-type medium	Bank-to-client or bank-to-bank
Secondary market	Continuous secondary market	No formal secondary market
Commissions	Negotiable	Negotiable but usually built into the premium
Participants	Exchange members and clients	Banks, corporations and financial institutions

- buy a sterling call option[1]
- buy a sterling option cylinder

Assume that the spot rate at the date when the treasurer is considering taking action amounts to $1.36 and that the forward rate for the maturity of the receivable is $1.35. Assume also that the premium for an option to sell dollars at $1.40 for the appropriate period is 4.50 cents. When he has been informed of the premium by his bank, the treasurer expresses the opinion that it is expensive, to which the bank replies that it will write a zero cost option. What this involves is as follows. To counter the premium payable on the $1.40 option bought, the client writes an option to sell dollars to the bank at $1.30 with a premium of 4.50 cents payable by the bank to the client. The two premia set off against each other giving rise to the zero cost. If the client takes the zero cost option he will be in a position to:

- carry the profit or loss himself for exchange rate movements between $1.30 and $1.40. If the rate moves to $1.32 on maturity the client takes the profit from the dollar strengthening from $1.36 to $1.32. Should the maturity rate be $1.38, the client takes the loss.
- limit profit or loss for himself should the exchange rate on maturity move outside the cylinder $1.40 to $1.30. So should the rate or maturity go to $1.42, the client bears a limited loss based on $1.40 less $1.36 and the bank bears the remainder of the loss, from $1.42 to $1.40. In a reverse direction, if the rate on maturity is $1.26, the client makes a gain based on $1.36 less

---

1. Note that he buys the call option. This may appear to be counter-intuitive to the beginner in currency options. The treasurer wishes to sell dollars and buy pounds. When buying pounds via a currency option, the action implied is to buy a sterling call. Similarly, for a financial futures hedge, the treasurer with a dollar receivable would buy sterling futures contracts.

$1.30 and the bank takes the remaining profit based on the dollar strengthening from $1.30 to $1.26.

Effectively, the cylinder option in the example provides the treasurer with total cover against the dollar weakening beyond $1.40 and gives a gain to the company from the dollar strengthening to $1.30; but the company limits its gain should the dollar strengthen beyond $1.30.

Ignoring interest rate considerations, Table 17.4 shows comparative results from leaving the dollars uncovered versus taking forward cover, versus buying a sterling option cylinder. Gains and losses shown in the table are in US cents against a base rate of $1.36. What the option cylinder hedge does is allow the corporate treasurer to fix an exchange rate within a narrow band for a nil net front-end premium. This is achieved by the treasurer writing an option in the opposite direction to that in which he desires cover. The rate at which the option is written is such that its premium is equal to the premium on the option to be bought or sold to give cover for the receivable or payable.

Table 17.4 Comparative Results of Option Cylinder (Data as Given in Text)

Maturity exchange rate	Dollar uncovered Gain (+) or loss (−)*	Forward sale Profit foregone (−) or loss saved (+)*	Buy sterling cylinder option Gain (+) or loss (−)*
1.42	−6	+7	−4
1.41	−5	+6	−4
1.40	−4	+5	−4
1.39	−3	+4	−3
1.38	−2	+3	−2
1.37	−1	+2	−1
1.36	0	+1	0
1.35	+1	0	+1
1.34	+2	−1	+2
1.33	+3	−2	+3
1.32	+4	−3	+4
1.31	+5	−4	+5
1.30	+6	−5	+6
1.29	+7	−6	+6
1.28	+8	−7	+6

Note: *Gains and losses shown in US cents versus spot of $1.36.

Summary

Currency options provide the right, but not the obligation, to buy or sell a specific currency at a specific price at any time prior to a specified date. That options give a right but not an obligation means that commercial users of the market are able to obtain insurance against an adverse movement in the exchange rate while still retaining the opportunity to benefit from a favourable exchange movement. At the same time the maximum risk to the buyer of an option is the actual cost of the option. Currency options have not been designed as a substitute for forward markets but as a new, distinct financial vehicle that offers significant opportunities and advantages to those seeking either protection or profit from changes in exchange rates.

Currency options come in two forms. There are traded currency options which are like traded options on shares and are for a standardised capital amount and have standardised delivery, or maturity, dates. There are also 'over the counter' options which are tailored by banks for their clients' individual requirements as to amount and maturity.

If a company wishes to leave open the possibility of making a currency gain on a receivable or payable, whilst protecting itself against adverse movements in the exchange rate, it can do so via the currency option market. Currency options are of particular interest to the treasurer when a future currency cash flow is uncertain, as in the case of putting in a contract tender. If the contract is not awarded, the company merely lets the currency option lapse – or, if it pays to do otherwise, it sells it on at a profit. If the company obtains the contract tendered for, it will exchange the currency option for a forward option running out to the payment dates under the contract.

Treasurers may also use currency options to hedge a contractually agreed deal to protect the downside exchange risk on a receivable or payable, whilst leaving open the upside potential. Currency options have become particularly attractive to corporate treasurers in times when there is substantial volatility in the foreign exchange markets. Currency options also provide an easy way for a company to take positions and to speculate in foreign currency.

References

Black, Fisher and Scholes, Myron (1973) 'The pricing of options and corporate liabilities', *Journal of Political Economy*, vol. 81, May/June, pp. 637–654.

Garman, Mark B. and Kohlhagen, Steven W. (1983) 'Foreign currency option values', *Journal of International Money and Finance*, vol. 2, pp. 231–237.

McFarlane, John (1985) 'Cylinder options reduce hedging cost', *The Accountant*, 23 October, pp. 12–13.

18

Financing International Trade and Minimising Credit Risk

Two problem areas dominate the financing of international trade; these concern foreign exchange risk and credit risk. The former topic is wide-ranging and is considered in detail in various sections of this book. This chapter focuses upon credit risk, that is, the risk that one may not be paid for goods or services supplied. Its complexities in an international arena arise because of the difficulties of taking repossession of goods following non-payment when they are outside the country of the supplier.

Before goods are shipped, the importer and exporter agree the terms of a transaction including price, insurance, freight, dates of shipment and so on. The banking system provides several methods of making or receiving payment in international trade. Choice of payment method usually lies between a number of alternatives including cash with order, or open account, or using bills of exchange, or documentary letters of credit, or drawing upon government assistance schemes. These alternatives are not mutually exclusive. For example, bills of exchange and letters of credit are often used as part of a package with government assistance as well. In this chapter we consider each of the five above methods of financing international trade. But it must be borne in mind that this whole topic is a broad one and the coverage here can only be superficial. Readers dealing with the topics of financing international trade and minimising credit risk in the real world would be advised to obtain advice from a banker or other specialist.

Cash with Order

From the standpoint of the exporter, this is the most desirable payment method. But in international trade it is the least used since some credit period is generally given to the importer. If the seller receives cash with order (CWO), he has possession of both the money and the goods for a limited period.

Cash with order is unattractive to the purchaser since he bears the whole burden of financing the shipment. He loses the use of funds for a significant time period, forcing him to finance working capital and to lose interest on funds.

Cash with order often has a stigma associated with it – namely, that the purchaser is less than credit-worthy. When it is used the buyer loses control of the situation. He is at the mercy of the supplier in terms of his honesty, solvency and ability to deliver goods promptly. The purchaser also has to be certain that the seller's country will not prohibit – for various reasons – the export of the goods concerned. Cash with order clearly creates risks for the buyer.

In international trade, cash with order is used where the importer is of doubtful credit standing and where the exporter is competitively very strong. This form of payment is extremely rare in exporting. It clearly involves an overseas buyer in extending credit to an exporter – the opposite procedure is the normal method of trade.

A variation of this form of payment is cash on delivery (COD). This is used for small-value goods which are sent via Post Office parcel post and are released only after payment of the invoice plus COD charges.

Open Account

Under this method of financing, exporter and importer agree that the account will be settled at a predetermined date. In the meantime, goods and shipping documents are sent to the buyer so that he may receive the goods and use them as he wishes. Open account has risks for the exporter since no documentary evidence of ownership or obligation is usually available. Differences of law and custom in various countries make it difficult to safeguard the interests of the exporter who loses control of the goods. If payment is not forthcoming, the exporter is in a weak position.

Using open account means that financing falls upon the exporter. The exporter needs enhanced working capital levels and loses interest on funds. Open account trading is used in international trade where there is a trusted business relationship between the parties and where the importer is of undoubted credit-worthiness.

Payment of indebtedness under open account may be made by telegraphic transfer, mail transfer, cheque or banker's draft. Telegraphic transfer involves an instruction from the importer's bank to the exporter's bank to transfer some funds on the importer's account to the exporter's credit. The importer has to pay his own bank the local currency equivalent to meet the amount of the invoice. The invoice may be expressed in the currency of either the exporter or importer or any other currency. Mail transfer payment involves the same process except that the payment from the importer is mailed by the importer's bank to the exporter's bank and is therefore a slower means of payment. Payment by cheque simply involves the importer in mailing his cheque to the exporter. Finally, payment under banker's draft involves the importer obtaining a banker's draft from his bank and sending it to the exporter's bank. It should be noted that under telegraphic transfer and mail transfer, cleared funds are released to the exporter. Cheque and banker's draft require collection and clearing and this can take time.

Thus, whilst an exporter receives the greatest security from cash with order or cash on delivery, open account is at the other extreme and it offers the least security to the exporter. The open account method of payment is increasingly popular within the EEC because it is simple and straightforward. 70 per cent of UK exports within the EEC are paid for under open account terms. It saves money and procedural difficulties but its risk to the exporter is obviously greater. It is only used when an exporter trusts the business integrity and ability of an overseas buyer, something that has probably been established through a sustained period of trading between many businesses within the EEC.

A variation of open account payment is the consignment account where an exporter supplies an overseas buyer in order that stocks may be built up in quantities sufficient to cover continued demand. The exporter retains ownership of the goods until they are sold, or for an agreed period, after which the buyer remits the agreed price to the exporter.

However, a large proportion of export contracts cannot be settled by payment in advance or by open account: this is particularly so for sales outside the EEC. So the trading community throughout the world has developed methods of payment which involve the transfer of documents for exported goods using the international banking system – with the aim of speedily settling export transactions at minimum risk to exporters and to overseas buyers.

Bills of Exchange

In our analysis, the third method of making payment in international trade is the bill of exchange. A bill of exchange is defined in UK law (Bills of Exchange Act 1882) as an unconditional order in writing addressed by one person to another, signed by the person giving it, requiring the person to whom it is addressed to pay on demand or at a fixed or determinable future time a sum certain in money to, or to the order of, a specified person, or to bearer.

An exporter can send a bill of exchange for the value of goods through the banking system for payment by an overseas buyer on presentation. Typically an exporter prepares a bill of exchange (which resembles a cheque; indeed a cheque is defined by the Bills of Exchange Act 1882 as a bill of exchange drawn on a banker, payable on demand) which is drawn on an overseas importer, or on a third party designated in the export contract, for the sum agreed as settlement (see Table 18.1 for an example of a bill of exchange).

The bill is called a sight draft if it is made out payable at sight, that is, on demand. If it is payable at a fixed or determinable future time, it is called a term draft, since the buyer is receiving a period of credit, known as the tenor of the bill. The buyer signifies an agreement to pay on the due date by writing an acceptance across the face of the bill.

By using a bill of exchange with other shipping documents through the banking system, an exporter can ensure greater control of the goods, because until the bill is paid or accepted by the overseas buyer, the goods cannot be released. Also, the buyer does not have to pay or agree to pay until delivery of the goods from the exporter.

An exporter can pass a bill of exchange to a bank in the UK. The UK bank forwards the bill to its overseas branch or to a correspondent bank in an overseas buyer's country. This bank, known as the collecting bank, presents the bill to whoever it is drawn upon, for immediate payment if it is a sight draft, or for acceptance if it is a term draft. This procedure is known as a clean bill collection because there are no shipping documents required. Clean bill collections have become more popular, particularly in European countries where the method is also used in internal trade. Such collections provide more security than open account terms if there is some doubt about a buyer's financial status.

Table 18.1 Example of a Bill of Exchange

No. *45/1.* Date *30ᵗʰ October 1984.* For *£2000*

At *sight* pay this *first* of Exchange

to the order of *ourselves*

Two thousand pounds only.

Value *in merchandise shipped to South Africa as per invoice*

number 84/69/2 which place to account

To: *Delany Capetown (Pty) Ltd.* For and on behalf of
Paarl Street *Jacksons Export (UK) Ltd.*
Rondebosch
Capetown
South Africa

However, it is more likely that bills are used in a documentary bill collection method of payment. In this case, an exporter sends the bill to the buyer by way of the banking system with the shipping documents, including the document of title to the goods, usually an original bill of lading. The bank only releases the documents on payment or acceptance of the bill by the overseas buyer.

An exporter may even use the banking system for a cash against documents (CAD) collection. In this case only the shipping documents are sent and the exporter instructs the bank to release them only after payment by the overseas buyer. This method is used in some European countries whose buyers prefer CAD to a sight draft if the exporter insists on a documentary collection for settlement of the export contract.

In all the methods of payment using a bill of exchange, a promissory note can be used as an alternative. This is issued by a buyer who promises to pay an exporter a certain amount of money within a specified time. It is also possible to send the documents and bill of exchange directly to an overseas buyer's bank thus by-passing the UK bank. This system of direct collection is widely supported by US banks.

In order to make clear what procedures an exporter wants from a particular collection and what action should be taken if an overseas buyer does not meet the payment terms of the contract, most UK banks ask exporters to fill out a bank lodgement form. This is a checklist which ensures that all the instructions are remembered in order to make a successful collection.

As an illustration of how bills of exchange work, Kahler and Kramer (1977) give the following example of a US exporter and a UK importer using a sixty-day sight draft:

1. The American exporter makes shipment to a British importer with the billing made out to the name of the exporter.
2. The exporter delivers the draft and shipping documents to the American bank which sends the draft and shipping documents to the British bank.
3. The British bank notifies the importer that the documents have arrived and presents the draft to the importer for acceptance, payment in 60 days.
4. Upon accepting the bill of exchange, the shipping documents are surrendered to the importer and the shipment can now be claimed.
5. The accepted bill of exchange is returned to the American bank by the British bank.
6. The exporter discounts the draft and receives advance payment.
7. The American bank, in turn, disposes of the bill of exchange in the acceptance market.
8. Upon receiving such funds, the American bank is now in a liquid position again.
9. When the 60-day maturity approaches, the bill of exchange is sent to the British bank by some financial institution that had purchased it from the American bank.
10. The British bank receives payment from the British importer in pounds sterling and the conversion of sterling to dollars is made by the British bank.
11. The funds are transmitted to the present holder of the trade acceptance.
12. The American exporter settles with the American bank to complete the transaction.

Kahler and Kramer summarise their example in a schematic form, as shown in Figure 18.1.

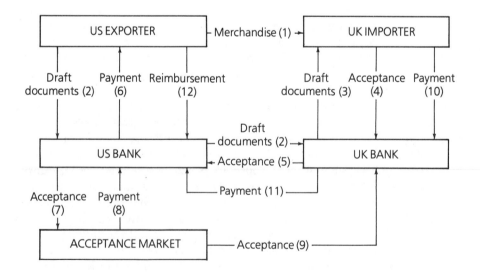

Figure 18.1   Example of International Trade Financing Under a Sixty-Day Sight Draft

Given that title documents may only be released upon payment, the exporter's position is superior to that achieved with open account exporting. Bills of exchange also have the advantage of being cheaper than documentary credits and they open further arenas for financing. Bills of exchange may be discounted by negotiation. This means that a bank buys its customer's outward collection (that is, the foreign currency proceeds of an export) at the time that the collection is remitted abroad. This provides the exporter with short-term funds. Banks may also give an advance against an outward collection of bills of exchange.

Exporters of substantial credit-worthiness may also use a merchant bank acceptance facility. Under this financing mechanism documentary drafts drawn by the exporter on the overseas buyer become security and are handled as documentary collections by the merchant bank. These documents are pledged to the merchant bank. The exporter draws a draft on the bank and, after acceptance by the bank, the draft, now known as an accommodation bill, is discounted, usually with a discount house, and the proceeds are paid to the exporter.

Using bills of exchange offers less security to the exporter than obtaining cash with order or using letters of credit. Bills of exchange provide the importer with a period of credit and he can be sure that the goods are what he ordered before he authorises payment. Transacting international trade via bills of exchange reduces the risk of non-payment. Although more expensive than cash with order and open account, bills of exchange are cheaper than trading via letters of credit.

Documentary Letters of Credit

A documentary letter of credit is a credit under which drawings are honoured, provided the beneficiary delivers the documents evidencing shipment of the goods ordered. With a documentary letter of credit, exporters are able to receive payment for goods in their own country once shipment has taken place. At the same time, the buyer is secure in the knowledge that payment will not have been made unless the terms and conditions of the credit have been met. With the security of the documentary credit, the exporter is able to produce goods knowing that he will receive payment promptly. At the same time the importer is as sure as he can be that he will receive the goods when they are required.

The first contractual step in an export transaction is the sale contract. If it is agreed as part of the contract that a documentary credit is to be used for payment of the goods, the buyer will make arrangements with his bank for its issue. The onus of drawing up the letter of credit lies with the importer. He gives his bank detailed instructions about the description of the goods, their quality and price, the total value of the credit, the documents required, the dates between which documents may be presented for payment and any special provisions which may have been agreed between purchaser and seller. These terms and conditions will be contained in the advice of issue of the documentary credit sent to the seller, who is technically referred to as the beneficiary. The documentary credit is separate from the sales contract. As such the beneficiary checks that the terms comply with those agreed in the sale contract. If they differ, the beneficiary contacts the buyer – technically known as the taker – and requests that he instruct his banker to issue an amendment to the credit.

Banks advise the beneficiary that a credit has been opened in his favour in one of three ways. They may advise him direct, indicating a bank in his country where he may obtain payment against the documents. Second, they may address the advice of opening to the beneficiary and send it to their branch or correspondent for onward transmission. Third, they may address it to their branch or correspondent in the beneficiary's country and request that he should be notified.

Letters of credit are of various types. The most frequently encountered are revocable, irrevocable and confirmed irrevocable credits. The differences between revocable and irrevocable credits are important.

A revocable credit may be amended or cancelled at any time without prior notice to the beneficiary. However, the issuing bank is bound to reimburse a branch or other bank to which such a credit has been transmitted and made available for payment, acceptance or negotiation, for any payment, acceptance or negotiation complying with the terms and conditions of the credit and any amendments received up to the time of the payment, acceptance or negotiation made by such branch or other bank prior to receipt by it of notice of amendment or cancellation.

An irrevocable credit constitutes a definite undertaking of the issuing bank – provided that the terms and conditions of the credit are complied with –

- to pay, or that payment will be made, if the credit provides for payment, whether against a draft or not;
- to accept drafts if the credit provides for acceptance by the payment at maturity if the credit provides for the acceptance of drafts drawn on the bank for the credit or any other drawee specified in the credit;
- to purchase/negotiate, without recourse to drawers and/or bona fide holders, drafts drawn by the beneficiary at sight or at a tenor on the applicant for the credit or on any other drawee specified in the credit, or to provide for purchase/negotiation by another bank, if the credit provides for purchase/negotiation.

A revocable credit is not a legally binding undertaking between the bank or banks concerned and the beneficiary, since it may be modified or cancelled at any time, without the beneficiary being notified, though payment made before receipt of a modification or cancellation remains valid. Thus it is never a confirmed credit.

An irrevocable credit may not be modified or cancelled without the consent of all the parties concerned.

The beneficiary of a credit may not know the standing of the opening bank. If the opening bank becomes bankrupt after the beneficiary's bank has negotiated the credit, but before it has been reimbursed, his bank has recourse to him. As a precaution, the beneficiary can ask his bank to confirm the credit for a fee, provided the bank is satisifed about the standing of the opening bank. Once confirmed, the confirming bank has no recourse to the beneficiary after negotiation of the credit. This constitutes a confirmed irrevocable documentary letter of credit.

After the beneficiary has received the documentary credit in the form he requires, and the goods are available for shipment, arrangements are made via an agent to draw up the documents. The agent receives a copy of the credit enabling him to ensure that the documents are prepared in accordance with it. After the goods have been shipped, the beneficiary delivers all the documents to his bank, with the credit. The bank compares the documents with the credit. If satisfied that they are in order, it pays the beneficiary.

When an exporter has negotiated in the contract with a buyer for a confirmed irrevocable letter of credit then security of payment, as far as humanly possible, is achieved.

Whether or not the credit is confirmed, it is essential that the exporter check the credit terms immediately to make sure that they are compatible with the sales contract made with the buyer. In dealing with documentary credits the bank is concerned only with the documents to be presented and not with the goods or services involved. Documentary credits may provide for payment at sight or for acceptance of a term bill of exchange by either the issuing bank in a buyer's country or the correspondent bank in the UK. A schematic representation of the typical series of steps involved in trading under a documentary credit is set out in Figure 18.2.

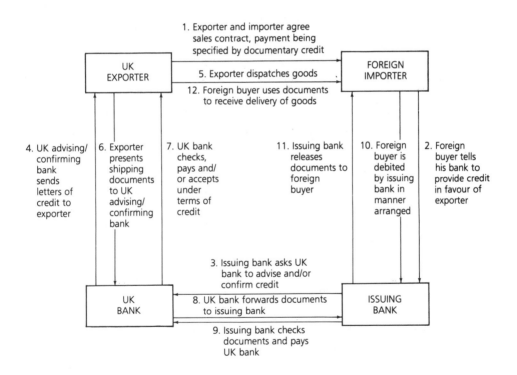

Figure 18.2 Documentary Credit Trading

Under a letter of credit transaction, the onus of financing falls squarely upon the buyer. The main benefit derived by the importer is the protection of a definite date by which the seller is required to ship goods. The buyer therefore expects prompt delivery. Also, the buyer may expect to receive lower prices when a letter of credit is submitted, since difficulties are so fully safeguarded that the exporter finds it unnecessary to cover them in the price. Advance orders, or orders running throughout a period of time, are well protected by the expiration date of the letter of credit, as well as by the limit of the sum of money for which it is drawn. Attractive discounts are frequently offered to importers for providing letter of credit payment.

Letters of credit are of great benefit when the parties involved are relatively unknown to each other, or where one of the parties is in a country where political risk of non-payment is high.

Over recent years, an increasing portion of world trade has been conducted between multinationals and their subsidiaries and associates or between well-established trading partners. In these cases the risk of default is greatly reduced and trading on open account has reasserted itself.

Letters of credit do have drawbacks and there are popular alternatives. For example, a small importer wishing to open a letter of credit may be called upon by his bank to provide partial − or even full − cash cover. The cash flow impact of this may be so acute as to force the importer to find other ways of arranging payment. This may be via a confirming house or an international credit union which arranges extended payment terms. Exporters are usually happy to deal with the confirming house, which makes payment on behalf of the importer, without the security of a letter of credit. Exporters can also improve cash flows by selling their debt books to a factoring house. Factoring houses give the seller credit insurance by taking over his invoices as the goods are supplied and provide cash − either immediately or at some agreed future date − for up to three quarters of the invoice value less various incidental charges.

Credit risk is at a maximum for the exporter when dealing on open account. Credit risk is minimised with an irrevocable confirmed letter of credit.

Before entering the arena of trading via documentary credit, it is worth noting that well over 50 per cent of the sets of documents lodged under letters of credit are rejected by banks upon first presentation because they are either incomplete or incorrect. Delays or refusals to pay inevitably ensue. The main reasons for this are that:

- the letter of credit has expired
- the documents are presented after the period stipulated in the letter of credit
- the shipment is late

But there are many other reasons. These are summarised in Appendix 18.1 at the end of this chapter. So important is it that documentation in letters of credit be complete that a checklist of fundamental areas to be covered is given in Appendix 18.2.

Government Assistance Schemes

Most countries operate a system of credit insurance through government agencies like the Export Credit Guarantee Department (ECGD) in the United Kingdom. The overall services of these departments vary from one country's agency to another's and for precise details it is necessary to refer to their booklets of services rendered. In the remainder of this chapter we concentrate upon ECGD's services in the export credit field.

ECGD insures exporters against the risk of not being paid, whether this results from the default of the purchaser or through other causes. It also offers unconditional guarantees of 100 per cent repayment to banks, thus creating security for banks to provide finance to exporters at favourable interest rates. ECGD insures new investment overseas against the risks of war, expropriation and the imposition of restrictions on remittance. It also provides protection against part of the increases in UK costs for large contracts with long manufacturing periods. For major contracts it supports the issue of performance bonds, and for members of a UK consortium it provides protection against losses arising through the insolvency of a member of the consortium.

ECGD classifies export trade into two categories. There is trade of a repetitive type, involving standard, or near standard, goods. Credit risk cover on these is provided on a comprehensive basis. The exporter must offer for cover all or most of his export business for at least one year in both good and bad markets. Second, there are projects and large capital goods deals of a non-repetitive nature, usually of high value and involving lengthy credit periods. This business is not suited to comprehensive treatment and specific policies are negotiated for each contract. Cover for this specific insurance is given in one of two ways. With a supplier credit, the manufacturer sells on deferred payment terms, borrowing from a UK bank to finance the period from shipment until payment is received. ECGD insures the exporter and often gives a guarantee direct to the bank. With a buyer credit, the exporter receives prompt payment from his buyer, who draws on a loan from a UK bank to provide this payment. The loan is repaid in instalments and ECGD guarantees the bank repayment by the overseas customer.

In the area of supplier credit, ECGD's comprehensive short-term guarantee provides an insurance on sales with credit periods of up to six months. The risks covered embrace:

1. insolvency of the buyer;
2. the buyer's failure to pay within six months of due date for goods which he has accepted;
3. the buyer's failure to take up goods which have been despatched to him (where not caused or excused by the policy holder's actions, and where ECGD decides that the institution or constitution of legal proceedings against the buyer would serve no useful purpose);
4. a general moratorium on external debt decreed by the government of the buyer's country or of a third country through which payment must be made;
5. any other action by the government of the buyer's country which prevents performance of the contract in whole or in part;
6. political events, economic difficulties, legislative or administrative measures arising outside the UK which prevent or delay the transfer of payments or deposits made in respect of the contract;
7. legal discharge of a debt (not being legal discharge under the proper law of the contract) in a foreign currency, which results in a shortfall at the date of transfer;

8. war and certain other events preventing performance of the contract provided that the event is not one normally insured with commercial insurers;
9. cancellation or non-renewal of a UK export licence or the prohibition or restriction on export of goods from the UK by law (ICC Series 1975).

ECGD covers 90 per cent of the loss where it arises through the first two categories of risk. With the third, the exporter bears the first 20 per cent of the original price, and ECGD bears 90 per cent of the remainder. For the other risks, ECGD covers 95 per cent of the loss, except where the loss arises before the goods are despatched overseas. Here the loss is limited to 90 per cent.

Under comprehensive policies, the exporter offers for insurance a broad spread of business to be transacted over a future period. But transactions involving large projects or contracts are negotiated individually between the exporter and ECGD. This gives rise to a specific guarantee where cover runs from either the date of contract or the date of shipment. Risks covered are similar to those covered under the comprehensive policies, except that the top percentage of cover remains at 90 per cent.

ECGD also offers guarantees for supplier credit financing. Here the credit period must be less than two years from the date of export of goods or completion of services and the buyer gives a promissory note or accepts a bill of exchange. ECGD may give an unconditional guarantee to the exporter's bank that it will pay 100 per cent of any sum three months overdue. ECGD agrees a limit for the finance it will guarantee based on experience and the exporter's financial standing. Operationally, the exporter presents the notes or bills to his bank after shipment of the goods with the appropriate documentary evidence and a standard form of warranty that his ECGD cover for the transaction is in order.

British banks have agreed to finance 100 per cent of the value of such transactions and charge interest at a very small spread over base rate. The exporter signs a recourse undertaking giving ECGD the right to recover from him should the bank claim sums due in advance of, or in excess of, claims payable under the standard policy. All classes of UK exports qualify for this facility.

With exports ranging from cash against documents to six-month credit, ECGD guarantees a straight loan from the bank to the exporter in respect of the export transaction and it guarantees 100 per cent of the bank loan.

A further area through which ECGD picks up credit risk is effectively via buyer credit financing. In many large contracts where specific supplier credit insurance is available, exporters may prefer to negotiate on cash terms and arrange a loan to the buyer with repayment terms similar to the credit he might expect from the supplier. ECGD buyer credit guarantees are available to banks making such loans in respect of contracts of £1 million or more.

A buyer credit guarantee normally involves the overseas purchaser in paying to the supplier, direct from his own resources, 15 to 20 per cent of the contract price, including a sufficient down payment on signature of the contract. The remainder is paid to the supplier direct from a loan made to the buyer or a bank in his country by a UK bank and guaranteed by ECGD as to 100 per cent of capital and interest, against non-payment for any reason. The contract may include some foreign goods and services, but the amount of the loan will then be less than the British goods and services to be supplied.

The operation of some of the above services is expanded upon in Appendix 18.3 at the end of this chapter. To obtain a complete picture of the full range of ECGD services, it is necessary to obtain their booklet on their work. A brief summary of the department's main services only is within the scope of this book.

Sources of Export Finance

Buying credit risk can be expensive. So it pays not to duplicate cover, for example by taking out ECGD cover together with an irrevocable letter of credit. On occasions this duplication may be unavoidable, such as where ECGD makes a confirmed irrevocable letter of credit a condition of its cover on a particular buyer. This happens when the buyer is especially risky and would not otherwise qualify for cover.

In Table 18.2 we summarise the various sources of short-term export finance. One of the headings in the table is important and deserves further comment on its implications. This is the term 'recourse'. Non-recourse finance means that the lender has no right of action against the exporter due to the overseas buyer failing to meet his obligations. However, it is worth mentioning that ECGD retains a right of recourse against the exporter on two grounds. The first relates to the extra percentage cover given to the bank. The bank advancing funds is indemnified 100 per cent by ECGD should the buyer fail to pay, but the exporter's cover is for only 90 or 95 per cent. Thus ECGD may claim back the difference of 5 or 10 per cent from the exporter. Also, the right of recourse may be retained in respect of the whole 100 per cent paid out by ECGD to the bank should ECGD consider that default has arisen due to a factor not covered in the comprehensive guarantee. In effect this is where there is a dispute about the exporter's performance of his contract. The exporter does, of course, continue to enjoy 90–95 per cent immunity to pure default risk, irrespective of whether the default is commercial, arising from the buyer's financial weakness, or political.

The accounting impact of non-recourse finance is interesting. If the finance is with recourse, it appears on the exporter's balance sheet as a liability financing the receivable on the assets side. But if the finance is without recourse, it is treated as an outright sale of the receivable to the bank. There is then no liability on the balance sheet. For the six categories of export finance in which the response of 'no' appears in the last column of Table 18.2 – that is, where the finance is with recourse to the exporter – receivables and liabilities would be greater on the balance sheet than would be the case with no recourse finance.

With reference to data in Table 18.2, various caveats should be noted. Regarding the column 'Is 100% advanced?', where less than 100 per cent is given under an export financing source it will usually be above 80 per cent of invoice credit insurance and is expensive. Nowadays factors increasingly hold their own ECGD cover. Many have overseas associates and they often restrict their factoring to customers approved by such associates. Export merchants and confirming houses operating in the traditional mode buy goods as a legal principal although the modern confirmer does not acquire title to the goods. Confirmers usually accept

Table 18.2 Sources of Export Credit

Source	Nature	Is buyer aware?	Is 100% advanced?	Is the exporter relieved of –		
				Sales ledger work?	Credit risk?	Recourse?
OVERDRAFT	Borrowing	No	Yes	No	No	No
ACCEPTANCE CREDIT	Borrowing	No	Yes	No	No	No
ADVANCE AGAINST BILLS	Borrowing	No	Less	No	No	No
NEGOTIATING BILLS	Sale of bills	No	Less	No	No	No
FACTORING	Sale of book debt	Yes	Less	Yes	Yes	Yes
INVOICE DISCOUNTING	Sale of invoices	No	Less	No	No	No
EXPORT MERCHANT	Sale of goods	Yes	Yes	Yes	Yes	Yes
CONFIRMING HOUSE						
– TRADITIONAL	Sale of goods	Yes	Yes	Yes	Yes	Yes
– MODERN	Sale of book debt	Yes	Yes	Yes	Yes	Yes
ECGD COMPREHENSIVE BANK GUARANTEE						
– BILLS	Sale of bills	No	Yes	No	90/95%	Yes
– OPEN ACCOUNT	Borrowing	No	Yes	No	90/95%	No
FORFAITING	Sale of bills	Yes	Yes	Yes	Yes	Yes

risks which exporters cannot deal with through their normal channels. Confirming is effectively a way of obtaining ECGD cover without incurring the substantial administrative cost of operating that cover. It should be noted that forfaiting normally differs from factoring by applying mainly to medium-term credit and by requiring that a guarantee, called an aval, be obtained from a local bank and this makes the credit costly. In some cases buyers are asked to obtain this aval without being informed of the forfaiting operation. Forfaiting and factoring are both relatively expensive media of export finance.

The forms of finance set out in Table 18.2 are all fairly complex and readers desirous of obtaining a detailed insight into their real-world operation are referred to the fairly substantial literature on their practical use. In-depth descriptions are outside the scope of a book of this nature.

Summary

The usual methods of payment in international trade involve either cash with order, open account, bills of exchange, documentary letters of credit or government assistance schemes.

Cash with order and irrevocable documentary letters of credit provide exporters with maximum security. If it is deemed necessary, government agencies, such as ECGD in Britain, will take up to 90 per cent of the credit risk on exports subject to the exporter paying a fee to ECGD. Government agencies also provide supplier credits and buyer credits which are sources of finance to ease smooth export trading.

Agencies similar to Britain's ECGD exist in most countries and offer very similar sorts of service. This job is done by Eximbank in the USA, COFACE in France, HERMES in West Germany, and so on. Full details of the services that they offer to exporters are available on request to the agency concerned.

Getting paid promptly in international trade has obvious and important implications for liquidity management in the export-orientated company. The checklists in Appendices 18.1 and 18.2 are important memory-joggers in this respect.

References

International Chamber of Commerce (1975) *Uniform Customs and Excise Practice for Documentary Credits*, ICC Series, London and Paris.

Kahler, R. and Kramer, R.L. (1977) *International Marketing*, South Western Publishing Company.

APPENDIX 18.1

MAIN REASONS FOR DELAYS IN PAYMENT AND REFUSALS TO PAY UNDER LETTERS OF CREDIT

The letter of credit has expired.

The documents are presented after the period stipulated in the letter of credit.

The shipment is late.

There is a claused (that is, an unclean or dirty) shipping document.

A charter party bill of lading is used when the letter of credit requires an on-board shipment.

The shipment is made between ports other than those stated in the documentary letter of credit.

The goods are shipped on deck when this is not permitted.

An insurance document of a type other than that required by the letter of credit is presented.

The insurance risks covered are not as specified in the letter of credit.

The insurance cover is expressed in a currency other than that of the letter of credit.

The goods are under-insured.

The insurance is not effective from the date of shipment.

The description, or spelling, of goods on invoice(s) differs from that in the letter of credit.

The weights differ between export documents.

The values shown on the invoice(s) and bill of exchange (draft) differ.

The marks and numbers differ between documents.

The drawing is for less than the letter of credit amount when part shipments are not permitted.

The letter of credit amount is exceeded by the value of the order.

The bill of lading does not evidence whether freight is paid or not.

The shipment is short.

There is an absence of document(s) called for in the documentary letter of credit.

The bill of exchange or draft is drawn on a wrong party.

The bill of exchange or draft is payable on an indeterminable date.

The bills of lading, insurance document or bill of exchange or draft are not endorsed correctly.

The copy of the freight account is not attached but is called for by the documentary letter of credit.

There is an absence of signatures of witnessings, where required, on documents presented.

Facsimile signatures are used when not allowed.

APPENDIX 18.2

CHECKLIST FOR LETTER OF CREDIT TRADING

Immediately upon receipt of the letter of credit, it should be read carefully and the terms should be checked against the contract of sale. The letter of credit should then be checked to ensure that:

It is of the type agreed, that is, irrevocable and confirmed, or just irrevocable.

It has an expiry date that is sufficiently far ahead for the goods to be shipped and the required documents obtained and presented in time.

It has terms and conditions that can be met and the required documents can be obtained exactly as called for.

It has correct spelling. Misspellings should be taken up immediately with the buyer.

It is irrevocable with the added confirmation of another bank (usually the advising bank).

It is to be paid either against documents, or against documents accompanied by a sight draft on the named paying bank, or by acceptance – against documents accompanied by a draft on a named bank draft at a usance (time), e.g. 30/60/90 days after date; or by negotiation – against documents accompanied by a sight draft or a time draft on the issuing bank or on the overseas buyer.

It is payable in the UK, or in the country of importation, or in a third country.

It includes the seller's name and address and that of the customer, complete and spelled correctly.

It has stated the amount and value correctly and is issued in the agreed currency.

It is in accordance with the terms of the sales contract, for example, ex-works, free carrier, f.o.b., c.&f., c.i.f. or other terms expressed in the original offer or pro forma invoice.

It lists the description, quantity and weight of the goods in accordance with the terms of the sales contract.

It includes drafts as agreed, for example at sight, at a stated usance (time), with the correct persons on whom they are to be drawn.

It has the right shipping and expiry dates; and allows a period of time for presentation of the shipping documents after their date of issuance which is sufficient for processing the order, making shipment and presenting the documents to the confirming bank.

It calls for the correct type of shipping document.

It enables the exporter to obtain insurance cover against the risks specified and states whether a policy or a certificate is required.

It requires or precludes any special declaration/statement or endorsements.

It involves any import or export licences.

It allows partial shipments.

It has correctly stated the shipping details such as the place and date of shipment and the port of destination.

It stipulates on-deck shipment allowed if the goods are of a type that might require on-deck stowage.

APPENDIX 18.3

EXPORT CREDITS

The Role of the Export Credit Agencies

The major export credit agencies of the world were either set up or were sponsored by their governments. Their primary function and main commercial objective is to encourage and facilitate the export of major capital goods, services and bulk materials. This policy is effected by offering the following kinds of programme:

- Guarantees to the banks who support exports of up to 100 per cent of the loan or lending part or all of the funds themselves.
- Insurance policies in favour of the exporter to cover certain types of commercial and political risks.
- Fixed rates of interest for certain currencies which will be below the commercial rate available for that currency.
- Additional protection such as cover against inflation and exchange risk.

The majority of export credit agencies prefer to act as an insurer and offer their support indirectly. For these reasons it is the banking community that usually offers, arranges and administers the loans.

Advantages of Utilising Export Credits

Financing by export credits is particularly attractive and convenient for buyers with major capital investment programmes involving long construction and payment periods.

The advantages of utilising export credit facilities far outweigh those available from the commercial financial markets and can be summarised as embracing:

- A fixed rate of interest, often subsidised to below market conditions. This fixed rate enables the prospective buyer to reduce his interest costs and allow more predictable economic projections and assessments of his future investment, cash flows and costs.
- Guaranteed availability of funds, even in periods of tight liquidity.
- Relatively long grace periods before repayment of principal. Such repayment usually commences six months from delivery of goods or the estimated date of commissioning of the project, depending on the supplier's contractual responsibility.
- Relatively long repayment periods, particularly for major turnkey contracts.

These further advantages must also be considered:

- Many export credit agencies offer financing in a number of currencies, giving the borrower some flexibility to match the borrowing currency with the currency of earnings, or to finance supplies from several countries in a single common currency, typically US dollars.
- Export credit agencies give funding banks guarantees of up to 100 per cent, which means that these banks regard the ultimate risk to be that of the export credit agency, not the borrower. In this sense export credit borrowing does not directly compete with or reduce a borrower's normal access to commercial funding.
- If commercial rates fall below the fixed export credit rate, the borrower at his sole option is able to prepay the loans, in most cases without any penalty or cost.
- The form of documentation is often less onerous for the borrower than that of a commercial borrowing.

Types of Export Credit Facility

There are a number of alternate financing structures which are used by the export credit agencies to support the payment terms of an export contract. The availability of each of these facilities which are described below is dependent on the overall programme of the export credit agency and the type and size of the relevant contract.

Supplier Credits

This is a form of financing in which the supplier takes the lead role. The credit is evidenced and offered by the supplier to the buyer by means of bills of exchange or promissory notes. These are repayable over a number of instalments commencing from the estimated commissioning of the plant and bear a fixed interest rate payable semi-annually in arrears. On receipt, these notes or bills of exchange are presented by the supplier to the commercial banks who then pay the supplier. The banks obtain guarantees from the export credit agency that, should the buyer not pay interest or principal, a percentage of the notes – usually between 90 per cent and 95 per cent – is refunded to the banks. Supplier credits are usually only offered in support of relatively small equipment contracts because of the balance sheet implications for suppliers taking the bank funding and passing it on to the buyer. The major exception is in Japan where, due to its industrial structure, supplier credits are often used by Japanese Trading Houses to support major turnkey projects.

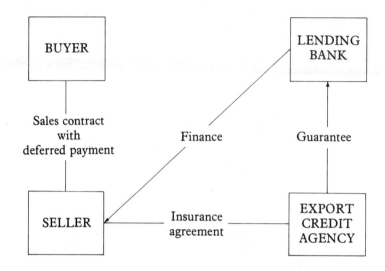

Buyer Credits

The supplier is not directly involved in the buyer credit arrangements and is paid from a loan agreement which is usually signed between a commercial banking syndicate and the buyer/borrower. The supplier is able to receive these funds on a similar payment system to that of a letter of credit. As the supplier is only indirectly involved in the financing of a buyer credit his risks, and the balance sheet implications arising from such risks, can often be significantly less than those under a supplier credit. Buyer credits are the most appropriate structure for major turnkey projects, particularly where the contractor is bidding on a lump-sum basis.

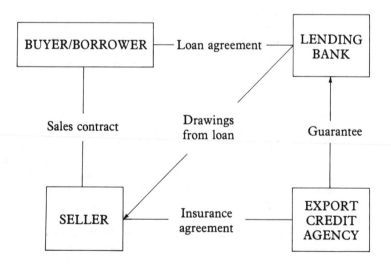

Project Lines of Credit

The structure of a project line of credit is similar to that of a buyer credit as outlined above – thus there is a form of loan agreement between a syndicate of banks and the buyer/borrower. However, unlike a buyer credit, where the loan agreement is structured to support one specific contract between the buyer and the contractor, a project line of credit can be set up prior to individual equipment contract awards and is to a greater extent controlled by the buyer or the buyer's representative. This enables the buyer/borrower, or the main contractor on behalf of the buyer, to know in advance the terms available from a particular export credit agency without having to make a final commitment to the purchase of individual items or packages of goods or services.

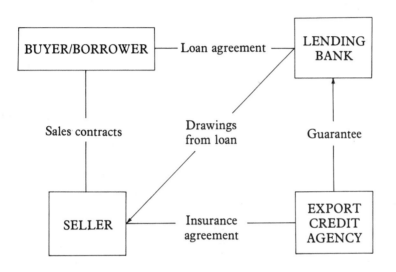

Outline Terms of Conditions

The minimum terms which will be offered through export credits will be dependent on the following criteria:

- The majority of the equipment and services to be supported must originate from the home country.
- The buyer/borrower concerned must be acceptable – the export credit agencies tend to take a more flexible attitude than the commercial market.
- The country category status of the buyer/borrower (see below) will dictate the terms which can be offered.
- The contractor must be able to perform his contractual obligations financially and commercially.
- The commercial contract must provide for an advance payment of at least 5 per cent with a further 10 per cent paid on or before delivery of the goods and services.

The category status of each country is reviewed from time to time by the OECD export credit agencies. The main criterion is GNP per capita. Status categorisations can be summarised as follows:

Borrowing country	GNP per capita	Maximum length of credit	Minimum rate for up to 5 years (%)	Minimum rate for over 5 years (%)	Eligible goods covered (%)
Category 1 (relatively rich)	Above $4,000 (1979)	5 years (exceptionally up to 8 years for very large contracts)	12.15	12.4	up to 80
Category 2 (middle income)	Between $1,000 and $3,000	8 years	10.85	11.35	up to 85
Category 3 (relatively poor)	Under $624 (1978)	10 years	10.00	10.00	up to 85

In addition to the above terms, export credit agencies are willing to consider, for major turnkey projects (particularly in category 3 countries), support for local cost (up to a maximum of 15 per cent of the value of supplying the country's goods and services) and occasionally capitalisation of interest during the construction period.

Non-OECD Export Credit Agencies

Major OECD export credit agencies offer fairly comparable services. Indeed, they are bound by a mutual agreement on minimum terms and conditions (The Consensus Agreement). There are also a number of developing countries who are now encouraging the export of their goods and services by providing credits below the consensus terms. In many cases their currency is not totally convertible and the benefit from the receipt of foreign convertible currencies far outweighs the timing of repayments and interest rate obtained. This means that extremely attractive credit terms may be offered which cannot always be matched by the Consensus agencies. Although the taking up of these attractive credits must be tempered with the contractor's technical and delivery considerations, there can be opportunities to take advantage of these credits for relatively unsophisticated equipment as part of the overall package. Examples of countries in this category include Brazil, Argentina, Mexico, Portugal, Poland, Hungary, USSR and South Korea.

TEST BANK
NUMBER THREE

MORE FOREIGN EXCHANGE RATES

Consider the tabulation below which is given by a bank to a customer. Required rates are for the stated foreign currency against the home currency.

	$	Guilders	Escudos
Spot	1.3915–25	4.70–4.70¼	263.15–25
	Premium	Premium	
1 month forward	1–0.90 cents	4½–4¼ cents	15 cents pm
			10 cents dis
2 months forward	1.60–1.50 cents	8½–8¼ cents	17 cents pm
			8 cents dis
3 months forward	2.10–2.00 cents	10½–10¼ cents	19 cents pm
			6 cents dis

The word 'premium' or 'discount' implies that the foreign currency quoted at the head of each column is at the premium or discount respectively.

1. At what rate will the bank sell escudos on a three-month forward option?
2. At what rate will the bank buy escudos on a three-month forward option?
3. At what rate will the customer sell guilders on a two-month forward option?
4. At what rate will the customer sell guilders on a three-month forward option?
5. At what rate will the customer buy dollars on a two-month forward option?

6. At what rate will the bank sell escudos three months forward, option over three months?
7. At what rate will the bank buy escudos three months forward, option over the third month?
8. At what rate will the customer sell guilders two months forward, option over the second month?
9. At what rate will the customer sell guilders three months forward, option over the second and third month?
10. At what rate will the customer buy dollars two months forward, option over the second month?

FOREIGN EXCHANGE RATES AGAIN

Quotations are:

Currency	Spot	1 month		2 months		3 months	
£/$	1.5015–25	3	6	7	11	13	17
$/SFr	2.0987–97	103	93	208	198	282	272
$/FF	7.8830–20	185	220	465	515	780	830

1. Calculate the annual % discount/premium at which the $ stands on the £ three months forward. Assume that you are buying £.
     For the remaining questions assume that your company is dealing in the FX markets with a dealer who has given the above quotations. At what rates would you deal the following:
  2. You sell $ for FF three months forward, option over third month.
  3. Dealer buys $ for SFr three months forward, option over second and third months.
  4. You buy $ for £ two months forward, option over first and second months.
  5. Dealers sells $ for FF two months forward.
  6. You sell $ for £ three months forward.
  7. Dealer sells SFr for $ one month forward.
  8. In the £/SFr forward market which currency is at a premium? Why?
  9. Calculate the £/FF spot quote.
  10. Calculate the rate at which you would deal were you to buy SFr for FF two months forward option over the whole period.

EXAMINATION QUESTIONS

1. Imagine that you work for a company wishing to deal in the

foreign exchange markets in Norwegian krone and US dollars against the pound. *The Financial Times* gives the following quotation $ and NKr against the £.

	US $	NKr
Spot	1.2775–1.2785	11.25–11.26
Forward		
1 month	0.56–0.53 cent pm	$\frac{1}{4}$ ore pm–$\frac{3}{8}$ dis
2 months	1.03–0.99 pm	$\frac{1}{2}$–1$\frac{1}{4}$ dis
3 months	1.50–1.45 pm	$\frac{7}{8}$–1$\frac{3}{4}$ dis

You notice that Eurocurrency interest rates are as follows according to the *FT*:

	Sterling	US$
Short-term	12$\frac{5}{8}$–12$\frac{7}{8}$	7$\frac{1}{4}$–7$\frac{3}{8}$
1 month	12$\frac{5}{8}$–12$\frac{3}{4}$	7$\frac{5}{16}$–7$\frac{7}{16}$
3 months	12$\frac{3}{8}$–12$\frac{1}{2}$	7$\frac{7}{16}$–7$\frac{9}{16}$

Assuming that your company's bank gives the same quotation as all of those tabulated above, answer the following:

(a) At what rate would your company sell NKr for sterling three months forward, option over the second and third months?
(b) At what rate would the bank sell NKr for sterling three months forward, option running 30 days to 90 days?
(c) At what rate would the bank sell $ for sterling three months forward, option over the third month?
(d) At what rate would your company sell $ for sterling three months forward, option over the third month?
(e) At what rate would the bank buy NKr one month forward?
(f) At what rate would the bank sell NKr one month forward?
Note: There are 100 ore in 1 krone.

2. A firm in the USA is due to receive payment of DM 10 million in two years' time. It would like to protect itself against a decline in the value of the Deutsche Mark but it finds it difficult to get forward cover for such a long period. Indicate the mechanics of two methods by which it might avoid the bulk of foreign exchange risk on this transaction.

3. Imagine that you work for a company wishing to deal in the foreign exchange markets in Danish kroner and US dollars against the pound. *The Financial Times* gives the following quotations $ and DKr against the £.

	US $	DKr
Spot	1.3820–1.3830	13.85¾–13.86¾
Forward		
1 month	0.26–0.29 dis	0.40 ore pm–0.40 ore dis
2 months	0.50–0.54 dis	0.45 ore pm–0.60 ore dis
3 months	0.80–0.85 dis	0.55 ore pm–0.55 ore dis

You notice that Eurocurrency interest rates are as follows according to the *FT*:

	Sterling	US $
Short-term	8¾–9	10¾–10⅞
1 month	9⅛–9¼	11⅛–11¼
3 months	9⅜–9½	11⁹⁄₁₆–11¹¹⁄₁₆

Assuming that your company's bank gives the same quotations as all of those tabulated above, answer the following:

(a) At what rate would your company sell DKr three months forward, option over the second and third months?

(b) At what rate would the bank sell $ three months forward?

(c) At what rate would the bank sell $ three months forward, option over the third month?

(d) At what rate would your company sell $ three months forward, option over the third month?

(e) At what rate would the bank buy DKr two months forward?

(f) At what rate would the bank sell DKr spot?

Note: There are 100 ore in 1 krone.

4. On 27 March 1985 the following applied:

   £/DM spot value 3.79–3.80
   £ three-month interest $13\frac{9}{16} - 13\frac{11}{16}$
   DM three-month interest $5\frac{15}{16} - 6\frac{1}{16}$
   £/DM three-month forward $7\frac{1}{8}$–7 pm
   (The ensuing three months consist of 90 days)

The treasurer of a £-based company decides to hedge a DM receivable due in three months' time. What are two alternative methods, and what are the effective interest rates for each? Why are they not the same?

(Association of Corporate Treasurers: Part II, Specimen paper in Currency Management)

5. A service company with 100% owned subsidiaries in four countries experiences major cash flows between these subsidiaries. The subsidiaries are in the UK, Netherlands, West Germany and Spain. The monthly cash flows are as follows:

UK pays	Dfl 500,000 to Netherlands
	Pta 40,000,000 to Spain
Netherlands pays	£250,000 to UK
	Pta 60,000,000 to Spain
	DM 400,000 to Germany
Germany pays	Dfl 600,000 to Netherlands
	Pta 50,000,000 to Spain
Spain pays	£200,000 to UK
	Dfl 400,000 to Netherlands
	DM 500,000 to Germany

where £1 = DM4 = Dfl4 = Pta 200
How might this system be improved, and what would be the benefits?

(Association of Corporate Treasurers: Part II, Specimen Paper in Currency Management)

6. The board of your company has decided not to be totally risk averse in covering all known currency transaction exposures. It has asked for your views on selective cover.
(a) What criteria should be considered when setting limits to the amount of currency risk to be accepted?
(b) What decision aids might be used to determine when to cover currency risk?

(Association of Corporate Treasurers: Part II, Specimen paper in Currency Management)

7. In early July, as the new manager of a branch, you call to see one of your corporate customers for the first time. He complains that he has received little help or advice from your predecessor concerning his payments and receipts in foreign currency. His business in this section is increasing, and you are asked for practical advice in connection with the following payments and receipts, including information on the protection available. The company normally has reasonable sterling credit balances but does swing into occasional overdraft.

Payments
1. US $100,000 by 30 September to Alnite Entertainments, Las Vegas.

2. Aus. $75,000 accepted bill in favour of Cobbers Pty Ltd, Brisbane, due 15 November.
3. Swiss francs 50,000 to Deutsche Suppliers GMBH, Hamburg, re goods sent to Holland, due during July.

Receivables
4. US $250,000 due 15 July from Pigalle Shows SA Paris.
5. Bank acceptance under a letter of credit for Aus. $55,000 for goods shipped to Irish Ashes Limited, Cork, due end of October.
6. Equivalent in Deutsche Marks of Swiss francs 50,000, due end of June from Swiss Rolls Limited.

Required:
(a) What immediate advice can you give your customer in connection with these payments/receipts?
(b) As the foreign business will grow, what further help/advice would you suggest that the bank should give?

(Institute of Bankers: Banking Diploma Stage 2. April 1982 Paper in Finance of International Trade)

8. Your customers, Blacksheep Limited, call to see you on 15 January to discuss a new contract they have signed with a French meat importer, Agneau-Mouton SA, Paris. The terms of the contract are as follows:

Quantity:	About 200 metric tons of chilled carcases, to be shipped in two equal lots, the first during the second half of January and the balance during the second half of March.
Price:	French francs 1600 per metric ton.
Terms:	Free delivered Paris by refrigerated road truck from the United Kingdom.
Payment:	To be effected in French francs through a documentary collection — one for each consignment — whereby the documents will be forwarded to the bankers of Agneau-Mouton SA through your office.

Your customers are satisfied with the credit rating of the buyers and expect that payment will be made within a few days of presentation of the documents through your correspondent in Paris. Blacksheep Limited requires forward exchange cover to be taken out to protect its sterling profit margin. You therefore arrange two forward exchange contracts to cover the two deliveries.

The rates of exchange for French francs on 15 January are as follows:

Spot	12.0966	– 12.1336
1 month	0.0275 cents dis	– 0.0375 cents dis
2 months	0.0575 cents dis	– 0.0775 cents dis
3 months	0.1050 cents dis	– 0.1250 cents dis
4 months	0.2350 cents dis	– 0.2650 cents dis

Shipments are effected in accordance with the contract, the first of 100 metric tons on 20 January and the second, also of 100 metric tons, on 18 March. However, *on 20 March* your customers call to see you again and inform you that, owing to industrial trouble in France, the March shipment has been delayed and they are unlikely to be paid on time since the carcases will now be subject to rigorous health inspection. The proceeds are unlikely, therefore, to be received until the third week in April. They ask you to cancel the March forward contract, which falls due towards the middle of April, and to arrange a new one for the value of *80 metric tons only* since a fifth of the consignment has 'disappeared' and will be subject to a separate insurance claim.

The rates for French francs on 20 March are as follows:

Spot	12.1350	– 12.1645
1 month	0.0245 cents dis	– 0.0355 cents dis

Required:

(a) Details of the forward contracts which your customers would take out on 15 January to protect their sterling receipts and calculations of the sterling proceeds of each contract.
(b) Calculation of the sterling entries which will be passed to your customers' account on 20 March in respect of the March close-out.
(c) Details of the extended forward contract which you arrange for your customers to cover the shipment of 80 metric tons, and a calculation of the expected sterling proceeds of the contract.

(Institute of Bankers: Banking Diploma, September 1984 Paper in Finance of International Trade)

9. Wavy Navy is a British company producing high-quality work boats which take approximately six months to build from date of order. In the past, the company has had a positive cash flow and has not demanded payment for the vessels until the time of delivery. Sales have been confined to the United Kingdom and to the Federal Republic of Germany. Payment for goods sold to Germany has been effected in Deutsche Marks. Wavy Navy has produced some components in its own yard and purchased the balance from UK

sources. Up to now, it has sold any surplus Deutsche Marks for sterling.

Recently, a buyer of undoubted standing has made a positive enquiry for a number of vessels indicating that it would pay for them in sterling on delivery. However, this potential buyer is insisting that the engines, which would have to be fitted at a very early stage in construction, should be supplied from Scandinavia. The Scandinavian engine manufacturer requires payment in Deutsche Marks but would grant Wavy Navy 90 days' credit terms.

Required:
(a) Brief notes indicating the areas in which Wavy Navy is at risk if it agrees to deliver vessels to the potential buyer.
(b) Advice, in note form, on how these specific risks can be reduced.

Note: Ignore normal payment risks and concentrate on the specific risks mentioned in the question.

(Institute of Bankers: Banking Diploma April 1985 Paper in Finance of International Trade)

10. Your customers, Ancient Mariners Limited, are sterling based and are negotiating with a major UK contracting company to transport building equipment and materials to a remote island in the Indian ocean. Payment is secure and will be made in US dollars, the contract being worth US $900,000. To complete the deal successfully, they will need to charter the following vessels:

(a) one roll-on/roll-off vessel from the USA;
(b) one tug and landing barge, complete with derrick, from Holland;
(c) one general cargo vessel, of about 5,000 tons cargo weight, from Singapore.

You know your customers will require bank finance and the directors call to see you to discuss the matter. Your enquiries reveal that Ancient Mariners Limited will obtain the contract subject to their agreeing to the following financial arrangements:

(i) Payment in respect of (a) above is to be $100,000 in all and is to be payable *to the US owners* upon the sailing of the vessel from the USA (the charter will be for one month from the date of the contract and sailing will take place immediately upon signing of the contract).
(ii) Payment in respect of (b) above is for a total of DM 300,000 payable *to the Dutch owners* in two equal lots. The first is to be made upon the sailing of the vessel, which will take place immediately the contract is signed, and the balance is to be paid

three months later. (The total charter time will be exactly six months.)

(iii) Payment in respect of (c) above is for a total price of US dollars 500,000, payable to *the Singapore owners* in two equal lots. The first payment is to be made one month after the signing of the contract and the second exactly six months after signing the contract.

(iv) Payment *from the main contractor* will be in three instalments as follows:

US $200,000 immediately upon signing the contract;
US $500,000 three months after signing the contract;
US $200,000 six months after signing the contract.

Additional information

(i) Assume that the contract is awarded and signed on 1 June and the bank is willing to support the customer.

(ii) Ignore commercial risks, such as chartering risks, weather and penalty clauses which might be included in the commercial contract.

(iii) Ignore any charges or interest payable in connection with any overdrawings.

(iv) Assume that the vessels sail on the same day as the contract is awarded, i.e. 1 June.

The rates applying on 1 June are as follows:

	£/US$	US$/DM
Spot	1.6100–1.6180	2.4096– 2.4145
1 month	0.21–0.16 cents pm	8.33–8.30 pf pm
2 months	0.38–0.33 cents pm	8.55–8.25 pf pm
3 months	0.51–0.46 cents pm	9.00–8.83 pf pm
6 months	0.66–0.61 cents pm	13.03–12.95 pf pm

Required:

Your advice to the company covering the following points:

(a) the risks that the company will have to face in accepting and arranging the contract described above;

(b) how the bank can help to minimise those risks, indicating quite clearly the technical description of the risks;

(c) a statement of the currency account and a calculation of the total sterling receipts the company will have at the end of the contract period, assuming that they will sell forward any surplus dollars to the bank.

(Institute of Bankers: Banking Diploma Stage 2, September 1983 Paper in Finance of International Trade)

11. Your customers, South Sea Traders Limited, have exported their products to the south seas and the Pacific coast of the United States for many years. Recently, they reached an agreement with their buyers in the United States which enables them to draw bills so that they fall due for payment 120 days after the shipment date. The documents are collected through your office. Because of restricted profit margins over the past few months and a shortage of working capital, the customers call to see you on 30 March to seek your advice on how best they can protect their profit margins on one immediate transaction and for future transactions. The bill amount specifically discussed is 100,000 US dollars, accepted by the buyer and falling due on 30 June. Past experience indicates that the buyer effects payment on the due date of the bills and so South Sea Traders does not have to worry about being out of funds for any length of time.

Additional information available on 30 March is as follows:

(i) US$ rates

Spot	$1.5180–$1.5260
1 month forward	Par–0.03 cents dis
2 months forward	0.05 cents dis–0.08 cents dis
3 months forward	0.09 cents dis–0.12 cents dis
4 months forward	0.20 cents dis–0.24 cents dis

(ii) UK base rate = 9.5%
(iii) US 3-month LIBOR rate = 10.25%
(iv) The customers are borrowing sterling from your office at 2% over the bank's base rate and you have agreed with them that, in the event of their requesting foreign currency, you would charge them at the rate of $1\frac{1}{2}$% over the US LIBOR rate.
(v) Your customers do not purchase goods for which they have to pay in foreign currency.

Required:
(a) By what methods can your customers be protected from foreign exchange risks whilst preserving their profit margins?
(b) Outline any contractual obligations in respect of foreign exchange that your customers would have to undertake.
(c) Show by calculation the costs of each method proposed in answer to (a) above, and the sterling proceeds which each method would produce.
(d) Set out a formula which your customers would use to compare sterling and foreign currency borrowing costs, taking into account, where appropriate, the advantages or disadvantages of forward cover.

Notes: (1) Ignore all bank charges in respect of commissions, etc.
(2) Base your calculations on a 30-day month and a 360-day year.

(Institute of Bankers: Banking Diploma April 1984 Paper in Finance of International Trade)

12. Tiger Moth Ltd, a customer of your bank, is a sterling-based aircraft charter company operating mainly in the UK, Western Europe, and the Caribbean. It has been awarded a contract to provide freight and passenger services for a number of remote islands in the mid-Atlantic and the Caribbean.

The contract, which is guaranteed by the governments of the various territories, is to be signed on 1 June 1985. The value of the contract to the customer is US $1.5 million, and it will be necessary for Tiger Moth Ltd to charter three aircraft at a total cost of US $900,000. Payment and receipt terms are as follows:

Payment by Tiger Moth:
(i)   One third upon signing the contract.
(ii) One third six months after signing the contract.
(iii) One third twelve months after signing the contract.

Receipts by Tiger Moth:
(i)   One third ($500,000) three months after signing the contract (guaranteed).
(ii) One third ($500,000) six months after signing the contract (guaranteed).
(iii) A third payment of up to $500,000 (one third of the contract value) 12 months after signing the contract. (According to the contract this payment may be reduced if Tiger Moth generates extra business on its own account.)

Your customer asks you to make the best possible financial arrangements to obviate any risks to the company.
US dollar rates on 1 June 1985 are as follows:

Spot	1.3195	1.3210
Three months	0.16 cents dis	0.21 cents dis
Six months	0.44 cents dis	0.72 cents dis
Twelve months	0.85 cents dis	1.05 cents dis
Spot 1 June 1986	1.4610	1.4670

Additional information and assumptions:

1. The full expected net receipts are sold forward on 1 June 1985 for delivery on 1 June 1986.
2. For the purpose of this question, ignore the possibility of any other forward contracts which might be arranged.

3. The contract is performed in its entirety except that, when the third payment falls due on 1 June 1986, it is calculated that Tiger Moth Ltd has generated extra business on its own account which requires a reduction in the contract payment from US $500,000 to US $250,000. (The 'extra earnings' should be ignored for the purpose of the calculations required in (c) below).
4. All commercial risks, such as chartering risks, credit risks, etc. which may be included in the commercial contract, may be ignored.
5. Any charges or interest payable in connection with any overdraft or transfers may be ignored.

Required:
The advice you would give to the company covering the following:

(a) The risk that the company has to face in accepting the contract which is awarded to it.
(b) The method that you would recommend to Tiger Moth Limited in order to minimise the risk mentioned in (a).
(c) A statement of the currency account you would operate on behalf of the customer, including a calculation at the end of the period showing the total sterling proceeds which would be credited to the customer's sterling account.

(Institute of Bankers: Banking Diploma, April 1985 Paper in Finance of International Trade)

13. In early May you are asked to confirm an irrevocable letter of credit on behalf of a Japanese correspondent bank. The terms are briefly as follows:

> *In favour of:* Associated Noxious Distributors, London
> *For account of:* Nippon Oriental Traders, Yokohama
> *Expiring:* 15 November 1982 in London
> *Amount:* About Japanese Yen 43,000,000 (forty-three million)
> *Covering:* About 1,000 metric tons of chemicals to be shipped in two approximately equal instalments, one during the first half of July and one during the first half of August.
> *Price:* Yen 43,000 per metric ton C.I.F. Yokohama, shipment from UK port.

Drawings will be made as follows:
95 per cent of the value of a provisional invoice upon presentation of documents strictly in order.
The remaining 5 per cent will be available against final invoice accompanied by an independent weight and analysis certificate showing the final weight and chemical analysis.

On 25 May the beneficiary asks you to cover the forward receivables in the foreign exchange market, as follows:

(i)   Arrange forward contracts immediately in respect of the value of each 500 metric ton shipment.
(ii) Upon presentation of documents close out any differences between the forward contract amounts and the actual values claimed.
(iii) Ignore forward cover for the balance to be claimed in October.

The documents were presented in order on the following dates:

15 July	– Documents showing a shipment of exactly 490 metric tons.
10 August	– Documents showing a shipment of exactly 526.316 metric tons.
31 October	– Final invoice claiming an agreed figure of Japanese Yen 43,550.

Required:
Using the following rates of exchange calculate the sterling sums your customer will receive on the appropriate presentation dates.

25 May	Spot	430.50	434.50
	1 month forward	2.50 pm	2.00 pm
	2 months forward	3.90 pm	3.10 pm
	3 months forward	6.75 pm	6.25 pm
	6 months forward	12.40 pm	11.65 pm
15 July	Spot	429.00	433.50
10 August	Spot	433.50	438.00
31 October	Spot	432.00	435.40

Notes: 1. For the purpose of this question, the bank and the beneficiary assume that shipment and presentation of documents will be made on the same day.
2. Ignore letter of credit charges as these are for the buyer's account.,
3. Ignore any close-out figures of less than 100 Yen.

(Institute of Bankers: Banking Diploma Stage 2, September 1982 Paper in Finance of International Trade)

19

International Capital Budgeting

Like domestic capital investment decisions, international capital budgeting focuses upon expected incremental cash flows associated with a project. The specification of these flows for the international project creates the usual difficulties found in a domestic capital project, but international project analysis is much more complex. Although the basic pattern follows the same model as that suggested by corporate financial theory, the multinational firm must consider factors peculiar to international operations.

A project may be estimated to produce very considerable cash flows in a foreign territory but, because of exchange control restrictions, the bulk of these foreign cash flows may not be distributable to the parent company. In these circumstances, looking at the project purely in terms of cash flows accruing in the foreign territory may indicate that it is worth investing. But is this good enough? Surely the present value to the parent company is a function of future cash flows accruing to it which are distributable to the parent company's shareholders. And we stated that for the project under review the bulk of foreign territory cash flows was blocked by exchange controls. Surely it is only the incremental cash flows which are remittable back to the parent company which add value for its share-holders. This means that our capital project might be looked at from at least two standpoints – incremental project cash flows and incremental parent cash flows – but to the international company it is only incremental parent cash flows that matter. Perhaps this is a straightforward concept relative to some other problems of multinational capital budgeting. Consider the situation exemplified below.

Complexities often arise in multinational companies because overseas invest-ment projects have substantial knock-on effects on other operations elsewhere within the group. For example, a motor manufacturer, contemplating the estab-lishment of a plant in Spain, may find that the proposed investment will affect the operations of other units within the multinational group. This may arise, in part, through the new project's effect on sales of other parts of the multinational in Europe – for example, sales deriving from the French and German plants. But it may also arise through vertical integration by, for example, affecting the output of a mining operation in South America which is owned by the multinational corpora-tion. It could be the case that the new plant is expected to absorb output from the mine. Where such knock-on effects exist, the firm needs to evaluate the project by aggregating all incremental cash flows accruing. Thus, whilst cash flows in Spain are clearly relevant, so are reduced cash flows accruing to the French and German operations, and so are increased flows accruing to the South American mine. In order fully to get to grips with the difficulties of multinational capital budgeting, it is necessary to progress slowly through a series of basic problems. This chapter uses one or two numerical examples to do so.

A Numerical Example

Consider the following situation. Multicorporation exports 120,000 widgets per annum to Alphaland, a fictional republic, at a price of £2 each. The variable cost of producing and delivering these widgets to Gamma, the capital and major trading area within Alphaland, is £1 per widget. Government officials in Alphaland have approached Multicorporation with a proposal that the firm build a small manufacturing plant in Gamma that would cost £1 million. Of this, £300,000 would be old equipment which Multicorporation has in its home country. Multicorporation would otherwise scrap this equipment which has a zero-tax written-down value. As a quid pro quo, an increase in tariffs against other importers of widgets would be associated with an agreement by Multicorporation to sell its product at £1.80 per widget and to buy certain raw materials from local suppliers and to use local managers. Total costs of local labour and materials are estimated at 50 pence per widget. At the end of 10 years, Multicorporation would sell out to the Alphaland Government for a nominal sum of £1.

With this background, Multicorporation estimates that it will sell about 240,000 widgets per annum. Some raw materials will continue to be bought from the parent and the price concerned is estimated at 30 pence per widget; on this, the parent will make a contribution estimated to amount to 10 pence per widget sold. Straight-line depreciation over 10 years is allowable for tax purposes on the whole amount of the £1 million of equipment. Corporate taxes are 50 per cent of profits in Alphaland and the parent company also has a 50 per cent tax rate at home and there is an allowance by way of a direct credit for taxes paid in Alphaland. No restriction exists on cash flow repatriations and the exchange rates are expected to remain constant. If it requires a 9 per cent DCF rate of return, should Multicorporation accept the Government's proposal? Table 19.1 details project cash flows and arrives at a DCF rate of return for the project of 7.2 per cent. This is below the 9 per cent requirement for this kind of project, so the company decides to reject the proposal. Influential civil servants in Alphaland hint that Internatcorp, a leading competitor, would be prepared to undertake the proposal should Multicorporation decide not to go ahead with the investment decision. If Multicorporation executives believe the civil servants' pronouncement, they must accept a probable loss in sales of the 120,000 widgets presently sold. The relevant incremental cash flow is then the basic cash flow of the project – namely, £182,000 per annum for 10 years. The DCF rate of return now becomes approximately 17 per cent. Clearly increment cash flows can be difficult to pin down on occasions. Maybe the kind of complexity exemplified in this problem is not just a function of the project being an international one. The same sort of difficulty could apply in a domestic capital budgeting problem. But there are complications which are truly the result of international operations. It is these that we shall now examine.

Table 19.1 Multicorp's Project in Alphaland

	£
Annual profit accruing in Alphaland	
Total sales 240,000 widgets × £1.80	432,000
Variable costs 240,000 widgets × £0.80	192,000
	240,000
Depreciation	100,000
Profit before tax	140,000
Tax	70,000
Profit after tax	70,000

	£	
Annual profit accruing in Multicorp's home country		
Contribution on raw materials sent to Alphaland 240,000 widgets × £0.10	£24,000	
Tax thereon	12,000	12,000
Total profit accruing to Multicorp		82,000
Add annual depreciation on equipment		100,000
Annual cash flow accruing to Multicorp		182,000
Cash flow foregone as a result of switching from export to direct manufacture		
Sales 120,000 widgets × £2	240,000	
Variable costs 120,000 widgets × £1	120,000	
	120,000	
Tax thereon	60,000	60,000
Annual net incremental cash flow		122,000
Investment		
Paid to third parties		700,000
Tax on profit on sale of equipment from parent to Alphaland		150,000
		850,000
DCF rate of return		7.2%

The International Complications

There are six main categories of complexity in international capital budgeting which analysts are advised to watch out for. These embrace situations where:

- project cash flows and parent cash flows differ;
- part of the parent input is via equipment (as per the above example);

- exchange rates are not expected to be constant throughout the project's life;
- different rates of tax apply in the country of the project and in the parent's country;
- royalties and management fees are involved;
- full remittance of cash flows arising from a project is restricted in terms of payment to the parent.

We shall now consider each of these complexities in turn.

In international capital budgeting, a significant difference may exist between the cash flow of a project and the amount that is remittable to the parent. The main reason for this is the existence of exchange controls in the host nation. Management in an overseas subsidiary can be excused for focusing only upon project cash flows accruing locally. Overseas managers often ignore the consequences of an investment upon the rest of the corporation – in particular the impact of the project at the level of distributable cash flows of the parent company. For the project, the appropriate incremental cash inflows are those additional cash outturns resulting from new operations after adjustment for local corporate taxes. From the parent's view, the critical incremental cash flow figures are the additional remittable funds to the parent treasury in London or New York. From the central treasury's point of view, the important cash flows relating to a new investment are incremental cash flows that are distributable to the multinational's shareholders. This means that management fees net of the costs of providing supervision, royalties, interest, dividend remittances, loan inputs and repayments and equity inputs are all key cash flows.

According to corporate financial theory, the value of a project is determined by the net present value of future cash flows available for the investor. The parent multinational corporation should therefore value only those cash flows that are available for repatriation. This should be done net of any transfer costs, since it is only these remaining funds that can be used to pay corporate dividends; it is only these funds that represent free cash flow available for shareholders. The estimation of parent cash flows involves us in focusing upon incremental remittable cash flows; whether they are actually remitted or not is immaterial – we need to home in on flows which may be remitted.

International project evaluation should embrace two key stages of analysis. First, project cash flows should be computed from the overseas subsidiary's standpoint, as if it were a separate free-standing entity. Focus in the second stage of analysis moves to the parent. Here analysis requires forecasts of the amounts and timing of distributable cash flows. It also requires information about taxes payable. The cash flow projections to the parent may be checked in terms of logic by considering what the parent distributable cash flows would be without the investment, and then considering the parent distributable post-investment cash flows and subtracting the former from the latter. In summary, then, it is distributable parent cash flows which matter.

For an overseas investment in a country where there are no restrictions on remittance, incremental cash flows accruing to the multinational corporation need to be forecast in local currency and then converted into the multinational corporation's home currency in accordance with expected exchange rates prevailing when such cash flows accrue. A framework is available towards the end of this chapter.

Where a project is in a country from which cash flow repatriation is restricted, the relevant focus should be upon remittable incremental parent cash flows. Analysis might embrace the cash flows set out in Table 19.2.

Table 19.2 Parent Cash Flows

Equity put into overseas project

Dividends back from overseas project

Equity capital remitted back to parent

Loans put into overseas project

Loan interest back from overseas

Loan repayments back from overseas

Management fees etc. received from overseas project net of supervision costs

Royalties

Equipment or inventory contributed to overseas project (here the opportunity cost is the relevant figure)

Contribution accruing to the parent or to a subsidiary in a country where repatriation of funds is not restricted (or to other subsidiaries whence repatriation is possible) on incremental sales to the project

Appropriate tax effect on remittance

Theoretically, the arguments in favour of considering only distributable parent cash flows in international capital budgeting decisions are overwhelming. However, one influential text, by Rodriguez and Carter (1979), casts some doubt upon this mode of analysis in respect of what its authors call the true multinational. And surveys show that firms give project cash flows more weight than parent cash flows. An investigation into the practices of 156 multinationals undertaken in 1978 by Vinod Bavishi (1979) reaches the conclusions summarised in Table 19.3.

The second major complication in international capital budgeting arises in situations in which the home-based company puts up part of its equity or loan

Table 19.3 Cash Flow Measures Used by US Multinationals in Foreign Project Appraisal

Pre-tax cash flow to foreign affiliate	12%
Post-tax cash flow to foreign affiliate	68%
Earnings remitted to the parent	12%
Earnings plus other cash flows, such as management fees, technical fees, royalties, etc. remitted to the parent	26%
Earnings plus other cash flows remitted to the parent, plus reinvested earnings	23%

capital in an overseas subsidiary by way of equipment or inventory. Clearly, the project should be debited with this input for the purpose of calculating project returns. But since it is parent returns that are of paramount importance, how should we treat this factor at the level of parent incremental cash flows?

The home territory company has surrendered value – in the form of equipment or inventory – in the expectation of obtaining greater value later on in terms of remittable, incremental parent cash flows. The problem that the financial analyst has is to put a value on the equipment or inventory surrendered. It is maintained that there is an ideally suited technique for valuing the property put in by the home territory company; it involves the use of the concept of deprival value. This was defined by Bonbright (1937, p. 71) as the 'adverse value of the entire loss, direct or indirect, that the owner might expect to suffer if he were to be deprived of the property'. Effectively, in subscribing equipment or inventory, the home territory company is voluntarily being deprived of assets in favour of the foreign business.

Bonbright advances three meaningful bases for valuation of an asset; these are:

- The current purchase price of an asset in a comparable state of wear and tear. This is replacement cost (RC).
- The net realisable value (NRV) of the asset. This is the current net disposable value.
- The present value of the expected future earnings stream flowing from the asset (PV).

An individual asset may be valued on each of these three alternative bases. But there are six ways in which values may be ranked in order of magnitude. These are:

1. NRV > PV > RC
2. NRV > RC > PV
3. PV > RC > NRV
4. PV > NRV > RC
5. RC > PV > NRV
6. RC > NRV > PV

In cases 1 and 2, the firm would be best advised to dispose of the asset concerned. However, the maximum loss suffered on disposal of the asset in these two cases is not NRV but RC. By purchasing another asset of the same type, the firm will restore the opportunity to obtain NRV. Thus the correct basis for valuation would be replacement cost.

In cases 3 and 4, the firm would be advised to use the asset in the business thus realising its present value which is the greatest payoff. However, if the firm were deprived of the asset concerned, it could simply replace it and thereby achieve the PV, which is the most advantageous outturn. In cases 3 and 4, the replacement cost is evidently the relevant deprival value alternative.

It should be reiterated that replacement cost in all of these circumstances would be the cost of replacing the asset in a condition similar to that deprived – this means in a comparable state of wear and tear and of comparable output capacity.

In case 5, if the firm were deprived of the asset, the amount foregone would be the PV. Evidently what the firm has foregone is the asset with which to earn future cash flow. Since the PV of future cash flows exceeds the NRV, the amount lost by the firm would be the PV. Note that, in this case, if the firm were deprived of the asset, there would be no point in replacing it – hence the RC is irrelevant.

Likewise in case 6, if the firm were deprived of the asset there would be no logical reason to replace it because RC exceeds both PV and NRV. This time, if deprived of the asset, the firm has surrendered the NRV rather than the PV. It would have paid the firm to obtain the NRV by selling it off rather than to concentrate upon PV by working the asset.

If this approach seems familiar to the reader, it is perhaps because it was the recommended method of asset valuation in the Sandilands Report on Inflation Accounting (1975, pp. 57–61) in the UK. Although inflation accounting is not the focus of this chapter, the Bonbright approach seems the relevant and logical way to assess the value foregone by the home territory company in surrendering assets to an overseas venture. The correct basis of valuation is summarised in Table 19.4.

Table 19.4 Basis of Asset Valuation

	Circumstances			*Correct basis*
1.	NRV > PV	> RC		RC
2.	NRV > RC	> PV		RC
3.	PV	> RC	> NRV	RC
4.	PV	> NRV	> RC	RC
5.	RC	> PV	> NRV	PV
6.	RC	> NRV	> PV	NRV

Cases 1, 2 and 4, where NRV exceeds RC, are likely to be relevant where inventory is input to a project.[1] These cases are much less likely to apply to fixed assets. The most common basis for equipment valuation is likely to derive from case 3, where the purpose for which the equipment is used in the home territory is likely to be ongoing. But cases 5 and 6 might also be encountered. Case 5 implies that the purpose to which the asset is put has a limited life since presumably when it was worn out it would pay to cease operations. Case 6 clearly implies that, rationally, the asset should be sold off immediately anyway.

Obviously, when an asset subscribed to an overseas venture is completely unnecessary to the home operations, the relevant valuation basis is NRV. Having

---

1. The assumption is that the input of inventory does not affect corporate sales at home. This would presumably be achieved by building up production prior to the shipment of inventory to the overseas project. It is reasonable to believe that most companies would wish to pursue this kind of production pattern. Likewise, with respect to case 3 (which is most likely to apply to fixed assets), the choice of RC as the appropriate valuation method presupposes that the home company would purchase a replacement asset before shipping the old one to the overseas territory, thereby avoiding disruption to home production and sales.

identified the appropriate valuation method in respect of the asset subscribed to an overseas project, this becomes the initial minus item in the parent cash flow projections against which subsequent estimated inflows are set. It is worth noting that, whether in a domestic or international situation, were one company to subscribe equipment and inventory to another company in return for a share of its equity, deprival value would provide the correct basis for valuing the input as part of the process of investment appraisal.

We would again stress that it is parent cash flows – not project flows – which are critical from the decision-making standpoint of the international company.

We shall now turn to the third area of complication: exchange rates. If exchange rates are in equilibrium at the time the project commences; if future exchange rates move in line with purchasing power parity; and if, further, project cash inflows and outflows move in line with general inflation in the overseas territory, then, assuming that there are no exchange control restrictions and assuming that host territory and home country taxes are at similar rates, project cash flow analysis will give exactly the same indication about investment viability as parent cash flow analysis. Rarely, if ever, will all of these conditions hold. Because of this, we recommend that estimated future project cash flows (net of local tax) be shown in money terms (that is, gross of expected host country inflation) and that the project net present value be calculated following the application of a money terms host country discount rate. Parent cash flows should be estimated by applying the expected future exchange rate to host country net cash flows if there are no exchange controls, or to remittable net cash flows if exchange controls are in place or are expected to be introduced. Due allowance must be made for host and home country taxation impacts and a parent net present value would be estimated following the application of a risk-adjusted parent discount rate. The question of appropriate discount rates is considered later in this chapter under the heading of 'Foreign Investment and the Cost of Capital'. Estimation of future exchange rates might follow projections of inflation rates with forecasting via purchasing power parity. Of course, it must be remembered that, whilst purchasing power parity is found empirically to hold in the long term, movements in exchange rates often follow discontinuous paths with governments supporting currencies for long periods before giving in and letting the economics of inflation rate differentials have their full effect. Thus exchange rate movements are often discontinuous and wise analysts will wish to reflect this in their forecasts – although the time at which purchasing power parity is likely to reassert itself is incredibly difficult to predict. Perhaps this problem is best handled via sensitivity analysis, with various sets of figures being prepared for different timings of purchasing power parity asserting itself.

The fourth area of complication concerns taxation. Clearly, project cash flows should be estimated net of local taxation and parent cash flows should be calculated net of parent taxation. On this point reference should be made to the chapter on International Taxation and especially to Table 24.1. Also, if royalties and management fees are charged by a home-based company to an overseas operating subsidiary, these should be shown as a debit to the project cash flow and as a credit in the parent cash flow analysis. Strictly speaking, of course, income to be foregone and/or incremental costs to be incurred in deploying management in pursuit of the project should be set against parent cash inflows.

To reiterate: situations where full remittance of net cash flow from project to parent is restricted are the major source of difficulty in international capital budgeting. They have briefly been referred to already, but the numerical example which follows may help the reader to understand the problem more fully.

Project Cash Flows v. Parent Cash Flows – A Numerical Example

In September 1985, the management committee of Whyco Inc. is considering an investment of US $5 million in a new subsidiary in Batavia, a fairly stable republic, where Whyco is presently making no sales. International marketing executives of Whyco have negotiated a monopoly supply of their product with the Batavian government in return for which Whyco will transfer ownership of the whole of the 100 per cent owned new subsidiary to the local government free of charge after five years of trading. Batavia has an expected inflation rate of 20 per cent per annum against the US expected rate of 5 per cent per annum. Approximately every month, to keep the currencies in line with purchasing power parity, the Batavian drac is devalued.

Batavia's exchange controls are such that the maximum annual dividend that Whyco will be allowed to remit (legally) to the USA will give dollar proceeds equal to 20 per cent per annum on the original investment from the USA. As mentioned above, the US company's investment is to be handed over to the Batavians in year 5, but immediately before this, the Whyco subsidiary may remit, as a special dividend, the balance of retained profits at the prevailing exchange rate.

Since Batavia has the same tax rate as the USA, the annual dividend remitted ($1 million per annum for five years) will not be subject to further taxes. As far as the remittance of cumulative retained profits is concerned, this will not be subject to further income taxes or corporate taxes either in Batavia or in the United States.

Table 19.5 Cash Flows – Batavian Venture

	Expected US $ dividend flow ($ mn)	Expected exchange rate (number of dracs to US $1)	Batavian forecast in money terms (expected inflation = 20%)		
			Free cash flow (mn dracs)	Net profit after tax (mn dracs)	Dividend (mn dracs)
Sept. 85	−5*	25	−125*		
Sept. 86	+1		50.0	40.0	
Sept. 87	+1		60.0	48.0	
Sept. 88	+1		72.0	57.6	
Sept. 89	+1		86.4	69.1	
Sept. 90	+1		103.7	82.9	
Sept. 90	?**				?**

Notes: * = original investment.
    ** = terminal retained earnings remitted as a special dividend.

Only if the amount of the special dividend remitted should exceed $5 million will the excess be subject to a capital tax of 25 per cent. There are no withholding taxes at all.

Forecasts of cash flows and profits for the new subsidiary have been sent to the Whyco treasurer – but there are some gaps. These forecasts are set out in Table 19.5. Whyco expects only to receive inflows in the USA on this project from annual dividend flows plus the final special dividend. These are expected to be remitted annually in September. Whyco's required real rate of return on this kind of project is 10 per cent per annum in the USA and 32 per cent per annum in Batavian drac terms. On the basis of the forecasts, what should Whyco's decision coalition do? The management committee views itself as a rational group aiming to maximise the present value of ordinary shareholders' interests.

The answer might follow along the lines set out below. According to purchasing power parity, the level of the drac can be forecast.

$$\frac{\hat{p}_\$ - \hat{p}_{Dc}}{1 + \hat{p}_{Dc}} = \frac{S_t - S_0}{S_0}$$

For September 1985, where S_t = expected drac exchange rate (USA quote using the direct method of quotation),

$$\frac{0.05 - 0.20}{1.20} = \frac{S_t - 0.04}{0.04}$$

$$-0.15 \times 0.04 = 1.20 \, (S_t - 0.04)$$
$$-0.006 = 1.20 \, S_t - 0.048$$
$$1.20 \, S_t = 0.042$$
$$S_t = 0.035$$

In dracs to the $ this is 28.57. Similar calculations can be done for later years giving the following values:

	Dracs to the $
Sept. 85	28.57
Sept. 86	32.65
Sept. 87	37.31
Sept. 88	42.64
Sept. 89	48.73

If the Batavian subsidiary remits a $1 million dividend each year, in dracs this will equal:

Sept. 85	Dc. 28.57 mn
Sept. 86	Dc. 32.65 mn
Sept. 87	Dc. 37.31 mn
Sept. 88	Dc. 42.64 mn
Sept. 89	Dc. 48.73 mn

Cumulative retained earnings at September 1989 can therefore be calculated as Dc. 107.76 mn. The tabulation in Table 19.5 now becomes:

	Dividend in US $ mn	Expected exchange rate (dracs to $)	Dividend (mn dracs)
Sept. 85	+1	28.57	28.57
Sept. 86	+1	32.65	32.65
Sept. 87	+1	37.31	37.31
Sept. 88	+1	42.64	42.64
Sept. 89	+1	48.73	48.73
Sept. 89	+2.21	48.73	107.76

The Batavian free cash flow is given in the question as is the discount rate of 32 per cent based on $(1 + r)(1 + \tilde{i}) - 1$ where r is real discount rate and $\tilde{i}$ is the expected inflation rate in Batavia. Thus the 32 per cent is based on $(1 + 0.10)(1 + 0.20) - 1 = 32\%$. So the US discount rate to be applied to US cash flows as set out in the above table should be:

$$(1 + 0.10)(1 + 0.05) - 1 = 15\%$$

Therefore the Batavian net present value is calculated thus:

Year (Sept.)	84	85	86	87	88	89
Free cash flow	−125	+50	+60	+72	+86.4	+103.7
32% discount factor	1.0	0.76	0.57	0.43	0.33	0.25
PVs	−125	38	34.2	31.0	28.5	25.9

$$\text{NPV} = 32.6 \text{ mn dracs}$$

The US net present value is calculated thus:

Year (Sept.)	84	85	86	87	88	89
	−5	+1	+1	+1	+1	+1 / +2.21
15% discount factor	1.0	0.87	0.75	0.65	0.56	0.49
PVs	−5	0.87	0.75	0.65	0.56	0.49 / 1.08

$$\text{NPV} = -0.6 \text{ mn } \$$$

On the basis of these forecasts distributable cash flows in the USA produce a negative net present value despite a positive local net present value. On the face of it, the implication is 'no go' unless Whyco executives can negotiate better terms with the Batavian government with respect to remittances, or terminal value, or duration before hand-over.

Foreign Investment and the Cost of Capital

A frequently asked question is whether foreign investment justifies a higher rate of return than does comparable domestic investment. Intuitively, students feel that a higher real return is justified for overseas investment given that the company is moving outside a geographical market which its executives know and in which it is presumably already successful. However, one might argue that international diversification lowers a firm's beta. Indeed, where there are barriers to international portfolio investment, it has been suggested that multinationals have accepted lower rates of return than firms operating in single countries because of their ability to diversify investment risks internationally.

For a company operating in Great Britain or the USA it may be argued that investment in less developed countries provides greater diversification benefits than investment in developed countries because their economies are less closely linked to those of industrialised nations. However, the systematic risk of projects in less developed countries is unlikely to be too far below the average for all projects since such countries are still ultimately tied in to the world economy. According to this view, the systematic risk of projects in less developed countries might only be marginally below comparable projects in industrialised countries. A Zambian copper mine may represent a capital project in a less developed country, but its systematic risk will be near to that in industrialised countries because the world demand and the world price of copper are functions of the state of economies in industrialised countries.

If stock markets take cognisance of and are influenced by domestic and international operations of firms, it follows that it is reasonable for foreign operations to be set required rates of return based upon systematic risk. Many researchers have attempted to test the hypothesis that investors take account of the foreign involvement of multinational firms. Severn (1974) found that the greater the foreign involvement of a firm, the lower the covariance of its earnings per share with the earnings per share of Standard and Poor's index. But multinationals are larger than most domestic corporations and the reduction in earnings variability found by Severn might have been due to size and greater product diversification rather than foreign earnings. Consistent with this view Haegele (1974) showed that, whilst multinationals' systematic risk is lower than for domestic corporations, these differences disappear once the results are adjusted for firm size. In this area, Agmon and Lessard (1977) examined the stock market behaviour of US multinational corporations. If investors recognise and reward international diversification, they argued, price movements of multinational shares should be more closely related to a world market factor and less to a domestic US market factor and this should be more pronounced the greater the degree of international operations. Whilst their regression analysis supports this hypothesis, their results are very low on statistical significance. Similarly, Aggarwal (1977) failed to locate any statistical relationship between multinationality and the cost of equity capital.

Perhaps, then, investors do not recognise the portfolio effects of a multinational corporation's foreign activities. Perhaps international diversification has an insignificant effect upon systematic risk. But perhaps there is a defect in the approach to the analysis. Beta calculations use the market return, R_M. But R_M already contains the impact of a large number of US multinationals. Corrections for this have been undertaken by Hughes, Logue and Sweeney (1975) who developed indices using portfolios of solely domestic and multinational firms. Their results suggest that the performance of the multinational is clearly superior to that of its purely domestic counterpart. This view is confirmed by work undertaken by Shapiro and Vinso (1979).

An interesting piece of work undertaken by Jacquillat and Solnik (1978) is worth mentioning. Comparing the results achieved in terms of reduction of variance by an international portfolio versus a portfolio of internationally diversified companies, they concluded that, whilst multinational firms do provide diversification for investors, international portfolio diversification is a far superior source of elimination of variance – and investors are able, in the absence of restrictions on portfolio investment, to action this superior diversification on their own. This seems to suggest that the required returns on foreign projects are unlikely to be much below the required returns on comparable domestic projects.

To all intents and purposes, then, there is no substantial evidence to suggest that we should use different required rates of return for comparable international and domestic projects.

Back to the Basic Model

Returning to the basic model applied to a situation where a multinational corporation is contemplating investment in a country which puts no restrictions on remittance of cash and profit flows, students are sometimes a little confused about the order of calculation necessary to arrive at a home country net present value for a project. In this section we show that at least four methods[1] may be followed to arrive at the present value. We show that mathematically they all give the same result so long as purchasing power parity holds throughout the period of analysis and so long as taxes are ignored. These assumptions are relaxed later. The four methods and the stages of evaluation involved in each are summarised in Table 19.6.

As shown in the table, method one arrives at a home currency present value in three steps. These steps are summarised mathematically below. The notation is as follows:

A_1, A_2, A_3 = local cash flows receivable at the end of years 1, 2 and 3.

e_1, e_2, e_3 = end-year exchange rates expressed in terms of number of units of home currency to one of away currency – that is the home country direct quote.

r_s = the home country (assumed to be the USA) money terms discount rate required.

Year	1	2	3
Stage 1 – Local cash flows in money terms	A_1	A_2	A_3
Stage 2 – Convert to $	$A_1 e_1$	$A_2 e_2$	$A_3 e_3$
Stage 3 – Calculation of $ present value	$\dfrac{A_1 e_1}{(1 + r_s)}$ +	$\dfrac{A_2 e_2}{(1 + r_s)^2}$ +	$\dfrac{A_3 e_3}{(1 + r_s)^3}$

Thus we have come up with a present value using method one.

---

1. The first two methods are as suggested by Brealey and Myers (1984).

Table 19.6 Framework for International Investment Decision Evaluation

	Method 1	Method 2	Method 3	Method 4
Stage 1	Estimate future cash flows in local currency and in money terms	Estimate future cash flows in local currency and in money terms	Estimate future cash flows in local currency and in money terms	Estimate future cash flows in local currency and in money terms
Stage 2	Convert to home currency using forecasting exchange rates	Calculate present value using local currency money terms discount rate	Reduce to real terms flows in local currency by discounting for local inflation	Reduce to real terms flows in local currency by discounting for local inflation
Stage 3	Calculate present value using home currency money terms discount rates	Convert to home currency present value using spot rate	Convert to home currency using spot exchange rate	Calculate real terms present value in local cash using real terms discount rate
Stage 4			Calculate present value using real terms discount rate	Convert to home currency present value using spot rate

We now turn to method two and here we use one further piece of notation, namely:

r_F = the foreign money terms discount rate required

For method two the steps to arrive at a present value can be shown as:

Year	1	2	3
Stage 1 – Local cash flows in money terms	A_1	A_2	A_3

Stage 2 – Calculation of local currency present value

$$\frac{A_1}{(1 + r_F)} + \frac{A_2}{(1 + r_F)^2} + \frac{A_3}{(1 + r_F)^3}$$

Stage 3 – Conversion to \$ present value

$$\left[\frac{A_1}{(1 + r_F)} + \frac{A_2}{(1 + r_F)^2} + \frac{A_3}{(1 + r_F)^3} \right] e_0$$

It will be recalled that the international Fisher effect yields the equation:

$$e_t = \frac{(1 + r_\$)}{(1 + r_F)} e_0$$

If we apply it to the present value we arrived at for method one, it will be shown to be equal to that in method two. Method one's present value expression becomes:

$$\frac{A_1}{(1 + r_\$)} \frac{(i + r_\$)}{(1 + r_F)} e_0 + \frac{A_2}{(1 + r_\$)^2} \frac{(i + r_\$)^2}{(1 + r_F)^2} e_0 + \frac{A_3}{(1 + r_\$)^3} \frac{(i + r_\$)^3}{(1 + r_F)^3} e_0$$

$$= \left[\frac{A_1}{(1 + r_F)} + \frac{A_2}{(1 + r_F)^2} + \frac{A_3}{(1 + r_F)^3} \right] e_0$$

So it is clear that methods one and two yield the same outturn.

In both methods three and four, we have begun from the estimation of future cash flows in money terms in foreign currency and then reduced these to real terms by discounting by anticipated inflation. Sometimes analysis begins from stage two, namely, being given real local cash flows. In our algebraic approach to method three we use some new notation, namely:

i_F = local anticipated inflation
$i_\$$ = US anticipated inflation
r_R = the real return requirement on a project

The Fisher effect would suggest that:

$(1 + r_\$) = (1 + r_R)(1 + i_\$)$ and
$(1 + r_F) = (1 + r_R)(1 + i_F)$

Expressed in words: the real return requirement should be constant from one country to another – certainly we would expect this where international capital movements are not restricted. Having said this, our cash flow steps for method three would be as shown below:

Year	1	2	3
Stage 1 – Local cash flows in money terms	A_1	A_2	A_3
Stage 2 – Local cash flows in real terms[1]	$\dfrac{A_1}{(1 + i_F)}$	$\dfrac{A_2}{(1 + i_F)^2}$	$\dfrac{A_3}{(1 + i_F)^3}$
Stage 3 – Convert to \$ using spot rate	$\dfrac{A_1 e_0}{(1 + i_F)}$	$\dfrac{A_2 e_0}{(1 + i_F)^2}$	$\dfrac{A_3 e_0}{(1 + i_F)^3}$
Stage 4 – Calculate \$ present value	$\dfrac{A_1 e_0}{(1 + i_F)(1 + r_R)}$ +	$\dfrac{A_2 e_0}{(1 + i_F)^2(1 + r_R)^2}$ +	$\dfrac{A_3 e_0}{(1 + i_F)^3(1 + r_R)^3}$

It will be observed that in stage three we have converted future cash flows from local currency to dollars using the spot rate. We have done this because we have eliminated inflation from our estimated flows at stage two. With inflation eliminated the appropriate exchange rate would be the spot rate. To move on from our stage four equation above, we substitute for $(1 + r_R)$ where:

$$(1 + r_R) = \frac{(1 + r_F)}{(1 + i_F)}$$

So the stage four expression becomes:

$$\left[\frac{A_1}{(1 + r_F)} + \frac{A_2}{(1 + r_F)^2} + \frac{A_3}{(1 + r_F)^3} \right] e_0$$

and this is the same as the final expression for methods one and two.

Finally we look at method four using the same procedures. We would begin from:

Year	1	2	3
Stage 1 – Local cash flows in money terms	A_1	A_2	A_3
Stage 2 – Local cash flows in real terms	$\dfrac{A_1}{(1 + i_F)}$	$\dfrac{A_2}{(1 + i_F)^2}$	$\dfrac{A_3}{(1 + i_F)^3}$
Stage 3 – Calculation of local present value	$\dfrac{A_1}{(1 + i_F)(1 + r_F)}$ +	$\dfrac{A_2}{(1 + i_F)^2(1 + r_F)^2}$ +	$\dfrac{A_3}{(1 + i_F)^3(1 + r_F)^3}$

---

1. We have assumed a constant inflation rate in our model. Even if we had not, our ultimate answer would come out the same although the mathematics would be more complicated.

Stage 4 – Convert to $ $\dfrac{A_1 e_0}{(1 + i_F)(1 + r_F)}$ + $\dfrac{A_2 e_0}{(1 + i_F)^2(1 + r_F)^2}$ + $\dfrac{A_3 e_0}{(1 + i_F)^3(1 + r_F)^3}$
present value

It will be noticed that this present value is the same as that obtained for method three.

Evidently whichever of the approaches in Table 19.6 we use, our present value in home currency terms comes out as identical. However, it must be clearly understood that alternative use of the above four approaches is based upon purchasing power parity holding throughout the life of the project – from beginning to end. And furthermore, the algebraic example takes no account of taxation. We now discuss which would be the appropriate method given allowance for each of the above market imperfections.

First of all we shall look at the implications of purchasing power parity not holding throughout the project's life. What if the overseas currency is not in equilibrium at the outset of the project? Would it make sense for a company to accept an otherwise poor overseas project simply because it was bullish about the strengthening of the overseas currency at a rate in excess of purchasing power parity? Or would it make sense to reject an overseas project that looked attractive in terms of operational cash outturns despite the fact that management was bearish about the overseas currency?

Brealey and Myers (1984) recommend that, assuming the project under investigation is in a country with a fully convertible currency, operating considerations are paramount. After all, they argue, if one has views about the strength or weakness of the overseas currency (and the home country has no exchange controls) one can back these judgements by taking positions in forward, futures or options markets. In this way one can obtain the benefit of backing judgements on project operating profitability and currency valuation. Referring to a multinational company investing in the Netherlands, Brealey and Myers comment that it would be foolish 'to reject a good project just because it is pessimistic about the guilder. The company would do much better to go ahead with the project and sell guilders forward. In that way, it would get the best of both worlds.' Brealey and Myers are presumably referring to a project which looks attractive in terms of guilder cash flow projections but which looks unattractive when assessed in terms of dollar cash flows following a weakening of the guilder in excess of purchasing power parity considerations. This might occur because the weakening made good a previous disequilibrium. If this is so, we would disagree with Brealey and Myers. The multinational company which habitually earns negative dollar net present values on projects, whether they be in the Netherlands or the USA, should suffer a decline in shareholder valuation. To get the best of both worlds would involve a combination of not implementing the project and selling guilders forward.

Brealey and Myers go on to say that the exchange rate that should be used to convert foreign flows to home currency should be the 'market's consensus forecast' based upon purchasing power parity holding throughout the life of the project with the current exchange rate as a base. We would reiterate that the Brealey and Myers view turns around a currency being fully convertible. Should the existence of relevant exchange controls create a market imperfection, then it is distributable parent cash flows based on remittable cash flows which should underpin the investment decision.

Brealey and Myers' view that corrections of previous disequilibria are effectively disregarded essentially assumes an efficient market/rational expectations perspective in which the four-way equilibrium immutably prevails. Whilst accepting the logic of their stated position, the evidence reviewed in Chapter 11 suggests that disequilibria continue for varying periods before correction. But correction seems ultimately to take place. And we would be naive to build financial models without allowing for correction of disequilibria. Most commentators accepted that the US dollar was undervalued in late 1978; virtually all commentators agreed that the dollar was overvalued early in 1985. The technique of selective hedging is based upon the existence of disequilibria in foreign exchange markets. In a real-world context, in which purchasing power parity is unlikely always to hold, we believe that it would be unwise to implement Brealey and Myers' prescription.

There is, further, the question of taxation. Clearly, free cash flows in the overseas territory are the starting point for analysing incremental inflows. These should be net of local taxation. Assuming that no exchange controls exist, the relevant increment cash flows in home currency terms are cash flows which are distributable to parent company shareholders. Thus all incremental foreign cash flows have (notionally) to be treated as if they were distributed as dividend to the parent. In turn, this means that overseas free cash flows net of local taxes have to be subjected (again notionally) to overseas withholding tax, then converted to home currency where they will (probably) bear further tax. Before tackling international capital budgeting problems in the real world, readers should peruse Chapter 24 on International Taxation up to, and in particular, Table 24.1.

We would suggest, therefore, that the right approach to capital budgeting, in countries with no regulations preventing the repatriation of funds, involves the following steps:

1. Forecasting local currency money terms free cash flows after local taxes.
2. Converting these to home currency, money terms free cash flows net of all taxes. Conversion should be based upon exchange rates which allow for corrections of past disequilibria in purchasing power parity (although the timing of such corrections is problematical) and incorporate subsequent inflation rate differentials.
3. Discounting of home currency, money terms free cash flows net of all taxes to net present value using a home currency, money terms, risk adjusted, net of tax discount rate.

It should be mentioned that the present author has come across real-world situations where the awareness that disequilibria in the four-way model do exist has led sophisticated companies to undertake overseas project analysis using two sets of calculations, one based on PPP holding through the life of the project and another based on the early correction of disequilibria followed then by PPP dictating subsequent exchange rate movements – in other words, a Brealey and Myers approach and an approach as recommended by the present author.

Summary

International capital budgeting, like its domestic counterpart, focuses upon expected incremental cash flows associated with a project. But international capital budgeting is more complex because of certain factors peculiar to international operations.

There are six main categories of complexity which analysts are well advised to look out for. These embrace situations where project cash flows and parent cash flows differ, where part of the parent input is by way of equipment, where exchange rates are not expected to be constant throughout a project's life (and this probably applies to all overseas projects), where different tax rates apply in the host and home country, where royalties and fees are to be paid out of income of the new investment to a group company in the home country, and where full remittance of project cash flows is restricted by exchange controls. Each of these situations is considered and the implications are discussed. These distinctive characteristics of international capital budgeting compared with domestic invest-ment appraisal are extremely important. They are rarely fully appreciated even within the most sophisticated of companies and the student can play a big part in helping his company grapple with the difficulties surrounding international invest-ment appraisal. Many poor international investment decisions have been made because of the failure of the multinational company fully to comprehend that it is distributable parent cash flows that matter rather than mere project cash flows.

References

Aggarwal, Raj (1977) 'Multinationality and stock market valuation', *Financial Review*, Summer, pp. 45–46.

Agmon, Tamir and Lessard, Donald R. (1977) 'Investor recognition of corporate international diversification', *Journal of Finance*, September, pp. 1049–1056.

Bavishi, Vinod (1979) *Capital Budgeting for US-based Multinational Corporations: An Assessment of Theory and Practice*, Working paper, University of Connecticut.

Bonbright, J.C. (1937) *The Valuation of Property*, McGraw-Hill.

Brealey, Richard and Myers, Stewart (1984) *Principles of Corporate Finance*, 2nd edn, McGraw-Hill.

Haegele, Monroe J. (1974) *Exchange Rate Expectations and Security Returns*, Ph.D. Dissertation, University of Pennsylvania.

Hughes, John S., Logue, Dennis E. and Sweeney, Richard J. (1975) 'Corporate international diversification and market assigned measures of diversification', *Journal of Finance and Quantitative Analysis*, November, pp. 627–637.

Jacquillat, Bertrand and Solnik, Bruno H. (1978) 'Multinationals are poor tools for diversification', *Journal of Portfolio Management*, Winter, pp. 8–12.

Rodrigues, Rita and Carter, Eugene (1979) *International Financial Management*, 2nd edn, Prentice-Hall.

Sandilands Committee, The (1975) *Inflation Accounting*, Cmnd 6225, HMSO.

Severn, Alan K. (1974) 'Investor evaluation of foreign and domestic risk', *Journal of Finance*, May, pp. 545–550.

Shapiro, Alan C. and Vinso, Joseph D. (1979) *The Value of International Diversification for the Multinational Corporation*, Working paper, University of Southern California.

Political Risk

In most countries, governments intervene in their national economies. This increases the political risk that multinational firms face. Political risk takes various forms, ranging from changes in tax regulations to exchange controls, ranging from stipulations about local production to expropriation, ranging from commercial discrimination against foreign-controlled businesses to restrictions on access to local borrowings. Political risk can be defined as the exposure to a change in value of an investment or cash position resultant upon government actions. When viewed from the multinational corporation's standpoint the effect of changes in government policies may be positive as well as negative.

Although political risk poses severe threats and may create profitable opportunities for multinational companies, firms have been found to view and to react to political risk without formal planning or systematic analysis. This is naive; a formal assessment of political risk and its implications for the multinational firm is important for decision making and it is towards the specification of such a framework that this chapter is aimed.

Formal assessment of political risk usually involves three key steps. These are:

1. The recognition of the existence of political risk and its likely consequences; this stage is concerned with measuring political risk.
2. The development of policies to cope with political risk; this stage is concerned with managing political risk.
3. Should expropriation occur, the development of tactics to maximise compensation; this stage is concerned with developing post-expropriation policies.

The Measurement of Political Risk

There are two ways to approach the measurement of political risk: there is the country-specific route (this is also called the macro approach), and there is also the firm-specific route (this is frequently called the micro approach).

Various political risk forecasting services are available. These services normally develop models leading to country risk indices which purport to quantify the level of political risk for each nation analysed. These indices generally reflect the stability of the local political environment. Such measures generally take cognisance of changes in government, levels of violence in the country, internal and external conflicts, and so on. Indices of this sort are intended to assess whether the government in power at a particular point in time will be there in the future and hence the extent to which the existing political status quo can be expected to continue.

The rating method developed by Haner (1979) is worth mentioning because its approach is systematic and its rationale is not dissimilar to many others. Haner rates, on a scale from 0 to 7, a number of factors which cause internal political stress. These include:

- fractionalisation of the political spectrum and power of resulting factions;
- fractionalisation by language, ethnic, or religious groups and power of resulting factions;
- restrictive measures required to retain power;
- xenophobia, nationalism, inclination to compromise;
- social conditions, including extremes in population density and the distribution of wealth;
- organisation and strength of a radical left government.

To these scores are added ratings arising from external factors. These include:

- dependence on or importance to a hostile major power;
- negative influence of regional political forces, possibilities of border wars and disruptions arising from such sources of conflict.

Finally, additional ratings relating to estimated symptoms of problems are computed and aggregated. These include:

- societal conflict;
- political instability.

Scores are aggregated and updated regularly as the world political environment changes. Countries are then rated as to:

- minimal risk: 0 to 19 rating points
- acceptable risk: 20 to 34 rating points
- high risk: 35 to 44 rating points
- prohibitive risk: over 45 rating points

A number of similar systems are available for subscription; however, their approaches vary slightly. Frequently their input data are different – for example inflation rates, balance of payment deficits, surpluses and other macroeconomic factors are used. Always the objective is to assess whether there is a high risk of adverse changes resulting from government intervention. The development of political risk models is becoming more sophisticated and most rely on a combination of objective data and subjective estimates. The ability of political risk models to forecast the timing of changes in the environment is important. Research in this area is at too rudimentary a stage to be anything like conclusive. As a rule, the models used by rating agencies have not been consistently successful. It is worth mentioning that such models have not evolved out of discriminant analysis techniques, which would, perhaps, be the most scientific approach to the rating of country-specific political risk.

The second avenue towards political risk rating is via the micro route. Studies of expropriation show that they are most likely to occur in the extractive, utility and financial services sectors of the economy rather than in the manufacturing sector. Based on David Bradley's study (1977) of expropriations by industry group over a period from 1960 to 1974, the league table of expropriations is shown in Table 20.1.

Table 20.1 Expropriation by Industry – 1960 to 1974

Industry	Number of expropriations	Percentage of total
Oil	84	12.0
Extractive industries	38	18.0
Utilities and transportation	17	4.0
Insurance and banking	33	4.0
Manufacturing	30	1.2
Agriculture	19	★
Sales and service	16	★
Land, property and construction	23	★

*Data not available

David Bradley's study also focused upon regions of the world where expropriation was most prevalent. It showed that Latin America, the Arab States and Black Africa featured at the top of the league table for the years from 1960 to 1974. His findings on this score are summarised in Table 20.2.

Table 20.2 Expropriation by Region – 1960 to 1976

	Number of expropriations	Expropriated companies as a percentage of all US companies in region
Latin America	144	2.6%
Arab States	78	20.4%
Black Africa	39	8.1%
Asia	31	2.2%

It needs to be stressed that some firms may gain by the same event that harms other firms. A firm relying on imports will be adversely affected by trade restrictions, but an import-competing firm may well be the beneficiary of such regulations.

Political risk has a different effect on different firms. Generalised political risk indices must be used cautiously and subjected to careful analysis in order to assess the full impact upon a particular company. Governments rarely expropriate foreign investments indiscriminately. The greater the benefits of a foreign operation to the host country and the more expensive the replacement of such facilities by a purely local operation, the lower the degree of political risk to the firm. Governments select expropriation targets according to criteria other than purely political ones.

Firms frequently incorporate the consequences of political risk into investment decisions via:

- shortening the minimum payback period;
- raising the required discount rate for the investment;
- adjusting cash flows for the cost of risk reduction, for example by charging a premium for overseas political risk insurance;
- adjusting cash flows to reflect the impact of a particular risk;
- using certainty equivalents in place of expected cash flows.

Of the above methods, the last is the least fraught with theoretical objections – but it is probably the least used, too.

Managing Political Risk

A firm may take action to control its exposure to political risk. Having analysed the political environment of a country and assessed its implications for corporate operations, it has to decide whether or not to invest there. If it decides to go ahead it should structure the investment so as to minimise political risk. It needs to be reiterated that the impact of political risk is a function of the firm's activities. The firm's overseas investments determine its susceptibility to political risk. Political risk may be controlled at the pre-investment stage or in the course of operations, or both. There are four approaches aimed at minimising risk in the pre-investment period. These can be classified as avoidance, insurance, negotiating the environment and structuring the environment.

The simplest approach to the management of political risk is to avoid it. Many firms do this by simply deciding against going ahead with investments in politically uncertain countries. If the international firm does decide to go ahead, the key question is the extent of political risk which a company is prepared to tolerate and whether the investment promises an appropriate return to compensate for it. Avoiding countries likely to be politically unstable ignores the possible high returns available from investment there. Business is all about taking risks and ensuring that sufficient returns are earned to compensate for them.

The second approach to pre-investment planning for political risk is insurance. Having insured assets in politically risky areas against expropriation and lesser risks of a political kind, the international firm can concentrate upon managing the business rather than worrying about political risk. Specific government departments of most developed countries sell political risk insurance to cover the foreign assets of domestic companies. In the UK, ECGD offers a confiscation cover scheme for new overseas investments only. Lloyds of London also offers the company opportunities to insure against political risk, including expropriation. Its cover applies to new and existing investments on a comprehensive, non-selective policy. Lloyds is, in fact, the only private insurer against expropriation. Fees vary according to country and the type of risk insured, with cover usually limited to 90 per cent of equity participation.

In addition to insurance, many firms try to reach an agreement with the host government before making an investment. This defines rights and responsibilities on the part of both parties. Effectively it specifies the rules under which the firm can operate locally and is called a concession agreement. Such agreements have been frequently resorted to by multinationals operating in less developed countries. They are often negotiated with weak governments. However, they have frequently been repudiated following a change in government and cannot therefore guarantee the international company avoidance of political risk. Concession agreements have carried less weight in the third world as time has gone by; nonetheless, they are usually observed in developed countries.

Having decided to invest in a country, a firm may minimise its exposure to political risk by structuring its operating and financial policies so as to make its posture acceptable and to ensure that it remains in charge of events. A strategy of keeping the foreign company dependent upon group companies for markets and/or supplies is one such tactic. With vertically integrated production in different countries, there is little point in the government of a host country expropriating assets since the company would continue to depend upon the multinational corporation for supplies. This policy is one of the approaches used by international motor companies.

For companies which depend heavily upon research and development facilities and proprietary technology it pays to concentrate these facilities in the home country thus enabling a firm to lower the probability of expropriation. Similarly, establishing a single global trademark that cannot legally be duplicated can be effective. Sourcing from various plants reduces the host nation's ability to hurt the worldwide firm by seizing a single plant. And encouraging external local shareholders is another risk-reducing policy. This may involve raising capital from the host government, international financial institutions and customers, rather than employing funds supplied or guaranteed by the parent company. But it may not necessarily be the cheapest way to raise capital.

Obtaining unconditional host government guarantees is another way of minimising financial aspects of political risk. Such guarantees enable creditors to initiate legal action in foreign courts against any commercial transactions between the host country and third parties should a subsequent government repudiate the original obligations. Such guarantees provide the international company with sanctions against a foreign nation without relying upon the support of its home government.

Operating policies may also be resorted to as a ploy to avoid political risk. In such a category we would put planned divestment, short-term profit maximisation, creating benefits for the host nation, developing local shareholders, and adaptation. Each of these is now briefly considered.

Planned divestment speaks for itself and is a frequently used policy for minimising political risk. Under short-term profit maximisation, we include policies of withdrawing the maximum amount of cash from the local operation. Cutting reinvestment to the bare minimum, deferring maintenance expenditures, cutting marketing expenditures, eliminating training programmes, are all tactics aimed at short-term cash generation. These policies are not unusual in the light of clear expropriation threats as they ensure that the company will have a short life locally. However, this behaviour is likely to hasten expropriation. International firms also try to manage political risk by changing the benefit/cost split between the multinational and the host country. If a local government's objectives are concerned with economic benefits and costs, then the international firm may attempt to reduce the perceived advantages of nationalisation or expropriation. Policies include ensuring that benefits accrue locally. Such approaches embrace training local workers and managers, developing export markets for the host nation and manufacturing a wide range of products locally as substitutes for imports. Another frequently employed strategy is the encouragement of local stakeholders including customers, suppliers, employees, bankers and so on, all based in the host nation. This policy includes concentrating operations upon joint venture partnerships with local firms. Another tactic for political risk management involves adaptation to potential expropriation and the development of policies to earn profits following expropriation. Many oil companies whose property has been nationalised or expropriated receive management contracts to continue exploration, refining and marketing. Such multinationals recognise that they do not have to own or control an asset in order to earn profits and create cash flow.

Financial tactics designed to minimise political risk embrace a whole spectrum. Threats exist both because of the possibility of confiscation of assets and because of the possibility that a foreign currency may become less convertible. If funds are not convertible it is best to borrow as much as possible locally rather than risk funds becoming permanently blocked overseas. Methods by which multinationals reduce political risk through financing tactics include the use of a very high proportion of local gearing, minimising intragroup sources of finance and avoiding parent or group guarantees. It also pays the multinational to try to ensure that profit arises in the UK, through such devices as royalty payments, transfer pricing and so on, rather than leaving surplus funds in a country where political risk may be perceived to be high. No medals should be won for building up blocked funds overseas.

Post-Expropriation Policies

Expropriation does not come out of the blue. Generally there are cues and signals which precede expropriation. Recognition of these gives the international firm the opportunity to open discussions with the host government. In anticipated expropriation situations, the international firm frequently moves from rational negotiation to applying power, to legal remedies and then to management surrender. When expropriation occurs, the aim of negotiation changes. Trying to persuade the host government of its folly comes first. The multinational corporation often quotes the future economic benefits that it will provide, but presumably the host government has already assessed these and its own actions have already taken them into account. If confiscation were merely a bargaining ploy on the part of the host nation to gain concessions, then this approach is likely to be successful. The multinational which perceives host government sabre-rattling to be of this kind may resort to a policy of retreat aimed at profitably keeping in the battle.

The firm may bargain with the government in an attempt to persuade it to reconsider. Mutual concessions may be suggested so that the firm might continue its operations. Such concessions may include the following:

- hire national managers
- raise transfer prices charged from the locally based firm to other parts of the group
- accept local partners
- change expatriate management
- invest more capital
- contribute to political campaigns
- release the host government from concessionary agreements
- support government programmes
- suspend payment of dividends
- surrender majority control
- remove all home country personnel
- reorganise to give greater benefit to the local company

Of the above concessions, the first four are the most attractive to the international firm. As a rule, the second four are the next most attractive and the final four are the least attractive.

If these concessions do not work, the firm begins to apply negative sanctions. These may take the form of supporting an opposition political party or invoking home government support for the firm's position; but such political tactics rarely work. By contrast, the international firm may agree at this stage to relinquish control in return for compensation, thereby saving the host government and the firm itself a considerable investment in negotiating time.

Whilst rational negotiation and the application of power continue, the firm may also begin to seek legal redress. It is a rule of law that legal remedy must first be sought in the courts of the host country. After this route has been exhausted, the international firm may proceed to put its case in the home country and in international courts. Where host courts are impartial, seeking local redress is likely to be moderately effective. But where the judiciary is subservient to the government, the international firm can expect little payoff here and it may be most expeditious to seek judgements against the host country's property in the home country or in third countries.

Efforts to sue national governments are frustrated by the doctrine of sovereign immunity and the act of state doctrine. The former says that a sovereign state may not be tried in the courts of another state without its consent. And the latter doctrine implies that a nation is sovereign within its own borders and its domestic actions may not be questioned in the courts of another nation, even if those actions violate international law. However, the doctrine of sovereign immunity is normally waived when it comes to a foreign country's commercial activities.

Another route is to lobby in the home country in an attempt to restrict the import of raw materials and other products from the host country. Arbitration of investment disputes is another alternative; this has been moderately effective since the establishment of the International Centre for Settlements of Investment Disputes, set up in 1966 by the World Bank. Created to encourage foreign direct investment by providing a forum for international investment disputes, the centre provides binding arbitration, although in practice its influence is small.

Should the firm have had little success at negotiating, applying power and seeking legal redress, eventual surrender follows and attempts to salvage some of the investment ensue. This usually involves settling for whatever insurance and other payments may be obtained.

Summary

Governments intervene in their national economies and, in so doing, increase the level of political risk that the multinational firm faces. Political risk ranges from exposure to changes in tax legislation, through the impacts of exchange controls, to restrictions affecting operations and financing in a host country. Political risk can be defined as the exposure to a change in the value of an investment or cash position resulting from government actions.

Multinationals are concerned with the measurement and management of political risk and this chapter has focused upon the generality of political risk measurement systems and upon managing political risk in the pre-investment stage, during the course of operations, and at the post-expropriation stage.

References

Bradley, David (1977) 'Managing against expropriation', *Harvard Business Review*, July–August, pp. 75–83.
Haner, F.T. (1979) 'Rating investment risks abroad', *Business Horizons*, vol. 22, no. 2, pp. 18–23.

21

Financing the Overseas Subsidiary

In addition to the general issues of financing which apply to any business, there are special factors which impinge upon the funding of an overseas subsidiary. With respect to the financing of any business, management needs to consider exactly what is being financed, the extent to which the problem can be solved by more efficient operation of the assets owned (for example, better working capital management can reduce the needs for funds), the extent of debt, the blend of short-term and long-term funds, the maturity structure and evaluation of the true relative costs of different sources of capital. But on the multinational financial stage there are more considerations which have to be borne in mind. In this chapter we present an analysis of the features peculiar to the financing of overseas operations. An approach to the problems of domestic financing can be found in any of the good standard texts on financial management.[1]

The special features of financing overseas subsidiaries that we shall cover in this chapter arise from the presence of political risk, exchange control risk, currency risk, losses earned by subsidiaries, intercompany credit, taxation effects, dividend policy, other methods of profit transfer, parent company guarantees and the problem of partly-owned subsidiaries. It is our contention that rational recommendations on the financing of an overseas subsidiary can only flow from a careful study of all the above special features and from an evaluation of how they are likely to impact upon a company confronted with an overseas opportunity which it wishes to finance. We shall now consider each of these special factors in turn.

Political Risk

Chapter 20 was devoted to the topic of political risk. In the context of financing an overseas subsidiary we need to consider confiscation risk, commercial political risk and financial political risk.

Subsidiaries operating in most stable, industrialised countries might consider themselves free from confiscation risk. However, even countries like the UK and

---

1. For example, Brealey and Myers (1984) or Franks, Broyles and Carleton (1985).

Canada have shown, for example in their postures on oil exploration, that US multinational companies run risk in this area. Obviously exposure in such countries is less than in, say, Nicaragua or Iran, but it nonetheless exists in advanced industrialised countries. The parent company may partially counter such risk by the way in which it finances its overseas subsidiaries. It may also resort to confiscation insurance. In Britain, ECGD offers confiscation cover for new overseas investments and Lloyds offers cover for existing and new investments in a comprehensive, non-selective form. Financial tactics designed to minimise this risk embrace the use of high levels of gearing (preferably local gearing), maximum use of local sources of funds including local debt and equity where a partly owned subsidiary is deemed acceptable, minimising the use of intergroup sources of finance, and avoidance of parent company guarantees. The essential idea is, of course, that should the subsidiary be confiscated, the host government takes over the liabilities as well as the assets of the multinational's local operations.

The second class of political risk is commercial political risk which is best explained by an example. Consider that an overseas country is taken over by a left-wing government which imposes regulations of high minimum wages and freezes price levels resulting in falling profit margins. This kind of exposure may affect all businesses in the country or it may be designed specifically to attack foreign-owned operations. Discrimination against foreign-owned businesses may take various guises such as not awarding government contracts to them, giving advantages and subsidies to local-owned competitors, restricting import licences for key raw materials, refusing to grant work permits to non-indigenous staff and so on. By taking in local shareholders it may be possible to create an influential body of opinion which would result in avoidance of some of the worst aspects of commercial political risk.

Financial political risk takes such forms as restricting access to local capital markets, restricting the repatriation of capital and dividends, imposing heavy interest-free import deposits, and so on. Financing tactics designed to beat such impediments are not always easy to access. If the problem is merely the non-availability of cheap local capital markets, the company must weigh up the relative merits of funds from outside the country versus the more expensive version of local funds. Restrictions on dividend remittance favour financing using parent debt or other debt borrowed from outside the host country. Interest and capital repayments will, in all probability, be remittable. If dividend remittances are severely restricted, analysis of parent cash flows, as recommended in Chapter 19, may show a lack of economic viability for the whole operation.

Exchange Control Risk

Frequently exchange controls affect the multinational company because an overseas subsidiary has accumulated surplus cash in the country in which it operates and this may not be remitted out of the overseas territory. This surplus cash may arise from profits earned or from sums owed for imports into the overseas country. As an example of how this latter constraint works, France had a regulation which stipulated that intergroup trade debts of a French subsidiary to an associated company, if not paid within one year of import, became blocked as an unremittable sum of capital invested in the subsidiary.

Goods shipped to some countries, notably Nigeria and India, which are denominated in the local currency, become blocked since the host country's currency is virtually inconvertible. The rule of thumb for the international company, irrespective of whether it is shipping to a subsidiary or to a third party, is not to ship goods without guaranteed clearance from exchange control and licensing authorities.

Where blocked funds are likely to accrue, the logical financing tactic for the international group is to finance overseas subsidiaries with as high a proportion of local borrowings as is possible. Blocked funds resulting from earning non-remittable profits may subsequently be used to repay these borrowings.

Currency Risk

Currency risk needs to be managed for the group as a whole and it is preferable if it is managed for the subsidiary too – even if this be by way of hedging with the group treasury. For the risk-averse company, the preferred policy is to match assets and liabilities in the same currencies both at group and at subsidiary level. In the overseas subsidiary, this would probably be assisted by drawing down as much local debt as is feasible. If local debt cannot be obtained by the overseas subsidiary because of its foreign ownership, the group treasurer may seek to borrow offshore the currency of the overseas subsidiary. If this cannot be drawn by the local company due to exchange controls it may be logical for the parent to do the borrowing.

If the only source of finance for the risk-averse overseas subsidiary is hard currency debt, for example US dollars or Swiss francs, then, if available, forward cover should be arranged for principal and interest payments. In evaluating competing sources of hard currency finance, if such has to be resorted to, it is assumed that the treasurer will not fall into the interest rate trap. Take the example of 'cheap' Swiss franc finance versus 'more expensive' US dollar funds. If the respective interest costs are 3 per cent per annum and 6 per cent per annum, the market is expecting the dollar to weaken over the borrowing period to eliminate this difference – this is what the international Fisher effect would be predicting. But remember that all this is on a pre-tax basis. To allow for tax effects, we have to take cognisance of the tax system under which the borrower is liable to pay tax on his income. According to most tax systems in the world, the total amount of interest (including any foreign exchange losses due to currency depreciation in the territory of operations relative to the currency of borrowing) is tax deductible. But in very many countries, currency losses on principal repayment are not – see Chapter 24 for more details. The conclusion is that in such circumstances, all other things being equal, it is cheaper and safer to pay the higher interest rate rather than to incur relatively large unrelieved losses on repayment of principal.

Losses Earned by Subsidiaries

Although there may be no currency exposure position for the group as a whole, it could be the case that local exchange controls mean that an overseas subsidiary carries an exposed position which could make the subsidiary insolvent should adverse currency movements materialise. This may result in trading becoming illegal.

The parent company may overcome this problem (and, for that matter, the general problem occasioned by local losses leading to insolvency) by injecting further capital or by advancing new loans and subordinating them to the other creditors. Alternatively, the parent may subordinate any existing intercompany debt to the other creditors, or it may guarantee all debts of the subsidiary, provided that these courses of action are acceptable under local legal rules. However, such policies leave any resultant losses unrelieved for tax purposes.

When trading losses have a high probability, it is perhaps better that the overseas business should be set up as a branch of the home operation – in which case losses would be tax-allowable against the home territory tax liability. Alternatively, an agreement may be made between a home territory exporting subsidiary, which is liable to tax, and the overseas operation to which it sells products, whereby it agrees to guarantee each year to meet the shortfall should overseas expenses exceed revenues. To be effective, this kind of revenue subvention must be defensible in the sense that the expense legitimately belongs in the home country. There is a defensible case where a substantial volume of goods is shipped from the home subsidiary to the overseas counterpart. It would not, of course, be a defensible argument were there no intercompany trade.

Intercompany Credit

The reader of this chapter so far is probably convinced that a very low parent input plus substantial local borrowing represents the ideal solution to the problem of financing the overseas subsidiary. Such a mix of funding creates problems should the subsidiary be subject to unforeseen setbacks. Whilst emergency lines of local credit may solve the short-term problem occasioned by a temporary reverse of profit or cash flow, it may be the case that these dry up in adverse circumstances. It then falls upon the group to provide funding.

Whilst the input of parent company equity or borrowing sourced from other than the local territory would solve the problem, the suddeness of the onset of the financing problem may favour another solution which may be recommended in the short term because it is more prompt and easy to set up. This short-term solution simply lies in a variation of the terms of intercompany credit. It means, in the context of the situation described, that the overseas subsidiary would pay inter-group creditors more slowly than originally prescribed and that intergroup receivables due to the overseas subsidiary would be paid more rapidly. The process is rather like leading and lagging, but this time it is triggered by an unforeseen deterioration of local outturns, rather than by an imminent movement of exchange rates. Resort to such a tactic must, of course, fall within the latitude on payment terms permitted by exchange control regulations.

Taxation Effects

International taxation is a complex topic. Its essence is summarised in Chapter 24 but, because the topic is so complicated, the coverage there can only be described as a general overview. Clearly, different countries have different tax systems with different rates of tax on profits. The scope for arranging an international group's affairs in order to minimise taxation is therefore extensive and this is true for tax corollaries of financing.

It is worth bearing in mind the almost immutable rule that there is no tax relief against consistent losses in any one country. The best approach therefore is to arrange a group's affairs so that losses are avoided in any one country. To the extent that such losses are caused by artificial practices, such as high transfer pricing, it is far better from a purely tax standpoint to discontinue such dysfunctional tactics.

Dividend Policy

As part of their exchange control regulations, many developing countries erect barriers which discriminate against dividends being paid to overseas shareholders. Whilst such practices tend to reduce the flow of funds out of the developing country, they also have the effect of discouraging direct investment inwards which might otherwise hasten the diffusion of technology, help the growth of the developing economy and provide much needed employment. Governments of developing countries argue that they prefer to keep a greater proportion of their industrial cake in the hands of local investors; multinationals argue that the cake becomes smaller than would otherwise be the case.

The critical question for the international company, though, is not an altruistic one: it concerns cash flows from and back to the parent. If a project fails to stand up when judged on these criteria – as advocated in Chapter 19 – the international company should not consider investing.

Other Methods of Profit Transfer

Because of their actions in the past, multinationals have gained a reputation for avoiding taxes and transferring cash around the world in spite of exchange controls by such devices as manipulating transfer prices, management fees, service charges, royalty payments and non-commercial interest payments. Over the last twenty years or so, tax authorities have become adept at frustrating such manipulation. It is frequently difficult to make even fair cross-frontier charges between group members without investigation. In short, the pendulum has swung so far in the direction of the taxing authorities that multinationals are basically very concerned about avoiding the payment of more than their fair burden of tax in many developing countries. Nowadays arm's length transfer pricing has become the preferred policy of most enlightened multinationals and the use of artificial means of profit transfer as a medium for shifting cash around a group has tended to fall into disrepute. That is not to say that it is non-existent, but it is practised much less frequently than the literature attacking multinationals would have us believe.

Parent Company Guarantees

The use of high levels of debt – especially local debt – to circumvent political risk has been recommended. Where parent company guarantees are given to an overseas subsidiary's creditors, the benefits gained by using high local debt levels tend to evaporate. Many multinationals make it a policy never to give parent company guarantees. But on occasions it is impossible to avoid giving them, for example if a contract tender is to be seriously considered. However, some treasurers would argue that the multinational company that walks away from its insolvent subsidiary is likely to have problems with lenders in all countries and that relatively little is gained by rigidly avoiding guarantees.

Letters of comfort are, of course, a different matter. These are letters given by the multinational parent to a lender, usually a bank, which acknowledge that the borrower is a subsidiary, that the parent is aware of the indebtedness and that the holding company intends to continue to own the subsidiary. Letters of comfort of this kind have no legal stature, but they do have a moral dimension. They are not guarantees and do not count as such for accounting purposes and for calculating covenant figures. However, letters of comfort which refer to the substitution of a guarantee in prescribed circumstances may be a different kettle of fish again. The key question is whether or not such letters constitute guarantees. Legal advice should be sought before signing a letter of this kind. Letters of comfort are sometimes called letters of awareness or letters of support.

The topic is debatable at length. However, it is our belief that as a device to reduce the impact of political risk, particularly confiscation risk, the avoidance of parent company guarantees certainly has substantial advantages for the international company.

Partly-owned Subsidiaries

Deciding about whether an overseas subsidiary should be wholly-owned or only partly-owned is probably the most critical and far-reaching decision on the financing of overseas operations. The major argument advanced against the presence of outside shareholders is that it makes single-minded management to meet the goals of the majority investor difficult without conflicts of interest with the minorities. The presence of the minority shareholder imposes a need to manage the subsidiary by the most careful application of the arm's-length principle. Any other approach results in constant friction with the outside shareholders who may become paranoid about the subsidiary's profits and cash flows being syphoned off for the benefit of the majority shareholder. This problem is frequently highlighted when one of the shareholders provides some local facilities for the subsidiary for which it requires financial recompense. At its worst, failure to apply the arm's-length principle results in substantially reduced motivation of local management – especially when such local managers are also minority shareholders. The key argument against the presence of outside shareholders is that the two sets of investors may have very different objectives on dividend policy. The dividend may be the only tangible reward for the minority who may also suffer much less tax on it than the majority shareholder. Furthermore, and most importantly, the minority shareholders may be reluctant to bear their fair share of the burdens of keeping the subsidiary financed or guaranteeing its obligations. At its most acute, this problem may effectively rule out new equity or guaranteed finance. It would, after all, be unfair to the majority shareholders to require them to bear a disproportionate share of such burdens. Such factors have to be carefully weighed against the opposite side of the argument.

The case for having local minority shareholders is that, in many countries, it is required by law and in many countries it is an absolute political necessity. It is often argued that in some countries influential local shareholders open vital doors to customers, contacts and government authorities and that they can protect the overseas subsidiary against political and commercial discrimination. Moreover, there are frequently very good commercial reasons for local participation in an overseas venture.

Where there are outside shareholders, important consequences ensue. Corporate objectives of the overseas subsidiary may differ from the wholly-owned case. We have referred to some obvious examples already, but there are others. For example, in the context of currency risk, local minority shareholders are not interested in group exposure; they are only concerned with that of the overseas subsidiary. Where the local minority shareholders are also the management group, views on perquisites and other managerial trappings are frequently bones of contention.

As a general rule, overseas subsidiaries with minorities are very lowly geared and it is often difficult to agree with the minority on profit retentions, extra capital or other finance from shareholders and guarantees from shareholders. Guarantees are altogether impracticable where the minority is held by the public. Indeed, where the partly owned overseas subsidiary is a company quoted on a local stock exchange the above problems are reinforced. Public investors cannot give guarantees for such a company, and it is costly and time-consuming to raise new capital from such shareholders. And where the law requires that local shareholders hold a minimum percentage of the capital, the parent company does not even have the option of merely subscribing new capital itself. All these difficulties favour a generous initial capitalisation and, probably, a policy of high retention of profits.

There is no single, ultimate answer to the problem of whether an overseas subsidiary company uses outside equity finance or not. In this section we have merely tried to point out the advantages and disadvantages of each policy. Real-world decisions on this topic require careful analysis and commercial judgement, but it must not be forgotten that an investment by a parent company in an overseas subsidiary must stand up in terms of parent cash flow analysis along the lines advocated in the chapter on capital budgeting.

Summary

The problem of financing an overseas subsidiary differs substantially from that of financing an independent company. The crucial question is whether it is wholly-owned by its foreign parent or not. Where it is only partly-owned, it should be capitalised generously and will probably be lowly geared. Where it is wholly-owned, the reverse policy is usually to be advised, with local borrowing providing a substantial proportion of capital. Multinational groups have special flexibility in that they can change intergroup credit terms to cope with temporary financial difficulties; but they must be careful not to allow an overseas subsidiary to incur unrelieved tax losses.

References

Brealey, Richard and Myers, Stewart (1984) *Principles of Corporate Finance*, 2nd edn, McGraw-Hill.

Franks, Julian R., Broyles, John E. and Carleton, William E. (1985) *Corporate Finance: Concepts and Applications*, Kent Publishing Company.

22

Measuring the Cost of International Borrowing

Companies may borrow in their own domestic capital markets or they may move further afield and tap international markets to finance their operations. The Eurocurrency market is the largest international source of funds; its mechanism and history are briefly surveyed in Chapter 23. Besides the Eurocurrency markets, the international company may decide to tap the domestic financial markets of overseas countries. In this respect, the international group may choose countries where it already has operations through associated companies or it may finance itself from countries where it does not carry on any operations. Many countries with extensive exchange controls restrict use of domestic capital markets to domestic companies only.

Tapping foreign capital markets may be done directly or indirectly. In the former case this may be achieved by the parent company or a subsidiary borrowing in local markets. In the latter case, this might involve a bilateral arrangement between an entity in the host country and the parent company in the home country. Such an arrangement might involve the exchange of the loan raised in the host country by the local entity in return for a loan in the home country from the parent company to the overseas entity. Loan arrangements of this kind are termed parallel loans or back-to-back loans or currency exchange agreements depending upon their exact nature; they are discussed further in Chapter 25.

Whenever a company decides to borrow uncovered in a foreign currency, it takes on a major complicating factor. This concerns the calculation of the cost of the loan. For a domestic borrowing the net-of-tax cost would simply be the net-of-tax interest expense. Preferably this should be expressed in discounted cash flow terms calculated by finding the discount rate which equates the sum raised under the borrowing with the net-of-tax interest costs and capital repayments allowing for their timing. For a foreign currency borrowing the framework for the calculation is the same but, because of changes in exchange rate, the interest payments and capital repayments can be expected to change over time when expressed in home currency terms. Since this difficulty is a distinctive feature of international borrowing, we shall devote this chapter to developing an approach for the calculation of the true cost of international borrowing.

The Advantages of Borrowing Internationally

Many companies carry on their main operations in countries whose domestic capital markets are comparatively small and possibly subject to drying up. Should the parent company be located in such a country and should that company have fairly substantial needs for cash to invest in order to compete in world markets, then its growth and competitive ability may be constrained by the existence of shallow domestic financial markets – unless it taps international financing sources. This was one of the major problems confronting Novo Industri A/S (see Stonehill and Dullum 1982), the pharmaceutical group based in Denmark, when in 1978 it launched its first dollar convertible Eurobond issue. The economics of the pharmaceutical industry with its high added value, high research and development levels, high capital intensity and its need for constant innovation, make access to deep capital markets a necessary precondition to successful competition on a world scale. Novo was aware that the scale of its corporate strategy turned around the availability of substantial cash resources on an ongoing basis. It saw its domestic capital market as being small and subject to periods of illiquidity which meant that, if it wanted to pursue its strategic plan, it was necessary to look outside domestic capital markets.

These kinds of consideration are not too critical for companies based in the UK or the USA, but they can be very relevant in many other countries. Indeed, the lack of depth coupled with the illiquidity of some countries' capital markets may be the historic reasons for most large multinational businesses being based in countries with sophisticated financing sources. This author believes that the lack of ready access to substantial domestic capital markets has constrained the growth of businesses in many smaller European countries and elsewhere in the world.

Besides the benefit of access to deeper financial markets, tapping capital markets outside its home country should enable the international company to take advantage of market imperfections that prevent the Fisher effect from holding in the short term. It will be recalled that, according to the four-way equivalence model developed in Chapter 5, real interest rates (that is, nominal rates adjusted for anticipated inflation) should tend towards equality. But, given that our model is rarely, if ever, totally in equilibrium, the company which has access to world financial markets, rather than just its domestic one, should be able to lower its cost of borrowing. Schematically we would suggest a relationship like that tabulated in Figure 22.1. It is worth mentioning, however, that when a company taps international financial sources for the first time it generally finds itself paying slightly more than an established borrower in terms of coupon rates plus underwriting fees.

The Risks of Borrowing Internationally

International financing can broadly be categorised as falling into three classes embracing the following situations:

1. financing in the currency in which cash inflows are expected;
2. financing in a currency other than that in which cash inflows are expected, but with cover in the forward market;

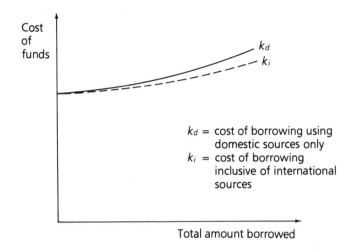

Figure 22.1 The International Cost of Borrowing

3. financing in a currency other than that in which cash inflows are expected, but without forward cover.

Financing by way of the first two methods avoids foreign exchange risk. But with funds raised via the third method, foreign exchange risk is taken on.

If the international Fisher effect were always to hold as an immutable iron law and if foreign exchange markets were always in equilibrium, then the benefit accruing to the company through lower nominal interest rates on financing in a hard currency would be exactly offset by the amount by which the harder currency appreciated relative to the other currencies. In other words, if international Fisher holds, the true cost of funds at the pre-tax level would be equal to the nominal interest rates in the home currency and this rate would apply irrespective of whence the international company were to draw its funds. As we know from the discussion in Chapter 11, the international Fisher effect does not hold in the short term in the real world. And there is some doubt about whether it holds in the long term. If it is the case that we cannot feel confident about international Fisher asserting itself in the long run, and if it is also the case that exchange rate markets and interest rates are not always in equilibrium, then the international treasurer may either seek to avoid financing risk by one or more of the techniques discussed in Chapters 14 to 17, or he may seek to profit in this area by his own insights. Thus he may seek to raise money denominated in overvalued currencies for relatively long maturities; and by the same token he will avoid raising funds in undervalued currencies.

Just as disequilibrium in international Fisher can give rise to financing opportunities for the astute corporation treasurer who is prepared to take on foreign exchange risk, so can market imperfections which flow from different tax regimes create opportunities. Tax legislation on foreign exchange gains and losses varies from one country to another. This topic is taken up again in more detail in Chapter 24. At this point, though, it is worth mentioning that two or more international financing propositions which appear to have the same pre-tax cost of funds after taking account of interest costs and expected strengthenings and weakenings of currencies may, on a post-tax basis, yield different costs. This phenomenon might result from the fact that corporate tax rates in different centres vary, but might also flow from the fact that countries have different rules as to whether a capital loss or gain on repayment of an international borrowing is respectively tax-deductible or comes into charge for tax. The US tax authorities allow losses and tax gains of this sort; UK tax legislation, as of 1985, does not allow tax deductibility of net losses nor does it seek to tax gains of this kind in respect of long-term borrowings; but see Chapter 24 for more details on this issue.

Most of the discussion to date in this text has focused upon exchange risk problems associated with international financial exposure in the short term − that is, up to one year. In reality, the majority of financing decisions have a time dimension beyond twelve months. But the further we extend this time horizon, the greater become two key problems which impinge upon the international financing decision. First, forward exchange markets become very thin; for the majority of currencies there is virtually no market beyond twelve months. Secondly, in many developing countries around the world, the availability of longer-term local currency financing becomes much more difficult to find.

The non-availability of forward markets for most currencies for periods beyond twelve months does not mean that the treasurer cannot obtain forward cover for long-term borrowings in foreign currencies. The astute treasurer can use the spot/forward method which was discussed in Chapter 15. Imagine a UK-based international company which has just made a SFr 50 million borrowing requiring repayment of the total sum borrowed in three years' time. If there were no forward market beyond twelve months, the treasurer could manufacture three-year cover by a spot/forward swap. The technique would involve the process shown in Table 22.1.

Table 22.1 Swap/Forward Cover for Three-Year Swiss Franc Borrowing

End of year		
0	Buy SFr 50 million versus £	12 months forward
1	Sell SFr 50 million versus £	spot
	Buy SFr 50 million versus £	12 months forward
2	Sell SFr 50 million versus £	spot
	Buy SFr 50 million versus £	12 months forward
3	Use proceeds of forward purchase at end-of-year 2 to repay borrowing	

Remember that the difference between the spot rate and the twelve-month forward rate is underpinned by interest rate differentials. This means that, using the technique summarised in Table 22.1, the treasurer has manufactured three-year cover for his borrowing at an exchange rate equal to the twelve-month forward rate at the end of year 0, plus/minus the twelve-month interest differential at the end of year 1, plus/minus the twelve-month interest differential at the end of year 2. It should be borne in mind that, when the treasurer begins this deal at the end of year 0, he is exposed in terms of not knowing what the interest rate differential for twelve months will be both at the end of year 1 and at the end of year 2. So this technique minimises risk but does not eliminate it totally.

What if the treasurer decides not to cover his long-term foreign borrowing? How should he use his knowledge to assess the relative merits of competing borrowing propositions? In short, how should the treasurer assess the cost of international borrowing?

Foreign Currency Financing Decisions

In a simple domestic financing situation, the true cost of finance may be derived by solving a straightforward discounted cash flow calculation. The amount borrowed, the cash inflow to the company, is set against the interest and principal repayments in each year, the outflows for the company, duly discounted. After a discounting process, the rate which equates the present value of total inflows with the present value of total outflows is the true cost of the borrowing. The general equation may be written as:

$$\text{Amount borrowed} = \frac{\begin{bmatrix} \text{Interest paid}_1 \\ + \\ \text{Capital repayment}_1 \end{bmatrix}}{(1 + r)} + \frac{\begin{bmatrix} \text{Interest paid}_2 \\ + \\ \text{Capital repayment}_2 \end{bmatrix}}{(1 + r)^2}$$

$$+ \ldots \frac{\begin{bmatrix} \text{Interest paid}_n \\ + \\ \text{Capital repayment}_n \end{bmatrix}}{(1 + r)^n}$$

where r is the true cost of the loan. The equation would derive from an incremental cash flow analysis in which additional inflows and outflows resulting solely from the financing decision would be specified. The true cost of the borrowing may be calculated on a pre-tax or post-tax basis. Clearly, if the post-tax cost is required, incremental cash flows must be expressed net of tax.

Where foreign exchange risk is undertaken in an international borrowing, the computation of the cost of the loan is somewhat more complex, but the calculations involve the same basic principles. Incremental cash flows arising under a borrowing are specified and the discounted cost is computed. But in this instance we need to recognise that incremental cash flows in home currency terms embrace the initial borrowing, interest to be paid and capital to be repaid with all of these cash flows duly adjusted to allow for expected or actual (if the analysis is an *ex post* one) exchange gains and losses. The general equation, in home currency terms, may be expressed as:

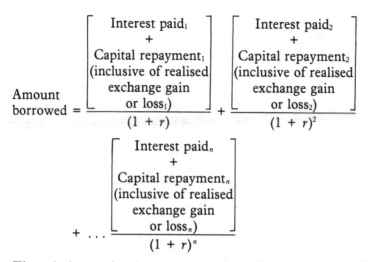

$$\text{Amount borrowed} = \frac{\begin{bmatrix} \text{Interest paid}_1 \\ + \\ \text{Capital repayment}_1 \\ \text{(inclusive of realised} \\ \text{exchange gain} \\ \text{or loss}_1) \end{bmatrix}}{(1 + r)} + \frac{\begin{bmatrix} \text{Interest paid}_2 \\ + \\ \text{Capital repayment}_2 \\ \text{(inclusive of realised} \\ \text{exchange gain} \\ \text{or loss}_2) \end{bmatrix}}{(1 + r)^2}$$

$$+ \ldots \frac{\begin{bmatrix} \text{Interest paid}_n \\ + \\ \text{Capital repayment}_n \\ \text{(inclusive of realised} \\ \text{exchange gain} \\ \text{or loss}_n) \end{bmatrix}}{(1 + r)^n}$$

The solution to the above equation for r gives us the true effective cost of a borrowing. Evidently, if the cost of a foreign borrowing is being made in advance of drawing down a loan, then estimates must be made of future exchange rate movements. For this purpose, the tools in the armoury of the international treasurer were discussed in earlier chapters. Where the currency of borrowing is overvalued or undervalued at the time the loan is drawn down the treasurer needs to make estimates of the timing and extent of movements towards equilibrium — and this is a major problem.

The true effective cost of a borrowing from international sources may be computed on a pre-tax or on a post-tax basis. The post-tax computation is more complex because we need to consider not only the net-of-tax interest cost, but also the foreign exchange gain or loss and whether this is recognised for tax purposes. Readers are referred to Chapter 24 which should be read before attempting any after-tax computations. The analyst also needs to be careful in his calculations about whether a borrowing is an amortising loan or one with a bullet repayment. A given currency movement virtually always results in a different true effective cost of funds if the loan is an amortising one as opposed to one involving a bullet repayment. The timing of an appreciation or depreciation of a currency can also be extremely material in the calculation of the true cost of borrowing. The sooner the appreciation of a borrowed currency takes place, the greater the increase in the true cost of borrowing. The sooner the devaluation of a borrowed currency occurs, the bigger the decrease to the net effective cost of funds.

As an example, consider a UK company financing itself in dollars. The company draws down a five-year $10 million borrowing in year 0 and the loan carries a 10 per cent per annum coupon. Assume that the dollar appreciates from $1.30 to the £ at the time of draw-down to $1.17. The true cost of the loan on a pre-tax basis is shown in Table 22.2. The table shows the true cost on the basis that the dollar revaluation takes place in one go either in year 1, or in year 2, or in year 3, and so on. The table shows the true effective pre-tax cost on a number of assumptions, as follows. First, the loan is repayable in equal instalments; second, the loan is assumed to be repaid by annual amortisation of $1 million plus a balloon in year 5 of $5 million; third, the loan is repaid by a bullet repayment at the end of year 5. The calculation of the figures which appear in Table 22.2 is shown in the Appendix at the end of this chapter.

Table 22.2   True Effective Annual Cost of Borrowing (%)

Year of $ appreciation	Equal amortisation	50% by equal amortisation 50% by balloon repayment	Bullet repayment
		Repayment terms	
1	14.5	13.7	12.8
2	13.3	13.0	12.6
3	12.3	12.2	12.3
4	11.3	11.7	12.1
5	10.6	11.3	12.0

The figures in the table emphasise the need to look beyond the coupon rate of interest. In our example the devaluation of sterling against the dollar is not a large one by the relative standards of past experience in a floating currency regime. But the impact of that depreciation in the case of the equally amortising loan is staggering. The impact of a revaluation of the dollar of only around 10 per cent coming early, rather than late, in the borrowing is to raise the coupon cost from around 10 per cent per annum to an effective cost of approaching 15 per cent per annum. The management of a company would have good reason to be critical of the treasurer who talked in terms of this dollar loan as only costing around 10 per cent per annum before tax.

Movements of the Swiss franc and the Deutsche Mark against sterling through the early seventies, and the strengthening of the dollar in the early eighties, show how naive many corporate treasuries have been in talking their companies into borrowing in cheap-interest currencies. Hopefully, such financial executives and their companies have learned by bitter, and expensive, experience.

It is also necessary to take account of expected currency movements when calculating the cost of debt as part of a company's exercise of calculating its weighted average cost of capital. This simple procedure is frequently overlooked by financial and planning executives. In many cases the effect can be very substantial indeed.

There is an increasing tendency for providers of finance in international capital markets to offer floating rate lending with interest tied to LIBOR (London Interbank Offer Rate) or some other convenient interest rate base. This creates complexities for the treasurer of an international company. There is a strong temptation to argue that, if international Fisher holds in the long term, the treasurer need not worry from where he obtains his borrowing. Devaluations and revaluations should, according to this theory, cancel out against floating interest rate differentials. This simplistic approach is only valid if the relevant exchange rates move in accordance with the prediction of purchasing power parity and the Fisher effect during the whole course of the loan from drawn-down to final repayment. Furthermore, interest and foreign exchange markets must be in equilibrium at the start of a borrowing period for this indifference to financial sourcing to be justified. This is a pretty tall order. Indeed, outside of text book models, it will never be found in the real world. This has practical implications for the international treasurer even in a world of floating interest rate finance. Imagine that a UK company is considering borrowing via a dollar floating rate loan at a time when the dollar is undervalued by reference to past movements of real effective exchange rates. Even though the loan carries a floating rate, should the dollar/ sterling exchange rate move once and for all to correct the previous disequilibrium in PPP and should the rates continue to move in line with international Fisher, then, if this is foreseen, the dollar borrowing will appear relatively expensive. So even with floating rate notes the treasurer needs to be very careful. The floating interest rate does not circumvent the problem of potential exchange rate movements.

This whole area of foreign currency financing without forward cover is one that is full of pitfalls. Short cuts are ill-advised. There is no substitute for careful analysis of the interaction between past movements of exchange rates, interest rates and inflation rates. And future estimates must be obtained if logical predictions of future exchange rates are to be made over the period of a borrowing. This process is an essential prerequisite to the task of estimating, *ex ante*, the cost of an international borrowing. It is hoped that the framework of analysis laid down in this text will be helpful to potential international borrowers.

Summary

International borrowing enables companies to lower their average cost of finance and it may be an important part of the funding equation for companies whose base is within countries with shallow capital markets, as well as for major multinational companies.

International financing can be categorised into three classes. Firstly, a company may borrow internationally in currencies in which it expects cash inflows to accrue. Secondly, it may borrow in a currency other than that in which cash inflows are expected but it may cover foreign exchange exposure through forward markets. Thirdly, the company may finance itself in a currency other than that in which cash inflows are expected but not take forward cover. The last of these funding alternatives is the most risky. Whilst the interest rate and capital repayments are fixed in foreign currency terms, the problem is that, because exchange rates may change, the home currency cost of borrowing is uncertain. It is possible to estimate the true cost of an uncovered foreign borrowing by taking into account expected exchange rate movements and timing of cash flows. This is done using the discounted cash flow technique with cash flows expressed in home currency terms after allowing for expected foreign exchange rate movements. The calculation of the true cost of the loan is the discounted cash flow rate which equates expected inflows and outflows. A framework for analysis is provided in this chapter.

Reference

Stonehill, Arthur I. and Dullum, Kare B. (1982) *Internationalising the Cost of Capital*, John Wiley.

APPENDIX 22

CALCULATION OF THE EFFECTIVE PRE-TAX COST OF FOREIGN BORROWING

Case 1

Amount borrowed by UK company: $10 million in year 0.
Coupon interest rate: 10%.
Repayment: equal annual amortisation.
Currency movement: $ moves from 1.30 to 1.17 to the pound at end of year 1.

Sterling flows (£000) in year	*0*	*1*	*2*	*3*	*4*	*5*
Borrowing	769					
Interest		−85	−68	−51	−34	−17
Capital repayment		−171	−171	−171	−171	−171
	769	−256	−239	−222	−205	−188
Try 15% Σ = 9	769	−223	−181	−146	−117	−93
Try 14% Σ = −8	769	−225	−184	−150	−121	−97

Effective cost of borrowing = 14.5%

Case 2

As per case 1, but with $ appreciation at end of year 2.

Sterling flows (£000) in year	*0*	*1*	*2*	*3*	*4*	*5*
Borrowing	769					
Interest		−77	−68	−51	−34	−17
Capital repayment		−154	−171	−171	−171	−171
	769	−231	−239	−222	−205	−188
Try 13% Σ = −4	769	−204	−187	−154	−126	−102
Try 14% Σ = 14	769	−203	−184	−150	−121	−97

Effective cost of borrowing = 13.3%

Case 3

As per case 1, but with $ appreciation at end of year 3.

Sterling flows (£000) in year	*0*	*1*	*2*	*3*	*4*	*5*
Borrowing	769					
Interest		−77	−62	−51	−34	−17
Capital repayment		−154	−154	−171	−171	−171
	769	−231	−216	−222	−205	−188
Try 12% Σ = −4	769	−206	−172	−158	−130	−107
Try 13% Σ = 14	769	−204	−169	−154	−126	−102

Effective cost of borrowing = 12.3%

Case 4

As per case 1, but with $ appreciation at end of year 4.

Sterling flows (£000) in year	0	1	2	3	4	5
Borrowing	769					
Interest		−77	−62	−46	−34	−17
Capital repayment		−154	−154	−154	−171	−171
	769	−231	−216	−200	−205	−188
Try 11% Σ = −6	769	−208	−175	−146	−135	−111
Try 12% Σ = 12	769	−206	−172	−142	−130	−107

Effective cost of borrowing = 11.3%

Case 5

As per case 1, but with $ appreciation at end of year 5.

Sterling flows (£000) in year	0	1	2	3	4	5
Borrowing	769					
Interest		−77	−62	−46	−32	−17
Capital repayment		−154	−154	−154	−154	−171
	769	−231	−216	−200	−185	−188
Try 10% Σ = −12	769	−210	−178	−150	−126	−117
Try 11% Σ = 7	769	−208	−175	−146	−122	−111

Effective cost of borrowing = 10.6%

Case 6

Amount borrowed by UK company: $10 million in year 0.
Coupon interest rate: 10%.
Repayment: Half by equal annual amortisation of $1.25 million per annum plus the remainder by a $5 million balloon at the end of year 5.
Currency movement: $ moves from 1.30 to 1.17 to the pound at the end of year 1.

Sterling flows (£000) in year	0	1	2	3	4	5
Borrowing	769					
Interest		−85	−75	−64	−53	−43
Capital repayment		−107	−107	−107	−107	−427
	769	−192	−182	−171	−160	−470
Try 14% Σ = 7	769	−168	−140	−115	−95	−244
Try 13% Σ = −16	769	−170	−143	−119	−98	−255

Effective cost of borrowing = 13.7%

Case 7

As per case 6, but with $ appreciation at end of year 2.

Sterling flows (£000) in year	0	1	2	3	4	5
Borrowing	769					
Interest		−77	−75	−64	−53	−43
Capital repayment		−96	−107	−107	−107	−427
	769	−173	−182	−171	−160	−470
Try 13% Σ = 1	769	−153	−143	−119	−98	−255

Effective cost of borrowing = 13.0%

Case 8

As per case 6, but with $ appreciation at end of year 3.

Sterling flows (£000) in year	0	1	2	3	4	5
Borrowing	769					
Interest		−77	−67	−64	−53	−43
Capital repayment		−96	−96	−107	−107	−427
	769	−173	−163	−171	−160	−470
Try 13% Σ = 16	769	−153	−128	−119	−98	−255
Try 12% Σ = −5	769	−154	−130	−122	−102	−266

Effective cost of borrowing = 12.2%

Case 9

As per case 6, but with $ appreciation at end of year 4.

Sterling flows (£000) in year	0	1	2	3	4	5
Borrowing	769					
Interest		−77	−67	−58	−53	−43
Capital repayment		−96	−96	−96	−107	−427
	769	−173	−163	−154	−160	−470
Try 12% Σ = 7	769	−154	−130	−110	−102	−266
Try 11% Σ = −16	769	−156	−132	−113	−105	−279

Effective cost of borrowing = 11.7%

Case 10

As per case 6, but with $ appreciation at end of year 5.

Sterling flows (£000) in year	0	1	2	3	4	5
Borrowing	769					
Interest		−77	−67	−58	−48	−43
Capital repayment		−96	−96	−96	−96	−427
	769	−173	−163	−154	−144	−470
Try 11% Σ = −6	769	−156	−132	−113	−95	−279
Try 12% Σ = 17	769	−154	−130	−110	−92	−266

Effective cost of borrowing = 11.3%

Case 11

Amount borrowed by UK company: $10 million in year 0.
Coupon interest rate: 10%.
Repayment: Bullet of $10 million at end of year 5.
Currency movement: $ moves from 1.30 to 1.17 to the pound at end of year 1.

Sterling flows (£000) in year	0	1	2	3	4	5
Borrowing	769					
Interest		−85	−85	−85	−85	−85
Capital repayment						−855
	769	−85	−85	−85	−85	−940
Try 13% Σ = 6	769	−75	−67	−59	−52	−510
Try 12% Σ = −23	769	−76	−68	−61	−54	−533

Effective cost of borrowing = 12.8%

Case 12

As per case 11, but with $ appreciation at end of year 2.

Sterling flows (£000) in year	0	1	2	3	4	5
Borrowing	769					
Interest		−77	−85	−85	−85	−85
Capital repayment						−855
	769	−77	−85	−85	−85	−940
Try 13% Σ = 13	769	−68	−67	−59	−52	−510
Try 12% Σ = −16	769	−69	−68	−61	−54	−533

Effective cost of borrowing = 12.6%

Case 13

As per case 11, but with $ appreciation at end of year 3.

Sterling flows (£000) in year	0	1	2	3	4	5
Borrowing	769					
Interest		−77	−77	−85	−85	−85
Capital repayment						−855
	769	−77	−77	−85	−85	−940
Try 13% Σ = 20	769	−68	−60	−59	−52	−510
Try 12% Σ = −9	769	−69	−61	−61	−54	−533

Effective cost of borrowing = 12.3%

Case 14

As per case 11, but with $ appreciation at end of year 4.

Sterling flows (£000) in year	0	1	2	3	4	5
Borrowing	769					
Interest		−77	−77	−77	−85	−85
Capital repayment						−855
	769	−77	−77	−77	−85	−940
Try 12% Σ = 13	769	−69	−61	−55	−54	−533
Try 13% Σ = 26	769	−68	−60	−53	−52	−510

Effective cost of borrowing = 12.1%

Case 15

As per case 11, but with $ appreciation at end of year 5.

Sterling flows (£000) in year	0	1	2	3	4	5
Borrowing	769					
Interest		−77	−77	−77	−77	−85
Capital repayment						−855
	769	−77	−77	−77	−77	−940
Try 12% Σ = 1	769	−69	−61	−55	−50	−533

Effective cost of borrowing = 12.0%

23

The Euromarkets

The Euromarkets are usually defined to include the markets for Eurocurrency, Eurocredits and Eurobonds. Each of these markets is described in this chapter.

The Eurocurrency market is that market in which Eurobanks accept deposits and make loans denominated in currencies other than the currency of the country in which the banks are located.

The traditional definition of Eurodollars is that they are dollars held in the form of time deposits in banks outside the United States. However, since 3 December 1981, US banks have been allowed to open international banking facilities (IBFs) within the USA which can transact international business free from most Federal Reserve Bank regulations. In essence, dollars deposited in an IBF become Eurodollars for all practical purposes. The IBF itself is a set of segregated asset and liability accounts maintained on the books of a banking organisation. IBF deposits must be for a minimum amount of $100,000 and for a minimum time of two days. Depositors and customers of IBFs must be foreign residents or other IBFs. By 1984, the IBFs had captured approximately 10 per cent of the total Eurocurrency banking market. From 1986, a similar scheme is likely to become operative in Tokyo. Since Japanese banks held £160 billion worth of Eurocurrency deposits at the end of 1984 in London, or 25 per cent of all Eurocurrency funds deposited in London, this deregulatory step poses a substantial threat to the City of London's command of the Euromarkets. But we digress: we should return to our preamble on the Eurocurrency markets.

Eurodeutsche Marks are Marks deposited in banks outside West Germany. The prefix 'Euro' really means 'external' and refers to funds that are intermediated outside the control of the central bank of the country of the currency in which the funds are denominated. The Eurocurrency market is made up of financial institutions that compete for dollar time deposits and make dollar loans outside the United States plus IBFs, financial institutions outside West Germany that bid for Deutsche Mark deposits and make Deutsche Mark loans, financial institutions outside the UK that bid for sterling deposits and loan sterling – and so on. The Eurocurrency market is by no means the same as the Eurobond market. The latter is defined further on in this chapter. There are a number of key Euromarket terms and concepts which need to be clarified before moving on to the complexities of Eurofinance; the following section aims to provide this clarification.

Definitions of Key Eurocurrency Terms

The Euromarkets are banking markets for deposits and loans. They are located outside the country of the currency in which the claims are denominated. These markets are prefixed as 'Euro' to indicate that they are not part of the domestic system, although they are closely linked to domestic systems through international transactions.

The term 'Eurodollar market' is sometimes used in the widest sense to encompass not only the market for dollars outside the USA, but also the market for Eurodeutsche Marks, Eurosterling, Eurofrench francs, etc. In this kind of usage the term 'Eurodollar market' becomes synonymous with 'Eurocurrency market'.

The gross size of the Eurocurrency market is the sum of all Eurocurrency liabilities, including the many interbank deposits on the books of Eurobanks. The total amount of credit extended to end users is best measured by the net figure, which excludes interbank deposits and considers only deposits or loan transactions between Eurobanks and non-bank users of funds.

Eurobonds are bonds denominated in currencies other than that of the country in which the bonds are sold, for example dollar-denominated bonds in London or Deutsche Mark-denominated bonds in Luxembourg. Although the Eurobond market achieves the same ends as the Eurodollar market, it is distinctly different. In the Eurodollar market, financial institutions have traditionally played an intermediate role by bearing the risk of lending; in the Eurobond market this risk is borne directly by the lender.

Eurobanks are financial intermediaries that bid for time deposits and make loans in currencies other than that of the country in which they are located.

LIBOR, the London Interbank Offered Rate, is the interest rate at which London Euromarket banks offer funds for deposit in the interbank market. It is the most usually quoted base for Eurocurrency transactions. The interest cost to the borrower is set as a spread over the LIBOR rate. Spreads over LIBOR have ranged from around 0.25% to 2%. There is, of course, a separate LIBOR for each of the many currencies in which interbank loans are made in London.

We shall now consider reserve asset requirements. Domestic and foreign banks taking deposits and lending in the currency of the country in which they operate are, in most financially sophisticated countries, required to hold asset reserves equal to a specified percentage of their deposit liabilities. These assets are usually required to be held in minimal interest-bearing forms. This situation contrasts with that relating to Eurocurrency deposits. Eurocurrency holdings are not subject to reserve asset requirements. Eurobanks are therefore able to lend at more competitive rates than their domestic counterparts since part of their portfolio of assets is not tied up in low interest-bearing reserve assets.

The term 'currency swap' also needs definition. A currency swap is an agreement to exchange specified amounts of two different currencies immediately on a spot basis and to reverse the transaction at an agreed exchange rate at a stated time in the future. In a swap transaction, the swap rate is all-important. This is the difference between the price at which a currency is bought and the price at which it is sold. The difference reflects the interest rate differential between the two currencies.

Market operators frequently talk of the Asian dollar market. This is simply that segment of the Eurocurrency market which is operated in the Far East and is centred primarily on Singapore and to a lesser extent on Hong Kong.

Finally in this section on definitions, we look briefly at syndicated Euro-credits. Eurocredit lending is the medium-term (and occasionally long-term) market for Eurocurrency loans provided by an organised group of financial institutions. Through grouping, with lenders each taking a small share of a loan, diversification can be achieved. The currencies lent need not be those of either borrower or lender. However, loans are made on a one-to-one basis and this has become more common in the bank lending to the corporate sector market.

Eurodollar Deposits and Loans

The most important distinction between the Eurodollar banking market and domestic banking is that Eurocurrency markets are not subject to domestic banking regulations. Because of the absence of this constraint on profitability, Eurobanks may obtain the same profit levels as domestic banks, even though they achieve lower spreads on lending depositors' funds than their domestic counterparts. This is, in fact, what happens in the market. The absence of reserve requirements and regulations enables Eurobanks to offer slightly better terms to both borrowers and lenders. Eurodollar deposit rates are somewhat higher, and effective lending rates a little lower, than they are in domestic money markets. The absence of regulations is the key to the success of the Eurocurrency markets.

Deep Euromarkets exist only in those currencies, such as the US dollar, the West German Mark and the pound sterling, that are relatively freely convertible into other currencies. Eurobanks are located in those centres that refrain from regulating foreign currency banking activities.

A Eurodollar deposit may be created and lent on in the manner set out below. A US corporation with $2 million surplus funds decides to take advantage of the more attractive Eurodollar rates on deposits relative to domestic dollars. The company's surplus funds were held originally in a time deposit in a local branch of a US bank. On maturity of this deposit the company replaces its time deposit with a demand deposit in the local US bank. The company transfers ownership, by payment, of the demand deposit in the local US bank to the US bank in London where a time deposit is made. This process creates a Eurodollar deposit, substituting for an equivalent domestic time deposit in a US bank. The London branch of the US bank deposits the cheque in its account in a US bank. The US company holds a dollar deposit in a bank in London rather than in the USA. The total of deposits of the banks in the US remains unchanged. However, investors hold smaller deposits in the US and larger deposits in London. The London bank now has a larger deposit in the USA. The increase in the London bank's deposits in the US bank is matched by the increase in dollar deposits for the world as a whole. The volume of dollar deposits in the USA remains unchanged, while the volume in London increases.

The London bank will not leave the newly acquired $2 million idle. If the bank does not have a commercial borrower or government to which it can lend the funds, it will place the $2 million in the Eurodollar interbank market. In other words, it will deposit the funds in some other Eurobank.

If this second Eurobank cannot immediately use the funds to make a loan, it will redeposit them again in the interbank market. This process of redepositing might proceed through several Eurobanks before the $2 million finds its way to a final borrower. At each stage the next bank will pay a slightly higher rate than the previous bank paid. But the margins involved in the interbank market are very small – of the order of 1/8%. As a rule, larger, better-known banks will receive initial deposits, while smaller banks will have to bid for deposits in the interbank market.

This interbank redepositing of an original Eurodollar deposit merely involves the passing on of funds from bank to bank. It does not, of course, add to the final extension of credit in the financial markets. Only when the $2 million is lent on to a corporation or a government or other non-bank borrower is credit eventually and effectively extended. To evaluate the true credit-creation capacity of the Eurodollar market, interbank deposits have to be netted out. The ultimate stage in the credit-creating process occurs when a Eurobank lends funds to a non-bank borrower.

Loans made in the Euromarket are similar to those made domestically by UK and US banks and so on. More lending is done on a corporate reputation or name basis, as it is sometimes called, to well-known entities with less credit investigation and documentation being involved than in domestic lending. When the amount needed is greater than one Eurobank is prepared to provide, borrowers obtain funds by tapping a syndicate of banks from different countries. Borrowers often have the option of borrowing in any of several currencies. Eurocurrency loans may be for short-term working capital or trade finance, or they may have maturities up to 10 years. The latter would be called medium-term Eurocredits, although they are basically no different from their short-term counterparts. When a Eurocurrency loan or commitment has a maturity of more than six months, the interest rate is usually set on a roll-over basis, that is, at the start of each three- or six-month period it is reset at a fixed amount (e.g. 1%) above the prevailing London interbank offered rate.

Eurocurrency deposits often carry interest rates a fraction higher than domestic deposits (since they avoid domestic interest rate ceilings where they exist) and borrowers can obtain cheaper money in Euromarkets than in domestic ones. So why do not all depositors and borrowers shift their business into the Eurocurrency market? One reason is the existence of exchange controls. Many governments make it difficult for depositors to invest abroad, and many restrict foreign borrowing by domestic companies. Another reason is the inconvenience and cost involved in maintaining balances or borrowing in a foreign country. Furthermore, the market is largely a wholesale one and deals in sums of under $1 million are not available. Eurobanks also prefer to lend to large, well-known corporations, banks, or governments. But the most important difference is that Eurodeposits, because they are located in a different country, are in some respects subject to the jurisdiction of that country. This is referred to as the sovereign risk characteristic of Eurocurrency markets, and is discussed later in the chapter.

Historical Underpinnings of the Eurocurrency Market

Ironically, the initial stimulus to the world's largest and least regulated international market for credit – the Eurocurrency market – was provided by the actions of the world's main socialist states. Shortly after the Second World War, the Soviet Union and its satellites and the Republic of China decided to hold their dollar assets in banks in Paris and London, rather than in banks in the USA. These communist countries feared first that their deposits in the USA might be blocked and second that their funds might be attacked by US residents with claims against communist country governments.

Growth of this rather small Eurocurrency market was stimulated in the late fifties. In 1957 the UK placed restrictions on the use of sterling for financing third-country trade. This policy followed the Suez crisis and one of the recurrent weaknesses of sterling. Encouraged to do so by the Bank of England, British bankers turned to the dollar to finance trade – hence their interest in tapping the Eurodollar market. Also, during the late fifties, many European countries relaxed their exchange controls for the first time since the war. Dollar convertibility was widely restored and the US domestic money market was reopened for the first time since the early thirties. These features led investors to move their funds more freely and gave lenders and borrowers more options.

But the take-off stage for the Euromarket did not come until the middle to late sixties when the net size of the market tripled. Three restrictions in the USA played a substantial part in this growth. The interest equalisation tax, which was brought in during 1963, imposed a penalty on US residents buying securities issued by foreigners. This encouraged the creation of alternative sources of medium-term and long-term financing and the Eurocurrency and newly emerging Eurobond markets grew in response to this demand. Furthermore, voluntary restrictions on direct foreign investment, which were set up in 1965 and made mandatory in 1968, forced US multinationals to raise funds for their overseas operations outside the USA. Also, the Federal Reserve Bank's foreign credit restraint programme closed off the opportunity for foreign borrowers, including foreign-based affiliates of US companies, to borrow medium-term debt in the USA.

These regulations had the effect of encouraging the use of the Euromarkets. Growth continued at a rapid pace even after the removal of the US restrictions in 1974. A further key influence in the market's growth was Regulation Q. This was first implemented in 1966. It limited the amount of interest which commercial banks in the USA were allowed to pay on time deposits. It resulted in very large shifts of corporate monies into non-bank financial assets and into the Eurodollar market. This gave an enormous boost to the Eurocurrency market in 1966, and again in 1969 and 1970, when regulations intensified. US banks began to set up foreign branches in order to have easier access to the Eurocurrency market. The liabilities of US banks to their foreign branches increased from $2 billion to $15 billion between 1967 and 1969. Subsequently, larger certificates of deposit – those over £100,000 – were exempted from Regulation Q. Nevertheless the Eurocurrency market, with its obvious attractiveness of higher rates for deposits and lower rates for borrowers than domestic markets, continued to grow despite the removal of the above restrictions. Regulation Q is being phased out, with its final demise scheduled for 1986. The net size of the Eurocurrency market (based on all outstanding Eurocurrency liabilities for the whole world, net of interbank holdings) grew from $21 billion in 1966 to $225 billion in 1975; by 1983 its size was estimated at $945 billion. Whilst growth rates of over 20 per cent per annum in the latter half of the seventies were common, these had fallen to 4 per cent by 1984.

Growth of the Eurodollar market has also been influenced by the US balance of payments deficits and the redistribution of international wealth towards the oil-producing countries since the early seventies. The recurrent US balance of payments deficit is not, however, viewed as itself being a reason for the growth of the Eurodollar market. Certainly, repeated and substantial deficits have transferred wealth from the US to other countries, but this does not mean that the dollars moving away from the US should necessarily find their way into the Eurodollar market. Were domestic US dollar rates on deposits superior to offshore rates, then these dollars would probably find their way into deposits within the USA. The fact is that, because the lower regulatory levels have meant that deposit rates are higher in the Eurodollar market, funds have found their way into the Eurocurrency arena. But why should these monies be allocated to the dollar-denominated segment of the Euromarket rather than to Eurodeutsche Marks or Euroyen and so on? First, political risk is viewed as being lower on dollar assets than on most others. Second, the market is much larger. Hence it is possible to move more funds into and out of US dollars without affecting rates than is the case for any other currency in the world. Thirdly (and possibly this is associated with the first factor) the dollar has been viewed as being as stable a currency as any other in the world. With the USA running a repeated and substantial balance of payments deficit during the early eighties, this fed the strength of the US dollar. The deficit was financed by attracting funds from overseas via high real interest rates – rather than by increasing the money supply excessively because of the expected impact of such a policy on inflation rates. As funds moved in, so the dollar tended to strengthen. Although the large US balance of payments deficit was not in itself related to the Euromarket's growth, the deficit had an indirect hand in its stimulus.

The same kind of reasoning applies to the impact of OPEC (Organisation of Petroleum Exporting Countries) wealth. The oil price increase in 1973 greatly increased the reserves of the oil-exporting OPEC countries. The most liquid part of the oil-exporting countries' claims on foreigners rose from $8.5 billion in 1972 to $73.6 billion in 1980. This growth in the OPEC countries' surpluses led to their placing large amounts of money in short-term Eurocurrency deposits, thus becoming the largest source of new funds for the Eurocurrency market. The large OPEC surpluses meant corresponding deficits in the oil-importing countries, which led to concern about recycling. Governments of countries suddenly experiencing large deficits were faced with a number of choices. They might recognise that their deficits would not be temporary and attempt to restructure their economies to lessen dependence on oil and to stimulate new exports, using reserves and borrowings to finance the restructuring. They might deflate their economies by holding down domestic consumption and investment, limiting demand, and thereby minimising borrowing. The option most widely chosen by developed countries involved a combination of financing and deflation.

The deflationary impact of higher oil prices was magnified by policies of government restraint on spending and domestic credit. The resulting recession in the developed countries shifted the burden forwards to the developing countries, as demand and relative prices became lower for less-developed countries' exports. The better-off developing countries were able to finance their deficits through borrowing in the international banking system, especially the Euromarket. Countries like Brazil and Mexico captured a larger share of Euromarket borrowing than did less developed countries. The poorest among the latter were deterred from entering the Euromarkets because of high interest rates and poor credit ratings. They were forced to limit current account deficits by restricting imports. Given the Euromarket's reluctance to provide financing to the very weak, low-income less developed countries, international organisations like the World Bank and the IMF increasingly became their main sources of funds.

The Players in the Market

The Eurocurrency market is entirely a wholesale market. Transactions are rarely for less than $1 million and sometimes they are for $100 million. Like the foreign exchange markets, the vast bulk is confined to interbank operations. The largest non-banking companies have to deal via banks. Borrowers are the very highest pedigree corporate names carrying the lowest credit risks. The market is telephone-linked or telecommunications-linked and is focused upon London which has a share of around one third of the Eurocurrency market. All Eurocurrency trans-actions are unsecured credits, hence the fact that lenders pay particular attention to borrowers' status and name.

Commercial banks form the institutional core of the market. Banks enter the Eurocurrency market both as depositors and lenders. Around twenty of the world's biggest banks play a dominant role in the Euromarket. They attract a disproportionate volume of primary deposits, which are then re-lent to other Eurobanks. These banks link the external with the domestic market, taking funds from one and placing them in other markets. The size, breadth and depth of the interbank market enable banks to adjust liquidity positions with great ease.

Corporations borrowing Eurocurrencies are mainly those whose name, size and good standing enable banks to make loans to them with little more than a superficial analysis of creditworthiness. But more recently the range of corporate and government borrowers has widened to embrace less worthy names. The main reason for this is the vast amount of funds available for lending. In the last decade the market has also seen an expansion in government and government-related borrowers. This is especially true of the medium-term Eurocredit market which has become widely tapped for infrastructure projects and for financing balance of payments deficits. Governments and central banks are also lenders in the Euro-currency markets. In addition, international institutions such as the World Bank and various regional development banks, and institutions associated with the EEC, have been regular borrowers. Private individuals are minor participants in the Eurodollar markets. High net worth people have, however, always been signifi-cant participants as investors in the Eurobond market where the fact that payment of interest is gross of tax and securities are bearer securities gives the market an anonymity and obvious attractiveness from a tax point of view.

Euromarket Deposits and Borrowings

Most deposits in the Eurocurrency market are time deposits at fixed interest rates, usually of short maturity. Around three quarters of deposits in London Eurobanks have maturities of less than three months. Many of these deposits are on call; thus they can be withdrawn without notice. Most of the time deposits are made by other banks, but many are made by governments and their central banks as well as multinational corporations. A few are made by wealthy individuals, often through a Swiss bank.

Deposits come in many forms. Besides negotiable Eurodollar certificates of deposit (sometimes termed London dollar CDs), there are various similar certificates of deposit. Floating rate notes (FRNs) have become popular for longer maturity deposits, including floating rate CDs.

Many Eurodollar loans are direct, bank-to-customer credits on the basis of formal lines of credit or customer relationships. However, the market has developed the technique of loan syndication for very large advances. The Eurocurrency syndication technique arose principally because of the large size of credits required by some government borrowers and multinational firms. The syndication procedure allows banks to diversify some of the unique sovereign risks that arise in international lending. Syndicated Euroloans involve formal arrangements in which competitively selected lead banks assemble a management group of other banks to underwrite the loan and to market participation in it to other banks.

Interest on syndicated loans is usually computed by adding a spread to LIBOR, although the US prime rate is also used as a basis for interest pricing. LIBOR interest rates change continuously, of course. The rate on any particular loan is usually readjusted every three or six months onto the prevailing LIBOR rate. This method of pricing is known as a rollover basis.

The Eurocredit Market

The Eurocredit market, sometimes called the medium-term Eurocredit market, or the medium-term Eurocurrency market, is defined as the market for loans in currencies which are not native to the country in which the bank office making the loans is located. The Eurocredit market is concerned with medium- and long-term loans and banks are the major lenders, with major borrowers being large multinational companies, international organisations and governments (frequently in developing countries). Generally, Eurocredits are extended by a large group of banks from many countries. The risk of loan default is thereby spread among many banks.

Loan Syndication

There are usually three categories of bank in a loan syndicate. There are lead banks, managing banks and participating banks. In large borrowings, there is a separate group called co-managers. This group comprises participating banks providing more than a specified amount of funds. Most loans are led by one or two major banks who negotiate to obtain a mandate from the borrower to raise funds. After the preliminary stages of negotiation with a borrower, the lead bank begins to assemble the management group who commit themselves to provide the entire amount of the loan, if necessary. Portions of the loan are then marketed to participating banks.

In the early stages of negotiation with a borrower, the lead bank assembles a management group to assure the borrower that the entire amount of the loan will be taken up. The management group may be in place before the mandate is received or may be assembled immediately afterwards. During this phase, the lead bank may renegotiate the terms and conditions of the loan if it cannot assemble a managing group on the initial terms. But, rather than renegotiate, many lead banks are willing to take more of the credit into their own portfolio than they had originally planned. The lead bank is normally expected to provide a share at least as large as any other bank. Once the lead bank has established the group of managing banks, it then commits the group to raise funds for the borrower on specified terms and conditions.

When the management group is established and the lead bank has received a mandate from the borrower, a placement memorandum is prepared by the lead bank and the loan is marketed to other banks which may be interested in taking up shares. Such lenders are termed the participating banks. The placement memorandum describes the transaction and gives information regarding the financial health of the borrower. The statistical information given in the memorandum is usually provided by the borrower.

The lead bank emphasises that the placement memorandum is not a substitute for an independent credit review by participating banks and such participating banks generally sign a statement that they have performed an independent analysis of the credit. However, smaller banks tend to rely heavily on the judgement of the lead and managing banks, arguing that large banks have better information and better analysts than smaller banks. Their behaviour seems to indicate that they argue that if the big banks are participating in the credit, it must be good.

Problems in this area were highlighted in the Coloctronis v. European American Bank case. European American Bank made a number of loans to shipping companies comprising the Coloctronis group and sold off participations in the credit. The loans were secured by mortgages on ships and assignments of their charter hire, and were guaranteed by various members of the Coloctronis family. A group of regional US banks took participations in the credit and when the Coloctronis group defaulted on its loans, the participants sued the lead bank. The regional banks stated that they knew little of Norwegian shipping and relied on the judgement of European American Bank, a substantial bank involved in shipping. The regional banks claimed that, since the sale of loan participations came under US security law, they were entitled to protection. The case was settled without a court decision. However, the fundamental issue of the responsibility of the lead bank to the participants raised by the case has caused large banks to review disclaimer clauses most carefully. And lead banks now examine placement memoranda very carefully before distribution to make sure that they are factual and do not involve subjective judgements.

The lead bank bears the chief responsibility for marketing the loan, although other members of the managing group assist in this respect. There are three main methods used to find participants for syndicated credits. The borrower may specify that a certain bank should be given the opportunity to participate because the borrower wishes to establish a relationship with that bank. Often banks contact the borrower expressing an interest in participating in a given credit. But the bulk of participants are banks invited by the lead bank to join the syndication. Each major bank maintains files on the syndicated lending activities of other banks. The files contain lists of banks that have joined various syndications. This information enables the loan syndication officers at the lead bank to estimate which banks might be interested in which borrowers. Once a first list of potential participants is assembled, the lead bank, operating through informal contacts, in London and elsewhere, will try to determine which of the banks are interested in expanding their portfolio to particular borrowers and on what terms, and which banks are unwilling to increase their credit exposure to particular countries. From this analysis the list is finalised.

When a bank is invited to participate in a syndication, the amount and the terms and conditions it is being asked to accept are set out in a telex sent by the lead bank. This short-cuts the negotiation process and expedites the credit.

The lead bank usually offers to sell off more of the credit than it really wishes, since some of the banks that receive invitations will opt not to participate. An experienced lead bank can usually gauge the appropriate number of participation invitations to be extended. If the credit is attractive, fewer banks will be contacted. If the credit (based on terms and conditions) appears hard to place, a greater number of invitations will be sent out. If the loan is over-subscribed, the borrower is usually given the opportunity to borrow more money than initially negotiated on the same terms. If the borrower does not choose to take advantage of this, the amounts assigned to each bank are scaled down pro rata.

In a successful loan syndication, once the marketing to participants is completed, the lead and managing banks usually keep 50 to 75 per cent of their initial underwritten share. The lead bank is generally expected to take into its portfolio about 10 per cent of the total credit. This rule of thumb does not apply to very large credits, where a 10 per cent commitment to a single borrower may, when taken with credits to the borrower already in the bank's portfolio, give the bank an excess exposure in relation to its capital. It is not acceptable market practice for a bank to lead and arrange a credit and not take any portion of the credit into its own portfolio. It takes from two weeks to three months to arrange a syndication, with six weeks as the norm – the more familiar the borrower, the quicker the terms can be set and the placement memorandum prepared.

The most common type of syndicated loan is a term loan, where funds can be drawn down by the borrower within a specified time of the loan being signed – this is called the drawdown period. Repayments are subsequently made in accordance with an amortisation schedule. Sometimes amortisation of loans commences almost immediately following drawdown. For other loans, amortisation may not commence until five or six years after drawing down the loan. Sometimes term loans have no amortisation over the life of the loan and all repayment is due on maturity – this kind of loan is termed a bullet loan. Loans which require repayment according to an amortisation schedule and include a larger final payment on maturity are termed balloon repayment loans. The period prior to the commencement of repayment is termed the grace period. The extent of the grace period is usually a major negotiating point between borrower and lead bank. Borrowers are usually willing to pay a wider spread in order to obtain a longer grace period.

Syndicated loans of the revolving credit type are occasionally encountered. In these, the borrower is given a line of credit which he may draw down and repay with greater flexibility than under a term loan. Borrowers pay a fee on the undrawn amount of the credit line.

Additional to interest costs on a loan, there are also front-end fees, commitment fees, and occasionally an annual agent's fee. Front-end management fees are one-off charges negotiated in advance and imposed when the loan agreement is signed. These fees are usually in the range of 0.5 to 1 per cent of the value of the loan. The fees may be higher if a particular borrower insists upon obtaining funds at a lower spread than warranted by market conditions and creditworthiness.

The relationship between spreads and fees is hard to quantify, as data on all fees are usually unobtainable. But there is some evidence to suggest that banks will accept lower spreads if compensated by higher fees, since they are interested in the total return on the loan. Some borrowers prefer to pay a higher fee, which is not published, while going on record as paying a low spread. Over time, demand and supply conditions determine both spreads and fees. During periods of easy market conditions, borrowers can command low fees and low spreads. During periods when banks are reluctant to extend credit, high spreads and high fees are the norm.

Front-end fees consist of participation fees and management fees. Each of these typically amounts to 0.25 to 0.5 per cent of the entire amount of the loan. Participation fees are divided among all banks in relation to their share of the loan. The management fees are divided between the underwriting banks and the lead bank. The lead bank usually takes a praecipium on the entire loan. The rest of the management fee is divided among the managing banks in proportion to the amount each agrees to underwrite prior to syndication.

An example may be useful in clarifying the division of front-end fees. Consider a $500 million syndicated credit, with the lenders consisting of a lead bank, ten other managing banks, and 20 participating banks. Assume that prior to syndication, the lead bank agrees to underwrite $100 million and each of the other managing banks agrees to underwrite $40 million. After syndication, the lead bank retains 10 per cent of the credit, or $50 million. Each of the other ten managing banks retains 4 per cent or $20 million, and each of the participating banks takes 2.5 per cent of the credit, or $12.5 million. Assume that front-end fees on the loan total 0.5 per cent. The lead bank receives 0.125 per cent of the whole amount as a praecipium; each of the managing banks receives 0.125 per cent of the portion initially under-written; the participation fee is 0.5 per cent on the amount each bank provides. The fee income, totalling $2.5 million, would be distributed as follows:

	Lead bank receives ($)	Each managing bank receives ($)	Each participating bank receives ($)
Lead bank praecipium (0.125%)	625,000	—	—
Management fee (0.125%)	125,000	50,000	—
Participation fee (0.25%)	125,000	50,000	31,250
	875,000	100,000	31,250

Of the front-end fees of $2.5 million, the lead bank receives $875,000; each managing bank receives $100,000 and each participating bank receives $31,250. Evidently, front-end fees are an important part of the managing bank's total return on a credit.

In addition to front-end fees, borrowers may pay commitment fees. These fees are charged to the borrower as a percentage of the undrawn portion of the credit in return for the bank tying up part of its credit capacity on behalf of the borrower, even though the loan has not yet been drawn down and does not earn any interest for the bank. Commitment fees of 0.375 to 0.5 per cent per annum are typically imposed on both term loans and revolving credits.

The agent's fee, if applicable, is usually a yearly charge but may occasionally be paid at the outset. The agent's fee is relatively small; on a large credit it may amount to $10,000 annually and is meant to cover administrative and minor incidental expenses related to the syndication.

To protect their margins, banks usually require all payments of principal and interest to be made after taxes imposed have been paid. If those taxes are not creditable against the banks' home country taxes, the borrower must adjust payments so that the banks receive the same net repayment. The decision as to whether the borrower or lender absorbs any additional taxes imposed by the country in which the loan is booked is negotiated between the parties. Additionally, a reserve requirement clause is generally inserted, stipulating that an adjustment will be made if the cost of funds increases because reserve requirements are imposed or increased.

There is generally no prepayment penalty on Eurocredits. The charges on syndicated loans may be summarised as:

Annual payments = (LIBOR + spread) × amount of loan drawn down and outstanding
+ commitment fee × amount of loan undrawn
+ annual agent's fee (if any)
+ tax adjustment (if any)
+ reserve requirement adjustment (if any)

Front-end charges = lead bank praecipium × total amount of loan
+ participation fee × face amount of loan
+ management fee × face amount of loan
+ initial agent's fee (if any)

Spreads and Maturities

The history of the amortisation credit market includes periods when lenders held the whip-hand and periods when borrowers were in charge. During borrowers' markets, spreads tend to be low and maturities long. During lenders' markets, the situation is reversed.

With other things being equal, a longer maturity loan should carry a wider spread in order to leave the lenders indifferent to the trade-off between profit and risk. Furthermore, if spreads widen over time, lenders are locked into a long maturity loan at the old spreads. If spreads narrow, the borrower can refinance and therefore should not object to accepting higher spreads for longer maturities. Bankers attempt to analyse both the economic and political risks associated with a loan. These are more difficult to analyse over a ten-year horizon than over a one-year horizon. So for each additional year of maturity, lenders require compensation in terms of spread, fees, or grace period. Borrowers prefer longer maturities and are willing to compensate lenders for such loans because they are assured of the availability of funds at a specified spread, even if market conditions tighten. If market conditions ease, a borrower can usually refinance. A number of researchers have attempted to estimate the trade-off between spreads and maturities. However, studies have suggested that whilst it does exist, it is neither stable nor predictable across time for particular country groupings and may differ substantially among country groupings at a given point in time. By and large, aggregate data on spreads and maturities over time suggest that there is an inverse relationship between the two variables. Spreads and maturities are heavily influenced by market conditions. During periods of low confidence in the market, when conditions are tight, spreads are wide and maturities short. In the two years following the Herstatt failure, banks were worried about the market and this was reflected in wide spreads and short maturities. In periods when market conditions are relatively easy, spreads decline and maturities lengthen.

Deductive reasoning suggests that a number of factors should be important in determining spreads. They should embrace the level of interest rates, the banks' capital/asset ratios, the volatility of interest rates, liquidity considerations attributable to the amount of non-bank deposits entering the Euromarket and relative loan demand pressures in domestic markets, changes in the competitive structure of the syndicated credit market, and borrower risk.

A high level of nominal interest rate implies a narrower absolute spread. There are several reasons for this. The first relates to considerations of return on capital. Banks are concerned about their overall return on capital. It has been shown that when LIBOR rises, their rate of return on capital increases. Consider the following example. A bank's return on a loan may be computed by assuming that the loan is funded by capital sources and deposits in proportion to the figures for capital and deposits on the bank's balance sheet. So, if a capital/total assets ratio of 5 per cent is hypothesised, the implication is that the average loan is funded 95 per cent from deposits and 5 per cent from capital. Assuming, for the purpose of simplicity, that the bank has no overhead or loan-processing costs and that it purchases funds in the interbank market at LIBOR, its return on capital is derived as follows:

$$\text{return on capital} = \left[\text{interest received on loan} - \left(\text{cost of servicing deposits} \times \frac{\text{deposits}}{\text{assets}} \right) \right] \times \frac{\text{assets}}{\text{capital}}$$

If the capital/asset ratio is 0.05, the spread is 1 per cent and the LIBOR is 16 per cent, then, applying the above equation, we would have:

$$
\begin{aligned}
\text{return on capital} &= [(\text{LIBOR} + 0.01) - (\text{LIBOR} \times 0.95)] \times 20 \\
&= [(0.16 + 0.01) - (0.16 \times 0.95)] \times 20 \\
&= (0.17 - 0.152) \times 20 \\
&= 0.018 \times 20 \\
&= 0.36 \\
&= 36\%
\end{aligned}
$$

If the capital/asset ratio and the spread remain constant, and LIBOR increases to 20 per cent, the before-tax rate of return is now 40 per cent. If the bank now wished to achieve a 36 per cent before-tax return on capital with a LIBOR of 20 per cent, it would charge a spread of 80 basis points, that is 0.8 per cent over LIBOR.

In terms of banks' financial planning processes, the above equation is often used to target loan spreads on the basis of required returns on capital. The equation can easily be made more complex by building in such factors as overhead costs and bad debt costs as proportions of loans advanced.

A second reason for an inverse relationship between nominal interest rates and spreads is that, if borrowers are sensitive to the total interest cost on syndicated loans (that is, LIBOR plus spread), banks may be forced to lower spreads to compensate for higher LIBOR when faced with an expected fall in demand.

The third possible explanation for an inverse relationship between interest rates and spreads is that banks are expected to equate the marginal cost of all sources of funds. In periods of high nominal interest rates, the opportunity cost of reserve requirements is higher. Hence the absolute differential between Euro-market and domestic market interest rates will widen because the former has no reserve requirements. More funds will therefore be shifted into the Euromarket and, with an unchanged demand for funds, this should be sufficient to reduce spreads.

Empirical attempts at estimating the relationship between the level of interest rates and spread have produced conflicting results. Goodman (1980) found the expected negative relationship between spread and interest rates; with each 100 basis point increase in interest rates (that is 1 per cent) he found a 7 basis point narrowing of spreads. However, Johnston (1980) found a slightly positive, but non-significant, relationship.

Over the last decade spreads and maturities on syndicated credits have fluctuated. The tabulation in Table 23.1 gives some idea of typical levels for different kinds of borrower according to their location by country.

Table 23.1 Spreads and Maturities on Syndicated Credits

	Spreads (%)	*Maturities (years)*
Industrial countries – range	0.51–1.72	5.3–10.2
– typically	0.60–0.80	6.0–8.0
High income developing		
countries – range	0.77–1.80	5.3–11.4
– typically	1.00–1.60	6.0–8.0
Low income developing		
countries – range	0.85–2.07	4.7–10.5
– typically	1.00–2.00	6.0–8.0
OPEC members – range	0.60–1.75	4.2–10.8
– typically	0.80–1.20	6.0–8.0

Securitisation

During the middle eighties, a number of influences affected the syndicated lending market and changed its nature. The value of new syndicated bank credits fell from around $130 billion in 1981 to around $75 billion in 1983, recovering to $106 billion in 1984. This did not mean borrowers were under pressure, it merely reflected a fundamental change in the nature of international capital markets. Indeed, the volume of funds intermediated through international capital markets remained firm but there was a switch away from the syndicated loan. Why should this have been so?

The underpinning reason is to be found in the fact that international banks' ratios were showing a sharp decline as they increasingly reported bad loans and provided for other doubtful debts. The key ratio of capital to assets deteriorated for a wide spectrum of banks towards levels which regulating central banks regard as imprudent. In syndicated lending, banks take a deposit and re-lend. The effect of this flows through to banks' ratios. The banks themselves therefore increasingly sought ways to make profit off-balance sheet. They looked for ways to transfer money from lenders to borrowers whilst collecting a fee for so doing, but without affecting their own balance sheets, and they came up with the formula of securitisation, or disintermediation, as it is sometimes called. Their approach involved the increasing use of the Eurobond and the Euronote issuance facility. Eurobonds are looked at later in this chapter but Euronotes are considered here.

The Euronote technique involves a reallocation of roles within the international capital market, the impact of which is to allow borrowers to raise what is effectively medium-term, say five- to seven-year, money at very low rates available traditionally only in the short-term money markets. A borrower who raises money in the Euronote market does so by the issue of short-term notes, with maturities of three and six months, that are negotiable like certificates of deposit and can be placed with non-bank investors such as corporate treasurers and central banks. As one issue of notes matures after three or six months, the borrower issues some more so that, while the holders of the debt change over time, the total amount outstanding in the market can be maintained in the medium term. But borrowers have to be sure that they will always be able to find buyers for their notes in the market. If they could not, they might find that they had to pay down the debt before the planned maturity. Because of this, a Euronote facility is normally backed up or underwritten by a group of commercial banks which stands ready to buy the paper at a specified price or to provide credit should the appetite of short-term investors wane.

The traditional function of commercial banks, which was to lend money over the medium term, has been split. Instead of lending money, commercial banks simply commit their resources, under Euronote issuance facilities, to guaranteeing that it will be available over the medium term. The actual funds are provided from elsewhere in the market, for example by non-bank investors looking for a short-term home for their surplus cash.

Linked to the deterioration of banks' capital ratios and the success of the Euronote issuance facility is the fact that prime companies and developed country governments have appeared as more attractive propositions to lenders than placing money with bankers. So much so that some have been borrowing in the Euronote markets at between five and ten basis points (between one twentieth and one tenth of a percentage point) below LIBOR.

Lead banks, in attempts at product differentiation in this market, have packaged Euronote deals in marginally different ways giving rise to numerous acronyms which include NIFs (note issuance facilities), RUFs (revolving underwriting facilities), MOFFs (multiple option funding facilities), TRUFs (transferable revolving underwriting facilities) and BONUS (borrower's option for notes and underwritten standby) – and there are more appearing all the time.

A threat to the Euronote market comes from possible regulation by central banks which have looked askance at its development. The market in Euronote issuance facilities has grown from virtually nothing in 1980 to an estimated $40 billion to $50 billion in 1985. Indeed, many central banks place restrictions on the issue of note facilities in their own currencies with the result that the US dollar and the uncontrolled ECU (European currency unit) remain two of the very few currencies in which Euronote facilities can, as of November 1985, be arranged.

What worries the central banks is that the underwriting banks are now carrying huge contingent commitments to provide money if the note sales or negotiation of them dry up. The critical question is whether, should these contingencies crystalise, the banks have adequate capital backing. It is precisely because the banks could be called upon to exercise their underwriting commitment at a time of world financial crisis that capital requirements are regarded as being so important. The Bank of England, for one, has become so concerned that it now insists that 50 per cent of these potential commitments should be included in measuring banks' capital adequacy ratios.

Eurocurrency Interest Rates and their Linkages with Domestic Rates

Each Eurocurrency market, whether it be Eurodollars, Eurosterling and so on, is linked through arbitrage to its domestic counterpart. Hence Eurocurrency rates are strongly influenced by domestic rates. Because there is no regulating authority to set interest rates in the Euromarkets and since no one set of banks enforces administered rates, Eurocurrency interest rates are determined by the forces of competition.

Furthermore, domestic and external markets compete for funds. The essential starting point to the analysis of the relationship between domestic and external interest rates is a clear understanding of what the Eurocurrency market is. Using the USA and the US dollar for illustration, the Eurodollar market (external) and domestic market (internal) are merely competing segments of the total market for dollar denominated credit, intermediated by financial institutions operating either internally (domestic banks) or externally (Eurobanks). The Eurodollar market competes with the domestic US credit market for deposits and for the making of loans. Within this competitive arena, the Eurocurrency segment possesses certain unique characteristics, namely:

- Eurobanks are not required to maintain reserves against their deposit liabilities.
- Eurobanks are less subject to regulation.
- Eurobanks are not subject to interest rate ceilings, whether imposed by government or by cartel.
- Eurobanks can take better advantage of low-tax locations.
- High degrees of competitiveness, and virtually unrestricted entry, force Eurobanks to keep margins small and overhead costs low.
- Eurobanks are less subject than domestic markets to pressure to allocate credit for socially valued but unprofitable purposes.

- Eurobanks are subject to greater risk than domestic banks (see later in this section).

Given that the Eurodollar market and the domestic dollar money markets deal in the same currency and that there is very considerable freedom for capital to move between these markets in response to interest rate diffrentials, it is no coincidence that interest rate structures are closely linked. In the absence of specific obstacles and barriers (such as exchange controls) arbitrage between the domestic and external segments of the dollar denominated money markets assures close correspondence both in terms of rate levels and in terms of timing and magnitude of rate changes. This close cleavage of rates has regularly been demonstrated in empirical work; but where exchange controls or the like are in place, the tendency for the close movement of rates in domestic and external markets is found to be much weaker. Indeed, an indication of the efficacy of capital controls can be seen in the degree of divergence of interest rates in the two markets. Wide divergences are associated with tight capital controls, and vice versa.

In our earlier discussions on the four-way equivalence model we found that the major influences upon Eurocurrency interest rates, currency expectations and forward exchange rates might be summarised as:

- Eurocurrency interest rate differential = forward premium or discount (this is known as interest rate parity).
- Forward premium or discount = expected change in exchange rate (expectations theory).
- Expected change in exchange rate = Eurocurrency interest rate differential (international Fisher effect).
- Eurocurrency interest rate differential = difference in expected inflation rates (Fisher effect).

It should be recalled – and this is most important – that when using the four-way equivalence model, interest rate differentials must be based upon Eurocurrency interest rates. It should also be recalled that, empirically, interest rate parity is the only one of the above equivalences which is found to hold in the short term.

That Eurocurrency rates do not exactly equal domestic interest rates is explained in the main by regulatory factors such as reserve requirements affecting one market but not the other. The extent to which reserve requirements impinge upon rates can be demonstrated by a simplified numerical example. Assume that a US bank receives $1 million in domestic deposits and the reserve requirement (which has to be deposited with the central bank and does not earn any interest) is 5 per cent. The effective funds received, then, amount to only $950,000 – that is, 95 per cent of the deposit. Assume further that the bank pays 15 per cent per annum on the full $1 million. The effective cost of the funds in the domestic deposit is therefore given by:

$$\text{Effective cost of domestic deposit} = \frac{\text{interest rate paid}}{1 - \text{reserve requirement}}$$

$$= \frac{15\%}{1 - 0.05}$$

$$= 15.79\%$$

The additional cost of the reserve requirement is therefore 79 basis points; this is the extra amount that the bank can afford to pay on Eurodollar deposits (which avoid reserve requirements) to achieve the same true cost of funds.

Another major reason for different interest rate levels in domestic and external markets arises because of perceived differences in risk. These risk differences can best be explained with the help of an example. A US depositor in the Eurodollar market holds a claim in one location, for example London, but may ultimately receive payment in the USA. The depositor might be deprived of his funds at maturity by an action of either the UK or the US government. In the case of a domestic deposit, it is only the actions of one government that can affect the deposit.

Of course, it is also possible to argue that Euromarkets may actually reduce risk. In countries where new capital controls upon disposition of residents' funds are feared, external deposits might well be considered less risky by residents than leaving funds on domestic deposits. As well as indirect interference through government regulations, depositors may be concerned with direct government intervention. The government of the country in which the Eurobank operates may seize the assets of the bank and block repayment of liabilities or otherwise restrict its activities through political action. The scenario might be as follows. In a fit of nationalism or in an attempt to alleviate foreign exchange difficulties, the government of a country where Eurocurrency deposits and loans are made intervenes in the operations of branches of foreign banks within its territory. This is the kind of risk which is termed sovereign risk in Eurobanking. And, by definition it is always present in the Eurocurrency business. Eurobanking involves attracting funds from non-residents and making loans to other non-residents. If very few of the Eurobank's assets are directly subject to the host country's jurisdiction, then offshore operations are at risk only if that government is able to press its claims in the jurisdictions of the borrowers against the competing claims of the parent bank. Another fear is that, while the central banks of various countries are often perceived as being ready to bail out any major bank whose domestic operations get into trouble, they might not do so for offshore branches. After all, who is the lender of last resort when difficulties originate from loans on the books of foreign affiliates?

In short, the risks associated with external dollar deposits and loans are usually greater than those associated with their domestic counterparts. These greater risks stem from the possibility of government intervention of not just one, but of two or more countries, and from the possibility that central banks might not function as lenders of last resort for Eurobanks.

Just as there is a relationship between domestic and external interest rates, so Eurodollar interest rates of different maturities follow similar term structures to domestic rates. Interest rates of the same maturity move in tandem in the two markets. Generally, long-term rates are less volatile than short-term rates. This is because short-term rates are very sensitive to the near-term outlook for credit conditions, whereas long-term rates are affected to a greater degree by long-term inflationary expectations.

The Term Structure of Interest Rates

The term structure of interest rates can be thought of as a graph of interest rates on securities of a particular risk class at a particular time, in which the interest rate is plotted on the vertical axis and time to maturity on the horizontal axis. Term structure theory is concerned with why the term structure has a particular shape at a particular time. Analysts sometimes refer to the term structure as being flat (same interest for all maturities), upward-sloping (long-term interest rates higher than short-term interest rates), or downward-sloping (short-term interest rates higher than long-term rates). Figure 23.1 illustrates these three situations.

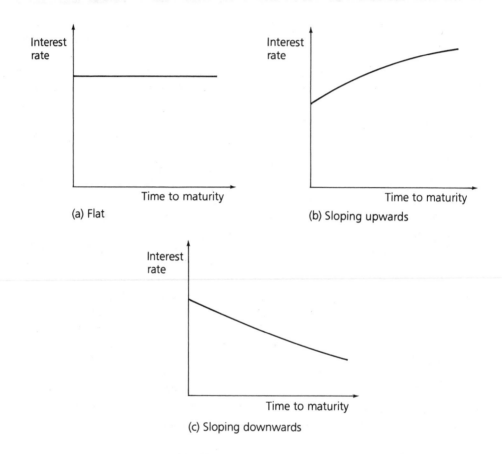

Figure 23.1   Types of Term Structure

The best known explanation of the term structure is the expectations theory. According to this hypothesis, expectations of future interest rates constitute the key determinant of the yield/maturity relationship. Each investor can buy either long-term securities and hold them or buy short-term securities and continually reinvest in shorts at each maturity over the holding period. In equilibrium, the expected return for each holding period will tend to be the same, whatever alternative or combination of alternatives was chosen. As a result, the return on a long-term bond will tend to equal an unbiased average of the current short-term rates and future short-term rates expected to prevail to maturity of the long-term bond. With this background, one can calculate the implicit or expected short-term rate for any future period based upon actual rates of interest prevailing in the market at a specific time. Expectations theory contends that the term structure of interest rates is entirely a function of investors' expectations about future interest rates. Most evidence underpins the importance of interest rate expectations in the term structure of interest rates. However, Hicks and others have argued that long-term rates in fact tend to differ from the average of expected short-term rates because market participants prefer to lend short unless offered a premium sufficient to offset the risk of lending long. Hicks (1946) argues that these liquidity premiums tend to be greater, the longer the maturity of the bond. His findings support the liquidity preference theory of the term structure of interest rates. Advocates of this theory believe that for the most part investors wish to lend short, and organisations aim to borrow long, so that liquidity premiums are positive − that is, the forward rate exceeds the expected future spot interest rate. If liquidity preference theory is right, the term structure should be upward-sloping more often than not. A positive liquidity premium rewards investors for lending long. The reward manifests itself in high long-term rates of interest. Of course, if future spot rates were expected to fall the term structure could still be downward-sloping − but liquidity preference theory would predict a less dramatic downward slope than expectations theory.

A third theory, the preferred habitat hypothesis of Modigliani and Sutch (1966), argues that bond markets are segmented by maturity, and that the maturity preferences of market participants are so strong that investors tend to borrow and lend only in a particular range of maturities. Therefore, in each different credit market, interest rates tend to be determined by supply and demand rather than by interest rate expectations. This explanation is sometimes called the market segmentation theory, or the hedging pressure theory.

Finally, there is the inflation premium theory. Like the liquidity preference explanation, this theory argues that long-term interest rates reflect investors' expectations about future short-term interest rates plus a premium for risk. However, advocates of the theory contend that the principal source of risk is the rate of inflation. They argue that investors are interested in real returns and that the primary determinant in the term structure of interest rates is investors' expectations of inflation over different holding periods which is the critical factor by which investors translate nominal interest rates into real expected returns.

Whichever theory of term structure seems to predominate in the domestic market should hold for the Euromarket. In the absence of capital controls, arbitrage would ensure the virtual equality of internal and external rates at each maturity, and whatever holds for the domestic market would also hold for Eurorates. In other words, there is normally no independent Eurodollar term structure of interest rates.

If capital controls are in place and they affect all maturities equally, the internal term structure might not be identical to the external one, but since Eurorates should tend to be at the same position relative to internal rates for each maturity, a nearly identical term structure should hold. As in the domestic market, if Euro-currency investors think interest rates will drop, they will try to lock into long-term deposits; this will tend to lower the long-term yield to maturity.

The term structure of Eurocurrency interest rates will be consonant with the market's interest rate forecasts if, and only if, the yield on a long-term deposit equals the expected yield obtained from investing in short-term securities and reinvesting the proceeds successively in short-term deposits at the interest rate expected to prevail during each future period.

The Eurodollar Credit Creation Process

The Eurocurrency market is often commented upon for its apparent ability to create vast amounts of credit. How this credit creation process takes place will now be analysed.

Consider the following example of the multiple deposit creation process with respect to the Eurodollar market. Our example follows on from the transfer of funds from a US bank to a London bank. Assume that a wealthy foreigner transfers $1 million from his New York Bank, Citibank, to his London Bank, Londbank. This bank will show an increase of deposit liabilities of $1 million. At the same time, it will gain an asset, namely, a claim on a US bank for $1 million. Assume that Londbank's correspondent bank is Citibank. Citibank will decrease its liabilities to the wealthy foreigner by $1 million and increase its liabilities to Londbank by $1 million. The change in their accounts can be summarised as follows:

Citibank

Assets	Liabilities
	− $1 million to wealthy foreigner
	+ $1 million due to Londbank

Londbank

Assets	Liabilities
+ $1 million due from Citibank	+ $1 million due to wealthy foreigner

The total deposit liabilities of Citibank have not changed, but the total of assets and liabilities of Londbank has increased by $1 million. If Londbank normally retains ten per cent of its assets as prudential reserves, it will now have an additional $900,000 to lend, whilst keeping $100,000 on demand deposit at Citibank. Assume that the recipient of the loan, a UK company called George Bull plc, requires the funds for future use in the USA and hence holds the money in a demand deposit at a US office of Citibank. Londbank has now replaced its $1 million deposit with Citibank by a $100,000 deposit with Citibank, and a $900,000 loan to George Bull plc. The total liabilities of Citibank again remain unchanged, as shown:

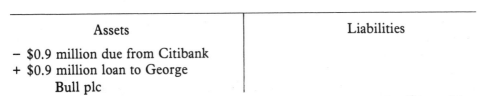

Citibank

Assets	Liabilities
	− $0.9 million due to Londbank
	+ $0.9 million to George Bull plc

Londbank

Assets	Liabilities
− $0.9 million due from Citibank	
+ $0.9 million loan to George Bull plc	

The position at the moment is as follows: Citibank's asset and liability position is unchanged − it had a $1 million liability to the wealthy foreigner; now it has a $100,000 liability to Londbank and a $900,000 liability to George Bull plc. However, the total of Eurodollars is up by $1,000,000. There has been no balance of payments deficit and no monetary expansion. The increase in Eurodollars occurred as a result of a transfer of funds. But because these funds were transferred from a non-bank to a bank (from our wealthy foreigner to Londbank) there is a potential for expansion. The expansion will take place if the borrowed funds are redeposited in the system, that is, in a Eurobank.

Suppose that George Bull plc, rather than holding the $900,000 in the USA, uses it to purchase wine from a French company, and this company chooses to hold the money in dollars at Westendbank, another bank in London, which again holds its dollars on deposit with Citibank in New York. Again Citibank's position is effectively unchanged, with a $100,000 liability to Londbank and a $900,000 liability to Westendbank rather than a $1,000,000 liability to Londbank. There have been $900,000 more Eurodollars created in this instance as Westendbank's liabilities are up by $900,000.

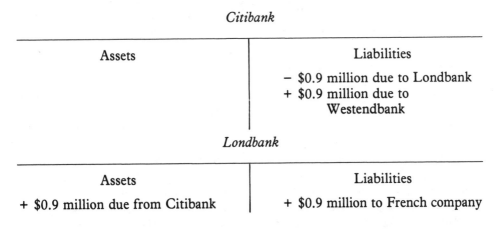

Citibank

Assets	Liabilities
	− $0.9 million due to Londbank
	+ $0.9 million due to Westendbank

Londbank

Assets	Liabilities
+ $0.9 million due from Citibank	+ $0.9 million to French company

If this process continued, with the proceeds of Eurodollar loans always being redeposited in Eurobanks, the final volume of obligations of Eurobanks denominated in dollars would be $10,000,000, all based on the $1,000,000 liability of Citibank.

The Eurodollar multiplier – the rate of the increase in Eurodollar deposits relative to the primary deposit – in the first case is one, and in the second case, ten. In the first example there was a maximum leakage and in the second there was zero leakage. In the first example the funds lent moved out of the Eurocurrency system back into domestic dollars; in the second the funds lent remained within the Eurocurrency market.

In a domestic banking system there is a fixed reserve requirement imposed by the authorities. There is also a relatively fixed leakage from the currency holdings of the public. Also, it is a feature of closed banking systems that their deposits cannot be extinguished by transfer to competing institutions such as building societies since they hold their funds within the banking system. But in the Eurodollar market there are no compulsory reserve requirements and there is no reason to suppose that funds lent in this market will automatically return to it.

In trying to estimate the value of the credit multiplier in such a market it is necessary to know by how much the market would grow given some initial inflow of funds. If the total size of the market increased by only the size of the inflow, the multiplier would be one. If it expanded as a result of credit multiplication by twice the amount of the inflow, the multiplier would be two. In fact, what limits the expansion to little more than the amount of the inflow is the fact that it has to compete with US domestic interest rates. An inflow of funds tends to reduce interest rates, and the resulting fall in the differential in favour of Eurodollars as against US domestic deposits and other domestic deposits tends to cause funds to flow out of the market. The banks, in order to loan out the additional funds, have to make loans more attractive, which means lowering the loan rate as well as the deposit rate. The market suffers heavy leakages when borrowers convert from Eurocurrencies into domestic currencies. In practice, given the low deposit ratio and the interest rate effect discussed above, the multiplier in the market is unlikely to be much more than one.

There are theoretical objections to the description of a multiple expansion of credits and deposits on a given reserve base with Eurocurrency markets. As Milton Friedman (1969) points out, 'if Eurodollar banks held zero prudential reserves, 100 per cent of outstanding deposits would be created deposits and the potential multiplier would be infinite. Yet the actual multiplier would be close to unity because only a small part of the funds acquired by borrowers from Eurodollar banks would end up as additional time deposits in such banks.' Furthermore, even within a domestic banking system with reserve requirements, the multiplier is misleading because, as Tobin (1963) has observed, 'an individual bank is not constrained by any fixed quantum of reserves; depositors' performance preferences do matter, so that an increase in reserves does not lead automatically to an expansion of deposits.' Thus, the application of bank reserve multipliers to the Eurocurrency market is not a realistic approach because the reserve multipliers can only show potential creation processes which say nothing about actually created deposits.

Despite these criticisms of the credit creation process there is no doubt that the Eurodollar system has gone a long way towards meeting increased liquidity requirements for routine financing of international trade in normal circumstances.

The Eurodollar market does tend to make for expansion through increasing the velocity of circulation of deposits. Formerly idle deposits become active deposits. By changing hands more frequently they finance a larger volume of activity.

The International Bond Market

Money may be raised internationally by bond issues and by bank loans. This is done in domestic as well as international markets. The difference is that in international markets the money may come in a currency which is different from that normally used by the borrower. The characteristic feature of the international bond market is that bonds are always sold outside the country of the borrower. There are three types of bonds, of which two are international bonds. A domestic bond is a bond issued in a country by a resident of that country. A foreign bond is a bond issued in a particular country by a foreign borrower. Eurobonds are bonds underwritten and sold in more than one country. A foreign bond may be defined as an international bond sold by a foreign borrower but denominated in the currency of the country in which it is placed. It is underwritten and sold by a national underwriting syndicate in the lending country. Thus, a US company might float a bond issue in the London capital market, underwritten by a British syndicate and denominated in sterling. The bond issue would be sold to investors in the UK capital market where it would be quoted and traded.

Foreign bonds issued outside the USA are called Yankee bonds, foreign bonds issued in Japan are called Samurai bonds. Canadian entities are the major floaters of foreign bonds in the USA.

A Eurobond may be defined as an international bond underwritten by an international syndicate and sold in countries other than the country of the currency in which the issue is denominated. An example of a Eurobond transaction would be an issue by a West German company of dollar denominated bonds through a consortium of UK merchant banks, a large German bank, and the overseas affiliate of an American investment bank.

US government restrictions introduced in 1964 gave the Eurobond market a considerable boost. Faced with a rising balance of payments deficit, the US authorities introduced the interest equalisation tax. The objective of this was to close off the New York capital market to borrowers from abroad. At the same time, restrictions were placed on the amount of funds that US multinationals could raise in the USA for overseas operations. These restrictions, which have since been lifted, caused borrowers and lenders to shift their activities from New York to Europe. This set the stage for the rapid growth of the Eurobond market.

In the Eurobond market the investor holds a claim directly on the borrower rather than on a financial institution. Eurobonds are generally issued by corporations and governments needing secure, long-term funds and are sold through a geographically diverse group of banks to investors around the world.

Eurobonds are similar to domestic bonds in that they may be issued with fixed or floating interest rates. But they possess a number of distinctive features:

- The issuing technique takes the form of a placing rather than formal issuing; this avoids national regulations on new issues.
- Eurobonds are placed simultaneously in many countries through syndicates

of underwriting banks who sell them to their investment clientele throughout the world.

- Unlike foreign bonds, Eurobonds are sold in countries other than that of the currency of denomination; thus dollar denominated Eurobonds are sold outside the USA.
- The interest on Eurobonds is not subject to withholding tax.

Prior to various changes in regulations introduced in 1984 it was usually necessary, for the interest on a Eurobond to be free of withholding tax, that the bond be issued through a special financing subsidiary, often in Luxembourg. The subsidiary issued the bonds, usually in the form of bearer bonds, with a parent company guarantee.

There are a number of different types of Eurobonds. A straight bond is one having a specified interest coupon and a specified maturity date. Straight bonds may be issued with a floating rate of interest. Such bonds may have their interest rate fixed at six-monthly intervals at a stated margin over the LIBOR for deposits in the currency of the bond. So, in the case of a Eurodollar bond, the interest rate may be based upon LIBOR for Eurodollar deposits. Floating rate notes have come to represent an increasing proportion of new issues on the Eurobond market. Interest on these bonds is paid at the end of each six-month period. Such bonds usually carry guaranteed minimum interest. If a bond has an interest rate of LIBOR plus 1 per cent with a minimum of 8 per cent and if LIBOR were to fall below 7 per cent, the interest would remain at 8 per cent. Floating rate notes (FRNs) help to eliminate risk for investors by keeping long-term interest receipts in line with prevailing short-term interest rates.

A convertible Eurobond is a bond having a specified interest coupon and maturity date, but it includes an option for the holder to convert his bonds into an equity share of the company at a conversion price set at the time of issue.

Medium-term Euronotes are shorter-term Eurobonds with maturities ranging from three to eight years. Their issuing procedure is less formal than for large bonds. Interest rates on Euronotes can be fixed or variable. Medium-term Euronotes are similar to medium-term rollover Eurodollar credits. The difference is that in the Eurodollar market lenders hold a claim on a bank and not directly on the borrower.

The issue of Eurobonds is normally undertaken by a consortium of international banks. The procedures for placing are similar to those detailed earlier in this chapter on syndicated loans. The borrower may be a large corporation or a government. The borrower normally asks a major international bank to arrange the issue. A managing syndicate, including at least four or five leading banks, plus a bank from the borrowing country, is then organised. Eurobonds are placed, rather than formally issued, with the banks' clientele of international investors. Typically, Eurobond underwriting and fee costs come out at between 2 and $2\frac{1}{2}$ per cent divided between three parts:

Management fee	0.375 − 0.5%
Underwriting fee	0.375 − 0.5%
Selling concession	1.250 − 1.5%
Total gross spread	2.000 − 2.5%

A record of the transaction called a tombstone is subsequently published in the financial press. An example of a tombstone for a floating rate note issue is given in Table 23.2. Those banks whose names appear at the top of the tombstone have agreed to subscribe to the issue. At a second level, a much larger underwriting syndicate is mentioned. The banks in the managing syndicate will have made arrangements with a worldwide group of underwriters, mainly banks and security dealers. After arranging the participation of a number of underwriters, the managing syndicate will have made a firm offer to the borrower, who obtains the funds from the loan immediately. At a third level, the underwriting group usually arranges for the sale of the issue through an even larger selling group of banks, brokers and dealers.

Eurobond issues have been made in a wide variety of currencies and composite currencies. These include US dollars, sterling, Deutsche Marks, French francs, Swiss francs, Belgian francs, Dutch guilders, ECUs, SDRs, and so on. Issues are generally for US $10 million upwards, towards US $1 billion.

Besides considering the Euromarkets, the UK-based international company has access to some domestic European debt markets and the US domestic market. Three of the domestic markets in continental Europe are open to non-resident borrowers. These are the German, Dutch and Swiss bond markets. They are often termed Euromarkets, but the use of this term is incorrect. In each case the domestic market is controlled by the local central bank which allocates a small number of positions in its issue queue to non-resident borrowers. Loan documentation follows that for domestic issues in each country. Of particular interest is the use of the sinking fund as a basis for loan redemption. Under this arrangement, which is neither used in the UK nor the US domestic market, the borrower may meet his obligations to make scheduled repayments in one of two ways. These are by surrendering bonds that he has previously purchased in the market or by redeeming bonds drawn according to their serial numbers in a lottery.

Since a large proportion of investors, particularly in the Swiss and German bond markets, comprises international lenders there would be a significant flow of funds across frontiers upon issue. This is not acceptable to the local authorities who require that borrowers sell the proceeds of the issue in the foreign exchange market immediately upon receipt. The borrower is usually required to carry out such transactions by way of the bank acting as lead manager and care has to be taken to ensure that a competitive rate is obtained. The size of the transaction will probably preclude the deal being done at the prevailing indicated market rate.

The domestic markets of other continental European countries are not generally open to foreign borrowers, although Luxembourg does permit a limited number of small issues.

In addition there is the US domestic debt market. Over six times as large as its UK counterpart it is, with the exception of the Euromarket, the largest in the world. It is also the most technically complicated in which to borrow. This means that only the largest foreign companies are able to justify the investment in set-up costs necessary to tap the market.

The US Securities and Exchange Commission (SEC) is responsible for setting standards and reviewing the content of all issue prospectuses. It also sets the standard for certain routine reports that companies must comply with if they are listed on one of the US stock markets or have public bonds in issue. As a result of

Table 23.2   Example of a Tombstone

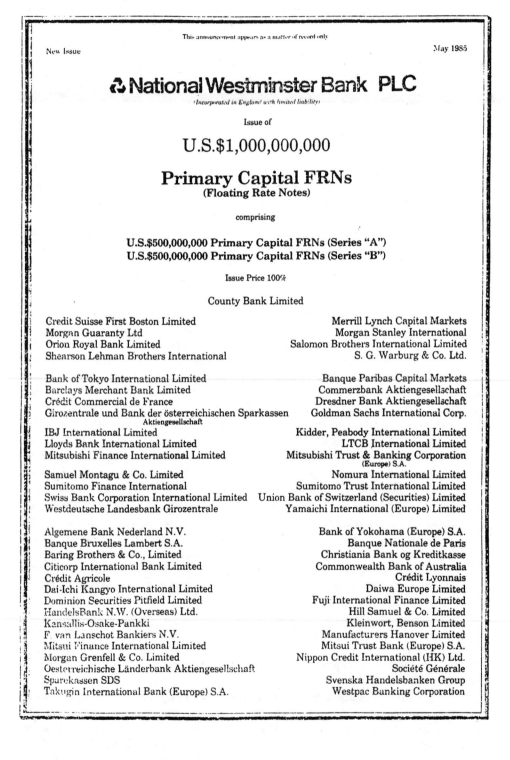

New Issue   May 1985

&. National Westminster Bank PLC

(Incorporated in England with limited liability)

Issue of

U.S.$1,000,000,000

Primary Capital FRNs
(Floating Rate Notes)

comprising

U.S.$500,000,000 Primary Capital FRNs (Series "A")
U.S.$500,000,000 Primary Capital FRNs (Series "B")

Issue Price 100%

County Bank Limited

Credit Suisse First Boston Limited	Merrill Lynch Capital Markets
Morgan Guaranty Ltd	Morgan Stanley International
Orion Royal Bank Limited	Salomon Brothers International Limited
Shearson Lehman Brothers International	S. G. Warburg & Co. Ltd.

Bank of Tokyo International Limited	Banque Paribas Capital Markets
Barclays Merchant Bank Limited	Commerzbank Aktiengesellschaft
Crédit Commercial de France	Dresdner Bank Aktiengesellschaft
Girozentrale und Bank der österreichischen Sparkassen Aktiengesellschaft	Goldman Sachs International Corp.
IBJ International Limited	Kidder, Peabody International Limited
Lloyds Bank International Limited	LTCB International Limited
Mitsubishi Finance International Limited	Mitsubishi Trust & Banking Corporation (Europe) S.A.
Samuel Montagu & Co. Limited	Nomura International Limited
Sumitomo Finance International	Sumitomo Trust International Limited
Swiss Bank Corporation International Limited	Union Bank of Switzerland (Securities) Limited
Westdeutsche Landesbank Girozentrale	Yamaichi International (Europe) Limited

Algemene Bank Nederland N.V.	Bank of Yokohama (Europe) S.A.
Banque Bruxelles Lambert S.A.	Banque Nationale de Paris
Baring Brothers & Co., Limited	Christiania Bank og Kreditkasse
Citicorp International Bank Limited	Commonwealth Bank of Australia
Crédit Agricole	Crédit Lyonnais
Dai-Ichi Kangyo International Limited	Daiwa Europe Limited
Dominion Securities Pitfield Limited	Fuji International Finance Limited
HandelsBank N.W. (Overseas) Ltd.	Hill Samuel & Co. Limited
Kansallis-Osake-Pankki	Kleinwort, Benson Limited
F. van Lanschot Bankiers N.V.	Manufacturers Hanover Limited
Mitsui Finance International Limited	Mitsui Trust Bank (Europe) S.A.
Morgan Grenfell & Co. Limited	Nippon Credit International (HK) Ltd.
Oesterreichische Länderbank Aktiengesellschaft	Société Générale
Sparekassen SDS	Svenska Handelsbanken Group
Takugin International Bank (Europe) S.A.	Westpac Banking Corporation

this involvement, the documentation associated directly and indirectly with a money-raising operation in the USA is much greater than in any comparable market. Although the amount of compulsory disclosure is high, it is not really significantly higher than that usually met voluntarily by most major UK companies.

Another novelty for the first-time borrower in the domestic debt market is the requirement that it must be rated by the two rating agencies. It is from this rating procedure that the term 'triple A' for the very highest quality of credit comes. Moodys writes Aaa, while Standard and Poors writes AAA. After triple A comes double A and then three gradations of single A: A+, A and A−. Then comes triple B which is the lowest rating acceptable in the bond market for a domestic credit. A foreign borrower would have to be rated single A to borrow but if it were an initial borrowing it would probably have to be A+. The rating largely determines the coupon rate but foreign borrowers can usually expect to pay around 50 basis points more than an equivalent rated and otherwise comparable domestic offer. It should be noted that it is the bond issue that is rated rather than the company; a company's whole spectrum of bond issues will usually carry the same rating but need not necessarily do so because of the varying quality of security. Each bond floated is rated prior to issue and the agencies monitor the rating, and may change it, through its life. This normally involves an annual review with occasional changes in rating.

The representatives of each rating agency require a comprehensive statement of affairs from the intending borrower. The data required will be greatly reduced if the borrower has already had bonds rated in the market. The statement is usually as strong on business strategy as on finance. It is reinforced by a number of senior executives submitting to a detailed interrogation. A new borrower would certainly be expected to field his chief executive and finance director. During this process, borrowers need the support of their investment bankers. Rating agency staff are extremely bright and sharp in debate. They specialise by industry. Given that they are being exposed to a great deal of confidential information, they have a very good insight into the strategies, structures and shares in market segments. The rating agencies give their rating decision to the borrower in confidence so that the company may withdraw the issue should the ratings be unacceptably low. The borrower may make representations at this stage, but the depth of analysis carried out makes it improbable that an agency will alter its rating. Agencies do not necessarily agree; split ratings are by no means unusual, but they only persist if they are one place apart. Should the gap be wider, a compromise will be reached with one or both agencies adjusting their rating. Where agreed, ratings are announced publicly and stand until they are adjusted on review.

The scale of the US domestic bond market makes it attractive to large borrowers but a significant sales effort is usually necessary, especially for first-time borrowers. Meetings to address investors are arranged with a road show visiting financial centres; the quality of such presentations is a significant factor in the success of an issue.

It always has to be remembered that the USA is a highly litigious society. It is not expensive to lose a law suit in the US because costs are not awarded in favour of the successful litigant. This means that it is always possible to find an attorney prepared to fight any fairly reasonable case on an opportunistic basis. If he wins, he takes a percentage of the damages, but he claims no basic fee, whether he wins or loses. The managers of companies entering the US financial markets should not forget this. It means that they are exposed to the risk of action for damages from any investor who can demonstrate that he was misled by a prospectus. Consequently, documentation is intensively studied by the issue managers, their solicitors and senior executives of the borrowing company to ensure its accuracy.

Before leaving this brief review of the US domestic market, reference must be made to the US commercial paper market. The term 'commercial paper' simply means an unsecured promissory note usually issued by corporations for maturities from one to 270 days. This market is open to foreigners and has been tapped at extremely fine rates by UK and continental European companies. The market's size can be assessed by the figure of some $280 billion outstanding at any one time with an average life of 22 days. The market works rather like acceptance credits, with paper held largely by non-bank investors, although there is no secondary market in US commercial paper. Rates are usually lower than US banks' prime rates. To tap the commercial paper market, credit rating is required and this is again carried out by Moodys and Standard and Poors, though the evaluation scale is a broader one and the depth of the investigation carried out is less penetrating. This market has been tapped by a wider range of non-US companies than the bond market and it is substantially less demanding in terms of cost and, since the SEC is not involved, of disclosure.

Dual Currency Issues

Before winding up this section on the Eurobond markets, it is worth mentioning dual currency bond issues. These are encountered in two distinct forms. The first type was developed around 1970 as a means of avoiding the German Bundesbank's queue of foreign borrowers waiting to tap the Deutsche Mark market. Permission was given for issues to be made outside the restrictions of that market but nonetheless denominated in Deutsche Marks, provided that interest and capital repayments were, at the investor's option, payable in an alternative currency. Usually sterling or the US dollar was the alternative. Investors were allowed to choose between the two currencies on each occasion that a payment was due. The catch is that all conversions between the two relevant currencies – say, the Deutsche Mark and sterling – are made at a fixed exchange rate which is usually that prevailing at the date of bond issue.

The bulk of the above kind of dual currency issues raised in Germany with a Deutsche Mark/sterling option dates back to a time when UK borrowers were constrained by exchange controls. Having obtained UK permission to borrow foreign currency, borrowers were prepared to raise finance where they could find it, with scant consideration of the possible demise of the fixed exchange rate regime. A bond issued at the time the exchange rate was DM8 = £1 would give the investor of DM8,000 (or £1,000) an interest income of DM400 or £50 with a 5 per cent coupon rate. Obviously, investors would choose the DM option as sterling weakened against the Mark through the seventies; equally obviously, the true cost of the bond escalated dramatically.

The second brand of dual currency bond developed more recently. Here, the investor has only a once-and-for-all option to convert to the alternative currency.

Having converted, he cannot revert to the original currency. Various hybrid bonds between the two types have been issued. For example, there have been issues denominated and repayable in US dollars but carrying interest optionally payable in Swiss francs.

From where he stands, the company treasurer needs to be convinced, at the evaluation stage of an issue of the above kind, that any foreign exchange exposure involved, in either or both currencies, can be hedged if necessary. He needs to ensure that the true interest burden that would arise on cnversion is not greater than that which would accrue on an alternative borrowing and he needs to feel convinced that value is derived from the dual currency funding option. We shall now return to our overview of the Eurobond market.

The Advantages of the Eurobond Market to Borrowers

The Eurobond markets possess a number of advantages for borrowers. These include the following:

- The size and depth of the market are such that it has the capacity to absorb large and frequent issues.
- The Eurobond market has a freedom and flexibility not found in domestic markets. The issuing techniques make it possible to bypass restrictions such as requirements of official authorisation, queuing arrangements, formal disclosure, exchange listing obligations and so forth, which govern the issue of securities by domestic as well as foreign borrowers in the individual national markets. All the financial institutions involved in Eurobond issues are subject to at least one national jurisdiction. National authorities can, and sometimes do, make their influence felt, especially when their own currency is used to denominate the issue.
- The costs of issue of Eurobonds, around 2.5 per cent of the face value of the issue, are relatively low.
- Interest costs on dollar Eurobonds are competitive with those in New York. Often US multinationals have been able to raise funds at a slightly lower cost in the Eurobond market than in the US domestic market.
- Maturities in the Eurobond market are suited to long-term funding requirements. Maturities may reach thirty years, but fifteen-year Eurobonds are more common. In the medium-term range, five- to ten-year Eurobonds run into competition with medium-term Eurodollar loans. But the longer maturities provide the assurance of funds availability at a known rate.
- A key feature of the Eurobond market is the development of a sound institutional framework for underwriting, distribution and placing of securities.

The Advantages of Eurobonds to Investors

There are a number of special characteristics of the Eurobond market which make it particularly attractive to investors. These include the following:

- Eurobonds are issued in such a form that interest can be paid free of income or withholding taxes of the borrowing countries. Also, the bonds are issued in bearer form and held outside the country of the investor, enabling the investor to evade domestic income tax. But some countries' exchange control regulations limit an investor's ability to purchase Eurobonds.

- Issuers of Eurobonds have, on the whole, an excellent reputation for credit-worthiness. Most of the borrowers, either governments, international organisations, or large multinational companies, have first-class reputations. The market is very much a name market.

- A special advantage to borrowers as well as lenders is provided by convert-ible Eurobonds. Holders of convertible debentures are given an option to exchange their bonds at a fixed price and within a specified period for the stock of the parent company of the financing subsidiary. A bond with a warrant gives the bondholder an option to buy a certain number of shares of common stock at a stated price. The more the price of the underlying stock rises, the more valuable the warrant becomes. Since warrants are usually detachable, the bondholder may retain the bond but sell the warrants.

- The Eurobond market is both active as a primary and as a secondary market. The secondary market expanded in the late sixties and early seventies. Eurobonds are traded over the counter both locally and internationally by financial institutions that are ready to buy or sell Eurobonds for their own accounts or on behalf of their clients. Just as telephone and telex linkages have integrated foreign exchange markets, so have they integrated the secondary market in Eurobonds. Since 1968, international trading in Euro-bonds has been greatly facilitated by a clearing house arrangement formed by Morgan Guaranty Trust Company in Brussels and called Euroclear. Participants in Euroclear can complete transactions by means of book entries rather than physical movements of the securities. This has removed the main barrier to secondary market trading, which had been the inability to deliver bonds on time. There are now various other clearing arrangements in the market.

Summary

The Eurocurrency market is that market in which Eurobanks accept deposits and make loans denominated in currencies other than that of the country in which the banks are located. Eurodollars[1] are dollars held in the form of time deposits in banks outside the United States. Eurodeutsche Marks are Marks deposited in banks outside West Germany. The prefix 'Euro' really means external and refers to funds that are intermediated outside the country of the currency in which the funds are denominated.

The Eurocredit market is defined as the market for loans in currencies which are not native to the country in which the bank officer making the loans is located. The Eurocredit market is concerned with medium- and long-term loans. Multi-national companies, international companies and governments are the main borrowers.

---

1. Except for the caveat raised in the third paragraph of this chapter.

A Eurobond is an international bond underwritten by an international syndicate and sold in countries other than the country of the currency in which the issue is denominated.

Chapter 23 has described the growth of the Euromarkets, the rationale for the growth, the players in the market place and the ways in which the markets operate.

References

Friedman, M. (1969) 'The Eurodollar markets: some first principles', *The Morgan Guaranty Survey*, New York.

Goodman, L.S. (1980) 'The pricing of syndicated Eurocurrency credits', *Quarterly Review*, Federal Reserve Bank of New York, Summer.

Hicks, J.R. (1946) *Value and Capital: An Enquiry into Some Fundamental Principles of Economic Theory*, 2nd edn, Oxford University Press.

Johnston, R.B. (1980) *Measuring Conditions in the Syndicated Medium-term Eurocredit Market: Some Attempts at Estimating a Spread-Maturity Trade-off*, Unpublished research paper.

Modigliani, F. and Sutch, R. (1966) 'Innovations in interest rate policy', *American Economic Review*, May, pp. 178–197.

Tobin, J. (1963) 'Commercial banks as creators of money', in Deane Carson (ed.), *Banking and Monetary Studies*, Homewood, Illinois.

24

International Taxation

The tax treatment of foreign exchange gains and losses varies from one country to another, and rules in different countries change from time to time. Great care is therefore necessary to ensure that local tax regulations are properly and comprehensively understood if optimal tax treatment is to be obtained for an international group of companies. Within the confines of a text which is not specifically devoted to taxation, it is only possible to give a general overview. For specific tax rules and regulations for particular countries, it is necessary to resort to local statutes and case law and it is necessary to use expert advice. Having said this, it is possible to describe a series of general principles, and the objective of this chapter is to do just that.

Foreign exchange transactions create profits or losses when the value of the home currency relative to the currency in which the transaction is denominated changes between the contract date and the date of payment. The transaction gain or loss on foreign exchange may affect the tax charge of the company at home or abroad. A translation gain or loss may arise when accounts expressed in one currency are translated into another.

Domestic taxation is complicated, but international tax is even more complex. Tax rates differ from country to country. An exchange gain may suffer a different tax charge depending upon where it is deemed, by inland revenue authorities, to be sourced. Some countries distinguish foreign exchange profits or losses of a revenue nature from those arising due to capital transactions. Exchange rate losses on a foreign currency loan may be an allowable charge against tax in some countries but not in others. Tax authorities in some countries ignore foreign exchange gains or losses unless they are realised. Others consider unrealised gains and losses to be fully taxable. Foreign currency gains or losses on currencies which are blocked by exchange control regulations are not usually taxed until they become realised following unblocking. These differences in tax regulations create market imperfections. By trading these imperfections through locating foreign exchange gains and other income in countries with low tax rates for this kind of revenue, and by channelling foreign exchange losses and other expenses into territories where they are tax allowable, where tax rates are high and where the multinational already has taxable income, the corporate treasurer and his tax adviser are able to minimise the tax bill of the company and undertake profitable tax arbitrages.

If tax rates and the underlying legislative framework were the same in every country, and if all types of income and capital gain were taxed similarly, opportunities for tax arbitrage would recede. That these features do not prevail means that tax and treasury planning are interlinked in international groups of companies. Failure to take cognisance of both tax and treasury impacts will lead to companies missing profit opportunities.

Many financing decisions are influenced by tax considerations – indeed, some are solely tax-based. By a similar token multinational tax planning may be constrained by the need for cross-border cash flows to service operational needs. For example, it may not be logical – although it might be tax-efficient – to lock up cash in a tax haven if it is needed elsewhere in the group.

Before proceeding we must define one or two technical terms. Ordinary income is defined for tax purposes as income arising in the normal course of trade. It is distinct from capital gains which accrue from the sale of fixed assets, etc. The distinction is significant in tax terms because countries frequently apply different tax rates to these two classes of income. Furthermore, taxation of foreign exchange distinguishes open and closed transactions. A transaction remains open until the final payment is acknowledged by the seller; then it becomes a closed transaction.

Profits or losses on foreign exchange transactions are termed realised gains or losses when the deal is closed by final payment. Many countries do not tax foreign exchange gains until they become realised gains.

The sourcing of income has important tax effects. A gain arising in a foreign tax territory is said to be sourced abroad. Such a gain is taxed in the overseas territory and the home tax charge may be eliminated or reduced by a foreign tax credit for the amount of tax paid in the foreign territory.

Broadly, four categories of foreign exchange gain or loss are distinguished for international tax purposes. These are gains or losses arising from:

- import/export transactions
- foreign currency loans
- forward foreign exchange transactions
- balance sheet translation

Each of these will now be considered in turn.

Import/Export Transactions

In most tax regimes throughout the world, foreign exchange gains or losses arising from an import/export contract denominated in a foreign currency are treated as if they were ordinary income. Gains are taxable and losses are allowable against other trading income.

In the UK, short-term gains and losses on normal trading transactions are treated as ordinary income for tax purposes. The UK authorities may ignore unrealised gains or losses on trading transactions (bringing them into charge for tax purposes upon realisation) if the company concerned has consistently ignored them in the past. This conforms with the accounting concept of prudence. But this question is a matter for negotiation with the British tax authorities. The tax-effective point may be either actual conversion of the currency or its translation for accounting purposes. But it is fair to say that translation – rather than realisation –

is the usual practice adopted by the UK Inland Revenue with respect to import/export gains or losses.

It is important to note that in respect of debts between companies within the same group the UK tax authorities may treat these as loans if the debt is outstanding for more than six months. This may have serious repercussions which are discussed in the next section, devoted to foreign currency loans.

Exchange rate gains or losses on transactions of a capital nature are treated as capital gains or losses. The gain or loss has a tax effect when it becomes a realised gain or loss. If fixed assets held abroad and denominated in a foreign currency are sold, the exchange gain or loss is incorporated with the gain or loss on the underlying purchase and sale transaction for UK tax purposes.

In many countries the separate transaction theory applies. This treats the foreign exchange portion of a gain or loss as being quite distinct from the purchase and sale transaction which it finances. The tax effect with respect to the foreign exchange gain or loss will then only accrue when the transaction is closed by payment rather than when the contract is signed. In contrast, the integrated approach ties the foreign exchange gain or loss into the contract which it finances. Profits or losses on exchange are then added to or deducted from the profit on the underlying transaction, whether it is of a capital or revenue nature. Under the separate transactions approach, the gain on the debt denominated in a foreign currency is not recognised for tax purposes until the transaction is closed by payment. So if a debt is unpaid at the accounting year end, the foreign exchange profit or loss has no tax effect until payment takes place in the following accounting period.

In the USA, tax legislation is such that foreign exchange gains or losses on trading transactions have a tax effect only when the transaction is closed by payment.

Foreign Currency Loans

Tax regimes in some countries treat gains and losses on repayment of loans denominated in foreign currencies as taxable or allowable against tax. Tax treatments of this type of gain or loss vary from country to country. In some, the gain or loss on both capital and interest is treated as ordinary income for tax purposes; gains are taxed, losses are allowable against tax. But in other countries the gain or loss has no tax effect until the payment is made, that is, when the loan is repaid (in part or in full) or when the interest payment is made. In some other countries gains are not taxed until realised, but losses are allowed on revalued foreign currency denominated loans.

In the United States of America, the gain or loss is usually not recognised for tax purposes until the deal is closed by repayment – either in full or in part if instalment repayments are involved – of the loan. The separate transactions theory applies; profits and losses on the underlying deal and foreign exchange gains are treated separately.

The tax situation in the UK is different and difficult. British tax legislation stresses the length of the loan. For a long-term loan, that is, beyond one year, exchange losses on capital are not allowable against income and exchange gains are not taxable. Such legislation caused problems for many British companies funded through Swiss franc loans and Deutsche Mark borrowings during the seventies when sterling halved in relative value against both currencies.

In connection with the question of measuring the period of a loan, it appears that an overdraft denominated in an overseas currency is regarded as circulating capital and as such is not regarded as a long-term loan. This is the general principle. But its application is by no means as clear-cut as that. At the root of the UK Inland Revenue's dilemma is the concept of fixed capital borrowing. Does such borrowing relate to the period of the borrowing or to the purpose for which the loan is raised? If it relates to the period of borrowing, what if a loan continues for many years but is repaid and renewed at short intervals? In response to this latter question, the Inland Revenue has taken the view that it is a long-term loan in principle and thus fixed capital. It has argued that a currency bank overdraft to fund fixed assets of a leasing company, repaid over three to five years, is fixed capital. However, in a case recently before the Special Commissioners, it was determined that five-year loans were circulating capital. Clearly, the problem is a complex one; and it is by no means a resolved one.

Problems in this area abound for the UK company. Imagine that a UK firm had acquired a capital asset, financed by Swiss francs. Assume that, when sold, the proceeds had yielded a 20 per cent profit, resulting in the UK company being taxed on the profit at its marginal tax rate. Now if, at the time of resale (assuming such resale had taken place later than twelve months after acquisition), the Swiss franc loan had been repaid but sterling had fallen in value by 30 per cent against the Swiss franc, the resultant exchange loss in repaying the debt from depreciated sterling would not have been allowable against tax. The UK company would have been taxed on the capital profit despite the fact that, in aggregate, the transaction would have yielded an overall loss. Had the asset purchased been a Swiss asset, the tax treatment would have remained the same. As can be seen, borrowing foreign currency to finance deals in the same currency in the belief that a company is achieving an internal hedge for tax purposes may be misguided. Significant tax exposure may exist.

Inevitably, discussion in this area must take cognisance of the decision in the case of Pattison v. Marine Midland Limited. Marine Midland, which was involved in banking activities, raised subordinated loans in foreign currency and lent the currency on, effectively on a matched basis. The Inland Revenue argued that there was a profit in terms of sterling when advances were repaid by customers and that this was assessable to UK tax. The tax authorities further argued that the matching loss upon repayment of the subordinated loans was a capital loss, and as such was not allowable. On appeal to the House of Lords, the Inland Revenue's argument was rejected: it was described as being misconceived and being fundamentally unsound. Of course, banks occupy a peculiar place in currency transactions inasmuch as almost all of their transactions are trading, with the exclusion of long-term borrowing and investment in fixed assets. As such, the Marine Midland case recognises the special character of a bank's matched book. But it appears that, in the context of tax precedent, matching would only be achieved by borrowing and lending in the same currency. Using currencies which tend to move together (being in the same currency zone, for example) would probably not achieve matching in tax legislation terms. It cannot be stressed too highly, though, that the decision in the Marine Midland case is concerned with the tax position of banks. In January of 1985, the Inland Revenue in the UK issued a provisional statement of practice in currency matters. It was hoped that this statement would resolve the question of whether the Marine Midland ruling could be extended beyond banking corporations. It is regretted that no such extension was contained in the statement.

Before moving on from foreign currency loans, it is worth considering a related problem created because cash balances are likely to build up in profitable companies and borrowings will probably arise in those companies with operating losses or high demands for cash. In tax terms, this will not be an effective situation because interest income will arise in companies which pay tax, and interest expense will arise in companies which are likely to have tax losses. The effect of this upon borrowing policy is that borrowings should be taken in companies which are currently tax-paying and likely to remain so. When taking financing decisions for overseas businesses, all other things being equal, equity may be preferred to debt where tax rates are low or zero. And debt/equity ratios may be set as high as possible in high tax rate countries. Having said this, the caveats referred to in earlier chapters about financing with as much local debt as possible as a means of avoiding political risk remain true.

It is also worth referring to thin capitalisation rules. Some countries have tax rules which state that, where overseas companies are deemed to have subsidiaries in the host country with an artificially low equity level – thin equity subsidiaries – interest may be classified as a distribution, with tax authorities refusing to allow it as a deduction in computing local tax payable.

Forward Foreign Exchange Transactions

Usually, when a company enters into a forward foreign exchange contract, the forward rate differs from the subsequent spot rate at the time the contract matures. Thus a loss or gain on exchange results. In most countries this is treated as ordinary income for tax purposes. Gains are taxable, losses are deductible. But variations on this theme occur. Some of these are as follows:

- The tax effect usually follows realisation of the gain or loss.
- The use to which the funds are put may affect the tax position. In Britain, gains or losses on forward contracts covering capital transactions have no short-term effect. In the USA, if the transaction is of an income nature, the gain or loss is treated for tax purposes like ordinary income; if the transaction is of a capital nature, the resultant gain is taxed at the capital gains rate. The USA rules that exchange gains or losses on translation hedges must be treated as capital gains or losses for tax purposes.
- The length of the forward contract may affect the position. Long-term contracts resulting in gains or losses may have no tax effect or may be taxed at a capital gains rate. In this context, 'long-term' is usually defined as being in excess of six months in the UK and twelve months in the USA.

These are merely some of the tax treatments relating to forward foreign exchange transactions. In the real world, the tax rules in individual countries need to be checked with great care.

The point to be borne in mind is that covering may create gains and losses which are treated differently for tax purposes from the losses and gains on the underlying transactions. Thus a hedge which is effective before tax may not be so after tax. Consider a UK company with a medium-term loan from Germany denominated in Deutsche Marks. If this is hedged with forward purchases of Deutsche Marks, and if sterling falls, there will be a loss on the loan. Normally, this has no tax effect in the UK because it is neither a trading item nor is it a chargeable asset for capital gains tax purposes. However, the forward purchase of currency is a chargeable asset and there will be a 30 per cent tax charge on the gain arising on this part of the hedging transaction. So the hedge will not have been effective after tax.

It may be argued at first sight that to obtain an effective post-tax hedge, the size of the deal should be grossed up by 30 per cent. But there is still a problem. If the Deutsche Mark were to fall, there would be a gain on the loan repayment and a loss on the forward cover. The loss would now be a capital one, so in the UK it would only be available for offset against current or future years' capital gains. So, although there would be a capital loss on the grossed-up hedge, it might not be usable, in which case the hedge would not be effective after tax.

Tax has an effect on hedging policy. It is also an important factor in other domains of foreign exchange planning. It may, for example, affect decisions on the best currency in which to invoice. Where it can, with a reasonable degree of confidence, be established that a particular cash flow will produce gains or losses, the currency of invoicing may be pertinent. This topic has already been considered in earlier chapters.

Balance Sheet Translation

On consolidation of subsidiaries' accounts into the home currency of the parent, a gain or loss on translation may arise. This gain or loss may have a tax effect. Most countries do not tax unrealised translation gains and losses, but a few do. Again, care must be taken to check out local taxation rules.

Dividends

The description in this section relates specifically to the holding company based in the UK. But since US tax rules applying to overseas dividends and branch income apply in an exactly similar manner to that in Britain, the exposition is equally applicable to the United States. This is also true for international companies based in most countries with interests abroad. However, the caveat that the reader needs to examine local tax rules carefully continues to apply.

If a UK resident company makes investments abroad, the company is liable to corporation tax on income received before deduction of foreign taxes. This rule applies to foreign branches and foreign subsidiaries and also to the chargeable fraction of any capital gains on the disposal of foreign assets.

If the UK resident company carries on business abroad through a branch or agency, it is chargeable to tax on all the profits of the branch or agency. Where a business is carried on through a foreign subsidiary, the UK company's liability arises only on actual amounts received from the subsidiary by way of interest or dividend. Double tax relief is available in respect of the foreign tax suffered on both income and other gains.

Normally, only direct foreign taxes are taken into account for double tax relief, but if a UK company receives dividends from a foreign company in which it owns ten per cent or more of the voting power, underlying taxes on the profits out of which the dividends are paid are taken into account as well. In this case the amount included in UK profits is the dividend plus both the direct and underlying foreign taxes. Double tax relief is given either unilaterally or under the provisions of a double tax agreement. It should be noted that the relief on overseas income cannot exceed the UK corporation tax payable on overseas income. Table 24.1 is included to show how this treatment works in numerical terms for a UK group which owns 100 per cent of a business in Ruritania, a fictional foreign country.

The assumptions at the head of Table 24.1 should be read carefully. They indicate the underlying position of the Ruritanian business relative to its UK parent and they set out UK and Ruritanian rates of corporate tax. In particular, it should be noted that, when the Ruritanian business is a subsidiary of the UK parent, the distribution before overseas dividend tax is grossed up to obtain the amount subject to UK tax – see halfway down columns 1 and 2 in the table. This sum is taxed at the UK corporate tax rate, but a foreign tax credit is available. This is given in respect of all the dividend-withholding tax borne and for a proportion of foreign-profits tax paid. In the example the foreign-profits tax credit, amounting to £214,000, is obtained by taking the amount of foreign-profits tax paid (the equivalent of £600,000) and multiplying it by the amount paid out as dividend (the equivalent of £500,000) divided by the profit available for distribution (the equivalent of £1,400,000).

Note also that if there are excess taxes paid – as in column 2 of Table 24.1 – the UK will impose additional taxes but will, in fact, allow the use of these excess taxes paid as an offset against UK taxes due on other foreign-sourced income. This tax treatment is equally applicable in the USA. The position where the foreign business is a branch of the UK company is exemplified in the right-hand columns. Note that all foreign profit, whether remitted to the UK or not, is liable to UK tax with a credit for overseas tax already paid.

Dividends[1] are, of course, one mechanism which groups of companies often use to remove cash from cash-rich subsidiaries. Subsidiaries which are already heavily geared will not normally be candidates for high dividend payouts.

Other things being equal, subsidiaries whose local currencies are anticipated to devalue by more than the interest rate differential between local currency deposits and parent currency deposits should pay relatively high dividends. The tax credit system, referred to above, is available in many countries for the underlying tax paid on profits sent by dividend from a subsidiary to the parent company. Consequently, it is often disadvantageous in tax terms to pay dividends from countries with lower tax rates than the parent. Sometimes, should the foreign tax credits exceed the parent's tax rate on the relevant income, the excess tax relief may be lost.

Foreign tax credits are not available in all jurisdictions and some countries

---

1. The remainder of this section on dividends is a little complex and may be skipped by those who want only a general overview. Such readers should pick up the text again at the heading 'Multicurrency Management Centres' later in this chapter.

Table 24.1 Tax Position of UK Company with Overseas Income

Holding company in UK owns 100% of the Ruritanian business.
Columns 1 and 3 assume that the UK corporation tax rate is 50%.
Columns 2 and 4 assume that UK corporation tax is only 35%.
Columns 1 and 2 assume that the Ruritanian business is a subsidiary.
Columns 3 and 4 assume that the Ruritanian business is a branch of the UK.
Ruritanian profits are, in sterling terms, £2 million pre-tax. In Ruritania, businesses are subject to a 30% tax. Where the local business is a subsidiary, the Ruritanian company pays a dividend of £500,000 and this is subject to a local withholding tax on dividends of 10%. In the case of the branch, there is no distribution.

Ruritania as a subsidiary (£000)			Ruritania as a branch (£000)	
50%	35%	UK corporation tax rate	50%	35%
2,000	2,000	Pre-tax profits	2,000	2,000
600	600	Foreign profits tax	600	600
1,400	1,400	Profit available for distribution	1,400	1,400
500	500	Paid out as dividend	—	—
900	900	Profit retained	1,400	1,400
450	450	UK net receipt of dividend	—	—
50	50	Withholding tax thereon	—	—
500	500	Distribution gross of dividend tax	—	—
714	714	Grossed up for UK tax purposes (multiply by 100/70)	—	—
714	714	Subject to tax	2,000	2,000
357	250	UK tax rate applied	1,000	700
		Foreign tax credit:		
(214)	(214)	Profits tax	(600)	(600)
(50)	(50)	Withholding tax	—	—
93	nil	Additional UK tax payable	400	100
—	14	Excess taxes paid	—	—

---

operate an exemption rather than a credit system, in which case dividend planning needs will be different.

One technique used by UK-based multinationals is to use a dividend mixer company, situated in an area of free exchange control and high political stability. Shareholdings and dividends are routed through the mixer company. The proportion of dividend income into the mixer company may be planned to produce the best underlying rate on dividend flows to the parent – see Figure 24.1.

Timing of dividends is another tax problem. If the effective overseas tax rates vary year by year, dividends are best paid when the rate is at its maximum. This will generate higher tax credits and is known by treasurers as saw toothing dividend streams, sometimes also called the rhythm method.

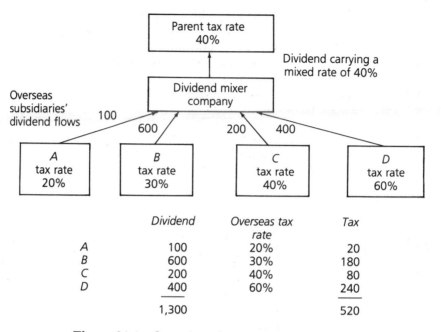

Figure 24.1   Operation of a dividend mixer company

In the UK, where the parent company has charges on income such as annual interest, these charges must be fully absorbed before double tax relief is given against UK tax on overseas dividends received. If the results suffer a downturn after interest, there may be insufficient UK tax charge to be covered by the double tax relief. This kind of situation may also result from the parent company incurring trading losses which must be offset against available profits before double tax relief is given. In the USA, foreign tax credits may be carried both back and forward within limits, but this is not allowed in the UK. Double tax relief may therefore be lost. Trading losses and charges on income can be carried forward, and this opportunity is the basis for saving tax by use of a dividend cleaning company. This dividend cleaning company, a UK resident one, accepts an overseas dividend, brings it into charge to corporation tax and offsets this tax charge via the double tax relief. On a subsequent distribution to the parent, no double tax relief is carried with it. The parent is consequently able to carry forward its excess losses or charges on income − see Figure 24.2 for an example.

Of course, the double tax relief in the dividend cleaning company may not equal the corporation tax liability on the dividend income exactly. It may then be possible to surrender to the company the exact amount of group relief necessary to eliminate the tax charge without producing excess double tax relief. But if the foreign tax rate exceeds the UK tax rate, this will not avoid excess double tax relief.

Another important feature of dividend planning is the operation of intermediate holding companies to accumulate investment income. For example, a holding company is formed and dividends received from lower-tier subsidiaries are retained there, rather than sending them by dividend to the parent company. Such treasury

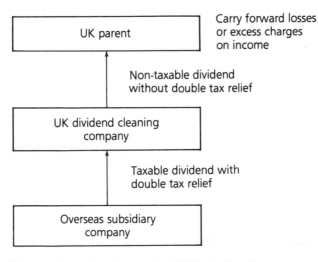

Figure 24.2 Operation of a dividend cleaning company

planning is, however, subject to anti-avoidance tax legislation in both the USA and in the UK. Intermediate holding companies are also used to take advantage of tax treaties in order to reduce withholding taxes. It may be possible, by correct choice of the intermediate company, to reduce a withholding tax rate to zero.

Evidently, the process is so complex that the treasurer and tax expert need to get together to consider the possibilities created by non-symmetrical tax treatment of dividends and other features as well. For example, the tax treatment of licence fees, royalties and similar charges may create opportunities for profitable exploitation. Thus the level of these payments may be set to ensure that they are allowed in full as a deduction from local taxable profits. Like dividends, the routing of such cash flows is important because it may reduce withholding tax rates.

Multicurrency Management Centres

Multinational corporations frequently set up currency management centres to focus and control currency management. Foreign exchange deals and covering by subsidiaries are usually routed through such centres. The mere existence of such centres often creates suspicion in the minds of local tax authorities. There may be problems in persuading tax authorities to accept such centres as legitimate business ventures rather than as tax-avoidance vehicles. Nonetheless, where a multicurrency management centre has been created, it can provide possibilities for tax minimisation.

The centre is likely to be the focus of foreign exchange transactions and it is likely to carry the currency exposure risk of the total corporation. Clearly, the tax implications of the location of such a centre need to be carefully studied. A tax haven may reduce the tax charge on foreign exchange gains but will not provide relief for any losses nor the cost of administrating the centre itself. The centre should be set in a location which has tax treaties with other countries and in which there are advantages for the corporation as a whole. Tax on interest or dividends withheld should be available to reduce local taxes and foreign tax credits should be similarly available. An extremely careful assessment of the world-wide tax burden of the corporation must precede choice of centre.

Should the multinational corporation wish to charge foreign exchange losses and administration costs of the centre to its various subsidiaries, it will probably have to prove the need for the centre other than as a tax avoidance device. The charging of a fee for the use of the centre's services to subsidiaries at a rate, for example, of half a per cent of the value of each deal helps in this context. Such charges should be in line with fees charged by independent consultancy services. However, tax authorities view with great suspicion fees paid to offshore multi-currency management centres located in areas where the corporation tax rate is very low.

Foreign Exchange Tax Strategy

The range of local tax rules on foreign exchange gains and losses makes the achievement of an optimal foreign exchange tax strategy difficult. Complexity is compounded by frequent changes in tax legislation.

The objective of tax strategy is to maximise distributable net of tax profit. As such, tax planning is part of the overall corporate strategy. But tax strategy may have important behavioural implications. If the multinational decides to devolve maximum autonomy to its foreign subsidiaries, it is not likely to permit a tax tactic of repaying loans to obtain tax credits to compromise its style of decentralised management. Low profits in certain foreign subsidiaries, created and manipulated for tax reasons, may lower morale of key staff of a foreign subsidiary.

Nonetheless, tax treatment of exchange gains and losses provides a rich and broad spectrum for the creative skills of the corporate treasurer. In this area, particular attention must be paid to the lack of symmetry in tax laws.

Devising a tax strategy involves tabulating tax rules, exchange controls and tax rates in each territory in which the multinational corporation operates. This represents the framework within which tax strategy operates. Another important step towards the specification of a fruitful tax strategy is the tabulation of expected cash flows and assets and liabilities held in each currency. This may already have been done as a stage in normal foreign exchange exposure management. Examination of tax effects of future transactions, in particular loans in foreign currencies, forward cover and translation gains or losses, plus a schedule of the benefits and costs of channelling such transactions through an offshore tax haven, should also be considered. Treatment of individual transactions will depend upon the local tax laws and existing exchange control regulations.

Examples abound of possible policies designed to maximise distributable post-tax cash flows. Financial assets may be moved between subsidiaries so that gains occur in countries where the tax on gains is nil or very low. Intercompany debt repayment may be accelerated (or retarded) to achieve optimal tax treatment. Subsidiaries may borrow from one another in weak foreign currencies if the exchange gain on the loan devaluation is not taxed in one centre and the loss is tax-allowable elsewhere; and they may borrow in strong currencies if the loss on loan revaluation is allowable in one centre while the profit is not taxable in the other.

The tax effect in either case may be a key factor in the decision as to where and in which currency to borrow. If the unrealised loss on a foreign loan is not allowed against tax until the loan is repaid, it may be tax-efficient to repay it and refinance. Allowable exchange losses should be located in those countries where tax rates are highest. Subsidiaries in weak currency countries may be funded by foreign loans if the exchange loss can be set against local profits. Financing a venture with short-term rollover funds (which are exchange-loss-allowable against tax) rather than with a long-term loan (which is only allowable on termination of the loan) may be tax-efficient. Making all currency contracts assignable may also be a useful tactic. Schemes of this sort have to conform to local exchange control regulations, but within such constraints there is plenty of scope to maximise post-tax profits.

It is to the topic of exchange controls that we shall turn in the next chapter.

Summary

In this chapter an attempt was made to summarise the main features of the key tax issues regarding foreign exchange gains and losses in the UK tax arena.

Exchange gains and losses can be split into those of a capital nature and those of a revenue nature. Revenue transactions constitute those relating to day-to-day trading, whilst capital transactions relate either to the financing structure of a company or to the fixed-asset base of the business. Exchange differences deriving from normal day-to-day trading will be chargeable as part of trading income assessable under Schedule D, Case I and normally subject to corporation tax at the income rate. Where exchange differences arise from transactions involving the capital structure of the business, they are usually chargeable under the capital gains rules. However, currency fluctuations arising from capital transactions are only chargeable or allowable under capital gains legislation if they relate to assets. The capital gains tax system does not apply to liabilities. Therefore it is possible for certain exchange differences to fall outside the scope of taxation and for a gain to arise tax-free or for no relief to be available for a loss. Examples of such gains or losses which fall outside the tax net are those relating to long-term liabilities denominated in a foreign currency.

Of key importance in terms of determining the tax status of exchange differences is the distinction between capital and revenue items. Discrimination between the two involves a careful study of the nature of the underlying asset or liability involved to see whether it is capital (fixed/long-term) or revenue (circulating/short-term) in the context of the overall business of the organisation. An asset or liability which may constitute a capital item for a manufacturing company may well be a trading asset or liability for a bank or other financial company.

A transaction entered into with the objective of hedging the effects of foreign exchange movements may fail in its objective if a gain on one leg of the transaction is taxable, but a corresponding hedge loss is not allowable. Thus, if a foreign currency borrowing is taken on to finance a capital investment in the same currency, and if sterling subsequently weakens, the currency gain arising on the eventual disposal of the asset will be subject to tax at the capital gains tax rate, whereas the corresponding loss on what would be designated a capital borrowing would not be allowable. A perfect pre-tax hedge may become an imperfect post-tax means of cover.

The Marine Midland case is an important one in UK tax precedent. A bank, Marine Midland, had borrowed US$15 million via an unsecured loan stock. The proceeds were used to lend dollars short-term to various bank customers. These loans were subsequently repaid and the proceeds were used to redeem the US$15 million loan stock. There were no net exchange gains or losses arising from this matched transaction and at no time were the dollars physically converted into another currency. During the term of the loan stock, sterling weakened against the dollar. The Inland Revenue contended that an exchange loss arose on redemption of the loan stock for book purposes which was a capital loss arising on repayment of a liability and consequently not tax-deductible. They further argued that the exactly offsetting exchange gain on repayment of the assets represented revenue profits derived from circulating assets which were taxable. On appeal, the House of Lords dismissed the Inland Revenue's arguments on the grounds that there could be no exchange profit or loss where there were no currency conversions and where steps had been taken to avoid exchange exposure by ensuring a fully matched position. Care must be taken not to apply the Marine Midland case out of context. The case relates to a bank and not to a manufacturing concern; the Inland Revenue authorities believe that Marine Midland is no precedent for a non-bank.

Forward exchange contracts entered into in a trading context will give rise to a tax treatment as part of trading income. Futures transactions and currency options are also distinguished according to their capital or revenue nature by reference to the transaction hedged. Speculative futures transactions will be given a capital gains treatment in all but exceptional circumstances. Speculative currency option gains and losses will be treated under capital gains tax rules if they derive from exchange-quoted options, but under Schedule D, Case VI if the option is not quoted.

The major difference between UK and US tax legislation as it relates to the international field is that in the USA losses and gains on long-term foreign borrowings are respectively relievable or chargeable to tax upon realisation of the loss or gain, whereas in the UK losses and gains usually fall outside the tax net.

25

Exchange Controls

Exchange controls refer to regulations which forbid or restrict the holding of assets denominated in foreign currency and the foreign exchange transactions of residents insofar as they affect the earning, holding and spending of foreign currencies or the acquisition, retention or disposal of assets and liabilities situated abroad and/or denominated in foreign currency. Exchange controls also circumscribe the actions of non-residents in the host country. In connection with controls, currency is said to be convertible if the authorities of the country allow it to be exchanged without restriction or the need for permission into currencies of other countries. Complete freedom for all residents of a country and for all holders of a national currency to buy foreign currency or foreign currency denominated assets is termed full convertibility or free convertibility. It exists only in a few countries and for only a few currencies.

A more restricted form of convertibility is used by many governments in respect of their national currency. It is referred to as partial convertibility, or non-residents' convertibility, or Article VIII Convertibility (named after Article VIII of the Articles of Agreement of the International Monetary Fund which specifies circumstances in which convertibility may be restricted). Partial convertibility allows only non-resident holders of the national currency to convert it into foreign currency or foreign currency assets but controls what residents may do. Thus the holding of foreign exchange by residents is controlled.

When faced with problems such as recurring deficits on balance of payments, governments frequently resort to various controls. Exchange control is one such form and, in this chapter, we shall focus upon controls of this kind because of their direct impact upon multinational finance.

Confronted with inadequate reserves to finance deficits, or faced with increasing liquid liabilities to foreigners on a scale that threatens to create future difficulties if redemption of these liabilities is requested, exchange controls are often invoked in an effort to prevent problems becoming worse. Exchange rate movements affect such broad segments of the economy that governments, faced with financial difficulties, often resort to supporting exchange rates within some range or band. Exchange controls take many forms and they affect international transactions. In balance of payments terms, they are intended to have positive effects – or perhaps less negative effects than would otherwise be the case – upon current account and capital account outturns.

The imposition of exchange controls usually follows a consistent pattern. Payments to foreigners exceed receipts from foreign countries. Depreciation of the value of the country's currency is anticipated and in an effort to strengthen the home currency, exchange controls are invoked. The government legislates that those who obtain foreign exchange through exports and other transactions must sell their foreign exchange to the government or designated banks. The government must allocate this foreign exchange to importers and other purchasers of foreign goods and services. The government usually keeps the home exchange rate at a level at which it is overvalued, even though this means that demand for imports increases and exporting becomes less profitable and more difficult. In turn this means that demand for foreign currency is greater than its supply. Hence some of those who wish to buy foreign exchange cannot be permitted to do so.

The situation is illustrated in Figure 25.1 in which it is assumed that the Coluvian government attempts to keep the exchange rate of the Coluvian peso equivalent to fifty pesos to the dollar. Demand and supply in a free market would result in an equilibrium rate of eighty pesos to the dollar. At the exchange rate of fifty pesos, holders of foreign exchange would be reluctant to surrender it: they know that the equilibrium rate is eighty pesos. So the government must force the sale of the supply of foreign exchange, *OA*, to itself or to designated banks, and it must allocate that supply to those who wish to buy it. At the official rate of fifty pesos to the dollar, rather than the equilibrium rate of eighty, demand for dollars and indeed goods priced in foreign currency will be greater than at the equilibrium rate. The government has therefore created a problem which it must solve by dictate. It has to nominate who may purchase foreign exchange or it must simply restrict purposes for which foreign currency may be purchased. In equilibrium, the quantity *OB* would be purchased, but this is legally prevented since the country only has *OA*. Hardly surprisingly, significant black markets begin to develop in foreign currency, with the black market price reflecting that rate which would hold in equilibrium rather than the official rate.

These kinds of exchange controls restrict imports to a level less than under free market conditions. When a country maintaining exchange controls devalues its currency, imports increase – if permitted. As is shown in Figure 25.1, if Coluvia devalued its currency from fifty pesos per dollar to eighty pesos per dollar, the supply of foreign exchange would tend to increase and therefore the purchase of foreign exchange for imports would also tend to increase.

The Spread of Exchange Controls

The widespread use of exchange controls is a phenomenon peculiar to the twentieth century. Although they were widely imposed during the First World War, exchange controls were relaxed shortly afterwards. Their imposition in peacetime followed the international financial crisis of 1931. It was in that year that Kredit-Anstalt, a large banking institution in Austria, became insolvent. Had banks in New York, London and Paris acted together they could have prevented a panic, but for various reasons they did not. Austria and Germany had just announced a customs union, eliminating duties between the two countries. German banks had relatively large deposits in Austria and the view in France and the UK was that to give aid to

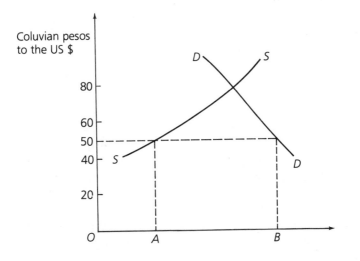

Figure 25.1 Foreign Exchange Market Under Exchange Controls

Austria was likely to aid Germany too. The French government and Paris banks were unwilling to take steps which might have this effect. Panic spread from Austria to Germany, and German banks began to restrict withdrawals. English banks, with large deposits in banks in Germany, also came under pressure as German bank failures were expected. At the same time, thousands of banks were failing in the USA and, although these failures were not related to the international situation, the impact throughout the world was negative. The value of sterling fell in foreign exchange markets. There was an outflow of gold from the UK and Britain was under heavy financial pressure. On Sunday, 20 September 1931, the UK abandoned the gold standard. Various countries followed suit and exchange rates began to fluctuate widely. As a response to this, many countries began to institute controls over foreign exchange transactions. These controls persisted and multiplied so that by the end of the Second World War almost all countries in the world, except the United States and a few others, had established direct controls over foreign exchange transactions.

These exchange controls could be distinguished by the extent to which they fell into three groups based upon their key characteristics. For example, some major countries, such as Britain (initially), relied upon indirect controls simply instituting mandatory purchase and sales of foreign exchange through the government. Some countries, including many in Europe and Latin America, established multiple rates of exchange depending upon the purpose for which foreign exchange was required. Exchange controls also evolved which incorporated restrictions on transfers of ownership of bank deposits.

Since the Second World War, many countries have relaxed their exchange controls and many have abolished them altogether. However, at the other extreme, many countries have imposed them and made them increasingly sophisticated. In many countries the local exchange control regulations are more complex than corporate taxation.

Where exchange controls exist, they are in an almost continuous state of change. Where they are not in operation, they may be introduced following various triggers such as changes in government or deterioration in balance of payments figures. The general guidelines summarised in this chapter are only very rough signposts through a complex minefield. Expert exchange control opinion always needs to be sought prior to overseas investment or divestment.

Exchange control regulations are particularly severe in many developing countries. Their attempts at takeoff into a period of self-sustaining growth require, as a prerequisite, the importation of large quantities of capital goods. This results in a heavy demand for foreign currency to pay for it. Exchange controls particularly aimed at maintaining the value of the home currency at an artificially high level should, so the argument goes, reduce the cost of imports. Many Latin American countries and some African countries have imposed draconian exchange controls as part of their packages of development.

We shall now present an overview of the typical mechanism of exchange controls and discuss some of the practical approaches to exchange control management.

Exchange Control Organisation

The responsibility for implementing exchange control regulations usually lies with the treasury function of the government of any given country. Although it decides the exchange control strategy, the tactics and management of exchange control are usually delegated to the central bank which, in its turn, delegates much of the day-to-day working to commercial banks.

The amount of delegation from the central banks to commercial banks depends upon the extent of the shortage of foreign exchange and, cynically, one must confess, the degree of corruption in the country concerned. Where foreign exchange is very scarce, the central bank tends to keep the issue of exchange control firmly in its own hands. This frequently causes excessive delays in negotiating imports into developing countries. Where the central bank does delegate the day-to-day running of the system to commercial banks, the release of foreign currency is much quicker and more efficient. Prior to the abolition of exchange controls in 1979, Britain operated with the Bank of England delegating a good deal of the day-to-day vetting of foreign exchange transactions to commercial banks and authorised dealers.

Exchange controls apply to residents of a country. The nature of the transaction for which foreign exchange is required is invariably important, as is the location to which foreign currency is to be transferred and the location of the party with whom the transaction is being carried out.

All companies operating in a given country are usually treated, for exchange control purposes, as resident in that country. That the head office or controlling staff reside in another country does not affect residence. Where financial institutions import and export large amounts of foreign currency, special rules usually apply. Residence for exchange control purposes is determined by a different set of rules from that which determines residence for tax purposes.

For currency purposes, the world may be looked upon as being divided into various zones. The countries within each zone tend to tie their currency to a dominant currency within that zone. Sterling, the US dollar and the French franc have all been used to fix the value of other currencies within their zone. Exchange control regulations for transactions between residents in the same zone are usually less rigorous than those applied to transactions with residents in different zones.

The applicability of exchange control rules is governed by the type of transaction involved, for example importing, exporting, hedging, investing, and so on. The classification – see Figure 25.2 – broadly accords with classifications for balance of payments purposes.

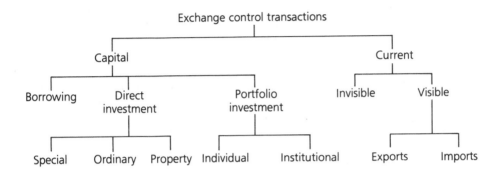

Figure 25.2   Exchange Control Transactions

Imports

Most countries with exchange controls require that a licence or certificate be obtained from an authorised bank or government department before goods can be imported. This licence may be either a specific licence or certificate which covers a specific contract, or a general licence to import goods of a generic type. Once the licence is obtained, the importer must provide documentary proof of the underlying transaction. This usually involves the original contract, shipping documents, invoices and so on, and these are submitted to an authorised bank to obtain the requisite amount of foreign currency. In some countries, import deposits have to be lodged with the authorised bank in advance of payment. These may involve an advance deposit at a zero interest rate of 100 per cent of the value of the transaction. Indeed, in Chile at one time the advance deposit was 10,000 per cent. Exchange control regulations frequently insist that the transaction should be denominated in a stated currency. The value of the import transaction may have to be confirmed and validated by a government agency which may, following evaluation, put a different value on the goods imported to that shown on the invoice. The official exchange rate for imports may differ from that for exports and it may be different for differing classes of import. Dealing on the forward exchange market may be permitted for some, but not all, types of transaction – and even then only after documentary proof of the underlying trade deal has been submitted. Obviously, with the existence of such complexities, companies involved in countries with exchange control regulations are advised to familiarise themselves with local regulations, customs and practices. Often this involves the need to purchase consultancy services.

Exports

Regulations relating to exports are usually less restrictive than those for imports. Governments try to encourage exports by reducing the paperwork involved. Normally, a general licence to export is all that is required, although in some countries governments maintain export monopolies of certain goods.

The timing of the payment for export is usually controlled. Payment is often required to be within six months of shipment although, in the case of capital equipment, special payment arrangements may be negotiated. Foreign exchange proceeds of an export deal must normally be offered to an authorised bank within a specified short period of being received. Conversion is frequently at a specified exchange rate. But it must be mentioned and borne in mind that many countries provide a form of subsidy on exports by remitting sales taxes or manipulating the exchange rate to provide favourable rates on export proceeds.

Invisibles

Management fees, insurance, royalties, foreign travel, consultancy fees and other invisibles often attract special rules. Buying insurance cover abroad is often forbidden and in many developing countries rules for the release of foreign currency for invisible imports such as consultancy fees, management fees and royalties are extremely tight. The reason for this is that international companies have sought to circumvent profit repatriation rules through the use of consultancy fees and royalty payments.

Investment Abroad

Capital transactions are classifed in terms of whether they represent borrowing, direct investment or portfolio investment. Direct investment embraces investment with the purpose of controlling the operation of a foreign firm. Portfolio investment includes investment whose primary purpose is the receipt of a stream of future income. The classification of investment as direct or portfolio turns on the question of whether the investor obtains an effective management interest in the overseas enterprise.

Most countries with exchange controls impose strict limitations on the outflow of capital, in particular for portfolio investment, and they carefully scrutinise direct investment. On inflows, the situation is reversed. Portfolio investment inwards is encouraged, but direct investment inwards is carefully screened. Even when inward investment is encouraged, developing countries impose strict rules as to repatriation of profits; this topic is considered under a separate heading later in this chapter.

Multiple Currencies

Most countries with exchange controls operate some kind of multiple currency. By a multiple currency is meant one which has at least two values at any point in time – normally there is an official exchange rate plus at least one, but often many more, special rates which vary according to the nature of the underlying transaction for which foreign currency is required. Portfolio investment abroad, property investment abroad and many other outflows which the home government does not wish to encourage attract a premium on the official rate. Rules vary considerably from one country to another and they need to be investigated and evaluated carefully by multinational companies.

Borrowing Abroad

The rules for borrowing in foreign currencies frequently change depending upon whether or not the home government wishes to encourage or restrict the inflow of foreign currency. Prior to the abolition of exchange controls in Britain in 1979, borrowing abroad was encouraged on occasions as an aid to filling balance of payments deficits.

Many developed countries, for example the US, the UK, Canada and West Germany, place virtually no restrictions on non-residents borrowing in their capital markets. But this posture is the exception rather than the rule. Most countries prohibit borrowing by non-residents. Furthermore, developing countries tend to restrict foreign subsidiaries resident in their countries in the extent to which they tap domestic financial markets. They prefer the investing company to ship in equity or loan investment from overseas.

Non-Resident and Foreign Currency Bank Accounts

Permission is usually required under exchange controls for a non-resident to open a bank account in the host country. Bank accounts of non-residents are usually segregated from those of residents. And different regulations are applied to the movement of funds into and out of them. Tighter regulations apply to residents' accounts. Residents are usually restricted from holding foreign currency denominated bank accounts.

Foreign Exchange Management Techniques

In an earlier chapter, we described internal exposure management techniques which may be helpful to the corporate treasurer of the international company. Exchange control regulations in many countries prohibit the use of some of these techniques, such as netting and leading and lagging.

Netting is the offsetting of an anticipated currency flow in one direction by an expected currency flow in the other direction. Bilateral netting is distinct from multilateral netting. Bilateral netting offsets currency A against currency B. Multilateral netting offsets currency A against currency B, currency B against currency C, and currency C against currency A – and more complex nettings are of course possible. Some countries restrict all netting; some restrict multilateral netting but not bilateral netting. So examination of local rules is necessary. In some countries, international companies must obtain permission if they are to use netting techniques; in other countries netting is not permitted at all; in other countries still, whilst it is necessary to apply for permission to carry out netting, such permission is virtually never given.

Leading and lagging are techniques used to take advantage of expected devaluations or revaluations. Since host countries' governments frequently perceive this as speculating against exchange adjustments, many lay down careful regulations limiting their use. Different sets of rules may apply to imports and to exports. Minimum and maximum leading or lagging times from shipment date, customs clearance date or invoice date are usually prescribed. Exact requirements (and exceptions allowed) are carefully specified in exchange control regulations. These may require that imports be paid for within a specified period from invoice date. Exchange control authorities usually require to know reasons for payments being made or deferred outside the standard timescale. A few major trading countries place no restrictions on netting and leading and lagging; these include the USA, Canada, West Germany and the UK.

Many countries with exchange control regulations allow residents to use forward exchange markets only when they have demonstrated that cover relates to genuine import or export transactions. Furthermore, they must use designated banks to undertake the cover.

Import and Export Contracts

Terms of payment are set out in the underlying contract. The exporter or importer must verify that these terms comply with exchange control regulations imposed by governments at both ends of the transaction. Important factors are currency denomination of contract, timing of payments, validation of value, use of the proceeds from the contract, licensing procedures, and so on. Rules on payment for export and import contracts are usually available from commercial banks or foreign consulates and need to be studied carefully.

Profits Repatriation

This is a critically important and complex topic. Profits made and cashflows earned in a foreign country are of no value to the international corporation if they cannot be repatriated to the home country for distribution to shareholders.

A small number of developed countries allow free repatriation of all profits and capital at any time. Normally under exchange control, capital put into a country may be repatriated, but the return of profits is strictly limited. Given that international companies have sought to circumvent the profits repatriation constraint by the use of billings for royalties, research and development, consultancy fees and so on, it is hardly surprising that countries with exchange controls have responded by limiting repatriations in general. Many countries with exchange controls limit the amount to be returned to a given percentage of total capital invested, or to a proportion of retained profit. This has the effect of forcing reinvestment of some of the profit in the host country. Frequently, profits which cannot be repatriated for a specified time – termed blocked profits – have to be invested in specified government bonds; upon maturity of the bonds, they may be sent abroad. Since such government bonds attract low interest rates, and since they are frequently used in high inflation countries, this creates a 'heads I win, tails you lose' situation.

Sometimes countries with exchange controls segregate investments according to whether they are of an approved or of an ordinary status. Approved status projects have a privileged profits repatriation position, or they may attract advantageous exchange rates on repatriation. From the international company's point of view such stipulations are of essence in evaluating overseas investment projects.

Rules on profit distribution are so complex and varied and subject to such frequent change that investing international companies make it a policy to scrutinise local regulations carefully and they often negotiate a specific watertight agreement with the host nation in respect of capital and profit repatriation. But even this may not be sufficient. Such agreements have been renounced by existing governments. And new incoming governments may also disregard agreements made by their predecessors. Compensation guarantees from home governments are available, though — in the UK through the Export Credit Guarantee Department; and in the USA through Eximbank.

Managing Overseas Funds

Various means are available to the international company for moving funds and profits from one country to another. These include:

- transfer pricing
- fees and royalty agreements
- leading and lagging
- dividends
- loans
- equity versus debt considerations
- currency invoicing
- re-invoicing centres

The first four of the above channels are either fairly straightforward or have been considered elsewhere in this text. Exchange control authorities have become well aware that multinational companies use transfer pricing, royalties and leading and lagging to move funds, and have themselves put impediments in the way of these techniques. Tight controls on invisibles, validation of import and export prices and constraints on leading and lagging are all examples of ways in which host governments have attacked this problem. We therefore turn to the other techniques involved.

The making and repaying of inter-company loans which originally involved the input of foreign finance into the host country is often the only legitimate way to transfer funds from a country with tight exchange controls. But, because foreign debt capital is subject to political risk and because funds may become blocked in foreign countries, multinationals have increasingly resorted to parallel loans, back-to-back loans and currency swaps.

Parallel loans means effectively a pair of loans made simultaneously in two countries. A parallel loan transaction involves two parties who simultaneously make loans of the same value to one another's foreign subsidiaries. The parent, company A, will extend a loan in its home country and currency to a subsidiary of company B, whose foreign parent will lend the local currency equivalent in its country to the subsidiary of company A. Drawdown of the loan, repayment of principle, and payments of interest are arranged to occur simultaneously. These loans may be depicted as shown in Figure 25.3. The following are the key characteristics of parallel loans:

1. There are two separate loans with no cross border movement of funds.
2. There is some arrangement whereby, legally, the loans may be set off one against the other. But loans cannot be offset in the respective consolidated balance sheets. Such loans appear as both assets and liabilities.
3. Payment of interest is made by both parties. This is based upon cost of money in each country and anticipated changes in currency values.

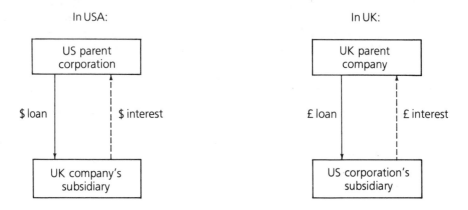

Figure 25.3   An Example of a Parallel Loan

The value of the parallel loan is usefully appreciated with the help of an example. Suppose the Coluvian associate of Company X Inc., the US parent, is generating peso flows which it is unable to repatriate. It may lend this money to the local associate of another multinational which requires peso finance to undertake investment. Thus the Coluvian subsidiary of Company X Inc. may lend blocked pesos to the Coluvian subsidiary of Company Y Inc. and, in return, Company Y Inc. would lend dollars to Company X Inc. in the USA. Thus Company X acquires the use of dollars in the United States whilst Company Y obtains pesos in Coluvia. By this mechanism Company X has obtained dollars and used its blocked pesos and it has also enabled Company Y to get local finance in Coluvia. Local finance might otherwise not be available to anything but local companies.

Back-to-back loans are often employed to finance associates located in countries with high interest rates or restricted capital markets – particularly when there is a danger of currency controls, or where different rates of withholding-tax are applied to loans from a financial institution. As an example, assume that the parent company deposits funds with a bank in country A, which in turn lends the money to a subsidiary in country B. In this sense, the back-to-back loan is an intercorporate loan channelled through a bank. The bank simply acts as an intermediary and from the bank's point of view the loan is risk-free because the parent's deposit collateralises the loan. Back-to-back loans of this sort create advantages where countries apply different withholding-tax rates to interest paid to a foreign parent and interest paid to a financial institution. Furthermore, should currency controls be imposed, governments usually permit the local subsidiary to honour the repayment schedule of a loan from a major multinational bank. However, host government monetary authorities may have few reservations about placing impediments in the way of repayment of a straight intercompany loan. Back-to-back financing therefore provides better protection than an intercompany loan against exchange controls or expropriation.

But there are other forms of back-to-back loan and these may work in a slightly different way. The term may signify reciprocal loans made in two different currencies between two companies. According to this approach, the back-to-back loan is a modification of the parallel loan. But it is different in two important respects. These are that there is a cross-border flow of funds which may raise withholding-tax questions and there is only one loan document. A back-to-back loan of this type may be depicted as shown in Figure 25.4.

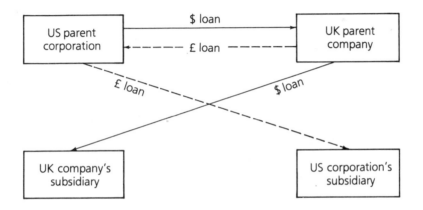

Figure 25.4 An Example of a Back-To-Back Loan

Currency swaps achieve similar objectives to parallel loans but they are somewhat simpler. They involve two parties and one agreement. The two companies involved may sell currencies to each other at the spot rate and undertake to reverse the exchange after a specified term. Unlike parallel loans, interest is not paid by both parties. In a currency swap, a fee is paid by one party to the other. This fee is equivalent to the forward foreign exchange premium or discount which in turn should reflect interest rate differentials. Currency swaps have one or two advantages over parallel loans. They are reported off balance sheet; they do not distort the profit and loss account with the reporting of both interest income and interest expense; they have simpler documentation and they afford greater protection in the event of a default.

A currency exchange agreement is a modification of the back-to-back loan and overcomes some of the disadvantages, particularly with regard to right of set-off. In a currency exchange, for example, a UK company would provide sterling to a US company in exchange for US dollars. At a later specified date after the initial exchange, the two companies will have the option, or sometimes the obligation, to require the other to re-exchange the same amounts of currency as on the initial exchange day. In consideration for the exchange, one party, normally the provider of the stronger currency, pays to the other an annual exchange fee, which is a reflection of the interest differentials and devaluation expectations between the two currencies. Currency exchange agreements are well explained in Heywood's (1985) text.

We now turn to considerations of debt versus equity in financing an overseas subsidiary. Generally speaking, financing an overseas subsidiary with debt from the parent company as opposed to equity provides greater flexibility. It is usually the case that a firm has greater latitude to repatriate funds in the form of interest and loan repayments than as dividends or reductions in equity. Furthermore, reductions in equity may be frowned upon by the host government. In addition, the use of loans as opposed to equity investment confers possibilities for reducing taxes. This arises on two fronts. Interest paid on a loan is usually tax-deductible in the host nation, whereas dividend payments are not. Also, unlike dividends, loan repayments do not normally constitute taxable income to the parent company. So, whilst host nations frequently require that certain proportions of an investment be financed from new monies brought into the country, the multinational needs to consider carefully whether the shipping in of such funds should be designated as debt or equity capital.

Capital controls may be circumvented by the judicious use of currency invoicing. The choice of currency in which an invoice is billed may enable a firm to remove blocked funds from a country which has exchange controls. Assume that a subsidiary is located within a country which restricts profit repatriation. If a devaluation of the host currency is forecast, this may provide the firm with an opportunity to move excess blocked funds elsewhere. This may be achieved by invoicing exports from that subsidiary to the rest of the corporation in the local currency of the devaluing country at a contracted price. As the local currency depreciates, profit margins are reduced in that subsidiary as opposed to what they would have been had billing been in a hard currency. But elsewhere within the corporation they are improved. Effectively, cash from the devaluing country will be shifted to another part of the group. Suppose that the subsidiary in the devaluing country were exporting £1 million worth of goods each month to the parent: a 10 per cent local devaluation each month would involve a monthly shift of £100,000 to the parent by means of invoicing in the devaluing currency. By the same token, funds may be moved into a country which imposes controls on capital inflows by invoicing exports to the associate in that country in a weak currency and billing exports from the country prohibiting capital inflows in a strong currency.

To complete our discussion on circumventing controls, we briefly consider the use of reinvoicing centres. Reinvoicing centres are mainly used by multi-nationals as part of the exposure management function, but they are sometimes used to disguise profitability, avoid government scrutiny and coordinate transfer pricing policy for tax purposes. The operation of reinvoicing centres was briefly explained in Chapter 13. To reiterate, the reinvoicing centre may be used to counter exchange controls by setting it in low-tax countries. These centres take title to all goods sold across frontiers, whether by one subsidiary to another or by sale to a third party customer, although the goods themselves move directly from the factory to the purchaser. The centre pays the seller and the centre receives payment from the purchaser. Whilst reinvoicing centres create obvious opportunities for using transfer pricing to the best advantage, they also give the international company considerable flexibility to utilise currency invoicing techniques. Needless to say, tax authorities and exchange control authorities are very suspicious of transactions which move through reinvoicing centres, especially when they are located in a tax haven.

Before we finish this section, it is worth mentioning four other techniques which are used for circumventing exchange controls. These are:

1. the purchase of capital goods with blocked currency where the equipment is for corporate-wide use;
2. the purchase of local services with blocked funds when such services are for use throughout the group;
3. conducting and paying for research and development in the host country when the benefits accrue throughout the group;
4. hosting corporate conventions, vacations and other expenses in the host country and paying for them with blocked currency.

The above techniques all involve purchasing goods or services locally, which may aid the firm in other countries, thus achieving unblocking. A multinational with blocked funds in Brazil may decide to purchase capital goods or services locally in Brazil despite the fact that they are intended to be used throughout the multinational. Similarly, it may decide to base group research and development, or group architectural and engineering personnel, in Brazil where funds are blocked. Another technique used by multinationals to unblock funds is to locate conventions and business meetings in countries where the company has blocked funds. Allied to this, multinationals frequently arrange holidays for employees in countries where funds are blocked. One other way of using blocked funds, which might be in Brazil, is to have employees of the multinational use, wherever possible, Varig, the Brazilian national airline, with tickets being purchased with cruzados held in Brazil by the Brazilian subsidiary.

Summary

Like taxation, exchange controls create market imperfections. They take many forms which range from requirements that residents surrender all holdings of foreign currency to restrictions on the acquisition of foreign currency denominated assets and liabilities; from the stipulation that foreign companies meet certain requirements for setting up business in the host country to restrictions on remittances out of the host country.

In response to exchange controls, international companies have developed techniques to mitigate some of the adverse impacts. These include the use of transfer pricing, fee and royalty payments, leading and lagging, matching, reinvoicing centres, parallel loans and many others. But close on their heels, host governments have tightened regulations to counter the multinationals' attempts at circumventing them.

Whilst this chapter has highlighted some of the issues in general terms, for the international treasurer contemplating an investment by his company in an overseas territory with exchange controls there is no substitute for a detailed knowledge of the actual exchange control regulations. Frequently, resort to a local consultant is necessary because of complexities and unwritten interpretations of regulations, and because of the scope for arranging individual agreements with host governments.

As of late 1985, the following countries had minimal or no exchange controls: Australia, Bahrain, Canada, Djibouti, Hong Kong, Japan, Kuwait, Lebanon, Macau, Maldives, Montserrat, New Zealand, Oman, Panama, Qatar, Sabah, St Helena, Sarawak, Saudi Arabia, Seychelles, Singapore, Sweden, Switzerland, United Arab Emirates, United Kingdom, United States of America, Vanuatu and West Germany.

Reference

Heywood, John (1985) *Foreign Exchange and the Corporate Treasurer*, 4th edn, Adam & Charles Black.

TEST BANK
NUMBER FOUR

EXAMINATION QUESTIONS

1. The Inter-Continental Hotel Company is considering investing in a new chalet hotel at Verbier in Switzerland. The initial investment required is for $2 million, or SFr 4 million at the current exchange rate of $1 = SFr 2. Profits for the first ten years will be reinvested, at which time Inter-Continental expects to sell out. Inter-Continental estimates that its interest in the hotel will realise SFr 6.5 million in six years' time.

(a) Indicate what factors you would regard as relevant in evaluating this investment.
(b) How will changes in the value of the Swiss franc affect the investment?
(c) Indicate possible ways of forecasting the $:SFr exchange rate ten years ahead.

2. Compare and contrast international investment and financing decisions with their domestic counterparts.

3. Waring Brothers, the London merchant bank, has a New York office. The following comments were overheard at the directors' dining-room table:

A: 'Lowering barriers to entry and breaking up monopolies and oligopolies always brings prices down.'
B: 'Not in banking. Deregulation will leave the cost of borrowing where it is at best. And it will probably even push it up.'
(a) Discuss the possible rationale for the comments made by speaker B.
(b) What other key consequences do you think will flow from US deregulation in banking? Why?

4. Discuss the concept of 'Currency Cocktail Issues'. In particular,

should the borrower be concerned with the apparent historical stability of the cocktail formula against his own currency? What are the major issues that the treasurer must be satisfied with?

(Association of Corporate Treasurers: Part II, Specimen paper in Funding Management)

5. You have recently been informed by the Central Bank of Zambia that a payment outstanding to you for some time from your subsidiary in Zambia has finally been approved, and that in three months' time the local currency will be exchanged for sterling at the prevailing rate and remitted to you. While you are pleased to learn of the impending payment, you have heard that the IMF has been in discussion with the Zambian Government and you know that they often insist on the devaluation of local currencies.

　　Against this background, you hear of an unconnected UK company whose subsidiary in Zambia is unable to borrow local currency due to a local disagreement, but which has no borrowing problems in the UK.

Required:
(a) How can you use this information to your company's advantage? What risks would you run?
(b) If the Zambian local currency stood at 1.856 to £1 today with an interest rate of 15%, while sterling 3-month interest was 12⅜–12½%, what forward rate would this imply?

(Association of Corporate Treasurers: Part II, September 1985 Paper in Currency Management)

6. Your customers, Europe Forever Limited, call to see you to discuss the renewal of their existing facilities for the coming 12 months. As a large import/export organisation, they are always interested in movements of foreign currency. Among the subjects they raised during your discussions is the rise in the use of European Currency Units (ECU). They are interested in this type of currency and also want to discuss the use of currency certificates of deposit and Eurobond issues, both of which they think might be expressed in ECUs.

Required:
A brief explanation for your customers of the salient features of:

(a) an ECU and the reasons for its rise in popularity over recent years;
(b) a currency certificate of deposit; and
(c) a Eurobond.

(Institute of Bankers: Banking Diploma, April 1984 Paper in Finance of International Trade)

7. Moving Parts Limited is a company specialising in power transmission equipment. It has a good export record selling either direct to overseas buyers or as a part of a consortium supplying major items of plant and capital equipment. Unfortunately, from its point of view, many of these sales are to companies operating in less credit-worthy parts of the world. This means that in many countries the support of a local bank cannot be relied upon, yet the contract terms usually call for credit periods of between two and five years and occasionally for more than five years. Contracts in the past have been expressed in sterling and usually range in value between £150,000 and £1 million.

The company has a basic ECGD Comprehensive Guarantee Policy.

Required:
A short memorandum outlining a scheme which is suitable for financing this type of deal.

Note: Ignore export house and confirming house schemes.

(Institute of Bankers: Banking Diploma, September 1984 Paper in Finance of International Trade)

8. What factors should influence a UK holding company when it considers how to finance a foreign subsidiary?

9. A US-based multinational is evaluating a new capital project in West Germany. The capital cost will be DM 30 million and it is forecast to produce cash inflows, in today's prices, of DM 7 million per annum for ten years. At the end of the project's life, DM 5 million — in today's prices — of working capital will be released; this is the only expected terminal value. The spot exchange rate is $0.5/DM; risk-free interest rates for dollars and Deutsche Marks are respectively 8% per annum and 5% per annum. The nominal return required for a US project of the class being considered is 15% in dollar terms and the expected US inflation rate is 6% per annum.

(a) On the basis of the date in the question, what inflation rate should we conclude would be effective in West Germany?
(b) Estimate the exchange rate in ten years' time. How have you arrived at your answer?
(c) Calculate the project's NPV.

10. Transworld Industries plc has been considering its position on currency exposure. The management board has come out in favour of currency neutrality. The group has, for a long time, had a net surplus of $50 million US assets over US liabilities. That it failed to take any action in the past is considered fortuitous because the exchange rate has moved from $2.30/£ in 1980 to $1.20/£ at the

time that the company has decided to take corrective action. The directors of Transworld Industries do not wish to increase the group's gearing ratio. What considerations would you bear in mind were you Transworld's treasurer, desirous of implementing a currency neutrality position? What actions could you take to achieve this objective?

The Ten Best Books on Multinational Finance

The references at the end of the chapters in this book can be pieced together to form a bibliography on multinational finance. What I have done here is to name the ten books on financial management in the multinational arena which I have found to be the most useful in my own studies of the subject. Some of these are academic books; some are aimed at practitioners and one is a case book.

Aliber, Robert Z. (1983) *The International Money Game*, 4th edn, Macmillan.
Carlson, Robert S., Remmers, H. Lee, Heckman, Christine R., Eiteman, David K. and Stonehill, Arthur I. (1980) *International Finance: Cases and Simulation*, Addison-Wesley.
Dufey, Gunter and Giddy, Ian H. (1978) *The International Money Market*, Prentice-Hall.
Eiteman, David K. and Stonehill, Arthur I. (1982) *International Business Finance*, 3rd edn, Addison-Wesley.
George, Abraham M. and Giddy, Ian H. (eds) (1983) *International Finance Handbook*, 2 volumes, John Wiley.
Kohlhagen, Steven W. (1978) *The Behaviour of Foreign Exchange Markets – a Critical Survey of the Empirical Literature*, New York University Press.
Lessard, Donald R. (ed.) (1979) *International Financial Management: Theory and Application*, Warren, Gorham and Lamont.
Rodriguez, Rita M. and Carter, E. Eugene (1984) *International Financial Management*, 3rd edn, Prentice-Hall.
Shapiro, Alan C. (1986) *Multinational Financial Management*, 2nd edn, Allyn and Bacon.
Walmsley, Julian (1983) *The Foreign Exchange Handbook: A User's Guide*, John Wiley.

Glossary

Absolute Purchasing Power Parity	A form of purchasing power parity which claims that under a fully floating exchange rate regime the ratio between domestic and foreign price levels equals the equilibrium rate of exchange between the domestic and foreign currencies.
Accommodating Accounts	A balance of payments term referring to those accounts that are triggered by the need to finance other transactions included in the balance of payments. Sometimes called Compensating or Financing Accounts.
Account Party	The party, usually the buyer, whose bank issues a letter of credit.
Accounting Exposure	Exposure which arises from the process of consolidating foreign currency denominated items into the parent currency denominated group financial accounts. Sometimes called Translation Exposure.
ADR	*See* American Depository Receipt.
Ad Valorem Tariff	Tariff calculated as a percentage of the value of goods entering the country.
Advisory Funds	Amounts of money left with a bank for investment on behalf of a customer after consultation with that customer.
After-Market	*See* Secondary Market.
AIBD	Association of International Bond Dealers.
All-Current Rate Method	A foreign currency translation method. All foreign currency denominated items are translated at current exchange rates. Sometimes called the Closing Rate Method or Current Rate Method − but not to be confused with the Current/Non-current Rate Method.
Allocation	The amount of new issue alloted to an investor or syndicate of investors.

American Depository Receipt (ADR)	Certificate of ownership issued by a US bank to investors in place of the underlying corporate shares which are held in custody.
American Option	An option which may be exercised on any business day within the option period.
Appreciation	An increase in the value of a currency.
Arbitrage	A purchase of foreign exchange, securities or commodities in one market coupled with immediate resale in another market in order to profit risklessly from price discrepancies. The effect of arbitrageurs' actions is to equate prices in all markets for the same commodity.
Arm's-Length Price	The price at which a willing seller and an unrelated willing buyer will freely agree a transaction.
Around	Term used in forward quotations by dealers. 'Ten-ten around' means ten points on either side of par – or ten points on either side of the present spot rate.
Ask Price	The larger price in a foreign exchange quotation. Sometimes called the Offer Price.
Association Cambiste Internationale	International society of foreign exchange dealers.
At Best	An instruction by a customer to his bank, agent or stockbroker to deal on his behalf at the best price obtainable in the market place.
Authorised Dealer	A dealer who is authorised by the monetary authority of a country to engage in specified foreign exchange activities. Such authority is usually required under exchange controls.
Autonomous Accounts	A balance of payments term referring to those accounts that are motivated purely by economic considerations rather than by the need to finance international transactions.
Back-to-Back Loan	*See* Parallel Loan.
Balance of Indebtedness	Statement prepared for a country summarising assets and liabilities that residents of the country have versus the rest of the world.
Balance of Invisibles	A balance of payments term. The balance on the services accounts.
Balance of Payments	A financial statement prepared for a country summarising the flow of goods, services, and funds between the residents of that country and the residents of the rest of the world during a particular period.

Balance of Trade	The net of imports and exports of goods reported in the balance of payments.
Balance Sheet Exposure	Exposure which arises from the process of translating foreign currency denominated balance sheet items into the parent currency denominated group accounts.
Bank for International Settlement	A bank for European central banks. It collects data on the size of Eurocurrency markets and central bank intervention in the foreign exchange market.
Bank Rate	The key interest rate in the banking system of many countries. It is effectively the rate at which the central bank of a country lends to its own money market institutions.
Bankhaus Herstatt	A West German bank that failed in the mid-seventies due to mismanaged foreign exchange trading. Its failure highlighted the lack of foreign exchange market regulation.
Banking Day	Any day on which a foreign exchange contract can be settled. A day on which banks at both ends of the deal must be open for business. Also called Business Day, Clear Day, Market Day or Open Day.
Basic Balance	The net of exports and imports of goods and services, unilateral transfers and long-term capital flows in the balance of payments.
Basis	The difference between cash and futures prices. Also the difference between yields on similar but different financial instruments.
Basis Point	A hundredth of a per cent. Used in relation to interest rates.
Bearer Instrument	A negotiable instrument on which title passes by mere delivery without endorsement or registration.
Bid Price	The smaller price in a foreign exchange quotation.
Big Figure	The first three digits of an exchange rate, for example $1.42 per pound, or DM2.72 per dollar. Sometimes dealers quote amongst themselves without using the big figure. Thus a quote of 20/30 for the Deutsche Mark would leave the big figure understood; the full quote might be DM2.7220/30.
Bilateral Netting	Two affiliated companies which offset their receipts and payments with each other, resulting in a single net intercompany receipt or payment to clear the balance.
Block Arrangements	A system where currencies of several countries float

jointly against other currencies, for example the European Monetary System.

Blocked Account	A bank account of a non-resident of a country with exchange controls where the amount in the account cannot be transferred to another country or currency without permission from the monetary authorities.
Blocked Currency	A currency that is not freely convertible to other currencies due to exchange controls.
Bond	A promise under seal to pay money. The term is generally used to designate the promise made by a corporation, either public or private, to pay money and it generally applies to instruments with an initial maturity of five years or more.
BONUS	Borrower's Option for Notes and Underwritten Standby. A form of Euronote. *See* Euronote.
Bracket	Banks involved in a new issue are grouped into brackets. The lead manager is on top, followed by co-managers, special underwriters, underwriters and other selling-group members. Banks in each bracket are either listed alphabetically or according to their commitments.
Bretton Woods Conference	A meeting of representatives of non-Communist countries in Bretton Woods, New Hampshire, USA, in 1944. Representatives agreed on the characteristics of the international monetary system, effectively the fixed exchange rate system, which prevailed until 1971.
Bridge Financing	A form of loan, usually at fluctuating interest rates, that takes the form of renewable overdrafts or discounting facilities. It is used as a continuing source of funds until the borrower obtains a medium- or long-term financing to replace it.
Broken Period	A deal which is not for a standard maturity, that is one, two, three, six or twelve months.
Broker	A foreign exchange intermediary who does not buy or sell currency on his own account, but arranges the buying or selling of currencies between third parties, usually banks.
Brokerage	Commissions due to a broker for his services.
Bullet	A straight debt issue with repayment in one go at maturity.
Business Day	*See* Banking Day.

Buyer's Option	The owner of a buyer's option contract may take delivery of the currency at any time between dates specified in the option.
Cable	Foreign exchange dealers' term for the sterling/dollar spot exchange rate. Term comes from cable transfer.
Call Option	The right, but not the obligation, to buy an amount of foreign exchange at a specified price within a specified period.
Capital Account	A balance-of-payments term. The part of the balance of payments which records the changes in financial assets and liabilities. The capital account is divided into long-term flows and short-term flows.
Capital Mobility	The extent to which private capital is free to be invested abroad. Capital mobility is predicated upon well-developed foreign exchange and financial markets, freedom from official restrictions on foreign investment, and confidence that future government policies will not obstruct the repatriation of invested funds.
Cash Flow Exposure	This is concerned with the effect of currency changes on the present value of future cash flows generated by a company's domestic and foreign operations. Sometimes called Economic Exposure.
CD	*See* Certificate of Deposit.
CEDEL	One of the Eurobond market's two clearing systems, owned by several European banks.
Central Bank	The institution with the primary responsibility to control the growth of a country's money stock. It may also have regulatory powers over commercial banks and over other financial institutions. It usually serves as the monetary agent for the government.
Certificate of Deposit (CD)	A placement of money for a specified period of time with a bank. The depositor receives a confirmation, the deposit receipt, which is a negotiable instrument. Bankers dealing in CDs make a secondary market where they may be sold and purchased prior to maturity. Investors usually accept a smaller interest rate on CDs than on regular time deposits because the investment has greater liquidity via the secondary market.
Chartism	Interpreting foreign exchange (and other) market activity and predicting future movements over the near term from graphic depictions of past prices and

volumes. It is sometimes called Technical Analysis or Momentum Analysis.

CHIPS	*See* Clearing House Interbank Payment System.
CIF	*See* Cost, Insurance and Freight Price.
Clean Float	An exchange rate system characterised by the absence of government intervention. Sometimes referred to as a Free Float.
Clear Day	*See* Banking Day.
Clearing House	An institution through which Eurobond contracts, futures contracts and other financial instruments, including cheques, are cleared.
Clearing House Interbank Payment System (CHIPS)	An automated clearing facility set up in 1970 and operated by the New York Clearing House Association which processes international money transfers for its membership which embraces over a hundred US financial institutions – mostly major US banks and branches of foreign banks.
Closing Exchange Rate	The exchange rate prevailing at a financial reporting date.
Closing Rate Method	*See* All-Current Rate Method.
Collateral	Security placed with a lender to assure the performance of the obligation; assuming that the obligation is satisfied, the collateral is returned by the lender.
Co-Managers	Banks ranking next after the lead manager in the marketing of a new issue of Eurobonds. They are chosen for their ability to place large amounts of new issues among customers. They may take more than the lead manager, whose position may arise because he is bringing a customer to the market as a borrower.
Commercial Paper	Unsecured promissory note issued usually for maturities of sixty days or less.
Commission	The amount of money, brokerage, compensation, or allowance given to a broker or agent for carrying on the business of the principal.
Commitment Fee	A percentage per annum rate charged by a lender on the daily undrawn balance of a borrowing facility.
Compensating Accounts	*See* Accommodating Accounts.
Compensatory Financing Facility	A lending programme administered by the IMF to finance short-term imbalances in members' inter-

	national payments caused by temporary shortfalls of exports.
Compound Tariff	A tariff that has *ad valorem* and specific components.
Compressibility Ratio	A ratio for assessing a country's liquidity position. It is the ratio of vital imports and debt service payments to exports, capital inflows and aid receipts.
Conditionality	The International Monetary Fund's practice of requiring members to adopt changes in their domestic economic policies as a condition for receiving balance of payments loans from the fund.
Confirmation	The written document confirming the oral foreign exchange contract agreed by telephone between either dealer and dealer or dealer and client.
Confirmed Irrevocable Letter of Credit	A type of credit issued by the importer's bank and confirmed by a bank in the exporter's country. The importer's bank commits itself irrevocably to pay the exporter's draft and the confirming bank (the exporter's bank) adds to this commitment by assuming the responsibility to pay the exporter's draft, provided that all conditions contained in the letter of credit are satisfied.
Consignment	An arrangement under which one exporter ships and delivers the product to the importer and receives payment only after the importer sells the product.
Consortium Bank	A group of banks whose objective is to provide joint financing to customers.
Continental Depository Receipt	A certificate of ownership issued by a Eurobank to investors in place of the underlying corporate shares which are held in custody.
Conversion Premium	The premium over an ordinary share's market price at which holders of a fixed-interest security may convert it into ordinary shares.
Convertibility	The ability to convert one currency into another without special permission from exchange control authorities.
Convertible	Fixed-interest borrowing convertible into the borrower's ordinary shares on stipulated conditions.
Convertible Bond	A fixed-interest security that is convertible into equity shares under stipulated conditions. The difference between the price of ordinary shares at the time of the issue of the bond and the rate at which they can be converted is the conversion premium. The attractiveness of convertible bonds is associated with the possibility

of a rise in the price of the ordinary shares or an appreciation in the currency in which the stock is quoted during the bond's life.

Convertible Eurobond — A Eurobond that can be converted into equity under prescribed conditions.

Correspondent Bank — A bank which handles the business of a foreign bank.

Cost, Insurance and Freight (CIF) Price — A price quotation by an exporter covering the cost of goods, any marine insurance, and all transportation charges to the foreign port of entry.

Cost of Capital — The rate of return expected by a party financing the firm.

Cost-Plus Loan Pricing — The interest rate on a loan is expressed as a function of some publicly available cost-of-funds measure, such as LIBOR (London Interbank Offered Rate).

Countervailing Duty — Taxes imposed on imports to offset the effects of foreign subsidies.

Country Risk — A wide range of risk, including political as well as economic risk. Corporate goals of multinationals and the national aspirations of host countries may not be congruent; the essential element in country risk is the possibility of some form of government action preventing the fulfilment of a contract.

Coupon — The fixed-interest rate attached to a lending.

Covenant — An obligation in writing. There are covenants in term loan agreements, deeds, mortgages and other similar instruments.

Covered Interest Arbitrage — A process of borrowing a currency, converting it to a second currency where it is invested, and selling this second currency forward against the initial currency. Riskless profits are derived from discrepancies between interest differentials and the percentage discount or premium between the currencies involved in the forward transaction. Covered interest arbitrage is based on disequilibrium in interest rate parity.

Covered Interest Differential — The deviation from interest rate parity.

Covering — Protecting the cash value of future proceeds of an international trade transaction, usually by buying or selling the proceeds in the forward market. Although used interchangeably with the term 'hedging', covering is, strictly speaking, protecting a future cash flow amount whereas hedging refers to the protection of foreign-denominated accounting assets or liabilities against pure translation losses.

Crawling Peg System	An exchange rate system in which the exchange rate is adjusted frequently and deliberately, maybe many times a year, usually to reflect prevailing rates of inflation.
Credit Risk	The likelihood, in lending operations, that a borrower will not be able to repay the principal or pay the interest.
Credit Tranche	The amount that a member country of the International Monetary Fund can borrow from the fund over and above the gold tranche.
Cross-Default Provision	A clause in a loan agreement that allows the lender to declare the loan immediately repayable and to terminate any further extension of credit if the borrower defaults on any other debt.
Cross Rate	The exchange rate between currencies A and B based upon the rates between currencies A and C and currencies B and C.
Currency Arbitrage	Taking advantage of differences between exchange rates in different markets involving the buying of one currency in one market and the selling of it in another.
Currency Area	Countries whose reserve holdings are denominated primarily in the currency of another, or whose currencies are either formally or informally linked to another and whose exchange control regulations parallel those in the dominant country.
Currency Band	A band within which a currency is allowed to fluctuate on both sides of its official parity. The central bank intervenes in order to maintain the value of the currency within the permissible range.
Currency Basket	A means of expressing the value of a financial asset or currency as a weighted average of more than one foreign exchange rate. The weights in this average are usually defined to be specific quantities of currencies, hence the term 'currency basket'.
Currency Option	A contract conferring the right, but not the obligation, to buy or sell a specified currency against another currency at a specific price at any time prior to a specified date.
Currency Swap	The simultaneous borrowing and lending operation in which parties transfer currencies from one to the other at the spot rate and agree to reverse the exchange after a fixed term at a fixed exchange rate.

Current Account	As used in the balance of payments, it is that section which records the trade in goods and services and the exchange of gifts among countries.
Current/Non-Current Method	A foreign currency translation method in which current items in balance sheets denominated in foreign currencies are translated at current exchange rates and long-term items are translated at historical rates.
Current Rate Method	*See* All-Current Rate Method.
Dealer	Specialist in a bank or company who is authorised to undertake foreign exchange transactions.
Debt Service Ratio	A ratio used to assess a country's creditworthiness. It is the ratio of a country's debt service payments to exports.
Deferred Payment	A payment under a letter of credit in which the exporter ships the goods to the importer but does not receive payment immediately. The payment is made at a specified time when all conditions stipulated in the letter of credit are met.
Demand Deposit	Funds in a current account that may be withdrawn at any time without notice. Demand deposits may or may not be interest-bearing deposits.
Depreciation	*See* Devaluation.
Details	Information a dealer requires following the completion of a transaction, such as rate and dates and so on.
Devaluation	A substantial decline in an exchange rate, usually effected in one go by government decree.
Direct Investment	Purchase of a foreign financial asset in which substantial involvement in the management of the foreign asset is presumed. In practice, it is any holding that represents more than 10 per cent ownership of the foreign asset. Also termed Foreign Direct Investment.
Direct Quote	A rate of exchange quoted in terms of X units of home currency to one unit of foreign currency.
Dirty Float	*See* Managed Float.
Discount Rate	(a) In capital budgeting, the rate which is applied to future cash flows to bring them to present value. (b) In trade terms, the rate which is applied to a non-interest-bearing obligation which can be translated into a rate for early payment. A bill of exchange payable at face

	value in 3 months' time might sell for 2 per cent less than its face amount, implying an annualised discount rate of 8 per cent. (c) In foreign exchange markets, the difference between the forward and the spot rate.
Discounting	Where a sale is to be settled by a bill of exchange, the seller may surrender it to a financial institution in exchange for immediate payment of an amount less than the face value to reflect interest.
Discretionary Funds	Funds placed with a bank by customers for investment on their behalf by the bank at the bank's own discretion.
Divergence	Signals that an EMS member's economic policies are out of line with its fellow members. Divergence is measured by fluctuations in the market value in terms of each member currency of the European Currency Unit relative to its central or par value.
Divergence Threshold	The critical value of each EMS member's divergence indicator that, when reached, establishes the point at which it is presumed that domestic economic policies will be adjusted.
Document of Title	This term includes the bill of lading, dock warrant, dock receipt, warehouse receipt, order for the delivery of goods, and any other document which in the regular course of business is treated as adequate evidence that the person in possession of it is entitled to own, hold, and dispose of the document and the goods it covers.
Documentary Draft	A draft, the honour of which is conditioned upon the presentation of a document. Here the term 'document' means any paper including document of title, security, invoice, certificate and the like. Also referred to as a Documentary Demand for Payment.
Doomsday Tax	US tax legislation provides that, when a foreign affiliate is set up in a tax-haven country to siphon income from a higher tax area, income from the tax-haven country is subject to US tax whether or not it is remitted to the United States. The proceeds from liquidating a tax-haven company may be subject to the doomsday tax.
Double Hedging	A foreign exchange technique used to hedge in which the size of the forward contract exceeds the exposed position, because the profits or losses on the forward contract are subject to tax.
Double Taxation	Taxes paid twice, once abroad where income is earned

and a second time in the UK, if the company is UK-owned. A principle of tax law is that double taxation should be avoided. If the UK company has already paid taxes abroad it should only pay enough taxes in the UK to bring the overall rate up to the UK rate.

Draft	An unconditional order in writing, signed by one party, usually the exporter, and addressed to the importer, requiring the importer or the importer's agent to pay, on demand (sight draft) or at a fixed future date (time draft), the amount specified on the face of the document.
ECGD	*See* Exports Credit Guarantee Department.
ECU	*See* European Currency Unit.
Economic Exposure	The extent to which the value of the firm will change due to an exchange rate change. This arises due to the effect of currency changes upon the parent currency present value of expected future cash flows to be generated by a company's operations.
Edge Act Corporation	A subsidiary of a US commercial bank whose income arises from operating in foreign countries. It is given powers not held by domestic US banks to operate in ways similar to the practices of the foreign banks.
Effective Exchange Rate	A rate measuring the overall nominal value of a currency over time in the foreign exchange market. It is calculated via a weighted average of bilateral exchange rates, using a weighting scheme that reflects the importance of each country's trade with the home country.
Efficient Market	A market in which there is a sufficiently large number of buyers and sellers to eliminate any incentive for arbitrage transactions, and in which the trade-off between return and risk is fully reflected in prices.
Elasticity	The degree of responsiveness in one variable to changes in another variable. Thus the price elasticity of exports would measure the degree of responsiveness in exports to changes in prices.
EMS	*See* European Monetary System.
Entrepot Financial Centres	World financial centres that play the role of bringing foreign lenders and foreign borrowers together. The countries in which these centres are located are channels through which international funds pass.
Eurobanks	Financial intermediaries that bid for time deposits and

make loans in currencies other than that of the country in which they are located.

Eurobond	A bond underwritten by an international syndicate of banks and marketed internationally in countries other than the country of the currency in which it is denominated. The issue is thus not subject to national restrictions.
Euroclear	One of the Eurobond market's two clearing systems. It is provided by Morgan Guaranty for over 100 banks.
Eurocurrency	A time deposit in a bank account located outside the banking regulations of the country which issues the currency.
Eurodollars	Dollars held in time deposits in banks outside the United States. These banks may be foreign-owned or overseas branches of US banks. But see International Banking Facilities.
Euronote	The Euronote market is one in which borrowers raise money by the issue of short-term notes, generally with maturities of three and six months, that are negotiable like certificates of deposit. As one issue of notes matures, the borrower issues some more so that whilst the holders of the debt change over time, the total amount outstanding can be maintained in the medium term. A group of commercial banks ensures that the borrower in a particular issue will be able to place such notes by standing by ready to purchase the paper should the appetite of short-term investors wane.
European Currency Unit (ECU)	A currency basket composed of specific quantities of the currencies of European Monetary System members.
European Monetary System (EMS)	A structure of agreements governing the exchange market activities of participating members of the European Economic Community. Agreements require members closely to manage the exchange values of their currencies relative to other members. The EMS eventually aims at the creation of a European Monetary Fund with the objective of moving towards monetary unification.
European Option	An option that can be exercised on the fixed expiration date only.
Exchange Contract	A contract to exchange one foreign currency for a given amount of another on a given date.

Exchange Controls	Restrictions imposed by the central bank or other government authorities on the convertibility of a currency or on the movement of funds in that currency.
Exchange Rate	The number of units of one currency expressed in terms of a unit of another currency.
Exchange Risk	The variability in a firm's net assets or value arising from uncertain exchange rate changes.
Exercise Price	The exchange rate at which a foreign exchange option may be exercised.
Export Finance Vehicle	A vehicle company set up to buy export receivables of affiliated companies. Export finance companies may conduct exposure or liquidity management functions.
Export–Import Bank (Eximbank)	US government agency established in 1934 to stimulate US foreign trade. The Eximbank supports commercial banks that are financing exports and provides direct financing, loan guarantees and insurance to exporters and foreign buyers of US goods. Similar to the ECGD in Britain.
Exports Credit Guarantee Department (ECGD)	A UK government department dedicated to facilitating UK exports primarily through subsidised export financing and offering export credit insurance to UK exporters.
Extended Facility	A long-term lending programme of the International Monetary Fund for the use of member countries with serious balance of payments problems that are not expected to be reversed in the near future.
External Exposure Management Techniques	Contractual agreements, external to the firm, designed to reduce or eliminate an existing foreign exchange exposure.
Factoring	A financing method in which the borrower assigns or sells his receivables as collateral to a firm, called a factor, which normally assumes responsibility for collection.
FASB 8	A US accounting standard in force from 1976 to 1981 that required companies to translate their foreign-affiliate financial statements using the temporal method. Foreign currency translation gains and losses were reported in the income statement as ordinary income.
FASB 52	A US accounting standard in force from December

1981, concerning translation of foreign currency financial statements. Results must be measured in the functional currency of the foreign entity, except in cases of high-inflation countries. Translation is done using the all-current method, with transaction losses showing up on the parent's income statement and translation losses on the parent's balance sheet.

Federal Funds

Money deposited with the Federal Reserve Bank, the central bank of the USA. This money is available on demand. Purchases of US Treasury bills and most other money market instruments in the domestic US money market may only be made with federal funds.

Filter Rule

A rule for buying and selling securities based on the premise that once a movement in a currency's exchange rate has exceeded a given percentage movement, it will continue to move in the same direction.

Financing Accounts

See Accommodating Accounts.

Firm

A dealer making a quotation on a firm basis commits his bank. But he usually puts some restriction on, such as 'firm for one minute' or 'firm for one million dollars only'. Can also be used to convey a strong currency, for example, 'the Deutsche Mark was firm today'.

Fisher Effect

The hypothesis that the nominal interest rate differential between two countries should equal the expected inflation differential between those countries. Also called Fisher's Closed Hypothesis.

Fisher's Closed Hypothesis

See Fisher Effect.

Fisher's Open Hypothesis

See International Fisher Effect.

Fix or Fixing

A daily meeting in certain countries at which exchange rates are officially fixed. These rates are then used for specific purposes such as tourist business.

Fixed Exchange Rate System

A system in which the value of a country's currency is tied to a major currency, such as the US dollar, gold or the SDR. The term usually allows for fluctuations within a range of one or two per cent on either side of the fixed rate.

Floating Exchange Rate System

A system in which the value of a currency relative to others is established by the forces of supply and demand in the foreign exchange markets. Strictly speaking, this implies that intervention by the governments involved should be absent.

Floating Lending Rate	A lending rate that is established at a fixed number of percentage points above a given rate, such as LIBOR, and which is adjusted periodically, often every six months. Adjustment occurs throughout the life of the loan.
Floating Rate Notes (FRNs)	Short-term floating interest rate securities. The interest rate is pegged to LIBOR, and is adjusted semi-annually. These securities are attractive to investors during periods of rising interest rates when fixed rate bonds are subject to depreciation.
For Information Only	Quotations which are not firm but are intended as an indication. Sometimes referred to as 'for information only quotes'.
Foreign Bond	A long-term security issued by a borrower in the capital market of another country. Usually under-written by a syndicate from one country and sold on that country's capital market, the bond is denominated in the currency of the country in which it is sold.
Foreign Credit Insurance Corporation	A private association of leading US insurance companies, affiliated with Eximbank, that provides short- and medium-term credit insurance to exporters, enabling them to obtain or offer better financing terms.
Foreign Currency Translation	The process of expressing those amounts that are denominated or measured in a foreign currency in terms of the reporting currency of the parent company.
Foreign Direct Investment	*See* Direct Investment.
Foreign Exchange	Currency other than the one used internally in a given country.
Foreign Exchange Broker	One who introduces two parties in a currency or deposit transaction. The parties might be a buyer and a seller of foreign currencies or a borrower and a lender of a given currency. The broker receives a fee for this service; brokers do not take positions for themselves; they only arrange transactions among other parties.
Foreign Exchange Option	A contract conveying the right, but not the obligation, to buy or sell a designated quantity of a foreign currency at a specified price during a stipulated period under stated conditions. The term is sometimes incorrectly used to mean an optional date forward contract.
Foreign Exchange Trader	One who stands ready to buy and sell currencies out of inventory and expects to earn a profit for the costs and risks incurred.

Foreign Tax Credit	Home country tax credit given against domestic tax in respect of foreign taxes already paid on foreign-source earnings.
Forfeiting	Acceptance by a bank of medium- or long-term bills of exchange without recourse to the seller.
Forward Contract	An agreement to exchange specified amounts of currencies of different countries at a specified contractual rate (the forward rate) at a specified future date.
Forward Differential	Percentage difference between spot and forward rates. Usually expressed as an annual percentage.
Forward Exchange Market	The market involved with forward contracts for exchange of currency at some future date. The usual forward maturities are for one, two, three, six and twelve months, although contracts for other maturities may be negotiated.
Forward/Forward Swap	A pair of forward exchange contracts involving a forward purchase and a forward sale of a currency, simultaneously entered into, but for different maturities. Sometimes called a Forward Swap.
Forward Margin	The difference between the forward rate and the spot rate of a currency.
Forward Option Contract	*See* Optional Date Forward Contract.
Forward Premium (or discount when negative)	The difference between the forward and spot rates, expressed either as an annualised percentage of the spot exchange rate or as so many cents or pfennigs. When forward currencies are worth more than the corresponding spot amount, the stronger currency is at a premium; the weaker currency is at a discount.
Forward Rate	The rate quoted today for delivery at a fixed future date of a specified amount of one currency against another.
Forward Swap	*See* Forward/Forward Swap.
Free Alongside (FAS)	An exporter's price quotation that includes delivery of goods alongside a designated transportation vehicle, with the importer responsible for all subsequent movement of the goods.
Free Cash Flow	The net figure obtained by deducting from cash generated by operations or by an investment that cash which has been absorbed by operations or by the investment. Free cash flow disregards all cash flowing

in from financing sources and it disregards remuneration of financing sources.

Free Float	*See* Clean Float.
FRNs	*See* Floating Rate Notes.

Fronting Loan
: A parent-to-affiliate loan channelled through a financial intermediary, usually an international bank. This type of loan reduces political risk since government authorities are more likely to allow the local affiliate to repay a loan to an international bank than to the parent company. Particularly appropriate in situations of high political risk or blocked funds.

Functional Currency
: The currency of the main economic environment in which a multinational operates. It is normally the currency of the environment in which the firm primarily generates and expends cash.

Futures Contract
: A standardised foreign exchange contract written against the exchange clearing house for a fixed number of foreign currency units and for delivery on a fixed date. Because of their standardisation, futures contracts have a deep secondary market.

General Resources Account
: The lending programme through which the IMF provides short-term balance of payments financing to its members.

Gold Standard
: A monetary agreement under which national currencies are backed by gold and gold is utilised for international payments.

Gold Tranche
: The amount that each member country of the IMF contributes in the form of gold as part of its membership quota in the fund.

Group of Ten
: Ten major industrial countries – West Germany, France, Belgium, The Netherlands, Italy, the United Kingdom, Sweden, Canada, Japan and the United States – that agreed in 1962 to stand ready to lend their currencies to the IMF under the General Arrangements to Borrow. The Group of Ten has taken the lead in subsequent changes in the international monetary system.

Hard Currency
: A strong, freely convertible currency. A strong currency is one that is not expected to devalue within the foreseeable future.

Hedging	The generation of a position in a given currency in the forward market or in the money market with the purpose of matching it against the net exposure position as evidenced by the balance sheet. The purpose of hedging is to make the net position for a particular currency at a given date equal to zero. The accounts included in the exposed balance sheet items are determined in accordance with accounting rules. *See also* Covering.
Historical Exchange Rate	The foreign currency exchange rate in effect on the date when an asset or liability was acquired.
Hot Money	Speculative bank deposits that are moved around the international money markets to take advantage of interest rate and currency movements.
IBFs	*See* International Banking Facilities.
IBRD	*See* International Bank for Reconstruction and Development.
IMF	*See* International Monetary Fund.
IMM	*See* International Monetary Market.
Income Statement Exposure	Arises as a result of the process of translating foreign-currency denominated income statement items into parent currency denomination group income statements.
Inconvertible Currency	A currency which cannot be converted into other currencies because of exchange control restrictions.
Indexing	In some countries the practice of adjusting debt by some measure of inflation to preserve the purchasing power of the debt in constant monetary units. In Brazil, indexing is applied to wages, business accounts and all debt.
Indication Rate	A rate which informs the enquirer of the prevailing exchange rate but the dealer is not prepared to deal at precisely this rate. *See* For Information Only.
Indicator Rules	Publicly announced rules that link adjustments in the value of exchange rates to movements in economic statistics.
Indirect Quote	A rate of exchange quoted in terms of X units of foreign currency per unit of home currency.
In-House Funds	Advisory and discretionary funds which banks invest for customers.

Intercompany Trade	Trade flows between fellow affiliates of the same group of companies.
Interest Arbitrage	The international transfer of funds to a foreign centre, or the maintenance of funds in a foreign centre with the intention of benefiting from the higher yield on short-term investment in that centre. *See* Covered Interest Arbitrage and Uncovered Interest Arbitrage.
Interest Equalisation Tax	A form of foreign exchange control, effective in the USA from 1963 until the end of 1973, that required US residents to pay a special tax on any purchase of foreign securities.
Interest Rate Differential	The difference between short-term interest rates prevailing in two money centres at a given moment. Sometimes called Interest Rate Spread.
Interest Rate Parity	The condition that the interest differential should equal the forward differential between two currencies.
Interest Rate Spread	*See* Interest Rate Differential.
Intermediary Company	A vehicle company used as a conduit for the transfer of funds between fellow affiliate companies.
Internal Exposure Management Technique	Tactics related to the business of the multinational which do not use third party contracts but are aimed at reducing exposed positions or preventing exposure from arising or exploiting possible future exchange rate movements.
International Bank for Reconstruction and Development (IBRD)	Usually known as the World Bank. The IBRD is owned by its member countries and makes loans at slightly below conventional terms to countries for projects of high economic priority.
International Banking Act 1978	US legislation designed to remove many of the competitive advantages that foreign banks had over their domestic US counterparts. Thus the Federal Reserve Bank is now authorised to impose reserve requirements on foreign banks and there are restrictions on their ability to take deposits nationwide.
International Banking Facilities (IBFs)	Free monetary zones in the United States that can be established by certain corporations and by US branches and agencies of foreign banks. The IBFs accepting foreign deposits are exempted from reserve requirements and interest rate restrictions and can make loans to foreign borrowers. The impact of their operations is that some dollars deposited in time deposits in the USA effectively become Eurodollars.

International Fisher Effect	The hypothesis that the interest differential between two countries should reflect the future change in the spot rate. Also called Fisher's Open Hypothesis.
International Monetary Fund (IMF)	International organisation created by the Bretton Woods Agreement in 1944 to promote exchange rate stability. The objectives of the Fund include supervising exchange market intervention of member countries, providing the financing needed by members to overcome short-term payments imbalances, and encouraging monetary cooperation and international trade among nations.
International Monetary Market (IMM)	A centralised market in Chicago where currency and financial futures contracts, amongst others, are traded.
Issue Price	The price at which securities are sold on issue.
Issuing Bank	The bank that issues a letter of credit. It is usually the buyer's bank.
Lag	To defer payment of a debt. A firm with a subsidiary in a hard-currency country that has capital controls may encourage the subsidiary to lag its payments in order to take advantage of a possible revaluation of the hard currency.
Law of Comparative Advantage	According to this hypothesis, a country will specialise in producing, and will export, those goods that it can produce cheaply relative to the costs of producing them in foreign countries. It will import those goods that it can produce only at relatively high cost.
Law of One Price	The hypothesis that unfettered trade between countries will equalise the price of any good in all countries.
Lead	To prepay a debt. A company with a subsidiary in a soft-currency country that has capital controls may encourage the subsidiary to prepay money due to harder currency countries to avoid the adverse impact in cash flow terms should the soft-currency country devalue.
Letter of Credit	A letter issued by a bank, usually at the request of an importer, indicating that the opening bank or another will honour drafts if they are accompanied by specified documents under specified conditions.
LIBOR	*See* London Interbank Offered Rate.
LIFFE	*See* London International Financial Futures Exchange.

Liquidity	The ability of a business to pay its debts as they fall due.
Lombard Rate	German term for the rate of interest charged for a loan against the security of a pledged promissory note. Particularly used by the Bundesbank, which normally maintains its Lombard rate at about 0.5 per cent above its discount rate.
London Dollar CDs	Negotiable certificates of dollar deposit issued by major Eurobanks. Denominations range from $10,000 to several million dollars and maturities range from a call basis to over five years.
London Interbank Offered Rate (LIBOR)	The interest rate at which prime banks offer deposits to other prime banks in London. This rate is often used as the basis for pricing Eurodollar and other Euro-currency loans. The lender and the borrower agree to a markup over LIBOR; the total of LIBOR plus the markup is the effective interest rate for the loan.
London International Financial Futures Exchange (LIFFE)	A centralised market in London where standardised currency, currency options and financial futures are traded.
Long Position	To have greater inflows than outflows of a given currency.
Managed Float	A floating exchange rate system in which some government intervention takes place. Also termed Dirty Float.
Market Day	*See* Banking Day.
Market Maker	An institution that stands willing to buy or sell an asset, or an institution that deals so frequently and in such volume in an asset that it makes it possible for others to buy or sell that asset at almost any time.
Matching	A process whereby a firm balances its long positions in a given currency (assets, revenues or cash inflows) with its offsetting short positions (liabilities, expenses or cash outflows). The remaining (unmatched) position is the net exposure in that currency.
Maturity (or Settlement) Date	The date on which a contract is due to be settled.
Maturity Gap Exposure	The risk arising from having assets and liabilities of the same amount in the same currency but for different maturities.
Medium Term	Credit periods of three to ten years.

Merchant Bank	A specialist bank that carries on a banking business and also acts as an advisor to companies, including assisting on flotations of new issues of shares and bonds.
Mismatch	A situation where assets and liabilities in a currency do not balance either in size or maturity.
MOFFs	Multiple option funding facilities. A form of Euronote. *See* Euronote.
Momentum Analysis	*See* Chartism.
Monetary/Non-Monetary Method	A foreign currency translation method. Non-monetary assets and liabilities are translated at their historical exchange rates whilst monetary items are translated at current exchange rates.
Money Market	Financial institutions and dealers in money and credit.
Moratorium	Authorisation of suspension of payments by a debtor for a stated time.
Multicurrency Clause	A clause which gives a Eurocurrency borrower the right to switch from one currency to another when a loan is rolled over.
Multilateral Netting	Affiliates within multinationals offset their debtor and creditor positions with the rest of the group as a whole, so that a single net intercompany receipt or payment is made each period to settle indebtedness.
Multiple Currency Pegging	An exchange rate management policy under which the weighted average exchange value of a currency against more than one other currency is held within a specified range through official intervention in the exchange market.
Negatively Sloping Yield Curve	A yield curve where interest rates in the shorter dates are above those in the longer. This occurs when interest rates are expected to fall.
Negotiable Instrument	Any financial instrument like bills of exchange, promissory notes, cheques, bank notes, CDs, share warrants, bearer shares or bearer bonds, the title of which passes by mere delivery, without notice to the party liable on the instrument, and in which the transferee in good faith and for a consideration of value acquires an indefeasible title against the whole world.
Net Exchange Position	Net asset or liability position in a given currency. Also termed a net long or short position.

Netting	A procedure by which affiliates within a multinational group net out intercompany trade or financial flows and only pass the net amount due.
NIFs	Note Issuance Facilities. A kind of Euronote. *See* Euronote.
Nominal Exchange Rate	The actual exchange rate.
Note	*See* Promissory Note.
Numeraire	The standard which is used for measurement. In multinational finance this refers to the currency chosen by the firm as reference against which all other currency cash flows are measured.
OECD	*See* Organisation for Economic Cooperation and Development.
Odd Date	Most forward currency contracts have maturities of one, two, three, six or twelve months ahead. Contracts for dates other than these standard periods are called 'odd date contracts'. They are generally relatively more costly than contracts for standard maturities.
Offer Price	*See* Ask Price.
Official Reserves	Holdings of gold and foreign currencies by official monetary institutions of a country.
Offshore Currency	*See* Eurocurrency.
Offshore Finance Subsidiary	A subsidiary company incorporated overseas, usually in a tax-haven country, whose function is to issue securities abroad for use in either the parent's domestic or foreign business.
Open Day	*See* Banking Day.
Open Position	The difference between the amount of a foreign currency owned or receivable and the total of the same currency payable under definite contracts. If one exceeds the other there is an open position. If the amount held and receivable exceeds the amount payable there is said to be a long position; if the amount held or receivable is less than the amount payable, it constitutes a short position.
Option Forward Contract	*See* Optional Date Forward Contract.
Option Premium	The price paid to the seller of a foreign exchange option for the rights involved.

Optional Date Forward Contract	A forward exchange contract in which the rate is fixed but the maturity is open, within a specified range of dates. Sometimes termed Forward Option Contract or Option Forward Contract.
Organisation for Economic Cooperation and Development (OECD)	An organisation that provides for intergovernmental discussion in the fields of economic and social policy. It collects and publishes data and makes short-term economic forecasts of its member countries.
Outright Forward Rate	The forward rate expressed in pounds or dollars per currency unit, or vice versa.
Par Value	Under the Bretton Woods fixed exchange rate system, the par value of a currency was that value measured in terms of gold or the US dollar which was maintained at a fixed rate relative to gold or the dollar.
Parallel Loan (a Back-To-Back Loan)	An arrangement in which two business firms in separate countries borrow each other's currency for a specific period of time. At an agreed future date they return the borrowed currencies.
Parallel Matching	A long or short position in one currency is matched against a short or long position in a different currency, this being reasonable since movements in the two currencies are expected to follow closely parallel paths.
Parent Country	The country in which the parent company of a multinational group is located.
Parent Currency	The currency of the parent company of a multinational group.
Parity	The official rate of exchange between two currencies.
Parity Grid	The matrix of bilateral par values for the currencies of members of the European Monetary System. This grid establishes the intervention prices between which member governments are obliged to maintain the exchange value of currency in terms of every other group currency.
Pip	The most junior digit in a currency quotation.
Placing Power	A bank's ability to sell securities to investors, usually applied to new issues.
Points	The number of units, often expressed in terms of 0.0001 of a unit of an exchange rate. It is customary to state that a currency has moved by so many points from a previous exchange rate. Forward quotes are often expressed in terms of so many points premium or discount above or below the spot rate.

Pooling	Transfer of excess affiliate cash into a central account – the pool – usually located in a low-tax country, where all corporate funds are managed by corporate staff.
Portfolio Investment	Purchase of a foreign financial asset with the purpose of deriving returns from the security without intervening in the management of the foreign operation.
Positively Sloping Yield Curve	A yield curve where interest rates in the shorter periods are below those in the longer. This is the normal form of yield curve.
PPP	*See* Purchasing Power Parity.
Praecipium	In the Euromarkets the manager of a bond or credit negotiates a fee payable by the borrower. From this the manager takes his own fee – the praecipium – before passing the remainder of the fee to the management group.
Premium	The amount by which a currency is more expensive in the forward market relative to the spot price.
Project Finance	Finance for a project without payment or guarantee obligations from the substantial parties, against the security of the future cash flows from the project itself.
Promissory Note	An unconditional promise in writing signed by one party engaging to pay on demand or at a fixed or determinable time a sum certain in money to or to the order of a specified person or to bearer, but not legally binding until delivered to the payee or bearer.
PUFs	Prime underwriting facilities. A form of Euronote. *See* Euronote.
Purchasing Power Parity (PPP)	The hypothesis that, over time, the difference between the inflation rates in two countries tends to equal the rate of change of the exchange rate between the currencies of the countries concerned.
Put Option	The right, but not the obligation, to sell an amount of foreign exchange at a specified price within a specified time.
Real Effective Exchange Rate	A rate calculated by dividing the home country's nominal effective exchange rate by an index of the ratio of average foreign prices to home prices. If purchasing power parity is holding, the real effective exchange rate should remain constant.
Real Exchange Rate	The value of a currency in terms of real purchasing power. It is calculated by comparing the price of a

hypothetical market basket of goods in two different countries, translated into the same currency at the prevailing exchange rate. Useful in measuring the price competitiveness of domestic goods in international markets.

Regulation Q

A US regulation, now phased out, of the Federal Reserve System that established a ceiling on interest rates on time deposits. Banks were forbidden to pay interest on deposits with maturities of less than 30 days. Regulations played a significant role in the original growth of the Eurodollar market.

Reinvoicing Vehicle

A vehicle company which performs group exposure or liquidity management functions. Goods exported from or imported to an associated company are shipped direct to the third party or to the associate as the case may be but invoicing is performed via the reinvoicing vehicle. Title to the goods and payment are thus channelled through the vehicle.

Relative Purchasing Power Parity

A form of purchasing power parity which claims that, in comparison to a period when equilibrium rates of exchange prevailed, changes in the ratio of domestic and foreign prices will indicate the necessary adjustment in the exchange rate between any pair of currencies.

Repurchase Agreement

A contract in which the seller of an asset agrees to buy back the asset sold on a specific date. The technique is frequently used when a bank, due to regulatory restrictions, cannot accept a deposit from a customer and pay interest on it. The bank may then sell a security to its customer and agree to repurchase it on the date the customer wants to have the money back.

Reserve Accounts

A balance of payments term referring to those accounts reflecting the changes in the amount of resources that the government of a country has at its disposal to settle international payments. These resources are composed of gold and foreign currency which is fully convertible into other currencies.

Revaluation

An increase in the spot value of a currency.

Revolving Loan

A loan with floating rates where rates and amounts, within the limits of the specified line of credit, are renegotiated periodically.

Rollover

When a forward exchange contract is about to mature a new forward contract is entered into to extend the original maturity date.

Rollover Ratio	A ratio used to assess a country's creditworthiness. It is given by the reciprocal of the average maturity of a country's external debt.
Round Tripping	An opportunity to arbitrage which arises when a bank's customer can use overdraft facilities to draw from and deposit the proceeds in the money markets at rates which exceed the cost of the overdraft.
RUFs	Revolving underwriting facilities. A form of Euronote. *See* Euronote.
SDRs	*See* Special Drawing Rights.
Second Amendment	This amendment to the Articles of Agreement of the International Monetary Fund, ratified in 1978, allows members more flexibility in the management of exchange rates than under the Bretton Woods system. It also increases the supervisory responsibilities of the IMF and makes the special drawing rights more attractive as reserve assets.
Secondary Market	Market in which securities are traded after issue. Also called 'the after-market'.
Selling Group	The banks marketing a new Eurobond issue.
Selling Period	A week or ten days during which managing banks canvass demand for a new issue of Eurobonds among underwriters and other selling banks on the basis of a provisional coupon and issuing price. Terms are formally agreed at the end of the selling period on the basis of demand expressed.
Short Dates	Dealing term meaning periods up to one week, but sometimes it is used to refer to periods up to a month.
Short Position	Situation in which anticipated outflows of a currency exceed the anticipated inflows of that currency over a period of time. Also refers to a net liability, net expense or net cash outflow position in a currency.
Sight Deposits	Current accounts, overnight deposits and money at call. Deposits with longer maturities are term deposits.
Sight Draft	A bill of exchange that is due when presented.
Smithsonian Agreement	Began the first stage of the multilateral exchange rate realignments that followed the collapse of the Bretton Woods system of international monetary relations.
Snake	The European system of exchange rate setting created in April 1972 and superseded in 1979 by the European Monetary System.

SNIFs	Short-term note issuance facilities. A form of Euronote. *See* Euronote.
Society for Worldwide Interbank Financial Transfers (SWIFT)	A standardised electronic message transfer service designed to send and confirm instructions concerning funds transfers associated with international payments in the major industrial countries.
Soft Currency	A weak currency whose convertibility is, or is expected to become, restricted.
Sovereign Risk	(a) The risk of government default on a loan made or guaranteed by it. (b) The risk that the country of origin of the currency being bought or sold will impose foreign exchange regulations that will reduce the value of the contract.
Space Arbitrage	The simultaneous purchase and sale of a currency in two different markets to take advantage of different exchange rates in those markets, the aim being to make a profit from the difference.
Special Drawing Rights (SDRs)	A form of international reserve asset created and ratified by the IMF in 1969. SDRs have their value based on a weighted average of five widely used currencies.
Spot/Forward Swaps	The simultaneous spot purchase or sale of a currency and a countering sale or purchase of the same currency in the forward market.
Spot Market	The currency market for immediate delivery, although, in the spot market, delivery is usually two working days after the transaction date.
Spot Rate	The price at which foreign exchange can be bought or sold for immediate delivery. In practice spot deals are settled two working days after the transaction date.
Spread	The difference between bid and ask prices in a price quote.
Square	Purchases and sales, or foreign currency assets and liabilities, which are equal; thus there is no position.
Square Position	The position when assets and/or cash inflows match liabilities and/or cash outflows in a given currency for a certain maturity.
Stop Loss	An order to sell a financial instrument when its price falls to a specified level.
Swap	A given currency is simultaneously purchased and sold, but the maturity for each of the transactions is different.

Swap Rate	The difference between spot and forward rates expressed in points – that is, in terms of 0.0001 of a currency unit.
SWIFT	*See* Society for Worldwide Interbank Financial Transfers.
Tax Haven	A country that imposes little or no tax on the profits from transactions carried on or routed through that country, especially income from dividends and interest.
Temporal Method	A foreign currency translation method. The translation rate adopted preserves the accounting principles used to value assets and liabilities in the original financial statements. Thus items stated at historical cost are translated at historical exchange rates; current exchange rates are used for items stated at replacement cost, market value or expected future value.
Term Deposit	Deposits, including certificates of deposit, for terms longer than sight deposits. *See* Sight Deposits.
Third Party Trade	Trade between companies which are not part of the same group.
Tombstone	Advertisement placed by banks shortly after a new Eurobond issue to record their part in its management and sale.
Transaction Date	Used in foreign exchange markets to record the date on which a foreign exchange contract is agreed.
Transaction Exposure	The extent to which a given exchange rate change will affect the value of foreign currency denominated transactions entered into.
Transfer Price	The price at which one affiliate in a group of companies sells goods or services to another affiliated unit.
Translation Exposure	*See* Accounting Exposure.
TRUFs	Transferable revolving underwriting facilities. A form of Euronote. *See* Euronote.
Uncovered Interest Arbitrage	A process of borrowing a currency and converting it to a second currency where it is invested. The arbitrageur aims to earn profit derived from the relative interest rates received and paid. Unlike covered interest arbitrage, the currency in which the arbitrageur invests is not sold forward; instead the arbitrageur waits until the maturity of his investment and then sells the second currency spot for the original currency. Also,

	unlike covered interest arbitrage, the uncovered version is risky.
Under Reference	A deal which cannot be finalised without reference to the bank which placed the order, whose name is not revealed without reference back to that bank.
Underwriting Group	Bankers who receive a commission for underwriting a new issue.
Unilateral Transfers	A balance of payments term referring to the accounts that measure gifts sent in and out of the reporting country.
Valeur Compensée	Principle governing foreign exchange transactions by which payments are made in both currencies on the same date. Also called Value Compensation.
Value Compensation	*See* Valeur Compensée.
Value Date	The date on which payment is made to settle a deal. A spot deal on Wednesday will be settled on Friday, so Friday is the value date.
Withholding Tax	A tax collected by the source originating the income as opposed to one paid by the recipient of the income after the funds are received. Thus a withholding tax on interest payments to foreigners means that the tax proceeds are deducted from the interest payment made to the lender and collected by the borrower on behalf of the tax authorities.
World Bank	*See* International Bank for Reconstruction and Development.
Xeno Currency	Another name for Eurocurrency.
Yard	Slang for 1,000 million. Comes from milliard.
Yield	The amount of interest payments as a percentage of the amount lent or borrowed.
Yield Curve	A diagrammatic representation of interest rates prevailing on a class of securities that are alike in every respect other than term to maturity. A yield curve may slope upward or downward or be flat.
Yield to Maturity	That discount rate which equates the sum of the present value of the future stream of income payments and the present value of the principal repayment at maturity with the market value of a security.

Present Value
Tables

Table A Present Value of $1

Years Hence	1%	2%	4%	6%	8%	10%	12%	14%	15%	16%	18%	20%	22%	24%	25%	26%	28%	30%	35%	40%	45%	50%
1	0.990	0.980	0.962	0.943	0.926	0.909	0.893	0.877	0.870	0.862	0.847	0.833	0.820	0.806	0.800	0.794	0.781	0.769	0.741	0.714	0.690	0.667
2	0.980	0.961	0.925	0.890	0.857	0.826	0.797	0.769	0.756	0.743	0.718	0.694	0.672	0.650	0.640	0.630	0.610	0.592	0.549	0.510	0.476	0.444
3	0.971	0.942	0.889	0.840	0.794	0.751	0.712	0.675	0.658	0.641	0.609	0.579	0.551	0.524	0.512	0.500	0.477	0.455	0.406	0.364	0.328	0.296
4	0.961	0.924	0.855	0.792	0.735	0.683	0.636	0.592	0.572	0.552	0.516	0.482	0.451	0.423	0.410	0.397	0.373	0.350	0.301	0.260	0.226	0.198
5	0.951	0.906	0.822	0.747	0.681	0.621	0.567	0.519	0.497	0.476	0.437	0.402	0.370	0.341	0.328	0.315	0.291	0.269	0.223	0.186	0.156	0.132
6	0.942	0.888	0.790	0.705	0.630	0.564	0.507	0.456	0.432	0.410	0.370	0.335	0.303	0.275	0.262	0.250	0.227	0.207	0.165	0.133	0.108	0.088
7	0.933	0.871	0.760	0.665	0.583	0.513	0.452	0.400	0.376	0.354	0.314	0.279	0.249	0.222	0.210	0.198	0.178	0.159	0.122	0.095	0.074	0.059
8	0.923	0.853	0.731	0.627	0.540	0.467	0.404	0.351	0.327	0.305	0.266	0.233	0.204	0.179	0.168	0.157	0.139	0.123	0.091	0.068	0.051	0.039
9	0.914	0.837	0.703	0.592	0.500	0.424	0.361	0.308	0.284	0.263	0.225	0.194	0.167	0.144	0.134	0.125	0.108	0.094	0.067	0.048	0.035	0.026
10	0.905	0.820	0.676	0.558	0.463	0.386	0.322	0.270	0.247	0.227	0.191	0.162	0.137	0.116	0.107	0.099	0.085	0.073	0.050	0.035	0.024	0.017
11	0.896	0.804	0.650	0.527	0.429	0.350	0.287	0.237	0.215	0.195	0.162	0.135	0.112	0.094	0.086	0.079	0.066	0.056	0.037	0.025	0.017	0.012
12	0.887	0.788	0.625	0.497	0.397	0.319	0.257	0.208	0.187	0.168	0.137	0.112	0.092	0.076	0.069	0.062	0.052	0.043	0.027	0.018	0.012	0.008
13	0.879	0.773	0.601	0.469	0.368	0.290	0.229	0.182	0.163	0.145	0.116	0.093	0.075	0.061	0.055	0.050	0.040	0.033	0.020	0.013	0.008	0.005
14	0.870	0.758	0.577	0.442	0.340	0.263	0.205	0.160	0.141	0.125	0.099	0.078	0.062	0.049	0.044	0.039	0.032	0.025	0.015	0.009	0.006	0.003
15	0.861	0.743	0.555	0.417	0.315	0.239	0.183	0.140	0.123	0.108	0.084	0.065	0.051	0.040	0.035	0.031	0.025	0.020	0.011	0.006	0.004	0.002
16	0.853	0.728	0.534	0.394	0.292	0.218	0.163	0.123	0.107	0.093	0.071	0.054	0.042	0.032	0.028	0.025	0.019	0.015	0.008	0.005	0.003	0.002
17	0.844	0.714	0.513	0.371	0.270	0.198	0.146	0.108	0.093	0.080	0.060	0.045	0.034	0.026	0.023	0.020	0.015	0.012	0.006	0.003	0.002	0.001
18	0.836	0.700	0.494	0.350	0.250	0.180	0.130	0.095	0.081	0.069	0.051	0.038	0.028	0.021	0.018	0.016	0.012	0.009	0.005	0.002	0.001	0.001
19	0.828	0.686	0.475	0.331	0.232	0.164	0.116	0.083	0.070	0.060	0.043	0.031	0.023	0.017	0.014	0.012	0.009	0.007	0.003	0.002	0.001	
20	0.820	0.673	0.456	0.312	0.215	0.149	0.104	0.073	0.061	0.051	0.037	0.026	0.019	0.014	0.012	0.010	0.009	0.005	0.002	0.001	0.001	
21	0.811	0.660	0.439	0.294	0.199	0.135	0.093	0.064	0.053	0.044	0.031	0.022	0.015	0.011	0.009	0.008	0.006	0.004	0.002	0.001		
22	0.803	0.647	0.422	0.278	0.184	0.123	0.083	0.056	0.046	0.038	0.026	0.018	0.013	0.009	0.007	0.006	0.004	0.003	0.001	0.001		
23	0.795	0.634	0.406	0.262	0.170	0.112	0.074	0.049	0.040	0.033	0.022	0.015	0.010	0.007	0.006	0.005	0.003	0.002	0.001			
24	0.788	0.622	0.390	0.247	0.158	0.102	0.066	0.043	0.035	0.028	0.019	0.013	0.008	0.006	0.005	0.004	0.003	0.002	0.001			
25	0.780	0.610	0.375	0.233	0.146	0.092	0.059	0.038	0.030	0.024	0.016	0.010	0.007	0.005	0.004	0.003	0.002	0.001	0.001			
26	0.772	0.598	0.361	0.220	0.135	0.084	0.053	0.033	0.026	0.021	0.014	0.009	0.006	0.004	0.003	0.002	0.002	0.001				
27	0.764	0.586	0.347	0.207	0.125	0.076	0.047	0.029	0.023	0.018	0.011	0.007	0.005	0.003	0.002	0.002	0.001	0.001				
28	0.757	0.574	0.333	0.196	0.116	0.069	0.042	0.026	0.020	0.016	0.010	0.006	0.004	0.002	0.002	0.002	0.001	0.001				
29	0.749	0.563	0.321	0.185	0.107	0.063	0.037	0.022	0.017	0.014	0.008	0.005	0.003	0.002	0.002	0.001	0.001	0.001				
30	0.742	0.552	0.308	0.174	0.099	0.057	0.033	0.020	0.015	0.012	0.007	0.004	0.003	0.002	0.001	0.001	0.001	0.001				
40	0.672	0.453	0.208	0.097	0.046	0.022	0.011	0.005	0.004	0.003	0.001	0.001										
50	0.608	0.372	0.141	0.054	0.021	0.009	0.003	0.001	0.001	0.001	0.001											

Table B Present Value of $1 Received Annually for N Years

Years (N)	1%	2%	4%	6%	8%	10%	12%	14%	15%	16%	18%	20%	22%	24%	25%	26%	28%	30%	35%	40%	45%	50%
1	0.990	0.980	0.962	0.943	0.926	0.909	0.893	0.877	0.870	0.862	0.847	0.833	0.820	0.806	0.800	0.794	0.781	0.769	0.741	0.714	0.690	0.667
2	1.970	1.942	1.886	1.833	1.783	1.736	1.690	1.647	1.626	1.605	1.566	1.528	1.492	1.457	1.440	1.424	1.392	1.361	1.289	1.224	1.165	1.111
3	2.941	2.884	2.775	2.673	2.577	2.487	2.402	2.322	2.283	2.246	2.174	2.106	2.042	1.981	1.952	1.923	1.868	1.816	1.696	1.598	1.493	1.407
4	3.902	3.808	3.630	3.465	3.312	3.170	3.037	2.914	2.855	2.798	2.690	2.589	2.494	2.404	2.362	2.320	2.241	2.166	1.997	1.849	1.720	1.605
5	4.853	4.713	4.452	4.212	3.993	3.791	3.605	3.433	3.352	3.274	3.127	2.991	2.864	2.745	2.689	2.635	2.535	2.436	2.220	2.035	1.876	1.737
6	5.795	5.601	5.242	4.917	4.623	4.355	4.111	3.889	3.784	3.685	3.498	3.326	3.167	3.020	2.951	2.885	2.759	2.643	2.385	2.168	1.983	1.824
7	6.728	6.472	6.002	5.582	5.206	4.868	4.564	4.288	4.160	4.039	3.812	3.605	3.416	3.242	3.161	3.083	2.937	2.802	2.508	2.263	2.057	1.883
8	7.652	7.325	6.733	6.210	5.747	5.335	4.968	4.639	4.487	4.344	4.078	3.837	3.619	3.421	3.329	3.241	3.076	2.925	2.598	2.331	2.108	1.922
9	8.566	8.162	7.435	6.802	6.247	5.759	5.328	4.946	4.772	4.607	4.303	4.031	3.786	3.566	3.463	3.366	3.184	3.019	2.665	2.379	2.144	1.948
10	9.471	8.983	8.111	7.360	6.710	6.145	5.650	5.216	5.019	4.833	4.494	4.192	3.923	3.682	3.571	3.465	3.269	3.092	2.715	2.414	2.168	1.965
11	10.368	9.787	8.760	7.887	7.139	6.495	5.937	5.453	5.234	5.029	4.656	4.327	4.035	3.776	3.656	3.544	3.335	3.147	2.752	2.438	2.185	1.977
12	11.255	10.575	9.385	8.384	7.536	6.814	6.194	5.660	5.421	5.197	4.793	4.439	4.127	3.851	3.725	3.606	3.387	3.190	2.779	2.456	2.196	1.985
13	12.134	11.343	9.986	8.853	7.904	7.103	6.424	5.842	5.583	5.342	4.910	4.533	4.203	3.912	3.780	3.656	3.427	3.223	2.799	2.468	2.204	1.990
14	13.004	12.106	10.563	9.295	8.244	7.367	6.628	6.002	5.724	5.468	5.008	4.611	4.265	3.962	3.824	3.695	3.459	3.249	2.814	2.477	2.210	1.993
15	13.865	12.849	11.118	9.712	8.559	7.606	6.811	6.142	5.847	5.575	5.092	4.675	4.315	4.001	3.859	3.726	3.483	3.268	2.825	2.484	2.214	1.995
16	14.718	13.578	11.652	10.106	8.851	7.824	6.974	6.265	5.954	5.669	5.162	4.730	4.357	4.033	3.887	3.751	3.503	3.283	2.834	2.489	2.216	1.997
17	15.562	14.292	12.166	10.477	9.122	8.022	7.120	6.373	6.047	5.749	5.222	4.775	4.391	4.059	3.910	3.771	3.518	3.295	2.840	2.492	2.218	1.998
18	16.398	14.992	12.659	10.828	9.372	8.201	7.250	6.467	6.128	5.818	5.273	4.812	4.419	4.080	3.928	3.786	3.529	3.304	2.844	2.494	2.219	1.999
19	17.226	15.678	13.134	11.158	9.604	8.365	7.366	6.550	6.198	5.877	5.316	4.844	4.442	4.097	3.942	3.799	3.539	3.311	2.848	2.496	2.220	1.999
20	18.046	16.351	13.590	11.470	9.818	8.514	7.469	6.623	6.259	5.929	5.353	4.870	4.460	4.110	3.954	3.808	3.546	3.316	2.850	2.497	2.221	1.999
21	18.857	17.011	14.029	11.764	10.017	8.649	7.562	6.687	6.312	5.973	5.384	4.891	4.476	4.121	3.963	3.816	3.551	3.320	2.852	2.498	2.221	2.000
22	19.660	17.658	14.451	12.042	10.201	8.772	7.645	6.743	6.359	6.011	5.410	4.909	4.488	4.130	3.970	3.822	3.556	3.323	2.853	2.498	2.222	2.000
23	20.456	18.292	14.857	12.303	10.371	8.883	7.718	6.792	6.399	6.044	5.432	4.925	4.499	4.137	3.976	3.827	3.559	3.325	2.854	2.499	2.222	2.000
24	21.243	18.914	15.247	12.550	10.529	8.985	7.784	6.835	6.434	6.073	5.451	4.937	4.507	4.143	3.981	3.831	3.562	3.327	2.855	2.499	2.222	2.000
25	22.023	19.523	15.622	12.783	10.675	9.077	7.843	6.873	6.464	6.097	5.467	4.948	4.514	4.147	3.985	3.834	3.564	3.329	2.856	2.499	2.222	2.000
26	22.795	20.121	15.983	13.003	10.810	9.161	7.896	6.906	6.491	6.118	5.480	4.956	4.520	4.151	3.988	3.837	3.566	3.330	2.856	2.500	2.222	2.000
27	23.560	20.707	16.330	13.211	10.935	9.237	7.943	6.935	6.514	6.136	5.492	4.964	4.524	4.154	3.990	3.839	3.567	3.331	2.856	2.500	2.222	2.000
28	24.316	21.281	16.663	13.406	11.051	9.307	7.984	6.961	6.534	6.152	5.502	4.970	4.528	4.157	3.992	3.840	3.568	3.331	2.857	2.500	2.222	2.000
29	25.066	21.844	16.984	13.591	11.158	9.370	8.022	6.983	6.551	6.166	5.510	4.975	4.531	4.159	3.994	3.841	3.569	3.332	2.857	2.500	2.222	2.000
30	25.808	22.396	17.292	13.765	11.258	9.427	8.055	7.003	6.566	6.177	5.517	4.979	4.534	4.160	3.995	3.842	3.569	3.332	2.857	2.500	2.222	2.000
40	32.835	27.355	19.793	15.046	11.925	9.779	8.244	7.105	6.642	6.234	5.548	4.997	4.544	4.166	3.999	3.846	3.571	3.333	2.857	2.500	2.222	2.000
50	39.196	31.424	21.482	15.762	12.234	9.915	8.304	7.133	6.661	6.246	5.554	4.999	4.545	4.167	4.000	3.846	3.571	3.333	2.857	2.500	2.222	2.000

Index

Notes